Essays of the Masters

Essays of the Masters

Edited with an Introduction by
CHARLES NEIDER

Cooper Square Press

First Cooper Square Press edition 2000

This Cooper Square Press paperback edition of *Essays of the Masters* is an unabridged republication of the edition first published in New York in 1956, with the addition of ten textual emendations. It is reprinted by arrangement with the editor.

Published by Cooper Square Press
An Imprint of Rowman & Littlefield Publishing Group
150 Fifth Avenue, Suite 911
New York, New York 10011

Distributed by National Book Network

Library of Congress Cataloging-in-Publication Data

Essays of the masters / edited with an introduction by Charles Neider.
    p. cm.
  Originally published: New York : Rinehart, 1956.
  ISBN 0-8154-1097-2 (alk. paper)
   1. Essays. I. Neider, Charles, 1915–

PN6142 .N4 2000
808.84—dc21   00-0345543

⊖™ The paper used in this publication meets the minimum requirements of American National Standard for Information Sciences—Permanence of Paper for Printed Library Materials, ANSI/NISO Z39.48–1992.
Manufactured in the United States of America.

Acknowledgments

The essays by Auden and Forster are reprinted from *I Believe,* edited by Clifton Fadiman, by permission of Simon and Schuster, Inc. Copyright, 1931, 1939, by Simon and Schuster, Inc.

The essay by Conrad is reprinted by permission of J. M. Dent & Sons Ltd.

The essay by Dostoevski is reprinted from Volume I, *The Diary of a Writer* by F. M. Dostoievsky, translated by Boris Brasol; copyright 1949 by Charles Scribner's Sons; used by permission of the publishers.

The essay by Eliot is reprinted from *Selected Essays 1917–1932* by T. S. Eliot, copyright, 1932, by Harcourt, Brace and Company, Inc., with the permission of Harcourt, Brace and Company, Inc., and of Faber and Faber Ltd.

The essay by Gide is reprinted from *My Theatre* by André Gide, by permission of Alfred A. Knopf, Inc. Copyright 1951 by Alfred A. Knopf, Inc.

The essay by Hemingway is reprinted from *Death in the Afternoon* by Ernest Hemingway; copyright 1932 by Charles Scribner's Sons. Reprinted by permission of the publishers.

The essay by Kafka is reprinted from *The Penal Colony* by Franz Kafka, translated by Willa and Edwin Muir, copyright 1948 by Schocken Books, Inc.

The essay by Lawrence is reprinted from *Mornings in Mexico* by D. H. Lawrence, by permission of Alfred A. Knopf, Inc. Copyright 1927 by Alfred A. Knopf, Inc.

The essay by Mann is reprinted from *Essays of Three Decades* by Thomas Mann, by permission of Alfred A. Knopf, Inc. Copyright 1947 by Alfred A. Knopf, Inc.

The essay by Maugham is reprinted from *The Summing Up* by W. Somerset Maugham, by permission of Mr. Maugham, A. P. Watt & Son, Doubleday & Co., Inc., and William Heinemann, Ltd.

The essay by Nexö is reprinted from *Days in the Sun* by Martin Andersen Nexö, copyright 1929 by Coward-McCann, Inc., by permission of Coward-McCann, Inc.

The essay by Proust is reprinted from *Swann's Way* from *Remembrance of Things Past* by Marcel Proust, translated by C. K. Scott-Moncrieff. Copyright 1934 by The Modern Library, Inc. Copyright 1924, 1925 by Thomas Seltzer. Reprinted by permission of Random House, Inc., and Chatto & Windus Ltd.

The essay by Sartre is reprinted by permission of *Town & Country* magazine.

The essay by Shaw is reprinted by permission of The Public Trustee and The Society of Authors, London.

The essay by Silone is reprinted by permission of *Partisan Review* and Mrs. Darina Silone. Copyright 1942 by *Partisan Review*.

The essay by Tagore is reprinted from *Creative Unity* by Rabindranath Tagore by permission of The Macmillan Company, the Trustees of Rabindranath Tagore, and Macmillan & Co., Ltd. Copyright 1922 by The Macmillan Company.

The essay by Tolstoi is reprinted from *What Is Art and Other Essays* by Leo Tolstoy, translated by Aylmer Maude, by permission of Oxford University Press.

The use of the trademarked name Mark Twain is made with the permission of Harper & Brothers.

The essay by Unamuno is reprinted from *Essays and Soliloquies* by Miguel de Unamuno, by permission of Alfred A. Knopf, Inc. Copyright 1924 by Alfred A. Knopf, Inc.

The essay by Woolf is reprinted from *The Second Common Reader* by Virginia Woolf, copyright, 1932, by Harcourt, Brace and Company, Inc., by permission of Harcourt, Brace and Company and Mr. Leonard Woolf.

The essay by Yeats is reprinted from *Essays* by William Butler Yeats by permission of The Macmillan Company. Copyright 1924 by The Macmillan Company. Also by permission of Mrs. William Butler Yeats, A. P. Watt & Son, and Messrs. Macmillan & Co., Ltd.

For the cooperation of all the above the editor expresses his thanks.

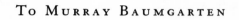

To Murray Baumgarten

Introduction

The present collection is not an orthodox one. It does not focus on the history or the development or the "form" of the essay and does not concentrate on the professional essayists at all—and by "professional" I refer to those writers, such as Lamb and de Quincey and, in modern times, Mencken and E. B. White, who find their best and fullest expression in the essay medium. What it does instead is show how the large creative minds, those which produced the novels, plays, and poems of the past century and a half, put the essay to their use.

Professional essayists commonly project their personalities directly onto paper—the flavor of their personalities is an important stock of their trade; whereas in their major works the writers in this volume generally project their personalities in disguised form. You are left to make out what you can about the authors when you read novels like *The Brothers Karamazov* or *The Counterfeiters,* and although in the long run the impression of personality is overwhelming, still it is tantalizingly indirect. Curiosity being what it is, we want a more direct view and a more intimate sampling. The hope to satisfy this desire is one of the chief inspirations for the existence of the present volume.

Every collection reflects—or ought to reflect—the bias of its editor. I say "ought to" because I know it is possible for a collection not to reflect this bias, particularly if the editor is intent on making selections according to some criterion of "impartiality." Bias is what gives a collection its tone and homogeneity—at least I have found this to be true of the good ones. As in other matters, there is "good" bias or "bad," catholic or provincial, aesthetic or mechanical. The ideal or perfect anthology no doubt exists in some literary heaven, but I have not yet found it on this publisher's, bookbuyer's, and editor's earth, for the sufficient reason that a perfect book by definition may not be circumscribed by external conditions. In an editor's life there are inevitably the imposed conditions of length, permission fees, copyright, translations, production costs, selling price, profit, variety of subject matter, style, length, et cetera. If the ten best essays turned out to be, in one's opinion, all travel essays dealing with Italy, they might make a charming collection for one's private use but would present great difficulties as a marketable item—unless the subject of the book were Italy rather than essays of the masters.

There are various other problems which an editor must face. I deplore, for example, the omission of Joyce in this volume; yet the only available essays by him were written when he was a very young man, precocious but not yet a master. Chekhov is a writer close to my heart; but his nonfictional prose writings that I am aware of are fragmentary and in the form of letters. Perhaps these points are not worth making. I make them only because in my experience too few people understand what is involved in compiling an anthology, most of them seeming to think it is chiefly a matter of a certain amount of clerical work. Those who have tried their hand at the task, thinking it a simple one, have usually been unpleasantly surprised by its complexity. And yet many people realize that the anthology as a form of communication and art has a long and honorable history, the Bible, the writings of Homer, the Greek Anthology, and many other great works being in essence collections of the work of many hands.

An editor, it seems to me, has a threefold responsibility in the making of a collection. First, he is responsible to the authors he is presenting. He must let them put their best foot forward and in a manner which most fully represents them. Second, he is responsible to the reader, in what he wants to show him and how he wants to entertain and influence him. And third, he is responsible to himself—to his own tastes and eccentricities, which he ought, as far as feasible, faithfully and honestly to reflect. It is a bit of a tightrope walk, as most editors have discovered. If I have slipped here or there it would not greatly surprise me.

CHARLES NEIDER

New York
January, 1956

Table of Contents

Acknowledgments   vii

Introduction   xi

W. H. AUDEN *My Belief*   1

HONORÉ DE BALZAC *The Physiology of Marriage*   13

JOSEPH CONRAD *Christmas Day at Sea*   23

CHARLES DICKENS *New York*   27

FËDOR DOSTOEVSKI *Something about Lying*   41

T. S. ELIOT *Tradition and the Individual Talent*   52

WILLIAM FAULKNER *On Receiving the Nobel Prize*   61

GUSTAVE FLAUBERT *Over Strand and Field*   62

E. M. FORSTER *What I Believe*   74

ANATOLE FRANCE *On Nunneries*   84

ANDRÉ GIDE *The Evolution of the Theater*   90

JOHANN WOLFGANG VON GOETHE *Shakespeare ad
Infinitum*   101

THOMAS HARDY *The Profitable Reading of Fiction*   113

NATHANIEL HAWTHORNE *Outside Glimpses of English
Poverty*   127

HEINRICH HEINE *London and the English*   155

ERNEST HEMINGWAY *Death in the Afternoon*   165

HENRY JAMES *Ivan· Turgénieff*   173

FRANZ KAFKA *The Aeroplanes at Brescia*   194

RUDYARD KIPLING *Chicago* 204

D. H. LAWRENCE *Market Day* 214

MAURICE MAETERLINCK *Chrysanthemums* 221

THOMAS MANN Anna Karenina 227

W. SOMERSET MAUGHAM *A Summing Up* 242

HERMAN MELVILLE *Hawthorne and His Mosses* 250

MARTIN ANDERSEN NEXÖ *Tangiers* 268

LUIGI PIRANDELLO *Eleonora Duse: Actress Supreme* 288

EDGAR ALLAN POE *Philosophy of Furniture* 299

MARCEL PROUST *Waking Dreams* 305

JEAN-PAUL SARTRE *Manhattan: The Great American Desert* 314

BERNARD SHAW *Chesterton on Shaw* 321

IGNAZIO SILONE *Ferrero and the Decline of Civilisations* 328

ROBERT LOUIS STEVENSON *The Old Pacific Capital* 334

RABINDRANATH TAGORE *East and West* 349

WILLIAM MAKEPEACE THACKERAY *On Being Found Out* 359

LEO TOLSTOI *On Art* 366

IVAN TURGENEV *Hamlet and Don Quixote* 379

MARK TWAIN *Traveling with a Reformer* 397

MIGUEL DE UNAMUNO *Large and Small Towns* 411

WALT WHITMAN *The Bible as Poetry* 417

OSCAR WILDE *Impressions of America* 421

VIRGINIA WOOLF *How Should One Read a Book?* 427

WILLIAM BUTLER YEATS *Magic* 438

Essays of the Masters

My Belief

by W. H. AUDEN [1907–1973]

Everything that lives is Holy—BLAKE

1§ GOODNESS is easier to recognize than to define; only the greatest novelists can portray good people. For me, the least unsatisfactory description is to say that any thing or creature is good which is discharging its proper function, using its powers to the fullest extent permitted by its environment and its own nature—though we must remember that "nature" and "environment" are intellectual abstractions from a single, constantly changing reality. Thus, people are happy and good who have found their vocation: what vocations there are will depend upon the society within which they are practised.

There are two kinds of goodness, "natural" and "moral." An organism is naturally good when it has reached a state of equilibrium with its environment. All healthy animals and plants are naturally good in this sense. But any change toward a greater freedom of action is a morally good change. I think it permissible, for example, to speak of a favorable mutation as a morally good act. But moral good passes into natural good. A change is made and a new equilibrium stabilized. Below man, this happens at once; for each species the change toward freedom is not repeated. In man, the evolution can be continued, each stage of moral freedom being superseded by a new one. For example, we frequently admire the "goodness" of illiterate peasants as compared with the "badness" of many townees. But this is a romantic confusion. The goodness we admire in the former is a natural, not a moral, goodness. Once, the life of the peasant represented the highest use of the powers of man, the farthest limit of his freedom of action. This is no longer true. The townee has a wider range of choice and fuller opportunities of using his power. He frequently chooses wrongly, and so becomes morally bad. We are right to condemn him for this, but to suggest that we should all return to the life of the peasant is to deny the possibility of moral progress. Worship of youth is another romantic pessimism of this kind.

2§ Similarly, there is natural and moral evil. Determined and unavoidable limits to freedom of choice and action, such as the necessity for destroying life in order to eat and live, climate, accidents, are natural evils. If, on the other hand, I, say, as the keeper of a boardinghouse, knowing that vitamins are necessary to health, continue, for reasons of gain or laziness, to feed my guests on an insufficient diet, I commit moral evil. Just as moral good tends to pass into natural good, so, conversely, what was natural evil tends, with every advance in knowledge, to become moral evil.

3§ The history of life on this planet is the history of the ways in which life has gained control over and freedom within its environment. Organisms may either adapt themselves to a particular environment—e.g., the fleshy leaves of the cactus permit it to live in a desert—or develop the means to change their environment—e.g., organs of locomotion.

Below the human level, this progress has taken place through structural biological changes, depending on the lack of mutations or the chances of natural selection. Only man, with his conscious intelligence, has been able to continue his evolution after his biological development has finished. By studying the laws of physical nature, he has gained a large measure of control over them and insofar as he is able to understand the laws of his own nature and of the societies in which he lives, he approaches that state where what he wills may be done. "Freedom," as a famous definition has it, "is consciousness of necessity."

4§ The distinguishing mark of man as an animal is his plastic, unspecialized "foetalized" nature. All other animals develop more quickly and petrify sooner. In other words, the dictatorship of heredity is weakest in man. He has the widest choice of environment, and, in return, changes in environment, either changes in nature or his social life, have the greatest effect on him.

5§ In contrast to his greatest rivals for biological supremacy, the insects, man has a specialized and concentrated central nervous system, and unspecialized peripheral organs, i.e., the stimuli he receives are collected and pooled in one organ. Intelligence and choice can only arise when more than one stimulus is presented at the same time in the same place.

6§ Man has always been a social animal living in communities. This falsifies any theories of Social Contract. The individual *in vacuo* is an intellectual abstraction. The individual is the product of social life; without it, he could be no more than a bundle of unconditioned reflexes. Men are born neither free nor good.

7§ Societies and cultures vary enormously. On the whole, Marx seems to me correct in his view that physical conditions and the forms of economic production have dictated the forms of communities: e.g., the geographical peculiarities of the Aegean peninsula produced small democratic city-states, while the civilizations based on river irrigation like Egypt and Mesopotamia were centralized autocratic empires.

8§ *But* we are each conscious of ourselves as a thinking, feeling, and willing whole, and this is the only whole of which we have direct knowledge. This experience conditions our thinking. I cannot see how other wholes, family, class, nation, etc., can be wholes to us except in a purely descriptive sense. We do not see a state, we see a number of individuals. Anthropological studies of different communities, such as Dr. Benedict's work on primitive American cultures, or that of the Lynds on contemporary Middletown, have shown the enormous power of a given cultural form to determine the nature of the individuals who live under it. A given cultural pattern develops those traits of character and modes of behavior which it values, and suppresses those which it does not. But this does not warrant ascribing to a culture a superpersonality, conscious of its parts as I can be conscious of my hand or liver. A society consists of a certain number of individuals living in a particular way, in a particular place, at a particular time; nothing else.

9§ The distinction drawn by Locke between society and government is very important. Again, Marx seems to me correct in saying that sovereignty or government is not the result of a contract made by society as a whole, but has always been assumed by those people in society who owned the instruments of production.

Theories of Rights arise as a means to attack or justify a given social form, and are a sign of social strain. Burke, and later thinkers, who developed the idealist theory of the state, were correct in criticizing the *a priori* assumptions of Social Contract and in pointing out that society is a growing organism. But, by identifying society and government, they ignored the power of the latter to interfere with the natural growth of the former, and so were led to denying the right of societies to revolt against their governments, and to the hypostatization of the *status quo.*

10§ A favorite analogy for the state among idealist political thinkers is with the human body. This analogy is false. The constitution of the cells in the body is determined and fixed; nerve cells can only give rise to more nerve cells, muscle cells to muscle cells, etc. But, in the transition from parent to child, the whole pack in inherited genetic characters is shuffled. The king's son may be a moron, the coal heaver's a mathematical genius. The entire pattern of talents and abilities is altered at every generation.

11§ Another false analogy is with the animal kingdom. Observed from the outside (how it appears to them no one knows), the individual animal seems to be sacrificed to the continuance of the species. This observation is used to deny the individual any rights against the state. But there is a fundamental difference between man and all other animals in that an animal which has reached maturity does not continue to evolve, but a man does. As far as we can judge, the only standard in the animal world is physical fitness, but in man a great many other factors are involved. What has survival value can never be determined; man has survived as a species through the efforts of individuals who at the time must often have seemed to possess very little biological survival value.

12§ Man's advance in control over his environment is making it more and more difficult for him, at least in the industrialized countries with a high standard of living, like America or England, to lead a naturally good life, and easier and easier to lead a morally bad one.

Let us suppose, for example, that it is sometimes good for mind and body to take a walk. Before there were means of mechanical transport, men walked because they could not do anything else; i.e., they committed naturally good acts. Today, a man has to choose whether to use his car or walk. It is possible for him, by using the car on an occasion when he ought to walk, to commit a morally wrong act, and it is quite probable that he will. It is despair at finding a solution to this problem which is responsible for much of the success of Fascist blood-and-soil ideology.

II

1§ A society, then, is good insofar as

a. it allows the widest possible range of choices to its members to follow those vocations to which they are suited;

b. it is constantly developing, and providing new vocations which make a fuller demand upon their increasing powers.

The Greeks assumed that the life of intellectual contemplation was the only really "good" vocation. It has become very much clearer now that this is only true for certain people, and that there are a great many other vocations of equal value: human nature is richer and more varied than the Greeks thought.

2§ No society can be absolutely good. Utopias, whether like Aldous Huxley's Brave New World or Dante's Paradiso, because they are static, only portray states of natural evil or good. (Someone, I think it was Landor, said of the characters in the *Inferno*: "But they don't want to get out.") People committing acts in obedience to law or habit are not being moral. As voluntary action always turns, with repetition, into habit, morality is only possible in a world which is constantly changing and presenting a fresh series of choices. No society is absolutely good; but some are better than others.

3§ If we look at a community at any given moment, we see that it consists of good men and bad men, clever men and stupid men, sensitive and insensitive, law-abiding and lawless, rich and poor. Our politics, our view of what form our society and our government should take here and now, will depend on

a. how far we think the bad is due to preventable causes;

b. what, if we think the causes preventable, we find them to be. If we take the extremely pessimistic view that evil is in no way preventable, our only course is the hermit's, to retire alto-gether from this wicked world. If we take a fairly pessimistic view, that badness is inherited (i.e., that goodness and badness are not determined by social relations), we shall try to establish an authori-tarian regime of the good. If, on the other hand, we are fairly op-timistic, believing that bad environment is the chief cause of bad-ness in individuals, and that the environment can be changed, we shall tend toward a belief in some sort of democracy. Personally I am fairly optimistic, partly for reasons which I have tried to outline above, and partly because the practical results of those who have taken the more pessimistic view do not encourage me to be-lieve that they are right.

4§ *Fairly* optimistic. In the history of man, there have been a few civilized individuals but no civilized community, not one, ever. Those who talk glibly of Our Great Civilization, whether European, American, Chinese, or Russian, are doing their coun-tries the greatest disservice. We are still barbarians. All advances in knowledge, from Galileo down to Freud or Marx, are, in the first impact, humiliating; they begin by showing us that we are not as free or as grand or as good as we thought; and it is only when we realize this that we can begin to study how to overcome our own weakness.

5§ What then are the factors which limit and hinder men from developing their powers and pursuing suitable vocations?

a. Lack of material goods. Man is an animal and until his imme-diate material and economic needs are satisfied, he cannot develop further. In the past this has been a natural evil: methods of production and distribution were too primitive to guarantee a proper standard of life for everybody. It is doubtful whether this is any longer true; in which case, it is a moral and remediable evil. Under this head I include all questions of wages, food, housing, health, insurance, etc.

b. Lack of education. Unless an individual is free to obtain the fullest education with which his society can provide him, he is being injured by society. This does not mean that everybody should have the *same* kind of education, though it does mean, I think, education of some kind or other, up to university age. Education in a democracy must have two aims. It must give vocational guidance and training; assist each individual to find out where his talents lie, and then help him to develop these to the full—this for some people might be completed by sixteen— and it must also provide a general education; develop the reason and the consciousness of every individual, whatever his job, to a point where he can for himself distinguish good from bad, and truth from falsehood—this requires a much longer educational period.

At present education is in a very primitive stage; we probably teach the wrong things to the wrong people at the wrong time. It is dominated, at least in England, by an academic tradition which, except for the specially gifted, only fits its pupils to be schoolteachers. It is possible that the time for specialization (i.e., vocational training) should be in early adolescence, the twelve-to-sixteen group, and again in the latter half of the university period; but that the sixteen-to-twenty age group should have a general education.

c. Lack of occupations which really demand the full exercise of the individual's powers. This seems to me a very difficult problem indeed. The vast majority of jobs in a modern community do people harm. Children admire gangsters more than they admire factory operatives because they sense that being a gangster makes more demands on the personality than being a factory operative and is therefore, for the individual, morally better. It isn't that the morally better jobs are necessarily better rewarded economically: for instance, my acquaintance with carpenters leads me to think carpentry a very good profession, and my acquaintance with stockbrokers to think stockbroking a very bad one. The only jobs known to me which seem worthy of respect, both from the point of view of the individual and society, are being a creative artist, some kind of highly skilled craftsman, a research scientist, a doctor, a teacher, or a farmer. This difficulty runs far deeper than our present knowledge or any immediate political change we can imagine, and is therefore still, to a certain extent, a natural rather than a moral evil, though it is obviously much aggravated by gross inequalities in economic reward, which could be remedied. I don't myself much like priggish phrases such as "the right use of leisure." I agree with Eric Gill that work is what one does to please oneself, leisure the time one has to serve the community. The most one can say is that we must never forget that most people are being degraded by the work they do, and that the possibilities of sharing the duller jobs through the whole community will have to be explored much more fully. Incidentally, there is reason for thinking that the routine manual and machine-minding jobs are better tolerated by those whose talents are for book learning than by those whose talents run in the direction of manual skill.

d. Lack of suitable psychological conditions. People cannot grow unless they are happy and, even when their material needs have been satisfied, they still need many other things. They want to be liked and to like other people; to feel valuable, both in their own eyes and in the eyes of others; to feel free and to feel responsible; above all, not to feel lonely and isolated. The first great obstacle is the size of modern communities. By nature, man seems adapted to live in communities of a very moderate size; his economic life has compelled him to live in ever-enlarging ones. Many of the damaging effects of family life described by modern psychologists may be the result of our attempt to make the family group satisfy psychological needs which can only be satisfied by the community group. The family is based on inequality, the parent-child relationship; the community is, or should be, based on equality, the relationship of free citizens. We need both. Fortunately, recent technical advances, such as cheap electrical power, are making smaller social units more of a practical possibility than they seemed fifty years ago, and people with as divergent political views as the anarchists and Mr. Ford are now agreed about the benefits of industrial decentralization.

The second obstacle is social injustice and inequality. A man cannot be a happy member of a community if he feels that the community is treating him unjustly; the more complicated and impersonal economic life becomes, the truer this is. In a small factory where employer and employees know each other personally, i.e., where the conditions approximate to those of family life, the employees will accept without resentment a great deal more inequality than their fellows in a modern large-scale production plant.

III

1§ Society consists of a number of individual wills living in association. There is no such thing as a general will of society, except insofar as all these individual wills agree in desiring certain material things, e.g., food and clothes. It is also true, perhaps, that all desire happiness and goodness, but their conceptions of these may and do conflict with each other. Ideally, government is the means by which all the individual wills are assured complete freedom of moral choice and at the same time prevented from ever clashing. Such an ideal government, of course, does not and could not ever exist. It presupposes that every individual in society possesses equal power, and also that every individual takes part in the government.

2§ In practice, the majority is always ruled by a minority, a certain number of individuals who decide what a law shall be, and who command enough force to see that the majority obeys them. To do this, they must also command a varying degree of consent by the majority, though this consent need not be and never is complete. They must, for example, have the consent of the armed forces and the police, and they must either control the financial resources of society, or have the support of those who do.

3§ Democracy assumes, I think correctly, the right of every individual to revolt against his government by voting against it.

It has not been as successful as its advocates hoped, firstly, because it failed to realize the pressure that the more powerful and better educated classes could bring to bear upon the less powerful and less educated in their decisions—it ignored the fact that in an economically unequal society votes may be equal but voters are not—and secondly, because it assumed, I think quite wrongly, that voters living in the same geographical area would have the same interests, again ignoring economic differences and the change from an agricultural to an industrial economy. I believe that representation should be by trade or profession. No one person has exactly the same interests as another, but I, say, as a writer in Birmingham, have more interests in common with other writers in Leeds or London than I have with my next-door neighbor who manufactures cheap jewelry. This failure of the geographical unit to correspond to a genuine political unit is one of the factors responsible for the rise of the party machine. We rarely elect a local man whom we know personally; we have to choose one out of two or three persons offered from above. This seems to me thoroughly unsatisfactory. I think one of our mistakes is that we do not have enough stages in election; a hundred thousand voters are reduced by a single act to one man who goes to Parliament. This must inevitably mean a large degree of dictatorship from above. A sane democracy would, I feel, choose its representatives by a series of electoral stages, each lower stage electing the one above it.

4§ Legislation is a form of coercion, of limiting freedom. Coercion is necessary because societies are not free communities; we do not choose the society into which we are born; we can attempt to change it, but we cannot leave it. Ideally, people should be free to know evil and to choose the good, but the consequences of choosing evil are often to compel others to evil. The guiding principle of legislation in a democracy should be, not to make people good, but to prevent them making each other bad against their will. Thus we all agree that there should be laws against theft or murder, because no one chooses to be stolen from or murdered. But it is not always so simple. It is argued by laissez-faire economists that legislation concerning hours of work, wages, etc., violates the right of individual wills to bargain freely. But this presupposes that the bargaining powers of different wills are equal, and that each bargain is an individual act. Neither of these assumptions is true, and economic legislation is justified because they are not.

But there are other forms of legislation which are less justified. It is true that the individual will operating in a series of isolated acts is an abstraction—our present acts are the product of past acts and in their turn determine future ones—but I think the law has to behave as if this abstraction were a fact, otherwise there is no end to legislative interference. Take the case, for instance, of drink. If I become a drunkard, I may not only impair my own health, but also that of my children; and it can be argued, and often is, that the law should see that I do not become one by preventing me from purchasing alcohol. I think, however, that this is an unjustifiable extension of the law's function. Everything I do, the hour I go to bed, the literature I read, the temperature at which I take my bath, affects my character for good or bad and so, ultimately, the characters of those with whom I come in contact. If the legislator is once allowed to consider the distant effects of my acts, there is no reason why he should not decide everything for me. The law has to limit itself to considering the act in isolation: if the act directly violates the will of another, the law is justified in interfering; if only indirectly, it is not. Nearly all legislation on "moral" matters, such as drink, gambling, sexual behavior between adults, etc., seems to me bad.

5§ In theory, every individual has a right to his own conception of what form society ought to take and what form of government there should be and to exercise his will to realize it; on the other hand, everyone else has a right to reject his conception. In practice, this boils down to the right of different political parties to exist, parties representing the main divisions of interest in society. As the different sectional interests cannot form societies on their own—e.g., the employees cannot set up one state by themselves and the employers another—there is always coercion of the weaker by the stronger by propaganda, legislation, and sometimes physical violence; and the more evenly balanced the opposing forces are, the more violent that coercion is likely to become.

I do not see how in politics one can decide *a priori* what conduct is moral, or what degree of tolerance there should be. One can only decide which party in one's private judgment has the best view of what society ought to be, and to support it; and remember that, since all coercion is a moral evil, we should view with extreme suspicion those who welcome it. Thus I cannot see how a Socialist country could tolerate the existence of a Fascist party any more than a Fascist country could tolerate the existence of a Socialist party. I judge them differently because I think that the Socialists are right and the Fascists are wrong in their view of society. (It is always wrong in an absolute sense to kill, but all killing is not equally bad; it does matter who is killed.)

Intolerance is an evil and has evil consequences we can never accurately foresee and for which we shall always have to suffer; but there are occasions on which we must be prepared to accept the responsibility of our convictions. We must be as tolerant as we dare—only the future can judge whether we were tyrants or foolishly weak—and if we cannot dare very far, it is a serious criticism of ourselves and our age.

6§ But we do have to choose, every one of us. We have the misfortune or the good luck to be living in one of the great critical historical periods, when the whole structure of our society and its cultural and metaphysical values are undergoing a radical change. It has happened before, when the Roman Empire collapsed, and at the Reformation, and it may happen again in the future.

In periods of steady evolution, it is possible for the common man to pursue his private life without bothering his head very much over the principles and assumptions by which he lives, and to leave politics in the hands of professionals. But ours is not such an age. It is idle to lament that the world is becoming divided into hostile ideological camps; the division is a fact. No policy of isolation is possible. Democracy, liberty, justice, and reason are being seriously threatened and, in many parts of the world, destroyed. It is the duty of every one of us, not only to ourselves but to future generations of men, to have a clear understanding of what we mean when we use these words, to remember that while an idea can be absolutely bad, a person can never be, and to defend what we believe to be right, perhaps even at the cost of our lives and those of others.

1939

The Physiology of Marriage

by HONORÉ DE BALZAC [1799–1850]

"MARRIAGE IS NOT an institution of nature. The family in the east is entirely different from the family in the west. Man is the servant of nature, and the institutions of society are grafts, not spontaneous growths of nature. Laws are made to suit manners, and manners vary.

"Marriage must therefore undergo the gradual development towards perfection to which all human affairs submit."

These words, pronounced in the presence of the Conseil d'État by Napoleon during the discussion of the civil code, produced a profound impression upon the author of this book; and perhaps unconsciously he received the suggestion of this work, which he now presents to the public. And indeed at the period during which, while still in his youth, he studied French law, the word ADULTERY made a singular impression upon him. Taking, as it did, a prominent place in the code, this word never occurred to his mind without conjuring up its mournful train of consequences. Tears, shame, hatred, terror, secret crime, bloody wars, families without a head, and social misery rose like a sudden line of phantoms before him when he read the solemn word ADULTERY! Later on, when he became acquainted with the most cultivated circles of society, the author perceived that the rigor of marriage laws was very generally modified by adultery. He found that the number of unhappy homes was larger than that of happy marriages. In fact, he was the first to notice that of all human sciences that which relates to marriage was the least progressive. But this was the observation of a young man; and with him, as with so many others, this thought, like a pebble flung into the bosom of a lake, was lost in the abyss of his tumultuous thoughts. Nevertheless, in spite of himself the author was compelled to investigate, and eventually there was gathered within his mind, little by little, a swarm of conclusions, more or less just, on the subject of married life. Works like the present one are formed in the mind of the author with as much mystery as that with which truffles grow on the scented plains of Perigord. Out of the primitive and holy horror which adultery caused him and the investigation which he had thoughtlessly made, there was born one morning a trifling thought in which his ideas were formulated. This thought was really a satire upon marriage. It was as follows: A husband and wife found themselves in love with each other for the first time after twenty-seven years of marriage.

He amused himself with this little axiom and passed a whole week in delight, grouping around this harmless epigram the crowd of ideas which came to him unconsciously and which he was astonished to find that he possessed. His humorous mood yielded at last to the claims of serious investigation. Willing as he was to take a hint the author returned to his habitual idleness. Nevertheless, this slight germ of science and of joke grew to perfection, unfostered, in the fields of thought. Each phase of the work which had been condemned by others took root and gathered strength, surviving like the slight branch of a tree which, flung upon the sand by a winter's storm, finds itself covered at morning with white and fantastic icicles, produced by the caprices of nightly frosts. So the sketch lived on and became the starting point of myriad branching moralizations. It was like a polypus which multiplies itself by generation. The feelings of youth, the observations which a favorable opportunity led him to make, were verified in the most trifling events of his after life. Soon this mass of ideas became harmonized, took life, seemed, as it were, to become a living individual and moved in the midst of those domains of fancy, where the soul loves to give full rein to its wild creations. Amid all the distractions of the world and of life, the author always heard a voice ringing in his ears and mockingly revealing the secrets of things at the very moment he was watching a woman as she danced, smiled or talked. Just as Mephistopheles pointed out to Faust in that terrific assemblage at the Brocken, faces full of frightful augury, so the author was conscious in the midst of the ball of a demon who would strike him on the shoulder with a familiar air and say to him: "Do you notice that enchanting smile? It is a grin of hatred." And then the demon would strut about like one of the captains in the old comedies of Hardy. He would twitch the folds of a lace mantle and endeavor to make new the fretted tinsel and spangles of its former glory. And then like Rabelais he would burst into loud and unrestrainable laughter, and would trace on the street-wall a word which might serve as a pendant to the "Drink!" which was the only oracle obtainable from the heavenly bottle. This literary Trilby would often appear seated on piles of books, and with hooked fingers would point out with a grin of malice two yellow volumes whose title dazzled the eyes. Then when he saw he had attracted the author's attention he spelt out, in a voice alluring as the tones of an harmonica, *Physiology of Marriage!* But, almost always he appeared at night during my dreams, gentle as some fairy guardian; he tried by words of sweetness to subdue the soul which he would appropriate to himself. While he attracted, he also scoffed at me; supple as a woman's mind, cruel as a tiger, his friendliness was more formidable than his hatred, for he never yielded a caress without also inflicting a wound. One night in particular he exhausted the resources of his sorceries, and crowned all by a last effort. He came, he sat on the edge of the bed like a young maiden full of love, who at first keeps silence but whose eyes sparkle, until at last her secret escapes her.

"This," said he, "is a prospectus of a new life-buoy, by means of which one can pass over the Seine dry-footed. This other pamphlet is the report of the Institute on a garment by wearing which we can pass through flames without being burnt. Have you no scheme which can preserve marriage from the miseries

of excessive cold and excessive heat? Listen to me! Here we have
a book on the *Art* of preserving foods; on the *Art* of curing
smoky chimneys; on the *Art* of making good mortar; on the *Art*
of tying a cravat; on the *Art* of carving meat."

In a moment he had named such a prodigious number of books
that the author felt his head go round.

"These myriads of books," says he, "have been devoured by
readers; and while everybody does not build a house, and some
grow hungry, and others have no cravat, or no fire to warm
themselves at, yet everybody to some degree is married. But come
look yonder."

He waved his hand, and appeared to bring before me a distant
ocean where all the books of the world were tossing up and down
like agitated waves. The octodecimos bounded over the surface
of the water. The octavos as they were flung on their way uttered
a solemn sound, sank to the bottom, and only rose up again with
great difficulty, hindered as they were by duodecimos and works
of smaller bulk which floated on the top and melted into light
foam. The furious billows were crowded with journalists, proof-
readers, paper-makers, apprentices, printers' agents, whose hands
alone were seen mingled in confusion among the books. Millions
of voices rang in the air, like those of schoolboys bathing. Certain
men were seen moving hither and thither in canoes, engaged in
fishing out the books, and landing them on the shore in presence
of a tall man, of a disdainful air, dressed in black, and of a cold,
unsympathetic expression. The whole scene represented the libraries and the public. The demon pointed out with his finger a
skiff freshly decked out with all sails set and instead of a flag
bearing a placard. Then with a peal of sardonic laughter, he read
with a thundering voice: *Physiology of Marriage.*

The author fell in love, the devil left him in peace, for he would
have undertaken more than he could handle if he had entered
an apartment occupied by a woman. Several years passed without
bringing other torments than those of love, and the author was
inclined to believe that he had been healed of one infirmity by
means of another which took its place. But one evening he found

himself in a Parisian drawing-room where one of the men among the circle who stood round the fireplace began the conversation by relating in a sepulchral voice the following anecdote:

A peculiar thing took place at Ghent while I was staying there. A lady ten years a widow lay on her bed attacked by mortal sickness. The three heirs of collateral lineage were waiting for her last sigh. They did not leave her side for fear that she would make a will in favor of the convent of Beguins belonging to the town. The sick woman kept silent, she seemed dozing and death appeared to overspread very gradually her mute and livid face. Can't you imagine those three relations seated in silence through that winter midnight beside her bed? An old nurse is with them and she shakes her head, and the doctor sees with anxiety that the sickness has reached its last stage, and holds his hat in one hand and with the other makes a sign to the relations, as if to say to them: "I have no more visits to make here." Amid the solemn silence of the room is heard the dull rustling of a snow-storm which beats upon the shutters. For fear that the eyes of the dying woman might be dazzled by the light, the youngest of the heirs had fitted a shade to the candle which stood near the bed so that the circle of light scarcely reached the pillow of the deathbed, from which the sallow countenance of the sick woman stood out like the figure of Christ imperfectly gilded and fixed upon a cross of tarnished silver. The flickering rays shed by the blue flames of a crackling fire were therefore the sole light of this sombre chamber, where the dénouement of a drama was just ending. A log suddenly rolled from the fire onto the floor, as if presaging some catastrophe. At the sound of it the sick woman quickly rose to a sitting posture. She opened two eyes, clear as those of a cat, and all present eyed her in astonishment. She saw the log advance, and before any one could check an unexpected movement which seemed prompted by a kind of delirium, she bounded from her bed, seized the tongs and threw the coal back into the fireplace. The nurse, the doctor, the relations rushed to her assistance; they took the dying woman in their arms. They put her back in bed;

she laid her head upon her pillow and after a few minutes died, keeping her eye fixed even after her death upon that plank in the floor which the burning brand had touched. Scarcely had the Countess Van Ostroem expired when the three co-heirs exchanged looks of suspicion, and thinking no more about their aunt, began to examine the mysterious floor. As they were Belgians their calculations were as rapid as their glances. An agreement was made by three words uttered in a low voice that none of them should leave the chamber. A servant was sent to fetch a carpenter. Their collateral hearts beat excitedly as they gathered round the treasured flooring, and watched their young apprentice giving the first blow with his chisel. The plank was cut through.

"My aunt made a sign," said the youngest of the heirs.

"No; it was merely the quivering light that made it appear so," replied the eldest, who kept one eye on the treasure and the other on the corpse.

The afflicted relations discovered exactly on the spot where the brand had fallen a certain object artistically enveloped in a mass of plaster.

"Proceed," said the eldest of the heirs.

The chisel of the apprentice then brought to light a human head and some odds and ends of clothing, from which they recognized the count whom all the town believed to have died at Java, and whose loss had been bitterly deplored by his wife.

The narrator of this old story was a tall spare man, with light eyes and brown hair, and the author thought he saw in him a vague resemblance to the demon who had before this tormented him; but the stranger did not show the cloven foot. Suddenly the word ADULTERY sounded in the ears of the author; and this word like a bell woke up in his imagination the most mournful countenances of that procession which before this had streamed by on the utterance of the magic syllables. From that evening he was haunted and persecuted by dreams of a work which did not yet exist; and at no period of his life was the author assailed with such delusive notions about the fatal subject of this book. But he bravely resisted the fiend, although the latter referred the most unimportant incidents of life to this unknown work, and like a customhouse officer set his stamp of mockery upon every occurrence.

Some days afterwards the author found himself in the company of two ladies. The first of them had been one of the most refined and the most intellectual women of Napoleon's court. In his day she occupied a lofty social position, but the sudden appearance of the Restoration caused her downfall; she became a recluse. The second, who was young and beautiful, was at that time living in Paris the life of a fashionable woman. They were friends, because, the one being forty and the other twenty-two years old, they were seldom rivals on the same field. The author was considered quite insignificant by the first of the two ladies, and since the other soon discovered this, they carried on in his presence the conversation which they had begun in a frank discussion of a woman's lot.

"Have you noticed, dear, that women in general bestow their love only upon a fool?"

"What do you mean by that, duchess? And how can you make your remark fit in with the fact that they have an aversion for their husbands?"

"These women are absolute tyrants!" said the author to himself. "Has the devil again turned up in a mob cap?"

"No, dear, I am not joking," replied the duchess, "and I shudder with fear for myself when I coolly consider people whom I have known in other times. Wit always has a sparkle which wounds us, and the man who has much of it makes us fear him perhaps, and if he is a proud man he will be capable of jealousy, and is not therefore to our taste. In fact, we prefer to raise a man to our own height rather than to have to climb up to his. Talent has great successes for us to share in, but the fool affords enjoyment to us; and we would sooner hear say 'that is a very handsome man' than to see our lover elected to the Institute."

"That's enough, duchess! You have absolutely startled me."

And the young coquette began to describe the lovers about whom all the women of her acquaintance raved; there was not a single man of intellect among them.

"But I swear by my virtue," she said, "their husbands are worth more."

"But these are the sort of people they choose for husbands," the duchess answered gravely.

"Tell me," asked the author, "is the disaster which threatens the husband in France quite inevitable?"

"It is," replied the duchess, with a smile; "and the rage which certain women breathe out against those of their sex, whose unfortunate happiness it is to entertain a passion, proves what a burden to them is their chastity. If it were not for fear of the devil, one would be Lais; another owes her virtue to the dryness of her selfish heart; a third to the silly behavior of her first lover; another still—"

The author checked this outpour of revelation by confiding to the two ladies his design for the work with which he had been haunted; they smiled and promised him their assistance. The youngest, with an air of gaiety, suggested one of the first chapters of the undertaking, by saying that she would take upon herself to prove mathematically that women who are entirely virtuous were creatures of reason.

When the author got home he said at once to his demon:

"Come! I am ready; let us sign the compact."

But the demon never returned.

If the author has written here the biography of his book he has not acted on the prompting of fatuity. He relates facts which may furnish material for the history of human thought, and will without doubt explain the work itself. It may perhaps be important to certain anatomists of thought to be told that the soul is feminine. Thus although the author made a resolution not to think about the book which he was forced to write, the book, nevertheless, was completed. One page of it was found on the bed of a sick man, another on the sofa of a boudoir. The glances of women when they turned in the mazes of a waltz flung to him some thoughts; a gesture or a word filled his disdainful brain with others. On the day when he said to himself, "This work, which haunts me, shall be achieved," everything vanished; and like the three Belgians, he drew forth a skeleton from the place over which he had bent to seize a treasure.

A mild, pale countenance took the place of the demon who had tempted me; it wore an engaging expression of kindliness; there were no sharp pointed arrows of criticism in its lineaments. It seemed to deal more with words than with ideas, and shrank from noise and clamor. It was perhaps the household genius of the honorable deputies who sit in the centre of the Chamber.

"Wouldn't it be better," it said, "to let things be as they are? Are things so bad? We ought to believe in marriage as we believe in the immortality of the soul; and you are certainly not making a book to advertise the happiness of marriage. You will surely conclude that among a million of Parisian homes happiness is the exception. You will find perhaps that there are many husbands disposed to abandon their wives to you; but there is not a single son who will abandon his mother. Certain people who are hit by the views which you put forth will suspect your morals and will misrepresent your intentions. In a word, in order to handle social sores, one ought to be a king, or a first consul at least."

Reason, although it appeared under a form most pleasing to the author, was not listened to; for in the distance Folly tossed the coxcomb of Panurge, and the author wished to seize it; but, when he tried to catch it, he found that it was as heavy as the club of Hercules. Moreover, the curé of Meudon adorned it in such fashion that a young man who was less pleased with producing a good work than with wearing fine gloves could not even touch it.

"Is our work completed?" asked the younger of the two feminine assistants of the author.

"Alas! madame," I said, "will you ever requite me for all the hatreds which that work will array against me?"

She waved her hand, and then the author replied to her doubt by a look of indifference.

"What do you mean? Would you hesitate? You must publish it without fear. In the present day we accept a book more because it is in fashion than because it has anything in it."

Although the author does not here represent himself as anything more than the secretary of two ladies, he has in compiling their observations accomplished a double task. With regard to marriage he has here arranged matters which represent what everybody thinks but no one dares to say; but has he not also exposed himself to public displeasure by expressing the mind of the public? Perhaps, however, the eclecticism of the present essay will save it from condemnation. All the while that he indulges in banter the author has attempted to popularize certain ideas which are particularly consoling. He has almost always endeavored to lay bare the hidden springs which move the human soul. While undertaking to defend the most material interests of man, judging them or condemning them, he will perhaps bring to light many sources of intellectual delight. But the author does not foolishly claim always to put forth his pleasantries in the best of taste; he has merely counted upon the diversity of intellectual pursuits in expectation of receiving as much blame as approbation. The subject of his work was so serious that he is constantly launched into an anecdote; because at the present day anecdotes are the vehicle of all moral teaching, and the anti-narcotic of every work of literature. In literature, analysis and investigation prevail, and the wearying of the reader increases in proportion with the egotism of the writer. This is one of the greatest misfortunes that can befall a book, and the present author has been quite aware of it. He has therefore so arranged the topics of this long essay as to afford resting places for the reader. This method has been successfully adopted by a writer, who produced on the subject of Taste a work somewhat parallel to that which is here put forth on the subject of Marriage. From the former the present writer may be permitted to borrow a few words in order to express a thought which he shares with the author of them. This quotation will serve as an expression of homage to his predecessor, whose success has been so swiftly followed by his death:

"When I write and speak of myself in the singular, this implies a confidential talk with the reader; he can examine the statement, discuss it, doubt and even ridicule it; but when I arm myself with the formidable WE, I become a professor and demand submission."
—Brillat-Savarin, Preface to the *Physiology of Taste*.

1829. This essay appeared as the introduction to *The Physiology of Marriage*.

Translated by
J. WALKER MC SPADDEN

Christmas Day at Sea

by JOSEPH CONRAD [1857–1924]

THEOLOGICALLY Christmas Day is the greatest occasion for rejoicing offered to sinful mankind; but this aspect of it is so august and so great that the human mind refuses to contemplate it steadily, perhaps because of its own littleness, for which of course it is in no way to blame. It prefers to concentrate its attention on ceremonial observances, expressive generally of good will and festivity, such, for instance, as giving presents and eating plum-puddings. It may be said at once here that from that conventional point of view the spirit of Christmas Day at sea appears distinctly weak. The opportunities, the materials too, are lacking. Of course, the ship's company get a plum-pudding of some sort, and when the captain appears on deck for the first time the officer of the morning watch greets him with a "Merry Christmas, sir," in a tone only moderately effusive. Anything more would be, owing to the difference in station, not correct. Normally he may expect a return for this in the shape of a "The same to you" of a nicely graduated heartiness. He does not get it always, however.

One Christmas morning, many years ago (I was young then and anxious to do the correct thing), my conventional greeting was met by a grimly scathing "Looks like it, doesn't it?" from my captain. Nothing more. A three-days' more or less thick weather had turned frankly into a dense fog, and I had him called according to orders. We were in the chops of the Channel, with the Scilly Islands on a vague bearing within thirty miles of us, and not a breath of wind anywhere. There the ship remained wrapped up in a damp blanket and as motionless as a post stuck right in the way of the wretched steamboats groping blindly in and out of the Channel. I felt I had

behaved tactlessly; yet how rude it would have been to have withheld the season's greetings from my captain!

It is very difficult to know what is the right thing to do when
one is young. I suffered exceedingly from my gaucherie; but imagine my disgust when in less than half an hour we had the narrowest possible escape from a collision with a steamer which,
without the slightest warning sound, appeared like a vague dark
blot in the fog on our bow. She only took on the shape of a ship as
she passed within twenty yards of the end of our jibboom, terrifying us with the furious screeching of her whistle. Her form melted
into nothing, long before the end of the beastly noise, but I hope
that her people heard the simultaneous yell of execration from
thirty-six throats which we sent after her by way of a Christmas
greeting. Nothing more at variance with the spirit of peace and
good will could be imagined; and I must add that I never saw a
whole ship's company get so much affected by one of the "close
calls" of the sea. We remained jumpy all the morning and consumed our Christmas puddings at noon with restless eyes and
straining ears as if under the shadow of some impending marine
calamity or other.

On shore, of course, a calamity at Christmas time would
hardly take any other shape than that of an avalanche—avalanche
of unpaid bills. I think that it is the absence of that kind of danger
which makes Christmas at sea rather agreeable on the whole. An
additional charm consists in there being no worry about presents.
Presents ought to be unexpected things. The giving and receiving
of presents at appointed times seems to me a hypocritical ceremony, like exchanging gifts of Dead Sea fruit in proof of sham
good-fellowship. But the sea of which I write here is a live sea; the
fruits one chances to gather on it may be salt as tears or bitter as
death, but they never taste like ashes in the mouth.

In all my twenty years of wandering over the restless waters of
the globe I can only remember one Christmas Day celebrated by
a present given and received. It was, in my view, a proper live-sea
transaction, no offering of Dead Sea fruit; and in its unexpected-
ness perhaps worth recording. Let me tell you first that it happened in the year 1879, long before there was any thought of wire-

less messages, and when an inspired person trying to prophesy broadcasting would have been regarded as a particularly offensive nuisance and probably sent to a rest-cure home. We used to call them madhouses then, in our rude, cave-man way.

The daybreak of Christmas Day in the year 1879 was fine. The sun began to shine sometime about four o'clock over the sombre expanse of the Southern Ocean in latitude 51; and shortly afterwards a sail was sighted ahead. The wind was light, but a heavy swell was running. Presently I wished a "Merry Christmas" to my captain. He looked still sleepy, but amiable. I reported the distant sail to him and ventured the opinion that there was something wrong with her. He said, "Wrong?" in an incredulous tone. I pointed out that she had all her upper sails furled and that she was brought to the wind, which, in that region of the world, could not be accounted for on any other theory. He took the glasses from me, directed them towards her stripped masts resembling three Swedish safety matches, flying up and down and waggling to and fro ridiculously in that heaving and austere wilderness of countless water-hills, and returned them to me without a word. He only yawned. This marked display of callousness gave me a shock. In those days I was generally inexperienced and still a comparative stranger in that particular region of the world of waters.

The captain, as is a captain's way, disappeared from the deck; and after a time our carpenter came up the poop ladder carrying an empty small wooden keg, of the sort in which certain ship's provisions are packed. I said, surprised, "What do you mean by lugging this thing up here, Chips?"—"Captain's orders, sir," he explained shortly.

I did not like to question him further, and so we only exchanged Christmas greetings and he went away. The next person to speak to me was the steward. He came running up the companion stairs: "Have you any old newspapers in your room, sir?"

We had left Sidney, N.S.W., eighteen days before. There were several old Sydney *Heralds, Telegraphs, Bulletins* in my cabin, besides a few home papers received by the last mail. "Why do you ask, steward?" I inquired naturally. "The captain would like to have them," he said.

And even then I did not understand the inwardness of these eccentricities. I was only lost in astonishment at them. It was eight o'clock before we had closed with that ship, which, under her short canvas and heading nowhere in particular, seemed to be loafing aimlessly on the very threshold of the gloomy home of storms. But long before that hour I had learned from the number of the boats she carried that this nonchalant ship was a whaler. She was the first whaler I had ever seen. She had hoisted the Stars and Stripes at her peak, and her signal flags had told us already that her name was: "*Alaska*—two years out from New York—east from Honolulu—two hundred and fifteen days on the cruising ground."

We passed, sailing slowly, within a hundred yards of her; and just as our steward started ringing the breakfast bell the captain and I held aloft, in good view of the figures watching us over her stern, the keg, properly headed up and containing, besides an enormous bundle of old newspapers, two boxes of figs in honour of the day. We flung it far out over the rail. Instantly our ship, sliding down the slope of a high swell, left it far behind in our wake. On board the *Alaska* a man in a fur cap flourished an arm; another, a much be-whiskered person, ran forward suddenly. I never saw anything so ready and so smart as the way that whaler, rolling desperately all the time, lowered one of her boats. The Southern Ocean went on tossing the two ships like a juggler his gilt balls, and the microscopic white speck of the boat seemed to come into the game instantly, as if shot out from a catapult on the enormous and lonely stage. That Yankee whaler lost not a moment in picking up her Christmas present from the English wool clipper.

Before we had increased the distance very much she dipped her ensign in thanks and asked to be reported "All well, with a catch of three fish." I suppose it paid them for two hundred and fifteen days of risk and toil, away from the sounds and sights of the inhabited world, like outcasts devoted, beyond the confines of mankind's life, to some enchanted and lonely penance.

Christmas Days at sea are of varied character, fair to middling and down to plainly atrocious. In this statement I do not include Christmas Days on board passenger ships. A passenger is, of course, a brother (or sister), and quite a nice person in a way, but his Christmas Days are, I suppose, what he wants them to be: the conventional festivities of an expensive hotel included in the price of his ticket.

From *Last Essays,* 1926.

New York

by CHARLES DICKENS [1812-1870]

THE BEAUTIFUL METROPOLIS of America is by no means so clean a city as Boston, but many of its streets have the same characteristics; except that the houses are not quite so fresh-coloured, the sign-boards are not quite so gaudy, the gilded letters not quite so golden, the bricks not quite so red, the stone not quite so white, the blinds and area railings not quite so green, the knobs and plates upon the street doors not quite so bright and twinkling. There are many by-streets, almost as neutral in clean colours, and positive in dirty ones, as by-streets in London; and there is one quarter, commonly called the Five Points, which, in respect of filth and wretchedness, may be safely backed against Seven Dials, or any other part of famed St. Giles's.

The great promenade and thoroughfare, as most people know, is Broadway; a wide and bustling street, which, from the Battery Gardens to its opposite termination in a country road, may be four miles long. Shall we sit down in an upper floor of the Carlton House Hotel (situated in the best part of this main artery of New York), and when we are tired of looking down upon the life below, sally forth arm-in-arm, and mingle with the stream?

Warm weather! The sun strikes upon our heads at this open window, as though its rays were concentrated through a burning-glass; but the day is in its zenith, and the season an unusual one. Was there ever such a sunny street as this Broadway! The pavement stones are polished with the tread of feet until they shine again; the red bricks of the houses might be yet in the dry, hot kilns; and the roofs of those omnibuses look as though, if water were poured on them, they would hiss and smoke, and smell like half-quenched fires. No stint of omnibuses here! Half-a-dozen have gone by within as many minutes. Plenty of hackney cabs and coaches too; gigs, phaetons, large-wheeled tilburies, and private carriages—rather of a clumsy make, and not very different from the public vehicles, but built for the heavy roads beyond the city pavement. Negro coachmen and white; in straw hats, black hats, white hats, glazed caps, fur caps; in coats of drab, black, brown, green, blue, nankeen, striped jean and linen; and there, in that one instance (look while it passes, or it will be too late), in suits of livery. Some southern republican that, who puts his blacks in uniform, and swells with Sultan pomp and power. Yonder, where that phaeton with the well-clipped pair of grays has stopped— standing at their heads now—is a Yorkshire groom, who has not been very long in these parts, and looks sorrowfully round for a companion pair of top-boots, which he may traverse the city half a year without meeting. Heaven save the ladies, how they dress! We have seen more colours in these ten minutes, than we should have seen elsewhere, in as many days. What various parasols! what rainbow silks and satins! what pinking of thin stockings, and pinching of thin shoes, and fluttering of ribbons and silk tassels, and display of rich cloaks with gaudy hoods and linings! The young gentlemen are fond, you see, of turning down their shirt-collars and cultivating their whiskers, especially under the chin; but they cannot approach the ladies in their dress or bearing, being, to say the truth, humanity of quite another sort. Byrons of the desk and counter, pass on, and let us see what kind of men those are behind ye: those two labourers in holiday clothes, of whom one carries in his hand a crumpled scrap of paper from which he tries to spell out a hard name, while the other looks about for it on all the doors and windows.

Irishmen both! You might know them, if they were masked, by their long-tailed blue coats and bright buttons, and their drab trousers, which they wear like men well used to working dresses, who are easy in no others. It would be hard to keep your model republics going, without the countrymen and countrywomen of those two labourers. For who else would dig, and delve, and drudge, and do domestic work, and make canals and roads, and execute great lines of Internal Improvement! Irishmen both, and sorely puzzled too, to find out what they seek. Let us go down, and help them, for the love of home, and that spirit of liberty which admits of honest service to honest men, and honest work for honest bread, no matter what it be.

That's well! We have got at the right address at last, though it is written in strange characters truly, and might have been scrawled with the blunt handle of the spade the writer better knows the use of, than a pen. Their way lies yonder, but what business takes them there? They carry savings: to hoard up? No. They are brothers, those men. One crossed the sea alone, and working very hard for one half-year, and living harder, saved funds enough to bring the other out. That done, they worked together side by side, contentedly sharing hard labour and hard living for another term, and then their sisters came, and then another brother, and lastly, their old mother. And what now? Why, the poor old crone is restless in a strange land, and yearns to lay her bones, she says, among her people in the old graveyard at home: and so they go to pay her passage back: and God help her and them, and every simple heart, and all who turn to the Jerusalem of their younger days, and have an altar-fire upon the cold hearth of their fathers.

This narrow thoroughfare, baking and blistering in the sun, is Wall Street: the Stock Exchange and Lombard Street of New York. Many a rapid fortune has been made in this street, and many a no less rapid ruin. Some of these very merchants whom you see hanging about here now, have locked up money in their strong-boxes, like the man in the Arabian Nights, and opening them again, have found but withered leaves. Below, here by the water-side, where the bowsprits of ships stretch across the footway, and almost thrust themselves into the windows, lie the noble American vessels which have made their Packet Service the finest in the world. They have brought hither the foreigners who abound in all the streets: not, perhaps, that there are more here, than in other commercial cities; but elsewhere, they have particular haunts, and you must find them out; here, they pervade the town.

We must cross Broadway again; gaining some refreshment from the heat, in the sight of the great blocks of clean ice which are being carried into shops and bar-rooms; and the pine-apples and water-melons profusely displayed for sale. Fine streets of spacious houses here, you see!—Wall Street has furnished and dismantled many of them very often—and here a deep green leafy square. Be sure that is a hospitable house with inmates to be affectionately remembered always, where they have the open door and pretty show of plants within, and where the child with laughing eyes is peeping out of window at the little dog below. You wonder what may be the use of this tall flagstaff in the by-street, with something like Liberty's head-dress on its top: so do I. But there is a passion for tall flagstaffs hereabout, and you may see its twin brother in five minutes, if you have a mind.

Again across Broadway, and so—passing from the many-coloured crowd and glittering shops—into another long main street, the Bowery. A railroad yonder, see, where two stout horses trot along, drawing a score or two of people and a great wooden ark, with ease. The stores are poorer here; the passengers less gay. Clothes ready-made, and meat ready-cooked, are to be bought in these parts; and the lively whirl of carriages is exchanged for the deep rumble of carts and waggons. These signs which are so plentiful, in shape like river buoys, or small balloons, hoisted by cords to poles, and dangling there, announce, as you may see by looking up, "OYSTERS IN EVERY STYLE." They tempt the hungry most at night, for then dull candles glimmering inside, illuminate these dainty words, and make the mouths of idlers water, as they read and linger.

What is this dismal-fronted pile of bastard Egyptian, like an enchanter's palace in a melodrama!—a famous prison, called The Tombs. Shall we go in?

So. A long narrow lofty building, stove-heated as usual, with four galleries, one above the other, going round it, and communicating by stairs. Between the two sides of each gallery, and in its centre, a bridge, for the greater convenience of crossing. On each of these bridges sits a man: dozing or reading, or talking to an idle companion. On each tier, are two opposite rows of small iron doors. They look like furnace-doors, but are cold and black, as though the fires within had all gone out. Some two or three are open, and women, with drooping heads bent down, are talking to the inmates. The whole is lighted by a skylight, but it is fast closed; and from the roof there dangle, limp and drooping, two useless windsails.

A man with keys appears, to show us round. A good-looking fellow, and, in his way, civil and obliging.

"Are those black doors the cells?"

"Yes."

"Are they all full?"

"Well, they's pretty nigh full, and that's a fact, and no two ways about it."

"Those at the bottom are unwholesome, surely?"

"Why, we *do* only put coloured people in 'em. That's the truth."

"When do the prisoners take exercise?"

"Well, they do without it pretty much."

"Do they never walk in the yard?"

"Considerable seldom."

"Sometimes, I suppose?"

"Well, it's rare they do. They keep pretty bright without it."

"But suppose a man were here for a twelvemonth. I know this is only a prison for criminals who are charged with grave offences, while they are awaiting their trial, or under remand, but the law here, affords criminals many means of delay. What with motions for new trials, and in arrest of judgment, and what not, a prisoner might be here for twelve months, I take it, might he not?"

"Well, I guess he might."

"Do you mean to say that in all that time he would never come out at that little iron door, for exercise?"

"He might walk some, perhaps—not much."

"Will you open one of the doors?"

"All, if you like."

The fastenings jar and rattle, and one of the doors turns slowly on its hinges. Let us look in. A small bare cell, into which the light enters through a high chink in the wall. There is a rude means of washing, a table, and a bedstead. Upon the latter, sits a man of sixty; reading. He looks up for a moment; gives an impatient dogged shake; and fixes his eyes upon his book again. As we withdraw our heads, the door closes on him, and is fastened as before. This man has murdered his wife, and will probably be hanged.

"How long has he been here?"

"A month."

"When will he be tried?"

"Next term."

"When is that?"

"Next month."

"In England, if a man be under sentence of death, even he has air and exercise at certain periods of the day."

"Possible?"

With what stupendous and untranslatable coolness he says this, and how loungingly he leads on to the women's side: making, as he goes, a kind of iron castanet of the key and the stair-rail!

Each cell door on this side has a square aperture in it. Some of the women peep anxiously through it at the sound of footsteps; others shrink away in shame. For what offence can that lonely child, of ten or twelve years old, be shut up here? Oh! that boy? He is the son of the prisoner we saw just now; is a witness against his father; and is detained here for safe keeping, until the trial; that's all.

But it is a dreadful place for the child to pass the long days and nights in. This is rather hard treatment for a young witness, is it not? What says our conductor?

"Well, it ain't a very rowdy life, and *that's* a fact!"

Again he clinks his metal castanet, and leads us leisurely away. I have a question to ask him as we go.

"Pray, why do they call this place The Tombs?"

"Well, it's the cant name."

"I know it is. Why?"

"Some suicides happened here, when it was first built. I expect it come about from that."

"I saw just now, that that man's clothes were scattered about the floor of his cell. Don't you oblige the prisoners to be orderly, and put such things away?"

"Where should they put 'em?"

"Not on the ground surely. What do you say to hanging them up?"

He stops and looks round to emphasize his answer:

"Why, I say that's just it. When they had hooks they *would* hang themselves, so they're taken out of every cell, and there's only the marks left where they used to be!"

The prison-yard in which he pauses now, has been the scene of terrible performances. Into this narrow, grave-like place, men are brought out to die. The wretched creature stands beneath the gibbet on the ground; the rope about his neck; and when the sign is given, a weight at its other end comes running down, and swings him up into the air—a corpse.

The law requires that there be present at this dismal spectacle, the judge, the jury, and citizens to the amount of twenty-five. From the community it is hidden. To the dissolute and bad, the thing remains a frightful mystery. Between the criminal and them, the prison-wall is interposed as a thick gloomy veil. It is the curtain to his bed of death, his winding-sheet, and grave. From him it shuts out life, and all the motives to unrepenting hardihood in that last hour, which its mere sight and presence is often all-sufficient to sustain. There are no bold eyes to make him bold; no ruffians to uphold a ruffian's name before. All beyond the pitiless stone wall, is unknown space.

Let us go forth again into the cheerful streets.

Once more in Broadway! Here are the same ladies in bright colours, walking to and fro, in pairs and singly; yonder the very same light blue parasol which passed and repassed the hotel-window twenty times while we were sitting there. We are going to cross here. Take care of the pigs. Two portly sows are trotting up behind this carriage, and a select party of half-a-dozen gentlemen hogs have just now turned the corner.

Here is a solitary swine lounging homeward by himself. He has only one ear; having parted with the other to vagrant-dogs in the course of his city rambles. But he gets on very well without it; and leads a roving, gentlemanly, vagabond kind of life, somewhat answering to that of our club-men at home. He leaves his lodgings every morning at a certain hour, throws himself upon the town, gets through his day in some manner quite satisfactory to himself, and regularly appears at the door of his own house again at night, like the mysterious master of Gil Blas. He is a free-and-easy, careless, indifferent kind of pig, having a very large acquaintance among other pigs of the same character, whom he rather knows by sight than conversation, as he seldom troubles himself to stop and exchange civilities, but goes grunting down the kennel, turning up the news and small-talk of the city in the shape of cabbage-stalks and offal, and bearing no tails but his own: which is a very short one, for his old enemies, the dogs, have been at that too, and have left him hardly enough to swear by. He is in every respect a republican pig, going wherever he pleases, and mingling with the best society, on an equal, if not superior footing, for every one makes way when he appears, and the haughtiest give him the wall, if he prefer it. He is a great philosopher, and seldom moved, unless by the dogs before mentioned. Sometimes, indeed, you may see his small eye twinkling on a slaughtered friend, whose carcase garnishes a butcher's door-post, but he grunts out "Such is life: all flesh is pork!" buries his nose in the mire again, and waddles down the gutter: comforting himself with the reflection that there is one snout the less to anticipate stray cabbage-stalks, at any rate.

They are the city scavengers, these pigs. Ugly brutes they are; having, for the most part, scanty brown backs, like the lids of old horsehair trunks: spotted with unwholesome black blotches. They have long, gaunt legs, too, and such peaked snouts, that if one of them could be persuaded to sit for his profile, nobody would recognise it for a pig's likeness. They are never attended upon, or fed, or driven, or caught, but are thrown upon their own resources in early life, and become preternaturally knowing in consequence. Every pig knows where he lives, much better than anybody could tell him. At this hour, just as evening is closing in, you will see them roaming towards bed by scores, eating their way to the last. Occasionally, some youth among them who has over-eaten himself, or has been worried by dogs, trots shrinkingly homeward, like a prodigal son: but this is a rare case: perfect self-possession and self-reliance, and immovable composure, being their foremost attributes.

The streets and shops are lighted now; and as the eye travels down the long thoroughfare, dotted with bright jets of gas, it is reminded of Oxford Street, or Piccadilly. Here and there a flight of broad stone cellar-steps appears, and a painted lamp directs you to the Bowling Saloon, or Ten-Pin alley; Ten-Pins being a game of mingled chance and skill, invented when the legislature passed an act forbidding Nine-Pins. At other downward flights of steps, are other lamps, marking the whereabouts of oyster-cellars—pleasant retreats, say I: not only by reason of their wonderful cookery of oysters, pretty nigh as large as cheese-plates (or for thy dear sake, heartiest of Greek professors!), but because of all kinds of eaters of fish, or flesh, or fowl, in these latitudes, the swallowers of oysters alone are not gregarious; but subduing themselves, as it were, to the nature of what they work in, and copying the coyness of the thing they eat, do sit apart in curtained boxes, and consort by twos, not by two hundreds.

But how quiet the streets are! Are there no itinerant bands; no wind or stringed instruments? No, not one. By day, are there no Punches, Fastoccini, Dancing-dogs, Jugglers, Conjurers, Orchestrinas, or even Barrel-organs? No, not one. Yes, I remember one. One barrel-organ and a dancing-monkey—sportive by nature, but fast fading into a dull, lumpish monkey, of the Utilitarian school. Beyond that, nothing lively; no, not so much as a white mouse in a twirling cage.

Are there no amusements? Yes. There is a lecture-room across the way, from which that glare of light proceeds, and there may be evening service for the ladies thrice a week, or oftener. For the young gentlemen, there is the counting-house, the store, the bar-room: the latter, as you may see through these windows, pretty full. Hark! to the clinking sound of hammers breaking lumps of ice, and to the cool gurgling of the pounded bits, as, in the process of mixing, they are poured from glass to glass! No amusements? What are these suckers of cigars and swallowers of strong drinks, whose hats and legs we see in every possible variety of twist, doing, but amusing themselves? What are the fifty newspapers, which those precocious urchins are bawling down the street, and which are kept filed within, what are they but amusements? Not vapid waterish amusements, but good strong stuff, dealing in round abuse and blackguard names; pulling off the roofs of private houses, as the Halting Devil did in Spain; pimping and pandering for all degrees of vicious taste, and gorging with coined lies the most voracious maw; imputing to every man in public life the coarsest and the vilest motives; scaring away from the stabbed and prostrate body-politic, every Samaritan of clear conscience and good deeds; and setting on, with yell and whistle and the clapping of foul hands, the vilest vermin and worst birds of prey. No amusements!

Let us go on again; and passing this wilderness of an hotel with stores about its base, like some Continental theatre, or the London Opera House shorn of its colonnade, plunge into the Five Points. But it is needful, first, that we take as our escort these two heads of the police, whom you would know for sharp and well-trained officers if you met them in the Great Desert. So true it is, that certain pursuits, wherever carried on, will stamp men with the same character. These two might have been begotten, born, and bred, in Bow Street.

We have seen no beggars in the streets by night or day; but of other kinds of strollers, plenty. Poverty, wretchedness, and vice, are rife enough where we are going now.

This is the place: these narrow ways, diverging to the right and left, and reeking everywhere with dirt and filth. Such lives as are led here, bear the same fruits here as elsewhere. The coarse and bloated faces at the doors, have counterparts at home, and all the wide world over. Debauchery has made the very houses prematurely old. See how the rotten beams are tumbling down, and how the patched and broken windows seem to scowl dimly, like eyes that have been hurt in drunken frays. Many of those pigs live here. Do they ever wonder why their masters walk upright in lieu of going on all-fours? and why they talk instead of grunting?

So far, nearly every house is a low tavern; and on the bar-room walls, are coloured prints of Washington, and Queen Victoria of England, and the American Eagle. Among the pigeon-holes that hold the bottles, are pieces of plate-glass and coloured paper, for there is, in some sort, a taste for decoration, even here. And as seamen frequent these haunts, there are maritime pictures by the dozen: of partings between sailors and their lady-loves, portraits of William, of the ballad, and his Black-eyed Susan; of Will Watch, the Bold Smuggler; of Paul Jones the Pirate, and the like: on which the painted eyes of Queen Victoria, and of Washington to boot, rest in as strange companionship, as on most of the scenes that are enacted in their wonderful presence.

What place is this, to which the squalid street conducts us? A kind of square of leprous houses, some of which are attainable only by crazy wooden stairs without. What lies beyond this tottering flight of steps, that creak beneath our tread?—a miserable room, lighted by one dim candle, and destitute of all comfort, save that which may be hidden in a wretched bed. Beside it, sits a man: his elbows on his knees: his forehead hidden in his hands. "What ails that man?" asks the foremost officer. "Fever," he sullenly replies, without looking up. Conceive the fancies of a fevered brain, in such a place as this!

Ascend these pitch-dark stairs, heedful of a false footing on the trembling boards, and grope your way with me into this wolfish den, where neither ray of light nor breath of air, appears to come. A negro lad, startled from his sleep by the officer's voice—he knows it well—but comforted by his assurance that he has not come on business, officiously bestirs himself to light a candle. The match flickers for a moment, and shows great mounds of dusky rags upon the ground; then dies away and leaves a denser darkness than before, if there can be degrees in such extremes. He stumbles down the stairs and presently comes back, shading a flaring taper with his hand. Then the mounds of rags are seen to be astir, and rise slowly up, and the floor is covered with heaps of negro women, waking from their sleep: their white teeth chattering, and their bright eyes glistening and winking on all sides with surprise and fear, like the countless repetition of one astonished African face in some strange mirror.

Mount up these other stairs with no less caution (there are traps and pitfalls here, for those who are not so well escorted as ourselves) into the housetop; where the bare beams and rafters meet overhead, and calm night looks down through the crevices in the roof. Open the door of one of these cramped hutches full of sleeping negroes. Pah! They have a charcoal fire within; there is a smell of singeing clothes, or flesh, so close they gather round the brazier; and vapours issue forth that blind and suffocate. From every corner, as you glance about you in these dark retreats, some figure crawls half-awakened, as if the judgment-hour were near at hand, and every obscene grave were giving up its dead. Where dogs would howl to lie, women, and men, and boys slink off to sleep, forcing the dislodged rats to move away in quest of better lodgings.

Here too are lanes and alleys, paved with mud knee-deep, underground chambers, where they dance and game; the walls bedecked with rough designs of ships, and forts, and flags, and American eagles out of number: ruined houses, open to the street, whence, through wide gaps in the walls, other ruins loom upon the eye, as though the world of vice and misery had nothing else to show: hideous tenements which take their name from robbery and murder: all that is loathsome, drooping, and decayed is here.

Our leader has his hand upon the latch of "Almack's," and calls to us from the bottom of the steps; for the assembly-room of the Five Point fashionables is approached by a descent. Shall we go in? It is but a moment.

Heyday! the landlady of Almack's thrives! A buxom fat mulatto woman, with sparkling eyes, whose head is daintily ornamented with a handkerchief of many colours. Nor is the landlord much behind her in his finery, being attired in a smart blue jacket, like a ship's steward, with a thick gold ring upon his little finger, and round his neck a gleaming golden watch-guard. How glad he is to see us! What will we please to call for? A dance? It shall be done directly, sir: "a regular break-down."

The corpulent black fiddler, and his friend who plays the tambourine, stamp upon the boarding of the small raised orchestra in which they sit, and play a lively measure. Five or six couples come upon the floor, marshalled by a lively young negro, who is the wit of the assembly, and the greatest dancer known. He never leaves off making queer faces, and is the delight of all the rest, who grin from ear to ear incessantly. Among the dancers are two young mulatto girls, with large, black, drooping eyes, and head-gear after the fashion of the hostess, who are as shy, or feign to be, as though they never danced before, and so look down before the visitors, that their partners can see nothing but the long fringed lashes.

But the dance commences. Every gentleman sets as long as he likes to the opposite lady, and the opposite lady to him, and all are so long about it that the sport begins to languish, when suddenly the lively hero dashes in to the rescue. Instantly the fiddler grins, and goes at it tooth and nail; there is new energy in the tambourine; new laughter in the dancers; new smiles in the landlady; new confidence in the landlord; new brightness in the very candles. Single shuffle, double shuffle, cut and cross-cut; snapping his fingers, rolling his eyes, turning in his knees, presenting the backs of his legs in front, spinning about on his toes and heels like nothing but the man's fingers on the tambourine; dancing with two left legs, two right legs, two wooden legs, two wire legs, two spring legs —all sorts of legs and no legs—what is this to him? And in what walk of life, or dance of life, does man ever get such stimulating applause as thunders about him, when, having danced his partner off her feet, and himself too, he finishes by leaping gloriously on the bar-counter, and calling for something to drink, with the chuckle of a million of counterfeit Jim Crows, in one inimitable sound!

The air, even in these distempered parts, is fresh after the stifling atmosphere of the houses; and now, as we emerge into a broader street, it blows upon us with a purer breath, and the stars look bright again. Here are The Tombs once more. The city watch-house is a part of the building. It follows naturally on the sights we have just left. Let us see that, and then to bed.

What! do you thrust your common offenders against the police

discipline of the town, into such holes as these? Do men and
women, against whom no crime is proved, lie here all night in
perfect darkness, surrounded by the noisome vapours which encircle that flagging lamp you light us with, and breathing this filthy
and offensive stench! Why, such indecent and disgusting dungeons
as these cells, would bring disgrace upon the most despotic empire
in the world! Look at them, man—you, who see them every night,
and keep the keys. Do you see what they are? Do you know how
drains are made below the streets, and wherein these human
sewers differ, except in being always stagnant?

Well, he don't know. He has had five-and-twenty young women
locked up in this very cell at one time, and you'd hardly realise
what handsome faces there were among 'em.

In God's name! shut the door upon the wretched creature who
is in it now, and put its screen before a place, quite unsurpassed in
all the vice, neglect, and devilry, of the worst old town in Europe.

Are people really left all night, untried, in those black sties?—
Every night. The watch is set at seven in the evening. The magis-
trate opens his court at five in the morning. That is the earliest
hour at which the first prisoner can be released; and if an officer
appear against him, he is not taken out till nine o'clock or ten.—
But if any one among them die in the interval, as one man did, not
long ago? Then he is half-eaten by the rats in an hour's time; as
that man was; and there an end.

What is this intolerable tolling of great bells, and crashing of
wheels, and shouting in the distance? A fire. And what that deep
red light in the opposite direction? Another fire. And what these
charred and blackened walls we stand before? A dwelling where
a fire has been. It was more than hinted, in an official report, not
long ago, that some of these conflagrations were not wholly accidental, and that speculation and enterprise found a field of exer-
tion, even in flames: but be this as it may, there was a fire last night,
there are two to-night, and you may lay an even wager there will be
at least one, to-morrow. So, carrying that with us for our comfort,
let us say, Good-night, and climb up-stairs to bed.

From *American Notes*, 1842.

Something about Lying

by FËDOR DOSTOEVSKI [1821–1881]

WHY IS EVERYBODY here lying—every single man? I am convinced that I will be immediately stopped and that people will start shouting: "Oh, what nonsense, by no means everybody! You have no topic, and so you are inventing things in order to begin in a more imposing fashion." I have already been upbraided for the lack of themes. But the point is that now I am earnestly convinced of the universality of our lying. One lives fifty years with an idea, one perceives and feels it, and all of a sudden it appears in such an aspect as to make it seem that one had hitherto not known it at all.

Lately, I was suddenly struck by the thought that in Russia, among our educated classes, there cannot be even one man who wouldn't be addicted to lying. This is precisely because among us even quite honest people may be lying. I am certain that in other nations, in the overwhelming majority of them, only scoundrels are lying; they are lying for the sake of material gain, that is, with directly criminal intent.

Well, in our case, even the most esteemed people may be lying for no reason at all, and with most honorable aims. We are lying almost invariably for the sake of hospitality. One wishes to create in the listener an æsthetical impression, to give him pleasure, and so one lies even, so to speak, sacrificing oneself to the listener.

Let anyone recall: has it not happened to anyone to add twenty times, let us say, the number of versts which, in one hour, horses have driven him, if only this be needed to strengthen a pleasurable impression on the listener. And, indeed, wasn't the listener pleased to such an extent that he would start at once to assure you that a certain troika, which he had known, on a bet outran a railroad train, and so on, and so forth.

Well, what about hunting dogs? Or how, in Paris, teeth were replaced in one's mouth? Or how, here, you were cured by Botkin? Regarding your illness, haven't you related such wonders that you started believing them yourself by the time you had reached the middle of your story (since by the middle of a story one always begins to believe it), but, when going to bed at night and recollecting with pleasure how agreeably your listener had been impressed, you would suddenly stop and involuntarily utter: "Eh, how I lied!"

However, this is not a convincing example, since there is nothing more agreeable than to talk about one's illness, if only a listener can be found; and once you start talking, it is no longer possible to refrain from lying; this will even cure a patient. But, returning from abroad, didn't you speak about a thousand things which you beheld "with your own eyes . . ."? No, I shall withdraw this example: for a Russian returning home it is impossible not to exaggerate things about "abroad," for otherwise why should he have been journeying thither?

But take, for instance, natural sciences! Did you not discuss natural sciences or bankruptcy cases and escapes over the border by different Petersburg, and other, Jews, understanding nothing about them and not knowing the A B C of natural sciences?

Excuse me—did you not relate some anecdote, as if it happened to you, to the very person who had told it to you as if it had happened to him? Did you possibly forget how, by the time you reached the middle of the story, suddenly you recalled and guessed this fact, which was clearly confirmed in the suffering look of your listener, who was intently staring at you (since in such cases people, I don't know why, stare at each other with an intensity magnified ten times)? Do you remember how, despite the loss of all your humor, nevertheless, with a courage worthy of the great cause, you continued to lisp your story? And then, when hurriedly you did get through with it, you both, with nervously hasty civilities, shook hands, smiled and ran in opposite directions from each other?—So that when, for no reason, in an ultimate convulsion, some demon drove you to cry to the listener, running down the staircase, a question about his auntie's health, he did not turn to you and made no reply—which fact stuck in your recollection as the most painful thing in the sum total of the incident that happened to you?

Briefly, if to all this anyone should answer me with a *nay,* namely, that he did not relate the anecdotes, did not touch upon Botkin, did not lie about Jews, did not shout on the staircase about auntie's health, and that nothing of the kind ever happened to him —I would simply not believe it. I know that the Russian liar, time and again, lies without even noticing it himself, so that one may not perceive the fact that he is lying. See what happens: no sooner will a man tell a successful lie, than he will include the anecdote among the unquestioned facts of his personal life, and then he acts quite conscientiously because he fully believes it; besides, it is unnatural sometimes not to believe it.

"Eh, rubbish!"—I will be told—"These are innocent lies; there is nothing universal about them." Be this as it may, I agree that all this is quite innocent, and merely hints at noble traits in one's character—for example, at a feeling of gratitude. Because if you were listened to when you were lying, it is impossible not to let the listener lie, if only from mere gratitude.

Courteous reciprocity in lying is virtually the prime condition of Russian society—of all Russian meetings, evening entertainments, clubs, scientific bodies, etc. Indeed, it is only a dull blockhead who, in cases of this kind, will suddenly begin to doubt the number of versts driven by you, or the miracles which Botkin performed when treating you. But these are heartless and hemorrhoidal creatures who themselves are forthwith punished, wondering thereafter why they have to suffer punishment. Men without talent.

Still all this lying, despite its innocence, hints at some very momentous fundamental traits of ours to such an extent that here the element of universality almost begins to reveal itself. For example: *first,* that we Russians are primarily afraid of truth—*i.e.,* we are not really afraid, if you please, but we always regard truth as something too weary in our intercourse, something prosaic, insufficiently poetic, too banal; and thereby, always evading truth, we, finally, made it something most extraordinary and rare in our

Russian world (I am not referring to the newspaper by this name).
Thus we have totally forgotten the axiom that truth is the most
poetic thing in the world, especially in its pure state. More than
that: it is even more fantastic than the ordinary human mind is
capable of fabricating and conceiving.

In Russia, truth almost invariably assumes a fantastic character. In fact, men have finally succeeded in converting all that the
human mind may lie about and belie into something more com-
prehensible than truth, and this prevails all over the world. For
centuries truth will lie right on the table before people but they
will not take it: they will chase after a fabrication precisely because
they look upon it as something fantastic and utopian.

Second, this is a hint at the fact that our wholesale Russian
lying suggests that we are all ashamed of ourselves. Indeed, every
one of us carries in him an almost innate shame of himself and
of his own face; and the moment Russians find themselves in company, they hasten to appear at all cost something different from
what they in reality are; everyone hastens to assume a different
face.

Already Hertzen has remarked about Russians abroad that
they don't know how to behave in public; they speak in a loud
manner, when everybody else is silent, and they cannot utter a
single word politely and naturally when it is necessary to speak.
And this is true: at once we observe a twist, a lie, a painful cramp;
at once there arises the urge for being ashamed of everything that
is actual, of concealing and effacing one's own face, given by God
to the Russian, and of assuming a different, an alien, as un-Russian
a face as possible. All this comes from the firm inner conviction
in every Russian that one's own face is necessarily trivial and shame-
fully comic, and that if he should assume a French, an English—
in brief, somebody else's—face, something more respectable would
come of it, and that in this guise he would not be recognized.

In this connection I will note something very characteristic:
this miserable petty shame of one's self and this vile self-negation
are, in most cases, unconscious; this is something convulsive and
unconquerable; yet, consciously, the Russians—even the most ardent self-negators among them—do not readily admit their trivi-

ality, and by all means demand respect for themselves: "I am, indeed, quite like an Englishman"—the Russian argues—"therefore, I should be respected, since everybody respects the English."

This fundamental type of our society has been moulding itself over a period of two hundred years, in accordance with the express principle formulated two centuries ago: "Never, under any circumstance, should one be himself; one should assume a different face, bespitting one's own face once and forever; one should always be ashamed of one's self and one should never resemble one's self." The results proved most complete. There is no German, no Frenchman, there is no Englishman in the whole world, who, when meeting other people, would be ashamed of his own face, provided he be honestly convinced that he had perpetrated nothing bad. A Russian is perfectly aware of the fact that there is no such Englishman, while an educated Russian also knows that the essential point of self-respect is not to be ashamed of one's own face, wherever it be. This is the reason why he hastens to assume the appearance of a Frenchman or of an Englishman, precisely so as to be taken as quickly as possible for a person who never, and nowhere, is ashamed of his face.

"Innocent things; old stuff; it has been told a thousand times already," people will say again. Be that as it may, but here is something even more typical. There is one point on which any Russian of the educated pattern, appearing in society or in public, is extremely exacting, and which he will yield under no circumstance. This point is intellect—the desire to appear more clever than he is, and—this is remarkable—this is in no sense a desire to seem more clever than the rest or even more clever than anyone in particular, but merely—*not more stupid than anyone.* "Concede," he means, "that I am not more stupid than anyone, and I will concede that you are not more stupid than anyone."

Here, again, we have something on the order of reciprocal gratitude. As is known, for instance, a Russian bows before European authority with happiness and haste, even without permitting himself to analyze: in such cases he is particularly opposed to analysis. Oh, it's different if a man of genius should descend from his pedestal, or merely cease to be in vogue: then, and with regard to such a person, there is no one harsher than the Russian intelligentsia; then there is no limit to its haughtiness, contempt and scoffing. Later, very naïvely we wonder if somehow we happen to learn that in Europe people still continue to look with respect upon the person who descended from his pedestal and to value him according to his merit. Yet that same Russian who had bowed before a genius in vogue, even without any analysis, nevertheless, under no circumstance and never, will admit that he is more stupid than this genius before whom he had just bowed, no matter how ultra-European he may be. "Well, Goethe—all right, Liebig—now then, Bismarck; why, all right; nevertheless, I too, am a somebody,"—so it necessarily seems to every Russian, even from among the most miserable and rascally, if it should come to that. And not that he may be pretending, because here there is hardly anything conscious, but only that he is pulled in that direction. There is an incessant feeling of idle ambition, knocking about the world, an ambition in no way justifiable. In a word, a Russian of the upper classes will never, and under no circumstance, reach that level—perhaps, the highest level —of the manifestation of human dignity, where a man admits that he is more stupid than another, when the latter is, in fact, more intelligent. I even do not know whether there are exceptions in this respect.

Let people refrain from laughing at my "paradox." Liebig's rival may not have terminated his high-school term, and, of course, he will not start arguing about his supremacy over Liebig should he be told and shown that this is Liebig. He will keep his mouth shut but, even so, he will be tempted even in Liebig's presence. . . . It would be different if, let us suppose, he should meet Liebig, without knowing it, somewhere in a railroad car. And should there ensue a conversation about chemistry, and should our fellow succeed in getting into the conversation, he would keep up the most learned dispute, knowing but one word in chemistry: chemistry. Of course he may surprise Liebig, but—who knows?—in the opinion of the listeners he might turn out the victor. Since in the Russian there is virtually no limit to the arrogance of his scientific language.

At this juncture there develops a phenomenon encountered

in the soul only of the Russian educated classes: in that soul, the moment it feels itself in public, not only is there no doubt about its intellect, but even about its supreme learnedness, if only it comes to erudition. One may, perhaps, understand such an attitude toward intellect, but it would seem that as regards one's erudition every man must possess the most accurate information on the subject. . . .

Of course, all this transpires only in public, when strangers are around. But at home, in one's mind . . . Why, at home, inwardly, no Russian ever troubles himself about his education and erudition; he never even raises a question regarding them. But even if he should raise it, most probably at home, too, he would decide it in his favor, notwithstanding the fact that he would have most accurate knowledge about his erudition.

Not long ago I personally, while sitting in a railroad car, chanced to listen during two hours of the journey to a whole treatise on classical languages. One man was speaking and all the others were listening. The speaker, unknown to the other passengers, was a middle-aged man, of an imposing, reserved and seigniorial appearance, who dropped his words weightily and slowly. He aroused everybody's interest. It was obvious from his very first words that not only did he speak but, probably, had thought about this theme for the first time. So this was merely a brilliant improvisation.

He emphatically rejected classical education, and its introduction into our schools he termed "historical and fatal folly"; but this was the only sharp word which he had permitted himself. He had adopted too lofty a tone which restrained him from flying into passion, from contempt itself for the subject. The grounds on which he stood were most primitive, permissible, perhaps, to a thirteen-year-old schoolboy—practically the same ones which up to the present are being adhered to by some of our newspapers campaigning against classical languages, to wit: "Since all Latin works have been translated, Latin is not needed," and so forth and so on, along these lines.

In our car he produced an extraordinary effect; many people, when parting with him, thanked him for the treat he had given them—especially, the ladies. I am convinced that he departed with the greatest respect for himself.

Nowadays in public (be it in railroad cars or elsewhere) conversations differ very much in comparison with olden times; now people are eager to listen and are craving for instructors in political and social subjects. True, our conversations ensue with but great effort; all keep back for a long time before making up their minds to start talking, but, once they have started, they will be seized sometimes with such a pathos that one almost has to hold their hands. More reserved and solid, so to speak, more elevated and isolated conversations pivot on stock exchange and governmental topics, but from a secret, travestied point of view, claiming knowledge of the highest mysteries unknown to the uninitiated public. The latter listen meekly and respectfully, while babblers gain in their demeanor. It stands to reason that few of them believe each other but, as a rule, they part quite content with each other and even in a somewhat grateful mood.

The problem of making a pleasant and joyous trip on our railroads consists in the skill of letting others lie and of believing as much as possible; then you, too, will be given a chance to tell a lie impressively if you, also, be tempted to do so. Thus it is a reciprocal advantage.

However, as I have stated, there are general, burning, pressing topics of conversation in which the whole public takes part, and not only for the purpose of enjoying their time. I repeat: they are thirsting for knowledge, for explanation of contemporary difficulties; they are craving for teachers, particularly women and especially mothers of families.

It is noteworthy that despite all this extraordinarily curious and most significant thirst for social advisers and guides—notwithstanding all these noble impulses, people are too easily satisfied, sometimes in a most unexpected manner; they believe everything; they are very poorly prepared and armed—much more weakly than one's most flaming fantasy could have imagined several years ago when it was more difficult to form a precise judgment on our Russian society than at present when more facts and information are available.

It can be positively asserted that every chatterbox with but moderately decent manners (our public, alas, up to the present has a prejudicial weakness for good manners, despite the ever-expanding education disseminated through feuilletons) may win out and convince his listeners of anything he pleases, receiving thanks and departing with deep respect for himself. It goes without saying—one doesn't even have to mention it—that he has got to be liberal: this is a condition *sine qua non*.

Another time, also in a railroad car, and also recently, I happened to hear a whole treatise on atheism. The orator—a man of a socialite and engineering, though gloomy, appearance, and with a pathological thirst for an audience—began with monasteries. About the monastery problem he understood nothing at all, not even the A B C of it. He regarded the existence of monasteries as something inseparable from the dogmas of faith, imagining that monasteries are maintained by the state, and cost much to the crown. Forgetting the fact that monks constitute an altogether voluntary association of persons, just like any other association, he insisted—in the name of liberalism—that they be abolished as a sort of tyrannical institution. He wound up with absolute and unlimited atheism on the basis of natural sciences and mathematics; to these he made abundant references without, however, citing in the course of his whole dissertation a single fact from these disciplines.

Again, this man alone talked, while all the others were merely listening. "I shall teach my son to be an honest man—that's all,"—he uttered in conclusion, with the full and obvious conviction that good deeds, morality and honesty are something given and absolute, depending upon nothing whatsoever; something that can always be found in one's pocket, whenever it be needed, without labor, doubts and misunderstandings.

This gentleman, too, scored an extraordinary success. Here there were officers, old men, ladies and grown-up children. When parting with him, the people thanked him warmly for the pleasure he had given them, and one lady—a mother of a family, smartly dressed and quite good-looking, with a charming giggle—declared that now she was fully convinced that in her soul "there was noth-

ing but vapor." This gentleman must have gone away with a feeling of unusual self-respect.

Now, this self-respect is the thing that confuses me. That there
are fools and chatterers is, of course, not surprising; but this
gentleman was obviously no fool and certainly, also, neither a villain nor a swindler; it may even be that he was an honest man and
a good father. Only, he understood nothing about the problems
which he ventured to solve. Is it possible that an hour, a day, or a
month later the thought would not occur to him: "My friend,
Ivan Vasilievich (or whatever his name is)—now, you have argued, but you understand nothing about the things you discussed.
You know this better than anyone. You referred to natural sciences
and mathematics, but you know better than anyone else that you
long ago forgot the scanty mathematics which you learned in
your technical school and which, even then, you did not know
thoroughly, while about natural sciences you never did have any
conception. How, then, did you venture to talk? How could you
teach?—Indeed, you must realize that you were only lying, and
you feel proud about yourself.—Aren't you ashamed of yourself?"

I am sure that he could have asked himself all these questions,
notwithstanding the fact that, perhaps, he is engaged in "business"
and that he has no time to spare on idle questions. I am quite certain that these questions, though in passing and mincingly, have
visited his brain. *But he was not ashamed! He did not blush!*

Now, this dishonesty of a certain kind in the educated Russian
is, to me, a decisive phenomenon. What is there in the fact that
with us it is so common and that all of us got used to it and it
seems so familiar? Even so, it remains an astonishing and extraordinary fact. It bears witness to such an indifference for one's
judgment of one's own conscience, or—which is the same thing—
such extraordinary disrespect for one's self, that one is seized with
despair, one loses all hope for something independent and salutary
for the nation—even in the future—from such people and such a
society.

The public—that is, the exterior—European appearance, the law
once and forever enacted by Europe—this public produces in every

Russian a crushing effect: in public he is a European, a citizen, a knight, a republican, with conscience and with his own firmly established opinion. At home, to himself: "Eh, what the devil do I care about opinions! Let them even whip me!" Lieutenant Pirogov, who forty years ago, on the Bolshaia Meschanskaia, was whipped by the locksmith Schiller, was a dreadful prophecy—a prophecy of a genius who had divined so terribly, since of the Pirogovs there is an immense quantity, so many that it is even impossible to whip them all. Please recall that after the incident the lieutenant forthwith ate a puff-paste patty, and that same evening, at a saint's day party of an important government official, he distinguished himself while dancing the mazurka. What would you think: when he capered that mazurka and exhibited, while performing the steps, his so recently offended limbs—did he think about the fact that only two hours earlier he had been whipped?— Unquestionably, he did. But was he ashamed?—Unquestionably, he was not!

Waking up next morning, he no doubt said to himself: "Eh, what the devil! Is it worth starting something if no one is going to find out! . . ." This "is it worth starting"—of course, on the one hand, suggests such a predisposition to accommodation to anything whatsoever, and at the same time, such a breadth of our Russian nature that, in the face of these qualities, even the unlimited is dimmed. The two-hundred-year disuse of the slightest independence of character and the two-hundred-year spitting upon our own Russian face have expanded Russian conscience to such a fatal boundlessness, from which may be expected . . . well, what would you think?

I am convinced that the lieutenant was, perhaps, capable of reaching such limits, or such an unlimitedness, as to avow his love that same evening and make a formal proposal to his partner in the mazurka—the host's elder daughter. Infinitely tragic is the image of that young miss fluttering with the fellow in a lovely dance and ignorant of the fact that only two hours before her cavalier had been whipped and that he does not mind it a bit. Well, and what would you think if she were to learn this fact, and the proposal, nevertheless, had been made anyway? Would she marry him (of course, on condition that no one would find out)?—Alas, unfailingly, she would marry him!

Even so, from among the Pirogovs and, generally, "the boundless ones," it seems, the overwhelming number of our women should be excluded. In our women one observes more and more sincerity, perseverance, seriousness and honor, sacrifice and search for truth, and in Russian women all these qualities have always been more pronounced than among the men. This cannot be doubted, notwithstanding all present-day deviations. The woman lies less, some of the women do not lie at all, whereas of the men who do not lie there are hardly any. I am speaking of the present moment in the life of our society.

The woman is more persistent and patient in work; she seeks, more *seriously* than the man, work for work's sake, and not merely for the sake of *pretending*. Perhaps it is from her that we must expect great help!

1873   Translated by
                                        BORIS BRASOL

Tradition and the Individual Talent

by T. S. ELIOT [1888–1965]

IN ENGLISH WRITING we seldom speak of tradition, though we occasionally apply its name in deploring its absence. We cannot refer to "the tradition" or to "a tradition"; at most, we employ the adjective in saying that the poetry of So-and-so is "traditional" or even "too traditional." Seldom, perhaps, does the word appear except in a phrase of censure. If otherwise, it is vaguely approbative, with the implication, as to the work approved, of some pleasing archaeological reconstruction. You can hardly make the word agreeable to English ears without this comfortable reference to the reassuring science of archaeology.

Certainly the word is not likely to appear in our appreciations of living or dead writers. Every nation, every race, has not only its own creative, but its own critical turn of mind; and is even more oblivious of the shortcomings and limitations of its critical habits than of those of its creative genius. We know, or think we know, from the enormous mass of critical writing that has appeared in the French language the critical method or habit of the French; we only conclude (we are such unconscious people) that the French are "more critical" than we, and sometimes even plume ourselves a little with the fact, as if the French were the less spontaneous. Perhaps they are; but we might remind ourselves that criticism is as inevitable as breathing, and that we should be none the worse for articulating what passes in our minds when we read a book and feel an emotion about it, for criticizing our own minds in their work of criticism. One of the facts that might come to light in this process is our tendency to insist, when we praise a poet, upon those aspects of his work in which he least resembles any one else. In these aspects or parts of his work we pretend to find what is individual, what is the peculiar essence of the man. We dwell with satisfaction upon the poet's difference from his predecessors, especially his immediate predecessors; we endeavour to find something that can be isolated in order to be enjoyed. Whereas if we approach a poet without this prejudice we shall often find that not only the best, but the most individual parts of his work may be those in which the dead poets, his ancestors, assert their immortality most vigorously. And I do not mean the impressionable period of adolescence, but the period of full maturity.

Yet if the only form of tradition, of handing down, consisted in following the ways of the immediate generation before us in a blind or timid adherence to its successes, "tradition" should positively be discouraged. We have seen many such simple currents soon lost in the sand; and novelty is better than repetition. Tradition is a matter of much wider significance. It cannot be inherited, and if you want it you must obtain it by great labour. It involves, in the first place, the historical sense, which we may call nearly indispensable to any one who would continue to be a poet beyond his twenty-fifth year; and the historical sense involves a perception, not only of the pastness of the past, but of its presence; the historical sense compels a man to write not merely with his own generation in his bones, but with a feeling that the whole of the literature of Europe from Homer and within it the whole of the literature of his own country has a simultaneous existence and composes a simultaneous order. This historical sense, which is a sense of the timeless as well as of the temporal and of the timeless and of the temporal together, is what makes a writer traditional. And it is at the same time what makes a writer most acutely conscious of his place in time, of his own contemporaneity.

No poet, no artist of any art, has his complete meaning alone. His significance, his appreciation is the appreciation of his relation to the dead poets and artists. You cannot value him alone; you must set him, for contrast and comparison, among the dead. I mean this as a principle of aesthetic, not merely historical, criticism. The necessity that he shall conform, that he shall cohere, is not one-sided; what happens when a new work of art is created is something that happens simultaneously to all the works of art which preceded it. The existing monuments form an ideal order among themselves, which is modified by the introduction of the new (the really new) work of art among them. The existing order is complete before the new work arrives; for order to persist after the supervention of novelty, the *whole* existing order must be, if ever so slightly, altered; and so the relations, proportions, values of each work of art toward the whole are readjusted; and this is conformity between the old and the new. Whoever has approved this idea of order, of the form of European, of English literature will not find it preposterous that the past should be altered by the present as much as the present is directed by the past. And the poet who is aware of this will be aware of great difficulties and responsibilities.

In a peculiar sense he will be aware also that he must inevitably be judged by the standards of the past. I say judged, not amputated, by them; not judged to be as good as, or worse or better than, the dead; and certainly not judged by the canons of dead critics. It is a judgment, a comparison, in which two things are measured by each other. To conform merely would be for the new work not really to conform at all; it would not be new, and would therefore not be a work of art. And we do not quite say that the new is more valuable because it fits in; but its fitting in is a test of its value—a test, it is true, which can only be slowly and cautiously applied, for we are none of us infallible judges of conformity. We say: it appears to conform, and is perhaps individual, or it appears individual, and may conform; but we are hardly likely to find that it is one and not the other.

To proceed to a more intelligible exposition of the relation of the poet to the past: he can neither take the past as a lump, an indiscriminate bolus, nor can he form himself wholly on one or two private admirations, nor can he form himself wholly upon one preferred period. The first course is inadmissible, the second is an important experience of youth, and the third is a pleasant and highly desirable supplement. The poet must be very conscious of the main current, which does not at all flow invariably through the most distinguished reputations. He must be quite aware of the obvious fact that art never improves, but that the material of art is never quite the same. He must be aware that the mind of Europe—the mind of his own country—a mind which he learns in time to be much more important than his own private mind —is a mind which changes, and that this change is a development which abandons nothing *en route,* which does not superannuate either Shakespeare, or Homer, or the rock drawing of the Magdalenian draughtsmen. That this development, refinement perhaps, complication certainly, is not, from the point of view of the artist, any improvement. Perhaps not even an improvement from the point of view of the psychologist or not to the extent which we imagine; perhaps only in the end based upon a complication in economics and machinery. But the difference between the present and the past is that the conscious present is an awareness of the past in a way and to an extent which the past's awareness of itself cannot show.

Some one said: "The dead writers are remote from us because we *know* so much more than they did." Precisely, and they are that which we know.

I am alive to a usual objection to what is clearly part of my programme for the *métier* of poetry. The objection is that the doctrine requires a ridiculous amount of erudition (pedantry), a claim which can be rejected by appeal to the lives of poets in any pantheon. It will even be affirmed that much learning deadens or perverts poetic sensibility. While, however, we persist in believing that a poet ought to know as much as will not encroach upon his necessary receptivity and necessary laziness, it is not desirable to confine knowledge to whatever can be put into a useful shape for examinations, drawing-rooms, or the still more pretentious modes of publicity. Some can absorb knowledge, the more tardy must sweat for it. Shakespeare acquired more essential history from Plutarch than most men could from the whole British Museum. What is to be insisted upon is that the poet must develop or procure the consciousness of the past and that he should continue to develop this consciousness throughout his career.

What happens is a continual surrender of himself as he is at the moment to something which is more valuable. The progress of an artist is a continual self-sacrifice, a continual extinction of personality.

There remains to define this process of depersonalization and its relation to the sense of tradition. It is in this depersonalization that art may be said to approach the condition of science. I, therefore, invite you to consider, as a suggestive analogy, the action which takes place when a bit of finely filiated platinum is introduced into a chamber containing oxygen and sulphur dioxide.

II

Honest criticism and sensitive appreciation are directed not upon the poet but upon the poetry. If we attend to the confused cries of the newspaper critics and the *susurrus* of popular repetition that follows, we shall hear the names of poets in great numbers; if we seek not Blue-book knowledge but the enjoyment of poetry, and ask for a poem, we shall seldom find it. I have tried to point out the importance of the relation of the poem to other poems by other authors, and suggested the conception of poetry as a living whole of all the poetry that has ever been written. The other aspect of this Impersonal theory of poetry is the relation of the poem to its author. And I hinted, by an analogy, that the mind of the mature poet differs from that of the immature one not precisely in any valuation of "personality," not being necessarily more interesting, or having "more to say," but rather by being a more finely perfected medium in which special, or very varied, feelings are at liberty to enter into new combinations.

The analogy was that of the catalyst. When the two gases previously mentioned are mixed in the presence of a filament of platinum, they form sulphurous acid. This combination takes place only if the platinum is present; nevertheless the newly formed acid contains no trace of platinum, and the platinum itself is apparently unaffected; has remained inert, neutral, and unchanged. The mind of the poet is the shred of platinum. It may partly or exclusively operate upon the experience of the man himself; but, the more perfect the artist, the more completely separate in him will be the man who suffers and the mind which creates; the more perfectly will the mind digest and transmute the passions which are its material.

The experience, you will notice, the elements which enter the presence of the transforming catalyst, are of two kinds: emotions and feelings. The effect of a work of art upon the person who enjoys it is an experience different in kind from any experience not of art. It may be formed out of one emotion, or may be a combination of several; and various feelings, inhering for the writer in particular words or phrases or images, may be added to compose the final result. Or great poetry may be made without the direct use of any emotion whatever: composed out of feelings solely. Canto xv of the *Inferno* (Brunetto Latini) is a working up of the emotion evident in the situation; but the effect, though single as that of any work of art, is obtained by considerable complexity of detail. The last quatrain gives an image, a feeling attaching to an image, which "came," which did not develop simply out of what precedes, but which was probably in suspension in the poet's mind until the proper combination arrived for it to add itself to. The poet's mind is in fact a receptacle for seizing and storing up numberless feelings, phrases, images, which remain there until all the particles which can unite to form a new compound are present together.

If you compare several representative passages of the greatest poetry you see how great is the variety of types of combination, and also how completely any semi-ethical criterion of "sublimity" misses the mark. For it is not the "greatness," the intensity, of the emotions, the components, but the intensity of the artistic process, the pressure, so to speak, under which the fusion takes place, that counts. The episode of Paolo and Francesca employs a definite emotion, but the intensity of the poetry is something quite different from whatever intensity in the supposed experience it may give the impression of. It is no more intense, furthermore, than Canto XXVI, the voyage of Ulysses, which has not the direct dependence upon an emotion. Great variety is possible in the process of transmutation of emotion: the murder of Agamemnon, or the agony of Othello, gives an artistic effect apparently closer to a possible original than the scenes from Dante. In the *Agamemnon,* the artistic emotion approximates to the emotion of an actual spectator; in *Othello* to the emotion of the protagonist himself. But the difference between art and the event is always absolute; the combination which is the murder of Agamemnon is probably as complex as that which is the voyage of Ulysses. In either case there has been a fusion of elements. The ode of Keats contains a number of feelings which have nothing particular to do with the nightingale, but which the nightingale, partly, perhaps, because of its attractive name, and partly because of its reputation, served to bring together.

The point of view which I am struggling to attack is perhaps related to the metaphysical theory of the substantial unity of the soul: for my meaning is, that the poet has, not a "personality" to express, but a particular medium, which is only a medium and not a personality, in which impressions and experiences combine in peculiar and unexpected ways. Impressions and experiences which are important for the man may take no place in the poetry, and those which become important in the poetry may play quite a negligible part in the man, the personality.

I will quote a passage which is unfamiliar enough to be regarded with fresh attention in the light—or darkness—of these observations:

> And now methinks I could e'en chide myself
> For doating on her beauty, though her death
> Shall be revenged after no common action.
> Does the silkworm expend her yellow labours
> For thee? For thee does she undo herself?
> Are lordships sold to maintain ladyships
> For the poor benefit of a bewildering minute?
> Why does yon fellow falsify highways,
> And put his life between the judge's lips,
> To refine such a thing—keeps horse and men
> To beat their valours for her? . . .

In this passage (as is evident if it is taken in its context) there is a combination of positive and negative emotions: an intensely strong attraction toward beauty and an equally intense fascination by the ugliness which is contrasted with it and which destroys it. This balance of contrasted emotion is in the dramatic situation to which the speech is pertinent, but that situation alone is inadequate to it. This is, so to speak, the structural emotion, provided by the drama. But the whole effect, the dominant one, is due to the fact that a number of floating feelings, having an affinity to this emotion by no means superficially evident, have combined with it to give us a new art emotion.

It is not in his personal emotions, the emotions provoked by particular events in his life, that the poet is in any way remarkable or interesting. His particular emotions may be simple, or crude, or flat. The emotion in his poetry will be a very complex thing, but not with the complexity of the emotions of people who have very complex or unusual emotions in life. One error, in fact, of eccentricity in poetry is to seek for new human emotions to express; and in this search for novelty in the wrong place it discovers the perverse. The business of the poet is not to find new emotions, but to use the ordinary ones and, in working them up into poetry, to express feelings which are not in actual emotions at all. And emotions which he has never experienced will serve his turn as well as those familiar to him. Consequently, we must believe that "emotion recollected in tranquillity" is an inexact formula. For it

is neither emotion, nor recollection, nor, without distortion of
meaning, tranquillity. It is a concentration, and a new thing resulting from the concentration, of a very great number of experiences which to the practical and active person would not seem to
be experiences at all; it is a concentration which does not happen
consciously or of deliberation. These experiences are not "recollected," and they finally unite in an atmosphere which is "tranquil" only in that it is a passive attending upon the event. Of
course this is not quite the whole story. There is a great deal, in
the writing of poetry, which must be conscious and deliberate. In
fact, the bad poet is usually unconscious where he ought to be
conscious, and conscious where he ought to be unconscious. Both
errors tend to make him "personal." Poetry is not a turning loose
of emotion, but an escape from emotion; it is not the expression of
personality but an escape from personality. But, of course, only
those who have personality and emotions know what it means to
want to escape from these things.

III   ὁ δὲ νοῦς ἴσως Θειότερόν τι χαὶ ἀπαθές ἐστιν.

This essay proposes to halt at the frontier of metaphysics or
mysticism, and confine itself to such practical conclusions as can
be applied by the responsible person interested in poetry. To divert interest from the poet to the poetry is a laudable aim: for it
would conduce to a juster estimation of actual poetry, good and
bad. There are many people who appreciate the expression of sincere emotion in verse, and there is a smaller number of people
who can appreciate technical excellence. But very few know
when there is an expression of *significant* emotion, emotion which
has its life in the poem and not in the history of the poet. The
emotion of art is impersonal. And the poet cannot reach this im-
personality without surrendering himself wholly to the work to
be done. And he is not likely to know what is to be done unless
he lives in what is not merely the present, but the present moment
of the past, unless he is conscious, not of what is dead, but of what
is already living.

1917

On Receiving the Nobel Prize

by WILLIAM FAULKNER [1897–1962]

I FEEL THAT this award was not made to me as a man but to my work—a life's work in the agony and sweat of the human spirit, not for glory and least of all for profit, but to create out of the materials of the human spirit something which did not exist there before. So this award is only mine in trust. It will not be difficult to find a dedication for the money part of it commensurate with the purpose and significance of its origin. But I would like to do the same with the acclaim, too, by using this moment as a pinnacle from which I might be listened to by the young men and women already dedicated to the same anguish and travail, among whom is already that one who will some day stand here where I am standing.

Our tragedy today is a general and a universal physical fear so long sustained by now that we can even bear it. There are no longer problems of the spirit. There is only the question: When will I be blown up? Because of this, the young man or woman writing today has forgotten the problems of the human heart in conflict with itself which alone can make good writing because only that is worth writing about, worth the agony and the sweat.

He must learn them again. He must teach himself that the basest of all things is to be afraid; and, teaching himself that, forget it forever, leaving no room in his workshop for anything but the old verities and truths of the heart, the old universal truths lacking which any story is ephemeral and doomed—love and honor and pity and pride and compassion and sacrifice. Until he does so he labors under a curse. He writes not of love, but of lust, of defeats in which nobody loses anything of value, of victories without hope and worst of all without pity or compassion. His griefs grieve on no universal bones, leaving no scars. He writes not of the heart but of the glands.

Until he relearns these things he will write as though he stood among and watched the end of man. I decline to accept the end of man. It is easy enough to say that man is immortal simply because he will endure; that when the last ding-dong of doom has clanged and faded from the last worthless rock hanging tideless in the last red and dying evening, that even then there will still be one more sound: that of his puny inexhaustible voice still talking. I refuse to accept this. I believe that man will not merely endure: he will prevail. He is immortal, not because he alone among creatures has an inexhaustible voice, but because he has a soul, a spirit capable of compassion and sacrifice and endurance. The poet's, the writer's, duty is to write about these things. It is his privilege to help man endure by lifting his heart, by reminding him of the courage and honor and hope and pride and compassion and pity and sacrifice which have been the glory of his past. The poet's voice need not merely be the record of man, it can be one of the props, the pillars to help him endure and prevail.

1950

Over Strand and Field

by GUSTAVE FLAUBERT [1821-1880]

IN QUIBERON, we breakfasted at old Rohan Belle-Isle's, who keeps the Hôtel Penthièvre. This gentleman had his bare feet stuck in old slippers, on account of the heat, and was drinking with a mason, a fact which does not prevent him from being the descendant of one of the first families of Europe; an aristocrat of the old stock! a real aristocrat! *Vive Dieu!* He immediately set to work to pound a steak and to cook us some lobsters. Our pride was flattered to its innermost fibre.

. . . . . .

The past of Quiberon is concentrated in a massacre. Its greatest curiosity is a cemetery, which is filled to its utmost capacity and overflows into the street. The head-stones are crowded together and invade and submerge one another, as if the corpses were uncomfortable in their graves and had lifted up their shoulders to escape from them. It suggests a petrified ocean, the tombs being the waves, and the crosses the masts of shipwrecked vessels.

In the middle, an open ossuary contain skeletons that have been exhumed in order to make room for other corpses. Who has said: "Life is a hostelry, and the grave is our home?" But these corpses do not remain in their graves, for they are only tenants and are ejected at the expiration of the lease. Around this charnel-house, where the heaps of bones resemble a mass of fagots, is arranged, breast-high, a series of little black boxes, six inches square, surmounted by a cross and cut out in the shape of a heart in front, so that one can see the skulls inside. Above the heart-shaped opening are the following words in painted letters: "This is the head of ———— ————, deceased on such and such a day, in such and such a year." These heads belonged to persons of a certain standing, and one would be considered an ungrateful son if, after seven years, he did not give his parents' skulls the luxury of one of these little black boxes. The remainder of the bodies is thrown into the bonehouse, and twenty-five years afterwards the heads are sent to join them. A few years ago they tried to abolish the custom; but a riot ensued and the practice continued.

Perhaps it is wicked to play with those round skulls which once contained a mind, with those empty circles in which passion throbbed. Those boxes surrounding the ossuary and scattered over the graves, over the wall and in the grass, without any attempt at order, may appear horrible to a few and ridiculous to many; but those black cases rotting even as the bones blanch and crumble to dust; those skulls, with noses eaten away and foreheads streaked by the slimy trails of snails, and hollow, staring eyes; those thigh-bones piled up as in the great charnel-houses mentioned in the Bible; those pieces of skulls lying around filled with earth, in which a flower springs up sometimes and grows through the holes of the eyes; even the vulgarity of those inscriptions, which are as similar as the corpses they identify—all this human rottenness appeared beautiful to us, and procured us a splendid sight.

If the post of Auray had arrived, we should have started at once for Belle-Isle; but they were waiting for it. Transient sailors with bare arms and open shirts sat in the kitchen of the inn, drinking to pass away the time.

"At what time is the post due here in Auray?"

"That depends; usually at ten o'clock," replied the innkeeper.

"No, at eleven," put in a man.

"At twelve," said M. de Rohan.

"At one."

"At half-past one."

"Sometimes it doesn't reach here until two o'clock."

"It isn't very regular!"

We were aware of that; it was already three. We could not start before the arrival of this ill-fated messenger, which brings Belle-Isle the despatches from *terra firma,* so we had to resign ourselves. Once in a while some one would get up, go to the door, look out, come back, and start up again. Oh! he will not come to-day.— He must have stopped on the way.—Let's go home.—No, let's wait for him.—If, however, you are tired of waiting, gentlemen. . . . After all, there may not be any letters. . . . No, just wait a little longer.—Oh! here he comes!—But it was some one else, and the dialogue would begin all over again.

At last we heard the beating of tired hoofs on the cobblestones, the tinkling of bells, the cracking of a whip and a man's voice shouting: "Ho! Ho! Here's the post! Here's the post!"

The horse stopped in front of the door, hunched its back, stretched its neck, opened its mouth, disclosed its teeth, spread its hind legs and rose on its hocks.

The animal was lean and tall, and had a moth-eaten mane, rough hoofs and loose shoes; a seton bobbed up and down on its breast. Lost in a saddle that swallowed him up, supported at the back by a valise and in front by the mail-bag, which was passed through the saddle-bow, its rider sat huddled on it like a monkey. His small face, adorned with straggling blond whiskers and as wrinkled and rough as a winter apple, was hidden by a large oil-cloth hat lined with felt; a sort of gray coutil coat was drawn up to his hips and bagged around his stomach, while his trousers stopped at the knees and disclosed his bare legs reddened by the rubbing of the stirrup-straps, and his blue hose, which hung over his shoes. The harness was held together with strings, the rider's clothes had been mended with threads of different colours; all sorts of patches and all kinds of spots, torn linen, greasy leather, dried mud, recent dust, hanging straps, bright rags, a dirty man and a mangy horse, the former sickly and perspiring, the latter consumptive and almost spent; the one with his whip and the other with its bells—all this formed but one object which had the same colour and movement and executed almost the same gestures, which served the same purpose, the conducting of the Auray post.

After another hour, when all the packages and commissions had been attended to and we had waited for several passengers who were to come, we finally left the inn and went aboard. At first there was nothing but a confused mass of people and luggage, oars that caused us to stumble, sails that dropped on our heads, men falling over each other and not knowing where to go; then everything quieted down, each one found his nook, the luggage was put in the bottom of the boat, the sailors got on the benches, and the passengers seated themselves as best they could.

There was no breeze and the sails clung limply to the masts. The heavy boat hardly moved over the almost motionless sea, which swelled and subsided with the gentle rhythm of a sleeping breast.

Leaning against one of the gunwales, we gazed at the water, which was as blue and calm as the sky, and listened to the splashing of the oars; sitting in the shadow of the sail, the six rowers lifted their oars regularly to make the forward stroke, and when they dipped them into the water and brought them up again, drops of crystal clung to their paddles. Reclining on the straw, or sitting on the benches, with their legs dangling and their chins in their hands, or leaning against the sides of the boat, between the big jambs of the hull, the tar of which was melting in the heat, the silent passengers hung their heads and closed their eyes to shut out the glare of the sun, that shone on the flat ocean as on a mirror.

A white-haired man was sleeping at my feet, a gendarme was sweltering under his three-cornered hat, and two soldiers had unfastened their knapsacks and used them as pillows. Near the bowsprit stood a cabin-boy looking into the stay-sail and whistling for wind, while the skipper remained aft and managed the tiller. Still no wind arose. Orders were given to haul in the sails; slowly and gently they came down and fell in a heap on the benches; then each sailor took off his waistcoat, stowed it away under the bow of the boat, and the men began to row again with all their might.

. . . . .

Our departure had been so delayed that there was hardly any water left in the harbour and we had great difficulty in landing. Our boat grated on the pebbles, and in order to leave it, we were compelled to walk on an oar as if it were a tight-rope.

Ensconced between the citadel and its ramparts, and cut in two by an almost empty port, the Palay appeared to us a useless little town overcome with military ennui, and put me in mind, I do not know why, of a gaping *sous-officier*.

One fails to see the low-crowned, broad-brimmed black felt hats of Le Morbihan, that give protection to the shoulders as well as the head. The women do not affect the big, white caps that stand out from their faces, and reach down their backs like those worn by the nuns, so that when worn by little girls they cover half of their bodies. Their gowns are made without the wide stripe of velvet applied on each shoulder and rounding away under the arms. Nor do they wear the low shoes with square toes, high heels, and long black ribbon streamers. Here, as elsewhere, we found faces that resemble other faces, costumes that really are no costumes at all, cobblestones, and even a sidewalk.

Was it worth while to expose ourselves to sea-sickness (which, by the way, we escaped, a fact that inclined us to leniency), only to see a citadel that we do not admire, a lighthouse that did not appeal to us in the least, and a rampart built by Vauban, of whom we were already heartily tired? But people had spoken to us of

Belle-Isle's rocks. So we started at once, and taking a short cut across the fields, walked to the beach.

We saw one grotto, only one (the day was near its close), but it appeared so beautiful to us (it was draped with sea-weed and decorated with shells, and water dripped from the top), that we resolved to spend a day in Belle-Isle, in order to discover more of them, if there were any, and feast our eyes leisurely upon their beauties.

The following day, at dawn, having filled our flasks and put some sandwiches in our knapsacks, we decided to go where we pleased; so, without a guide or information of any sort (this is the best way), we set out to walk, having resolved that we would go anywhere, provided it were far, and would return home at any time, provided it were late.

We began by a path which led to the top of a cliff, then followed its asperities and valleys and continued around the whole island. When we reached places where landslips had obliterated it, we struck out into the country and let our eyes roam over the horizon of the sea, the deep blue line of which touched the sky; then we walked back to the edge of the rocks, which had suddenly reappeared at our side. The perpendicular cliff, the top of which we were treading, concealed the flank of the rocks, and we could only hear the roaring of the breakers below us.

Sometimes the rock was split in its entire length, disclosing its two almost straight sides, streaked with layers of silica, with tufts of yellow flowers scattered here and there. If we threw a stone, it appeared suspended in the air for a time, would then strike the sides of the cliff, rebound from the one to the other, break into a thousand bits, scattering earth and pebbles in its course, and finally land at the bottom of the pit, where it frightened the cormorants, which shrieked and took flight.

Frequent storms and thaws have pushed a part of the upper grounds into these gorges, and so their steep slope has grown less abrupt, and one is able to climb down to the bottom. We attempted to do so by sliding down like children, holding ourselves back with our hands and feet, and finally we landed safely on the soft, wet sand.

The tide was going out, but in order to be able to pass, we had to wait until the breakers receded. We watched them approach us. They dashed against the rocks, swirled in the crevices, rose like scarfs on the wind, fell back in drops and sprays, and with one long, sweeping libration, gathered their green waters together and retreated. When one wave left the sand, its currents immediately joined, and sought water levels. The sea-weed moved its slimy branches; the water bubbled between the pebbles, oozed through the cracks of the rocks and formed a thousand rivulets and fountains. The drenched sand absorbed it all, and soon its yellow tint grew white again through the drying action of the sun.

As soon as we could, we jumped over the rocks and continued on our way. Soon, however, they increased in numbers, their weird groups being crowded together, piled up and overturned on one another. We tried to hold on with our hands and feet, but we slid on their slippery asperities. The cliff was so very high that it quite frightened us to look up at it. Although it crushed us by its formidable placidity, still it fascinated us, for we could not help looking at it and it did not tire our eyes.

A swallow passed us and we watched its flight; it came from the sea; it ascended slowly through the air, cutting the luminous, fluid atmosphere with its sharp, outstretched wings that seemed to enjoy being absolutely untrammelled. The birds ascended higher and higher, rose above the cliff and finally disappeared.

Meanwhile we were creeping over the rocks, the perspective of which was renewed by each bend of the coast. Once in a while, when the rocks ended, we walked on square stones that were as flat as marble slabs and seamed by almost symmetrical furrows, which appeared like the tracks of some ancient road of another world.

In some places were great pools of water as calm as their greenish depths and as limpid and motionless as a woodland stream on its bed of cresses. Then the rocks would reappear closer than before and more numerous. On one side was the ocean with its breakers foaming around the lower rocks; on the other, the straight, unrelenting, impassive coast.

Tired and bewildered, we looked about us for some issue; but the cliff stretched out before us, and the rocks, infinitely multiplying their dark green forms, succeeded one another until their unequal crags seemed like so many tall, black phantoms rising out of the earth.

We stumbled around in this way until we suddenly perceived an undulating series of rough steps which enabled us to climb up to flat land again.

It is always a pleasure, even when the country is ugly, to walk with a friend, to feel the grass under one's feet, to jump over fences and ditches, to break thistles with one's stick, to pull leaves from the bushes and wheat from the fields, to go where one's fancy dictates, whistling, singing, talking, dreaming, without strange ears to listen to one's conversation, and the sound of strange footsteps behind one, as absolutely free as if one were in the desert!

Ah! Let us have air! air! And more space! Since our contracted souls suffocate and die on the window-sill, since our captive spirits, like the bear in its cage, turn around and around, and stagger against the walls of their prison, why not, at least, let our nostrils breathe the different perfumes of all the winds of the earth, why not let our eyes rove over every horizon?

No steeple shone in the distance, no hamlet with thatched roofs and square yards framed by clusters of trees, appeared on the side of a hill; not a soul was to be seen, not even a peasant, a grazing sheep, or a stray dog.

All those cultivated fields look uninhabited; the peasants work in them, but they do not live there. One is led to believe that they benefit by them but do not care about them in the least.

We saw a farm and walked in; a ragged woman served us some ice-cold milk in earthen cups. The silence all around was peculiar. The woman watched us eagerly, and we soon took our departure.

We walked into a valley, the narrow gorge of which appeared to extend to the ocean. Tall grass with yellow flowers reached up to our waists, and we had to take long strides in order to advance. We could hear the murmur of flowing water near by, and we sank ankle-deep into the marshy soil. Presently the two hills parted; their barren sides were covered with short, stubby grass and here and there were big yellow patches of moss. At the foot of one hill a stream wends its way through the drooping boughs of the stunted shrubs that grow on its edges, and loses itself in a quiet pond where long-legged insects disport themselves on the leaves of the water-lillies. The sun beat down on us. The gnats rubbed their wings together and bent the slender ends of the reeds with the weight of their tiny bodies. We were alone in the tranquillity of this desert.

At this point, the valley curved and widened and formed a sharp bend. We climbed a little hill, in order to locate ourselves, but the horizon either ended abruptly, enclosed by another hill, or else stretched out over new plains. We did not lose courage, however, and continued to advance, while we thought of the travellers on desert islands who climb on promontories in the hope of sighting some vessel setting sail towards them.

The soil was growing less moist, and the grass less high; presently the ocean came in view, ensconced in a narrow bay, and soon the shore, strewn with débris of shells and madrepores, crunched beneath our footsteps. We let ourselves drop to the ground and as we were exhausted, we soon fell asleep. An hour later the cold woke us up, and we started homeward without any fear of losing our way this time. We were on the coast facing France, and Palay was on our left. It was here, the day before, that we had discovered the grotto we admired so much. It did not take us long to find others, higher and deeper even than the first one.

They always opened through large, pointed arches which were either upright or inclined, their bold columns supporting enormous pieces of rock. Black, veined with purple, fiery red, or brown streaked with white, these beautiful grottoes displayed for their visitors the infinite variety of their shapes and colouring, their graces and their grand caprices. There was one all of silver veined with deep red; in another, tufts of flowers resembling periwinkles had grown on glazings of reddish granite, and drops of water fell from the ceiling on the fine sand with never-ceasing regularity. In the background of another grotto, beneath a long semi-circle, a bed of polished white gravel, which the tide no doubt turns and makes fresh every day, seemed to be waiting to receive the body of a mermaid; but the bed is empty and has lost her forever! Only the moist sea-weed remains on which she used to stretch her delicate nude limbs when she was tired of swimming, and on which she reclined till daybreak, in the pale light of the moon.

The sun was setting, and the tide was coming in over the rocks that melted in the blue evening mist, which was blanched on the level of the ocean by the foam of the tumbling waves. In the other part of the horizon, the sky streaked with orange stripes looked as if it had been swept by a gale. Its light reflected on the waters and spread a gleaming sheen over them, and projected on the sand, giving it a brownish tinge and making it glitter like steel.

Half a mile to the south, the coast is covered by a line of rocks that extends to the sea. In order to reach them, we should have been compelled to tramp as we had already done that morning. We were tired, and it was far; but a temptation seemed to push us forward. The breeze played in the cracks of the rocks and wrinkled the surface of the pools; the sea-weed, cleaving to the sides of the cliff, shook in the wind, and from the part of the sky where the moon was to rise, a pale light spread over the waters. It was the hour when the shadows lengthen. The rocks appeared larger, and the breakers a deeper green. The sky seemed to expand, and all nature assumed a different appearance.

So we started, without giving a thought to the incoming tide or whether or not we should find later a way to get back to land. We wished to enjoy our pleasure to the fullest extent. We seemed lighter than in the morning, and ran and jumped without the slightest feeling of fatigue. An abundance of animal spirits impelled us onward and we felt a peculiarly robust twitching in our muscles. We shook our heads in the wind and touched the grasses with our fingers. We breathed the salt air of the ocean, and noted and assimilated every color, every sunbeam, every sound, the design of the sea-weed, the softness of the sand, the hardness of the rocks that echoed under our footsteps, the height of the cliffs, the fringe of the waves, the accidents of the coast, and the voice of the horizon; and the breeze that passed over our faces like intangible kisses, the sky with its passing clouds, the rising moon, the peeping stars. Our souls bathed in all this splendour, and our eyes feasted on it; we opened our ears and nostrils wide; something of the very life of the elements, forced from them undoubtedly by the attraction of our eyes, reached us and was assimilated, so that we were able to comprehend them in a closer relation and feel them more keenly, thanks to this complex union.

By thus entering and penetrating into nature, we became a part of it, diffused ourselves in it, and were claimed by it once more; we felt that it was overpowering us, and we rejoiced; we desired to be lost in it, to be borne away, or to carry it away with us. As in the raptures of love, one wishes more hands with which to caress, more lips with which to kiss, more eyes with which to see, more soul with which to worship; spreading ourselves out in nature, with a joyful and delirious abandon, we regretted that our eyes could not penetrate to the innermost parts of the rocks, to the bottom of the sea, to the end of the heavens, in order to see how the stones grow, how the breakers are made, how the stars are lighted; we regretted that our ears could not catch the rumour of the fermentation of the granite in the bowels of the earth, could not hear the sap circulate in the plants and the coral roll in the solitudes of the ocean. And while we were under the spell of that contemplative effusion, we wished that our souls, radiating everywhere, might live all these different lives, assume all these different forms, and, varying unceasingly, accomplish their metamorphoses under an eternal sun!

But man was made to enjoy each day only a small portion of food, colours, sounds, sentiments and ideas. Anything above the allotted quantity tires or intoxicates him; it becomes the idiocy of the drunkard or the ravings of the ecstatic. O, God! How small is our glass and how large is our thirst! What weak heads we have!

.   .   .   .   .   .

In order to return to Quiberon, we were compelled, on the following day, to rise before seven o'clock, a feat which required some courage. While we were still stiff from fatigue and shivering with sleep, we got into a boat along with a white horse, two drummers, the same one-eyed gendarme and the same soldier who, this time, however, did not lecture anybody. As drunk as a lord, he kept slipping under the benches and had all he could do to keep his shako on his head and extricate his gun from between his feet. I could not say which was the sillier of the two. The gendarme was sober, but he was very stupid. He deplored the soldier's lack of manners, enumerated the punishments that would be dealt out to him, was scandalised by his hiccoughs and resented his demeanour. Viewed from the side of the missing eye, with his three-cornered hat, his sabre and his yellow gloves, the gendarme presented one of the sorriest aspects of human life. Besides, there is something so essentially grotesque about gendarmes that I cannot help laughing at them; these upholders of the law always produce the same comic effect on me, and so do attorneys for the king, magistrates, and professors of literature.

Tipped to one side, the boat skimmed lightly through the foaming waves. The three sails were comfortably swelled; the masts creaked and the wind rattled the pulleys. A cabin-boy stood at the helm singing. We could not catch the words, but it was some slow, monotonous lay which neither rose nor fell and was repeated again and again, with long-drawn-out inflections and languid refrain. And it swept softly and sadly out over the ocean, as some confused memory sweeps through one's mind.

The horse stood as straight as it could on its four legs and pulled at a bundle of hay. The sailors, with folded arms, looked absently at the sails and smiled a far-away smile.

. . . . .

So we journeyed on without speaking a word and as best we could, without reaching the edge of the bay, where it looked as if Plouharnel might be. However, after a while we arrived there. But when we did, we were confronted by the ocean, for we had followed the right side of the coast instead of the left, and were forced to turn back and go over a part of the route.

A muffled sound was heard. A bell tinkled and a hat appeared. It was the Auray post. Again the same man, the same horse, the same mail-bag. He was ambling quietly towards Quiberon; he would be back directly and return again the next day. He is the guest of the coast; he passes in the morning and again at night.

His life is spent going from one point to another; he is the only one who gives the coast some animation, something to look forward to, and, I was almost going to say, some charm.

He stopped and talked to us for a few minutes, then lifted his hat and was off again.

What an ensemble! What a horse, and what a rider! What a picture! Callot would probably have reproduced it, but it would take Cervantes to write it.

After passing over large pieces of rock that have been placed in the sea in order to shorten the route by cutting the back of the bay in two, we finally arrived at Plouharnel.

The village was quiet; chickens cackled and scratched in the streets, and in the gardens enclosed by stone walls, weeds and oats grew side by side.

While we were sitting in front of the host's door, an old beggar passed us. He was as red as a lobster, dirty and unkempt and covered with rags and vermin. The sun shone on his dilapidated garments and on his purple skin; it was almost black and seemed to transude blood. He kept bellowing in a terrible voice, while beating a tattoo on the door of a neighbouring house. . . .

From *Over Strand and Field*, 1886. Written probably in 1847, the year in which Flaubert and his friend Maxine du Camp journeyed through Brittany. They composed the book jointly. According to du Camp, he wrote the even chapters and Flaubert the odd ones. Translator unidentified.

What I Believe

by E. M. FORSTER [1879–1970]

I DO NOT BELIEVE in belief. But this is an age of faith, where one is surrounded by so many militant creeds that, in self-defense, one has to formulate a creed of one's own. Tolerance, good temper, and sympathy are no longer enough in a world which is rent by religious and racial persecution, in a world where ignorance rules, and science, who ought to have ruled, plays the subservient pimp. Tolerance, good temper, and sympathy—well, they are what matter really, and if the human race is not to collapse they must come to the front before long. But for the moment they don't seem enough their action is no stronger than a flower, battered beneath a military jack boot. They want stiffening, even if the process coarsens them. Faith, to my mind, is a stiffening process, a sort of mental starch, which ought to be applied as sparingly as possible. I dislike the stuff. I do not believe in it, for its own sake, at all. Herein I probably differ from most of the contributors to this volume,* who believe in belief, and are only sorry they can't swallow even more than they do. My lawgivers are Erasmus and Montaigne, not Moses and St. Paul. My temple stands not upon Mount Moriah but in that Elysian Field where even the immoral are admitted. My motto is "Lord, I disbelieve—help thou my unbelief."

I have, however, to live in an Age of Faith—the sort of thing I used to hear praised and recommended when I was a boy. It is damned unpleasant, really. It is bloody in every sense of the word. And I have to keep my end up in it. Where do I start?

With personal relationships. Here is something comparatively solid in a world full of violence and cruelty. Not absolutely solid, for psychology has split and shattered the idea of a "person," and has shown that there is something incalculable in each of us, which may at any moment rise to the surface and destroy our normal balance. We don't know what we're like. We can't know what other people are like. How then can we put any trust in personal relationships, or cling to them in the gathering political storm? In theory we can't. But in practice we can and do. Though A isn't unchangeably A or B unchangeably B, there can still be love and loyalty between the two. For the purpose of living one has to assume that the personality is solid, and the "self" is an entity, and to ignore all contrary evidence. And since to ignore evidence is one of the characteristics of faith, I certainly can proclaim that I believe in personal relationships.

* *I Believe,* edited by Clifton Fadiman.

Starting from them, I get a little order into the contemporary chaos. One must be fond of people and trust them if one isn't to make a mess of life, and it is therefore essential that they shouldn't let one down. They often do. The moral of which is that I must myself be as reliable as possible, and this I try to be. But reliability isn't a matter of contract—that is the main difference between the world of personal relationships and the world of business relationships. It is a matter for the heart, which signs no documents. In other words, reliability is impossible unless there is a natural warmth. Most men possess this warmth, though they often have bad luck and get chilled. Most of them, even when they are politicians, *want* to keep faith. And one can, at all events, show one's own little light here, one's own poor little trembling flame, with the knowledge that it's not the only light that is shining in the darkness, and not the only one which the darkness doesn't comprehend. Personal relations are despised today. They are regarded as bourgeois luxuries, as products of a time of fair weather which has now passed, and we are urged to get rid of them, and to dedicate ourselves to some movement or cause instead. I hate the idea of dying for a cause, and if I had to choose between betraying my country and betraying my friend, I hope I should have the guts to betray my country. Such a choice may scandalize the modern reader, and he may stretch out his patriotic hand to the telephone at once, and ring up the police. It wouldn't have shocked Dante, though. Dante places Brutus and Cassius in the lowest circle of Hell because they had chosen to betray their friend Julius Caesar rather than their country Rome. Probably one won't be asked to make such an agonizing choice. Still there lies at the back of every creed something terrible and hard for which the worshiper may one day be required to suffer, and there is even a terror and a hardness in this creed of personal relationships, urbane and mild though it sounds. Love and loyalty to an individual can run counter to the claims of the state. When they do—down with the state, say I, which means that the state will down me.

This brings me along to democracy, "even Love, the Beloved Republic, which feeds upon Freedom and lives." Democracy isn't a beloved republic really, and never will be. But it is less hateful than other contemporary forms of government, and to that extent it deserves our support. It does start from the assumption that the individual is important, and that all types are needed to make a civilization. It doesn't divide its citizens into the bossers and the bossed, as an efficiency regime tends to do. The people I admire most are those who are sensitive and want to create something or discover something, and don't see life in terms of power, and such people get more of a chance under a democracy than elsewhere. They found religions, great or small, or they produce literature and art, or they do disinterested scientific research, or they may be what is called "ordinary people," who are creative in their private lives, bring up their children decently, for instance, or help their neighbors. All these people need to express themselves, they can't do so unless society allows them liberty to do so, and the society which allows them most liberty is a democracy.

Democracy has another merit. It allows criticism, and if there isn't public criticism there are bound to be hushed-up scandals. That is why I believe in the press, despite all its lies and vulgarity, and why I believe in Parliament. The British Parliament is often sneered at because it's a talking shop. Well, I believe in it because it is a talking shop. I believe in the private member who makes himself a nuisance. He gets snubbed and is told that he is cranky or ill-informed, but he exposes abuses which would otherwise never have been mentioned, and very often an abuse gets put right just by being mentioned. Occasionally, too, in my country, a well-meaning public official loses his head in the case of efficiency, and thinks himself God Almighty. Such officials are particularly frequent in the Home Office. Well, there will be questions about them in Parliament sooner or later, and then they'll have to mend their steps. Whether Parliament is either a representative body or an efficient one is very doubtful, but I value it because it criticizes and talks, and because its chatter gets widely reported.

So two cheers for democracy: one because it admits variety and two because it permits criticism. Two cheers are quite enough:

there is no occasion to give three. Only Love, the Beloved Republic
deserves that.

What about force, though? While we are trying to be sensitive
and advanced and affectionate and tolerant, an unpleasant question pops up: Doesn't all society rest upon force? If a government
can't count upon the police and the army, how can it hope to
rule? And if an individual gets knocked on the head or sent to a
labor camp, of what significance are his opinions?

This dilemma doesn't worry me as much as it does some. I
realize that all society rests upon force. But all the great creative
actions, all the decent human relations, occur during the intervals
when force has not managed to come to the front. These intervals are what matter. I want them to be as frequent and as
lengthy as possible and I call them "civilization." Some people
idealize force and pull it into the foreground and worship it,
instead of keeping it in the background as long as possible. I think
they make a mistake, and I think that their opposites, the mystics,
err even more when they declare that force doesn't exist. I believe
that it does exist, and that one of our jobs is to prevent it from
getting out of its box. It gets out sooner or later, and then it destroys us and all the lovely things which we have made. But it isn't
out all the time, for the fortunate reason that the strong are so
stupid. Consider their conduct for a moment in the Nibelung's
Ring. The giants there have the guns, or in other words the
gold; but they do nothing with it, they do not realize that they
are all-powerful, with the result that the catastrophe is delayed
and the castle of Walhalla, insecure but glorious, fronts the storms
for generations. Fafnir, coiled around his hoard, grumbles and
grunts; we can hear him under Europe today; the leaves of the
wood already tremble, and the Bird calls its warnings uselessly.
Fafnir will destroy us, but by a blessed dispensation he is stupid
and slow, and creation goes on just outside the poisonous blast of
his breath. The Nietzschean would hurry the monster up, the
mystic would say he didn't exist, but Wotan, wiser than either,
hastens to create warriors before doom declares itself. The Val-
kyries are symbols not only of courage but of intelligence; they
represent the human spirit snatching its opportunity while the

going is good, and one of them even finds time to love. Brunhilde's last song hymns the recurrence of love, and since it is the privilege of art to exaggerate she goes even further, and proclaims the love which is eternally triumphant and feeds upon freedom, and lives.

So that is what I feel about force and violence. It is, alas! the ultimate reality, on this earth, but—hooray!—it doesn't always get to the front. Some people call its absences "decadence"; I call them "civilization" and find in such interludes the chief justification for the human experiment. I look the other way until fate strikes me. Whether this is due to courage or to cowardice in my own case I cannot be sure. But I know that if men hadn't looked the other way in the past nothing of any value would survive. The people I respect most behave as if they were immortal and as if society were eternal. Both assumptions are false: both of them must be accepted as true if we are to go on eating and working and loving, and are to keep open a few breathing holes for the human spirit. No millennium seems likely to descend upon humanity; no better and stronger League of Nations will be instituted; no form of Christianity and no alternative to Christianity will bring peace to the world or integrity to the individual; no "change of heart" will occur. And yet we needn't despair, indeed we cannot despair; the evidence of history shows us that men have always insisted on behaving creatively under the shadow of the sword; that they have done their artistic and scientific and domestic stuff for the sake of doing it, and that we had better follow their example under the shadow of the airplanes. Others, with more vision or courage than myself, see the salvation of humanity ahead, and will dismiss my conception of civilization as paltry, a sort of tip-and-run game. Certainly it is presumptuous to say that we *can't* improve, and that man, who has only been in power for a few thousand years, will never learn to make use of his power. All I mean is that, if people continue to kill one another at the rate they do, the world cannot get better than it is, and that since there are more people than formerly, and their means for destroying one another more diabolic, the world may well get worse. What's good in people—and consequently in the world —is their insistence on creation, their belief in friendship, in loyalty, for its own sake; and though violence remains and is indeed the major partner in this muddled establishment, I believe that creativeness remains too, and will always assume direction when violence sleeps. So, though I am not an optimist, I cannot agree with Sophocles that it were better never to have been born. And although I see no evidence that each batch of births is superior to the last, I leave the field open for this happier view. This is such a difficult time to live in, especially for a European, one can't help getting gloomy and also a bit rattled.

There is of course hero worship, fervently recommended as a panacea in some quarters. But here we shall get no help. Hero worship is a dangerous vice, and one of the minor merits of a democracy is that it does not encourage it, or produce that unmanageable type of citizen known as the Great Man. It produces instead different kinds of small men, and that's a much finer achievement. But people who can't get interested in the variety of life and can't make up their own minds get discontented over this, and they long for a hero to bow down before and to follow blindly. It's significant that a hero is an integral part of the authoritarian stock in trade today. An efficiency regime can't be run without a few heroes stuck about to carry off the dullness—much as plums have to be put into a bad pudding to make it palatable. One hero at the top and a smaller one each side of him is a favorite arrangement, and the timid and the bored are comforted by such a trinity, and, bowing down, feel exalted by it.

No, I distrust Great Men. They produce a desert of uniformity around them and often a pool of blood too, and I always feel a little man's pleasure when they come a cropper. Every now and then one reads in the newspapers some such statement as, "The *coup d'état* appears to have failed, and Admiral Boga's whereabouts is at present unknown." Admiral Boga had probably every qualification for being a great man—an iron will, personal magnetism, dash, flair—but fate was against him, so he retires to unknown whereabouts instead of parading history with his peers. He fails with a completeness that no artist and no lover can experience, because with them the process of creation is itself an achievement, whereas with him the only possible achievement is success. I believe in aristocracy though—if that's the right word, and if a democrat may use it. Not an aristocracy of power, based upon rank and influence, but an aristocracy of the sensitive, the considerate, and the plucky. Its members are to be found in all nations and classes, and all through the ages, and there is a secret understanding between them when they meet. They represent the true human tradition, the one permanent victory of our queer race over cruelty and chaos. Thousands of them perish in obscurity; a few are great names. They are sensitive for others as well as for themselves, they are considerate without being fussy, their pluck is not swankiness but the power to endure, and they can take a joke. I give no examples—it is risky to do that—but the reader may as well consider whether this is the type of person he would like to meet and to be, and whether (going further with me) he would prefer that the type should *not* be an ascetic one. I'm against asceticism myself. I'm with the old Scotchman who wanted less chastity and more delicacy. I don't feel that my aristocrats are a real aristocracy if they thwart their bodies, since bodies are the instruments through which we register and enjoy the world. Still, I don't insist here. This isn't a major point. It's clearly possible to be sensitive, considerate, and plucky and yet to be an ascetic too, and if anyone possesses the first three qualities, I'll let him in! On they go—an invincible army, yet not a victorious one. The aristocrats, the elect, the chosen, the best people—all the words that describe them are false, and all attempts to organize them fail. Again and again authority, seeing their value, has tried to net them and to utilize them as the Egyptian priesthood or the Christian Church or the Chinese civil service or the Group Movement, or some other worthy stunt. But they slip through the net and are gone; when the door is shut they are no longer in the room; their temple, as one of them remarked, is the holiness of the heart's imagination, and their kingdom, though they never possess it, is the wide open world.

With this type of person knocking about, and constantly crossing one's path if one has eyes to see or hands to feel, the experiment of earthly life cannot be dismissed as a failure. But it may well be hailed as a tragedy, the tragedy being that no device has been found by which these private decencies can be transferred to public affairs. As soon as people have power they go crooked and sometimes dotty, too, because the possession of power lifts them into a region where normal honesty never pays. For instance, the man who is selling newspapers outside the Houses of Parliament can safely leave his papers to go for a drink, and his cap beside them: anyone who takes a paper is sure to drop a copper into the cap. But the men who are inside the Houses of Parliament —they can't trust one another like that; still less can the government they compose trust other governments. No caps upon the pavement here, but suspicion, treachery, and armaments. The more highly public life is organized the lower does its morality sink; the nations of today behave to each other worse than they ever did in the past, they cheat, rob, bully, and bluff, make war without notice, and kill as many women and children as possible; whereas primitive tribes were at all events restrained by taboos. It's a humiliating outlook—though the greater the darkness, the brighter shine the little lights, reassuring one another, signaling, "Well, at all events I'm still here. I don't like it very much, but how are you?" Unquenchable lights of my aristocracy! Signals of the invincible army! "Come along—anyway let's have a good time while we can." I think they signal that too.

The savior of the future—if ever he comes—will not preach a new gospel. He will merely utilize my aristocracy; he will make effective the good will and the good temper which are already existing. In other words he will introduce a new technique. In economics, we are told that if there was a new technique of distribution, there need be no poverty, and people would not starve in one place while crops were dug under in another. A similar change is needed in the sphere of morals and politics. The desire for it is by no means new; it was expressed, for example, in theological terms by Jacopone da Todi over six hundred years ago. *"Ordina questo amore, O tu che m'ami,"* he said. "O thou who lovest me—set this love in order." His prayer was not granted and I do not myself believe that it ever will be, but here, and not through a change of heart, is our probable route. Not by becoming better, but by ordering and distributing his native goodness, will man shut up force into its box, and so gain time to explore the universe and to set his mark upon it worthily. At present he only explores it at odd moments, when force is looking the other way, and his divine creativeness appears as a trivial by-product, to be scrapped as soon as the drums beat and the bombers hum.

Such a change, claim the orthodox, can only be made by Christianity, and will be made by it in God's good time: man always has failed and always will fail to organize his own goodness, and it is presumptuous of him to try. This claim—solemn as it is—leaves me cold. I cannot believe that Christianity will ever cope with the present world-wide mess, and I think that such influence as it retains in modern society is due to its financial backing rather than to its spiritual appeal. It was a spiritual force once, but the indwelling spirit will have to be restated if it is to calm the waters again, and probably restated in a non-Christian form. Naturally a great many people, and people who are not only good but able and intelligent, will disagree with me here; they will vehemently deny that Christianity has failed, or they will argue that its failure proceeds from the wickedness of men, and really proves its ultimate success. They have Faith, with a large F. My faith has a very small one, and I only bring it into the open because these are strenuous and serious days, and one likes to say what one thinks while speech is still free: it may not be free much longer.

These are the reflections of an individualist and a liberal who has found his liberalism crumbling beneath him and at first felt ashamed. Then, looking around, he decided there was no special reason for shame, since other people, whatever they felt, were equally insecure. And as for individualism—there seems no way out of this, even if one wants to find one. The dictator-hero can grind down his citizens till they are all alike, but he can't melt them into a single man. That is beyond his power. He can order them to merge, he can incite them to mass antics, but they are obliged to be born separately and to die separately and, owing to these unavoidable termini, will always be running off the totalitarian rails. The memory of birth and the expectation of death always lurk within the human being, making him separate from his fellows and consequently capable of intercourse with them. Naked I came into the world, naked I shall go out of it! And a very good thing too, for it reminds me that I am naked under my shirt. Until psychologists and biologists have done much more tinkering than seems likely, the individual remains firm and each of us must consent to be one, and to make the best of the difficult job.

1939

On Nunneries

by ANATOLE FRANCE [1844-1924]

IT IS PAINFUL to see a young girl die voluntarily to the world. The Nunnery is terrifying to all who do not enter its doors. In the middle of the Fourth Century of the Christian era, a young Roman lady, Blæsilla by name, undertook such a severe course of fasting in a Convent that she died of the effects. The populace followed her coffin to the grave, shouting furiously: "Drive out, drive out this odious tribe of Monks from the city! Why do we not stone them? Why do we not throw them into the Tiber?" And when, fourteen hundred years afterwards, Chateaubriand, by the mouth of the Père Aubry, extolled the women who have "sanctified their beauty to the masterpieces of repentance and mortified the rebellious flesh whose pleasures are only pains," the Abbé Morellet, an old man and a philosopher, listened with impatience to this panegyric of the cloistered life, and exclaimed: "If this is not fanaticism, I ask the author to give me his definition of what fanaticism is!" What do we learn from these interminable disputes, if not that the religious life alarms the natural man, but that nevertheless it has reasons for its existence and continuance? Neither populace nor philosophers always appreciate these reasons. They are deep-seated and touch the greatest mysteries of human nature. The Cloister has been taken by storm and its walls thrown down. Its deserted ruins have been repeopled afresh. There are certain souls that gravitate thither by a natural bias; *claustral* souls they are. Because they are innately inhuman and pacific, they quit the world and go down rejoicing into silence and peace. Many souls are born weary; they have no curiosity; they drag out a sluggish existence without a wish for one thing more than another. Not knowing either how to live or die, they embrace the religious life as a lesser life and a lesser death. Others are led to the Cloister by indirect motives; they never foresaw whither they were going. Wounded innocents, an early disappointment, or secret grief, has spoilt the scheme of things for them. Their life will never bear fruit; the cold has blighted the blossom. They have realized too soon how evil the world is. They hide away in corners to weep. They would fain forget. . . . Or rather, they cherish their grief and set it in a place of shelter away from men and men's activities. Yet again there are others attracted to the Convent by the zeal of sacrifice, souls that are eager to give themselves wholly to heaven, in a self-abandonment more ardent than love itself knows. These last, the smallest class of all, are the true brides of Christ. The grateful Church bestows on them the sweet names of *lily* and *rose, dove* and *lamb,* promising them, by the mouth of the Queen of Virgins, the crown of stars and the throne of purity. But we should beware of going further than the theologians warrant. In the Ages of Faith, there was no greater enthusiasm about the mystic virtues of Nuns. I am not speaking of the people, who always looked upon the denizens of Convents with a certain suspicion and told facetious tales about them. I speak of the Secular Clergy, whose opinions were very mixed. We must not forget that the poetry of the Cloistered life only dates from Chateaubriand and Montalembert.

Another point to be considered—religious communities differ altogether according to the varying conditions of period and country; they cannot all be massed together in one and the same judgment. The Religious House was for centuries, in the West of Europe, farm, school, hospital, and library combined. There were Houses for the preservation of knowledge, others for the encouragement of ignorance. Some were designed for work, as others were for a life of idleness.

I visited some years ago the hill on which St. Odile, daughter of a Duke of Alsace, raised in the middle of the twelfth century a Convent, the memory of which has lingered ever since in the soul of the Alsatian people. She was a brave and good woman, who sought and found means to soften for those about her the curse of living, which then weighted sore on poor folks. Aided by clever fellow-workers of her own sex and served by numerous serfs, she cleared the ground, tilled the fields, reared stock, secured the harvests against pillagers. She was a special providence to the improvident. She taught the mead-drinkers sobriety, the violent gentleness, all men carefulness and good management. What resemblance can we discern between these robust, pure-hearted virgins living in a barbarous age, these daughters of kings and tillers of the soil, and the dainty Lady Abbesses who, under Louis xv, went to Mass in paint and patches, and left a scent of *poudre à la maréchale* on the lips of the Abbés who kissed their fingers?

And even then, even in those scandalous days, when the Abbeys served as refuge and prison for the younger daughters of noble houses who had proved recalcitrant, there were good, pious souls to be found behind the bars of Convents. It so happens I have surprised the secrets of one of them. It was last year at Legoubin's, the bookseller on the Quai Malaquais, amongst whose treasures I lighted on an old Manual of Confession for the use of nuns. An inscription on the title-page written in a formal hand informed me that in 1779 the book was the property of the Sœur Anne, a Nun of the Order of the Feuillantines. It was in French, and had this special peculiarity—that each sin was printed on a little square slip attached to the leaf by the edge merely. While examining her conscience in the Convent Chapel, the penitent needed neither pen nor pencil to jot down her faults, whether grave or venial. All she had to do was to turn down the little strip mentioning any particular sin she had committed. Then in the confessional, by help of her book, which she went through systematically, from one turned-down slip to another, Sœur Anne ran no risk of forgetting any breach of God's commandments or the Church's ordinances.

Now, at the time when I discovered the little book on my friend Legoubin's shelves, I noticed that a number of offences showed only a single crease where they had been turned down. These were Sœur Anne's extraordinary sins. Others had been folded in again and again, so that the corners of the paper were all worn and dog's-eared. Here we had Sœur Anne's pet peccadilloes.

There was no doubt about it. The book had never been used since the dispersion of the Nuns in 1790. It was still stuffed with religious pictures and illuminated prayers, which the good Nun had slipt in between the pages.

In this way I came to know Sœur Anne's soul. I found it held only the most innocent of sins, and I have great hopes that Sœur Anne is seated to-day at the right hand of the Father. No purer heart ever beat beneath the white robe of the Feuillantine Sisters. I can picture to myself the pious sister with her clear eyes and stoutish figure, as she walks slowly up and down between the cabbage beds of the Convent-garden. She is quite calm and self-possessed as her white hand marks down in her book her sins, which are as regular and as orderly as her life—vain words, wandering thoughts in Chapter and in Church, trivial acts of disobedience, and greediness at meals. This last touch moved me to tears; Sœur Anne was greedy at her repast of roots boiled in plain water! She was not unhappy. She had no doubts. She never tempted God. Sins such as these have left no mark in the little book. She was a Nun, and her heart was in the Convent. Her destiny was in accord with her nature. That is the secret of Sœur Anne's good life.

I do not know, but I quite think there are many Sœur Annes at the present day in Nunneries. I could find not a few things to say against the Monks; I think it best to own frankly that I am not very fond of them. As to the Nuns, I believe they have most of them, like Sœur Anne, a conventual spirit, in which the graces of their estate flourish and abound.

Why otherwise should they have taken the veil? In these days they are not driven into the Cloister by the pride and avarice of

relations. They take the vow because they like to. They could repudiate them, if they chose; yet you see they do not. The free-
thinking dragoons we see in farces of the Revolutionary period
breaking down Convent doors soon had enough of invoking nature and marrying the Nuns. Nature is of vaster scope than free-
thinking dragoons quite realize; she unites the sensuous and the
ascetic both in her comprehensive bosom. For the Cloister, the
monster must needs be lovable, seeing it is loved, and no longer
devours any but voluntary victims. The Convent has charms of its
own. There is the Chapel, with its gilded vessels and paper roses,
a Blessed Virgin painted in the colours of life and bathed in a pale,
mysterious radiance as of moonlight, the chants and the incense
and the Priest's voice; these are some of the most obvious fascina-
tions of the Cloister, and they often carry the day against the attractions of the world.

After all, there is a soul in these things, and they contain the
sum total of poetry certain natures are capable of. Sedentary by
nature and disposed to a discreet, unassuming, retiring life, women
are from the first in their element in a Convent. The atmosphere
is cosy and comforting, a trifle stifling; it affords the pious dames
who breathe it all the delights of a long-drawn asphyxiation.
They fall into a half-sleep, and soon lose the habit of thinking. This is a fine thing to get rid of. In exchange, they gain certainty. An excellent transaction, surely, from the practical point
of view.

I do not lay much stress on titles such as the *bride of Jesus, vessel
of election, immaculate dove.* Enthusiasm, mysticism, plays no
great part in religious communities. The virtues jog quietly along
a humdrum path. Everything, even including the sentiment of the
divine, keeps a judicious course near the ground, attempts no
heavenward flights. Spirituality is world-wise and takes a material
form so far as it can, and the possibilities in this direction are far
greater than is commonly supposed. The great business of life is so
minutely divided up into a series of little trivial transactions that
punctuality satisfies all needs. Nothing ever breaks the even
thread of existence. Duty is reduced to its simplest terms; the rule
of the House defines it. There is much in this to satisfy timid

souls, gentle, tractable natures. Such a life kills imagination, but not gaiety of heart. It is a rare thing to see an expression of deep-seated melancholy on a Nun's face.

At the present day, we should search in vain in the Convents of France for a Virginie de Leyva or a Giulia Carraciolo, unwilling victims of a hated system, craving frantically for a breath through the Cloister gratings of the free air of nature and the world of men. Nor yet should we find, I think, a St. Theresa or a St. Catherine of Siena. The heroic age of the Cloister is gone for ever. The mystic ardour of an earlier time waxes faint. The motives that impelled so many men and women to adopt the monastic life have ceased to exist. In those times of violence, when a man was never sure of reaping the fruits of his labour, when he was liable to be awakened at any moment by the screams of the dying and the flames of burning homesteads, when life was a nightmare, souls of softer temper were fain to retire to dream of heaven in the Religious Houses that rose like great arks above the waves of hate and malice. But these days are past. The world has grown almost bearable, and people are more willing to stay in it. At the same time, such as find it still too rough and too insecure are at liberty, after all, to leave it. The Constituent Assembly was wrong to dispute the right, and we have done well to allow it in principle.

I have the privilege to know the Lady Superior of a Community the Mother House of which is in Paris. She is a woman of excellent principles who inspires me with sincere respect. She was telling me, a little while since, about the last moments of one of her Nuns, whom I had known as a merry-hearted and pretty girl in society, and who had entered the Convent to die a lingering death from consumption.

"She made an edifying end," the Lady Superior told me. "She used to get up every day all through her long illness, and two lay sisters would carry her to the Chapel. She was praying there on the very morning of her release. A taper burning before the image of St. Joseph was guttering on to the pavement. She directed one of the lay sisters to set the candle straight. Then she threw herself back, heaved a deep sigh, and the death agony began. She received the last consolations of religion. She could only testify

by the movement of her eyes to the pious satisfaction the sacra-
ments of the dying afforded her."

The little narrative was given with an admirable simplicity.
Death is the most important transaction of the religious life. But
so good a preparation for it is the existence of the Cloister that
nothing more momentous is left to do at that hour than at any
other. The dying Nun sets a taper straight—and expires. It was
the one act lacking to round off the blessedness of a minute and
meticulous piety.

1894   Translated by
                                          ALFRED ALLINSON

The Evolution of the Theater

by ANDRÉ GIDE [1869-1951]

THE EVOLUTION of the art of drama is a particularly difficult subject. I should like to begin by telling you why. Perhaps you will
then allow me to talk rather than to lecture, and to talk around
the subject rather than on the subject itself.

Since I consider that dramatic works do not find, nor mean to
find, their aim and end in themselves (and this makes for one of
the worst difficulties of the subject), but that the dramatist sets his
work up, so to speak, between the audience and the actor, I propose to take, in succession, first the author's, then the actor's, and
then the spectator's point of view, in an effort to consider, each in
turn, these three aspects of one and the same evolution.

Another difficulty, not among the least, comes from the fact that
in the success of a play, or even of a whole genre of plays, many
considerations may be involved which have nothing to do with
literature. I speak not only of the manifold elements that dramatic
works must draw on in order to be successfully performed: the
wealth of scenery, brilliant costumes, beautiful women, the talent

and celebrity of actors; I speak especially of certain preoccupations, social, patriotic, pornographic, or pseudoartistic, of the author.

The successful plays of today are often tissues of just these preoccupations; so much so that by dropping them one at a time we almost annihilate the play.*

But for the most part it is precisely to these preoccupations that the play owes its popularity; the author who does not give in to them, but who writes solely out of a preoccupation with art, is quite likely not even to see his work performed.

Now, since dramatic works live only potentially in books, live completely only on the stage, the critic who today would take an interest in the evolution of the theater would be obliged, in order not to neglect the parallel evolution of actor and audience, to speak of works that have only a very distant relation to literature, and on the other hand to neglect plays of purely literary merit; here I refer not only to works like Francis Viélé-Griffin's *Phocas,* Henri de Régnier's *La Gardienne,* or Francis Jammes's *Un Jour,* which I agree may be considered as poems only, but to the early plays of Maeterlinck, the dramas of Claudel, Henri Ghéon's *Le Pain,* and others (I was about to say *Le Cloître* of Verhaeren, but remembered the happy success it has won in Brussels and elsewhere). Or if our critic does speak of these works, it can only be as events in the world of books, unknown to the stage and to the theater audience; their evolution not only remains apart from the other, quite apart, but even runs counter to it.

---

* The same preoccupations exist, it is true, for the novel also; but besides the fact that they are a great deal less harmful to it because the novel is a vague, multiform, and omnivorous literary species, the novelist who allows himself to be guided by them turns his back on literature in a franker fashion. And however bumptious the publicity that may precede or follow it, a bad book, written to be sold, is not, after all, presented in a much more impertinent manner than a good one. Better still: boosting puts us on guard; when a writer like Champsaur announces that his *Arriviste,* even before publication, has reached its . . . 30th thousand, the public knows what to think, of book and author alike. We are never taken in by novels as we are by works in the theater; the playwright, moreover, is never alone involved; there are also the actors, the producer, and his expenses. A serious literary critic never mentions, never even reads, books of the mediocrity of many plays to which our leading dramatic critics think they are obliged to devote several columns.

"In social animals," writes Darwin, natural selection "will adapt the structure of each individual for the benefit of the whole community; if the community," he adds, "profits by the selected change." Here the community does not profit; it does not wish to profit. The artist whose work is not performed buries himself in his work, escapes the general evolution, and ends by reacting against it. The works of which I speak are all works of reaction.

Reaction against what? I should readily say against realism, were it not that the word *realism,* which has already been given so many different senses, would quickly prove a serious handicap to me as well. The cleverest hypocrisy I could use would not suffice to convict the works of Monsieur Rostand, for example, of realism, nor the comedies of Molière nor the dramas of Ibsen of antirealism. Let us say, rather, a reaction against episodism. Yes, for the lack of a better, *episodism* seems to me the preferable word. For art does not consist in the use of herioc, historical, or legendary figures; nor is it necessarily inartistic to put contemporary bourgeois figures on the stage. Yet there is some truth in Racine's words, which I read from the preface to *Bajazet:* "Characters in tragedy must be regarded with a different eye than we ordinarily regard those persons we have seen close to. It may be said," he adds, "that the respect we have for heroes increases as they are farther from us." It may be said, however, I venture to add in turn, that respect for characters on the stage is perhaps not indispensable. The artist chooses figures distant from us for the reason that time, or any kind of distance, allows an image to reach us only after it has been stripped of everything episodic, bizarre, and transitory, leaving only its portion of profound truth for art to work on. And the sense of strangeness that the artist seeks to produce by putting his characters at a distance from us indicates just this desire: to give us his work of art as a work of art, his drama as drama simply, and not to run after an illusion of reality which, even if it were attained, would only serve to form upon reality a pleonasm. Was it not this very desire that urged our classical writers, almost without their knowledge, to be bound by the three unities: to make drama deliberately and plainly artistic.

Whenever art languishes we order it back to nature, as we take a sick person to a watering-place. This is a mistake: nature, alas, cannot help. I agree that it may be good sometimes for art to go to the country; if it is pale from exhaustion, that it go to the fields,— that is, to life—to regain its strength. But our masters, the Greeks, knew well enough that Aphrodite was not born of any natural fecundation. Beauty will never be produced by natural means; it can only be obtained by artificial constraint. Art and nature are rivals on earth. Yes, art embraces nature, and holds it; but citing the celebrated line, art might well say:

"J'embrasse mon rival; mais c'est pour l'étouffer." *

Art is always the result of constraint. To believe that it rises higher as it becomes freer is to believe that what keeps a kite from rising is its string. Kant's dove, which thought it could fly better without the air to trouble its wings, did not realize that in order to fly, it had to have the air's resistance to support its wings. Likewise art must be supported by resistance in order to rise. I have mentioned the three dramatic unities, but what I am saying at present is quite as true also for painting, sculpture, music, and poetry. Art aspires to freedom only in periods of illness, when it would prefer to live easily. Whenever it feel vigorous, it seeks struggle and obstacle. It loves to burst out of its sheath, and for that reason it prefers a tight one. Is it not in periods when life is most overflowing that the need of the strictest forms torments our most moving geniuses? Hence the use of the sonnet during the luxuriant Renaissance, by Shakespeare, Ronsard, Petrarch, and even Michelangelo; hence Dante's use of *terza rima;* Bach's love of the fugue; and the restless need of the constraint of the fugue in the later works of Beethoven. How many more examples could be cited! Should we be astonished that the lyrical impulse's power of expansion is due to its compression; or that the weight to be supported is what makes architecture possible?

The great artist is one who is exalted by his difficulties, who uses an obstacle as a springboard. It has been said that Michelangelo owed to the very flaw in the marble his creation of the compact movement of his Moses. It was the limited number of speakers at his disposal on the stage that constrained Æschylus to imagine

* I embrace my rival, but only to choke him.

the silence of Prometheus being chained to the rock in the Caucasus. Greece banished the man who added a string to the lyre. Art is born of constraint, lives by struggle, dies of freedom.

The dramatist little by little diminished the space that separates the stage from the audience, boasting at first that he was gaining for drama in power of expression what it lost at once in beauty. It seems that this evolution was fated; the actor also did his best to diminish that "distance" which Racine required between the spectator and the figure on the stage, and to humanize the hero. He threw away, in turn, mask and buskin—in short, everything that made of him something strange, to be regarded, if I may repeat Racine's words, "with a different eye than we ordinarily regard those persons we have seen close to." He did away even with the conventional costume which, by taking the dramatic character out of its historical period, by abstracting him so to speak, allowed only that precisely to remain which was general and human. If there was any progress in that, it was at least very dangerous progress. Under the pretext of truth, the actor sought accuracy. Costumes, properties, scenery, all did their best to identify exactly the place and time of the action, with never a care that Racine, for example, had taken care to do the opposite. We read in Goethe: "There are, properly speaking, no historical figures in poetry; only, when the poet wishes to portray the world that he has conceived, he chooses certain persons he has met with in history and does them the honor of borrowing their names and applying them to the beings of his own creation." * I have taken these lines just as they are quoted by Victor Hugo in one of the notes to his *Cromwell:* "One is astonished," he says, "to read these lines from Herr Goethe." Today we are perhaps less astonished.

But on this point the dramatist has the actor against him. Talma, when he was supposed to play the *Mahomet* of Voltaire, thought it well to study the Mahomet of history first, for a whole month. He himself relates how, "having found too many and too great discrepancies between the one he had conceived and the one Voltaire presented, he had immediately renounced the

* *Über Kunst und Alterthum.*

role because it would have been impossible for him to render it without departing from the truth." I quote from the text of Guiraud's memoirs; I could not have invented a better example. That was all very well because Voltaire's *Mahomet* is not a good play; but—during a rehearsal of *Britannicus,* when someone reproached one of our greatest actors of today for not interpreting his role in a manner Racine would no doubt have desired, he cried: "Racine?—who is he? I know only Nero." *

The actor's collaboration, then, which is indispensable, gives particularity where the author wanted generality. I cannot blame the actor; a dramatic work is not a work in abstraction: the characters are a pretext for generalization, but they are always of a particular truth; and the theater as well as the novel is the place for characters.

Ladies and gentlemen, the theater is an extraordinary thing. People like you and me gather in a hall in the evening to watch other people feign passions that none of us have the right to have, because our laws and our manners are against them. I propose for your meditation a remark of Balzac's found in the *Physiologie du mariage:* "Manners," he says, "manners are the hypocrisy of nations." Does he mean, perhaps, that our manners do not stamp out those passions which the actor displays, but only hide them? Does he mean that our moderate conduct is only meant to mislead others; that we are the actors (*hypokrites* in Greek, you know, means actor); that our politeness is only feigned and that, in short, virtue, the "politeness of the soul" as Balzac calls it, virtue is most of the time only decoration? Could it be that

* There is much indignation over the arrogance of actors. Their arrogance seems to me natural enough, and I find that dramatists condemn it much too easily; for we must remember the dramatist's work aims to last for eternity, whereas the actor can create only fleeting figures like those snow statues which Pietro de' Medici forced Michelangelo to model all one winter in his garden. The following words are reported of a great actor who one evening went to a box in the theater to slap the face of an illustrious critic whose article the same morning had treated him severely, and unjustly, so he claimed. "You writers have all time before you, but with actors it is different; if you do not do us justice on the day we perform, to what court can we appeal? What will the future think of us?"

Should we be astonished if the actor tries, beyond everything else, to live, even at the author's expense?

our pleasure in the theater comes partly from this: hearing voices speak out what in us is stifled by propriety? Sometimes. But more often a man regards passions on the stage as frightful monsters that have been tamed. He has the admirable faculty of becoming before long what he pretends to be, and that is what caused Condorcet to write (I am happy to take cover behind so imposing a name): "The hypocrisy of manners, a vice peculiar to the nations of modern Europe, has contributed more than we think to destroy the energy of character that distinguished ancient nations." * So the hypocrisy of manners has not always existed.

Yes, man becomes what he pretends to be; but to pretend to be what one is not is a thoroughly modern pretense; more to the point, it is a peculiarly Christian pretense. I do not say that the intervention of will counts for nothing in the formation or deformation of the human being; but the pagan did not believe he should be different from what he was. Then the human being did not constrain himself to be commonplace, but drove himself to excel by virtue; each man exacted of himself only what was in him, and without deformation modeled himself on his god. Hence the great number of gods, as numerous as the instincts of men. It was not by free choice that man devoted himself to a particular god; the god recognized his own image in the man. Sometimes it happened that the man refused to see it; and the god unrecognized in the man took vengeance; this happens most terribly to Pentheus in the *Bacchantes* of Euripides.

Pagans rarely considered qualities of the soul as goods that could be acquired, but rather as natural properties like those of the body. Agathocles was good, or Charicles courageous, quite as naturally as one had blue eyes, the other black. For them religion did not hold up on a cross, or set up before them on earth, any bundle of virtues or any moral phantom that it was important to resemble, under pain of being considered ungodly; the typical man was not one, but legion; or rather there was no typical man. In those days, since the mask had no use in life, it was worn only by the actor.

* *Vie de Voltaire.*

When one speaks of the history of drama, it is important, perhaps more important than anything else, to ask: *Where is the mask?* In the audience, or on the stage? In the theater, or in life? It is here *or* there, never both at once. The most brilliant periods of drama, those in which the mask is triumphant on the stage, are those in which hypocrisy ceases to mask life. On the contrary, those in which what Condorcet calls "the hypocrisy of manners" is triumphant are the very periods in which the mask is snatched from the face of the actor and he is required to be not beautiful but natural; that is to say, if I rightly understand, that he must take his models from reality, or at least from the semblances of it to be seen in his audience; and that is to say, from a monotonous and already masked humanity. The author, meanwhile, also priding himself on being natural, will undertake to furnish the actor a drama suited to his purposes: a drama both monotonous and masked—in short, a drama in which the tragedy of situations (since we must have tragedy of some sort) will gradually replace the tragedy of character. Just consider, for example, the disquieting dearth of characters in the naturalistic novel, the very one that pretends to copy reality. But is this surprising? Our modern society with its Christian morality does all it can to hamper the development of character. "Ancient religion," wrote Machiavelli long ago, "beatified only men of worldly glory like captains of armies and founders of republics, whereas our own has glorified humble and contemplative men rather than men of action. It has found the sovereign good in humility, in abjection, in contempt of worldly things, whereas the other found it in greatness of soul, in strength of body, in all that makes men bold. Our religion wants men strong to endure, not to do great deeds." With characters like these, if we can still call them characters, what kind of dramatic *action* is still possible? Whoever says drama says character; Christianity is against character, proposing to all men a common ideal.

Therefore, purely Christian drama, to tell the truth, does not exist. Such plays as *Saint-Genest* and *Polyeucte* may be called Christian dramas, if they wish. They are of course Christian by virtue of the Christian element that has gone into their making, but they are dramas only because of the struggle between their Christian and non-Christian elements.

Another reason why Christian theater is not possible is that the last act, in all necessity, must take place off stage—I mean in the other life. Goethe was quite well aware of this: the second part of *Faust* ends in heaven; likewise, I suppose, the sixth act of *Polyeucte* and the sixth act of *Saint-Genest* are played in heaven. If neither Corneille nor Rotrou wrote his sixth act, it was not only out of respect for the three unities, but rather because Polyeucte, Pauline, and St. Genest, at the threshold of paradise, having put away all passion by which the drama was sustained, having become perfect Christians, completely decharacterized, had in truth nothing more to say.

Ladies and gentlemen, I am not proposing a return to paganism. I am simply noting the thing of which our tragedy is dying: want of characters. Christianity, alas, is not solely responsible for this process of leveling which led Kirkegaard to say: "Leveling is not of God, and every upright man must have moments in which he is tempted to weep over this work of desolation." Those over whom their desires are victorious do not find it difficult to believe in the gods. Desires are true gods so long as they rule; they are proved to be false only when the unity of despotic reason has already supplanted them. It was the invention of morals that turned Olympus into a desert. Monotheism exists in man before it becomes a god outside him. Man serves one or several gods in himself before he projects his faith into the skies. Paganism and Christianity were first psychology before they were metaphysics. Paganism was at one and the same time the triumph of individualism and the belief that man cannot become other than he is. This was the school of the theater.

But once again it is not the impossible return to paganism that I am here to propose; nor am I here to remark coldly on the death of the theater; but rather to examine what in our time is killing it, in order to deduce what might make it live; for it is not the decadence of the art of drama that matters to me, but rather its rebirth, which I believe in, and foresee.

The way to save the theater from episodism is to rediscover its restrictions. The way to people it again with characters is to separate it again from life. I should readily say: give us back moral freedom and the restrictions of art will follow; do away with hypocrisy in life and the mask will return to the stage. But since moral convention will heed nothing, the artist must take the initiative. I have some hope that convention will follow; let me tell you why.

It is obvious that new forms of society, new distributions of wealth, unforeseen contributions from the outside account for much in the formation of character; nevertheless I believe we are led to overestimate the formative role of such things; I rather believe their role is one of discovery, merely. All things have always existed in man, sometimes seen, more or less, and sometimes hidden; what in recent times has been discovered in him is newly disclosed to sight but had been there asleep in man from the beginning. Just as I believe there still exist in our time people like the Princesse de Clèves, or Onuphre, or Celadon, I am also quite ready to believe that long before they appeared in books, Adolphe, Rastignac, and even Julien Sorel existed in life. Furthermore, I believe that just as humanity is after all stronger than any particular race, we can find elsewhere than in St. Petersburg (I mean in Brussels or in Paris) such characters as Nezhdanov, Myshkin, and Prince André. But as long as their voices have not sounded in books or on the stage, they languish or fret under the mantle of custom, awaiting their hour. We do not hear them because the world hears only those voices it can recognize; and because their voices are drowned out, being too new. We look at the black mantle of custom and do not see them under it; better still (I mean worse still), these new forms of humanity do not recognize themselves. How many secret Werthers were unaware of themselves, waiting only for the bullet of Goethe's Werther, to kill themselves! How many hidden heroes there are, only awaiting the example of the hero of some book, a spark of his life to make them live, a word of his to make them speak! Is that not, ladies and gentlemen, what we likewise hope from the theater: that it offer humanity new forms of heroism and new heroes?

The soul requires heroism; but our society scarcely allows today more than a single form of heroism (if it is heroism), and that is the heroism of resignation, of acceptance. When a powerful creator of characters, like Ibsen, drapes the figures of his theater in the dreary mantle of our manners, at the same stroke he condemns his most heroic heroes to bankruptcy. Yes, his admirable theater, necessarily, shows us from one end to the other the bankruptcy of heroism. How could he have done otherwise without deserting reality, since, for that matter, if reality allowed any heroism (I mean apparent or theatrical heroism) we should know it, we should indeed know these real heroes personally.

That is why I believe the bold task of Pygmalion or Prometheus is only for those who will deliberately turn the orchestra pit into a moat, widen the gap between stage and audience, between fiction and reality, between actor and spectator, and between the hero and the mantle of manners.

That is why my eyes, full of expectation and joy, are turned toward those unplayed plays of which I spoke awhile ago; they are becoming year by year more numerous and soon I hope will find their stage. Every turn of the wheel of history brings to light what before was invisible in the darkness.

"Time in its slow, illimitable course," says the Ajax of Sophocles, "brings all to light and buries all again; strange things it brings to pass. . . ." We expect of humanity new manifestations. Sometimes those who take the floor keep it for a terribly long time; generations that have yet to speak, however, are growing impatient in their silence. It seems that those who are now speaking, despite their pretense to represent all mankind in our time, must realize that others are waiting, and when these take the floor, those will not get it again—for a long time. The floor today belongs to all who have not yet spoken. Who are they?

The theater will tell us.

I am reminded of the "deep sea" of which Nietzsche speaks, of those unexplored regions of man, full of new dangers and surprises for the heroic navigator. I am reminded of what voyages must have been before there were maps and without our exact and limited record of the known. And I reread the words of Sinbad: "And, lo, the master of the ship vociferated and called out,

threw down his turban, slapped his face, plucked his beard, and
fell down in the hold of the ship by reason of the violence of his
grief and rage. So all the merchants and other passengers came
together to him and said to him: 'O master, what is the matter?'
And he answered them: 'Know, O company, that we have wandered from our course, having passed forth from the sea in which
we were, and entered a sea of which we know not the routes.' "
I am thinking of Sinbad's ship, and how today the theater is turning its back on reality and lifting anchor.

This essay was delivered as a lecture   Translated by
at the Société de la Libre Esthétique,   JACKSON MATHEWS
Brussels, March 25, 1904.

Shakespeare ad Infinitum

by JOHANN WOLFGANG VON GOETHE
[1749–1832]

THERE HAS ALREADY been so much said about Shakespeare that it
would seem as if there was nothing left to say; and yet it is the
characteristic of genius ever to be stimulating other men's genius.
In the present case I wish to consider Shakespeare from more
than one point of view—first as a poet in general, then in comparison with the classic and modern writers, and finally as a
writer of poetic drama. I shall attempt to work out what the imitation of his art has meant to us, and what it can mean in the future. I shall express my agreement with what has been written
by reiterating it, and express my dissent briefly and positively,
without involving myself in conflict and contradiction. I proceed
to the first topic.

I. SHAKESPEARE AS POET IN GENERAL

The highest achievement possible to a man is the full consciousness of his own feelings and thoughts, for this gives him the

means of knowing intimately the hearts of others. Now there are men who are born with a natural talent for this and who cultivate it by experience towards practical ends. From this talent springs the ability to profit in a higher sense by the world and its opportunities. Now the poet is born with the same talent, only he cultivates it not for his immediate worldly purposes but for a loftier spiritual and universal purpose. If we call Shakespeare one of the greatest poets, we mean that few have perceived the world as accurately as he, that few who have expressed their inner contemplation of it have given the reader deeper insight into its meaning and consciousness. It becomes for us completely transparent: we find ourselves at once in the most intimate touch with virtue and vice, greatness and meanness, nobility and infamy, and all this through the simplest of means. If we ask what these means are, it seems as if they were directed towards our visual apprehension. But we are mistaken; Shakespeare's works are not for the physical vision. I shall attempt to explain what I mean.

The eye, the most facile of our organs of receptivity, may well be called the clearest of the senses; but the inner sense is still clearer, and to it by means of words belongs the most sensitive and clear receptivity. This is particularly obvious when what we apprehend with the eye seems alien and unimpressive considered in and for itself. But Shakespeare speaks always to our inner sense. Through this, the picture-world of imagination becomes animated, and a complete effect results, of which we can give no reckoning. Precisely here lies the ground for the illusion that everything is taking place before our eyes. But if we study the works of Shakespeare enough, we find that they contain much more of spiritual truth than of spectacular action. He makes happen what can easily be conceived by the imagination, indeed what can be better imagined than seen. Hamlet's ghost, Macbeth's witches, many fearful incidents, get their value only through the power of the imagination, and many of the minor scenes get their force from the same source. In reading, all these things pass easily through our minds, and seem quite appropriate, whereas in representation on the stage they would strike us unfavorably and appear not only unpleasant but even disgusting. Shakespeare gets his effect by means of the living word, and it is for this reason that one should hear him read, for then the attention is not distracted either by a too adequate or a too inadequate stage-setting. There is no higher or purer pleasure than to sit with closed eyes and hear a naturally expressive voice recite, not declaim, a play of Shakespeare's. According to the delineation of the characters we can picture to ourselves certain forms, but more particularly are we able by the succession of words and phrases to learn what is passing in their souls; the characters seem to have agreed to leave us in the dark, in doubt, about nothing. To that end conspire heroes and lackeys, gentlemen and slaves, kings and heralds; indeed even the subordinate characters are often more expressive in this way than the leading figures. Everything which in an affair of great importance breathes only secretly through the air, or lies hidden in the hearts of men, is here openly expressed. What the soul anxiously conceals and represses is here brought freely and abundantly to the light. We experience the truth of life—how, we do not know!

Shakespeare associates himself with the World-Spirit; like it, he explores the world; from neither is anything hidden. But whereas it is the business of the World-Spirit to keep its secrets both before and after the event, it is the work of the poet to tell them, and take us into his confidence before the event or in the very action itself. The depraved man of power, the well-intentioned dullard, the passionate lover, the quiet scholar, all carry their heart in their hand, often contrary to verisimilitude. Every one is candid and loquacious. It is enough that the secret must out, and even the stones would publish it. The inanimate insists upon speaking; the elements, the phenomena of sky, earth and sea, thunder and lightning, wild animals, lift their voice, often apparently symbolically, but all joining in the revelation.

The whole civilized world too brings its treasures to Shakespeare; Art and Science, Commerce and Industry, all bear him their gifts. Shakespeare's poems are a great animated fair; and it is to his own country that he owes his riches.

For back of him is England, the sea-encircled and mist-covered country, whose enterprise reaches all the parts of the earth. The poet lives at a noble and important epoch, and presents all its glory and its deficiencies with great vivacity; indeed, he would hardly produce such an effect upon us were it not just his own life-epoch that he was representing. No one despised the outer costume of men more than he; but he understood well the inner man, and here all are similar. It is said that he has delineated the Romans with wonderful skill. I cannot see it. They are Englishmen to the bone; but they are human, thoroughly human, and thus the Roman toga presumably fits them. When one takes this into consideration, one finds his anachronisms entirely admirable; indeed, it is just his neglect of the outer form that makes his works so vital.

Enough of these slight words, which cannot begin to sound the praises of Shakespeare. His friends and worshipers will have to add many a word to them. But one more remark: it would be hard to find a poet each of whose works was more thoroughly pervaded by a definite and effective idea than his.

Thus *Coriolanus* is permeated by the idea of anger at the refusal of the lower classes to recognize the superiority of their betters. In *Julius Cæsar* everything hinges on the idea that the upper classes are not willing to see the highest place in the State occupied, since they wrongly imagine that they are able to act together. *Antony and Cleopatra* expresses with a thousand tongues the idea that pleasure and action are ever incompatible. And so one will ever find, in searching his works, new cause for astonishment and admiration.

II. SHAKESPEARE COMPARED WITH THE ANCIENTS AND THE MODERNS

THE INTERESTS which vitalize Shakespeare's great genius are interests which centre in this world. For if prophecy and madness, dreams, omens, portents, fairies and gnomes, ghosts, imps, and conjurers introduce a magical element which so beautifully pervades his poems, yet these figures are in no way the basic elements of his works, but rest on a broad basis of the truth and fidelity of life, so that everything that comes from his pen seems to us genuine and sound. It has already been suggested that he belongs not so much to the poets of the modern era, which has been called "romantic," but much more to the "naturalistic" school, since his work is permeated with the reality of the present, and scarcely touches the emotions of unsatisfied desire, except at his highest points.

Disregarding this, however, he is, from a closer point of view, a decidedly modern poet, separated from the ancients by an enormous gulf, not perhaps with regard to his outer form, which is here beside our point, but with regard to his inner and most profound spirit.

Here let me say that it is not my idea to use the following terminology as exhaustive or exclusive; it is an attempt not so much to add another new antithesis to those already recognized, as to indicate that it is already contained in these. These are the antitheses:

Ancient	Modern
Natural	Sentimental
Pagan	Christian
Classic	Romantic
Realistic	Idealistic
Necessity	Freedom
Duty (*sollen*)	Will (*wollen*) *

The greatest ills to which men are exposed, as well as the most numerous, arise from a certain inner conflict between duty and will, as well as between duty and its accomplishment, and desire

* "Goethe, in a thoughtful essay, *Shakespeare und kein Ende,* written many years later than his famous criticism of Hamlet in *Wilhelm Meister,* says that the distinction between the two [ancient and modern drama] is the difference between *sollen* and *wollen,* that is, between *must* and *would.* He means that in the Greek drama the catastrophe is foreordained by an inexorable Destiny, while the element of free will, and consequently choice, is the very axis of the modern. The definition is conveniently portable, but it has its limitations. Goethe's attention was too exclusively fixed on the fate tragedies of the Greeks, and upon Shakespeare among the moderns. In the Spanish drama, for example, custom, loyalty, honor, and religion are as imperative and as inevitable as doom. In the *Antigone,* on the other hand, the crisis lies in the character of the protagonist."—James Russell Lowell, *Shakespeare Once More.*

and its accomplishment; and it is these conflicts which bring us so often into trouble in the course of our lives. Little difficulties, springing from a slight error which, though taking us by surprise, can be solved easily, give the clue to situations of comedy. The great difficulties, on the other hand, unresolved and unresolvable, give us tragedy.

Predominating in the old poems is the conflict between duty and performance, in the new between desire and accomplishment. Let us put this decided divergency among the other antitheses and see if it does not prove suggestive. In both epochs, I have said, there predominates now this side, now that; but since duty and desire are not radically separated in men's characters, both will be found together, even if one prevails and the other is subordinate. Duty is imposed upon men; "must" is a bitter pill. The Will man imposes upon himself; man's will is his kingdom of heaven. A long-continued obligation is burdensome, the inability to perform it even terrible; but a constant will is pleasurable, and with a firm will men can console themselves for their inability to accomplish their desire.

Let us consider a game of cards as a kind of poem; it consists of both those elements. The form of the game, bound up with chance, plays here the rôle of necessity, just as the ancients knew it under the form of Fate; the will, bound up with the skill of the player, works in the other direction. In this sense I might call whist "classic." The form of play limits the operation of chance, and even of the will itself. I have to play, in company with definite partners and opponents, with the cards which come into my hand, make the best of a long series of chance plays, without being able to control or parry them. In Ombre and similar games, the contrary is the case. Here are many openings left for skill and daring. I can disavow the cards that fall to my hand, make them count in different ways, half or completely discard them, get help by luck, and in the play get the best advantage out of the worst cards. Thus this kind of game resembles perfectly the modern mode of thought and literature.

Ancient tragedy was based on inescapable necessity, which was only sharpened and accelerated by an opposing will. Here is the seat of all that is fearful in the oracles, the region in which Œdipus lords it over all. Less tragic appears necessity in the guise of duty in the "Antigone"; and in how many forms does it not appear! But all necessity is despotic, whether it belong to the realm of Reason, like custom and civil law, or to Nature, like the laws of Becoming, and Growing and Passing-away, of Life and of Death. Before all these we tremble, without realizing that it is the good of the *whole* that is aimed at. The will, on the contrary, is free, appears free, and is advantageous to the *individual*. Thus the will is a flatterer, and takes possession of men as soon as they learn to recognize it. It is the god of the modern world. Dedicated to it, we are afraid of opposing doctrines, and here lies the crux of that eternal division which separates our art and thought from the ancients. Through the motive of Necessity, tragedy became mighty and strong; through the motive of Will, weak and feeble. Out of the latter arose the so-called Drama, in which dread Necessity is overcome and dissolved through the Will. But just because this comes to the aid of our weakness we feel moved when, after painful tension, we are at last a little encouraged and consoled.

As I turn now, after these preliminaries, to Shakespeare, I must express the hope that the reader himself will make the proper comparisons and applications. It is Shakespeare's unique distinction that he has combined in such remarkable fashion the old and the new. In his plays Will and Necessity struggle to maintain an equilibrium; both contend powerfully, yet always so that Will remains at a disadvantage.

No one has shown perhaps better than he the connection between Necessity and Will in the individual character. The person, considered as a character, is under a certain necessity; he is constrained, appointed to a certain particular line of action; but as a human being he has a will, which is unconfined and universal in its demands. Thus arises an inner conflict, and Shakespeare is superior to all other writers in the significance with which he endows this. But now an outer conflict may arise, and the individual through it may become so aroused that an insufficient will is raised through circumstance to the level of irremissible necessity. These motives I have referred to earlier in the case of Hamlet; but the motive is repeated constantly in Shakespeare—Hamlet through the agency of the ghost; Macbeth through the witches, Hecate, and his wife; Brutus through his friends gets into a dilemma and situation to which they were not equal; even in Coriolanus the same motive is found. This Will, which reaches beyond the power of the individual, is decidedly modern. But since in Shakespeare it does not spring from within, but is developed through external circumstance, it becomes a sort of Necessity, and approaches the classical motive. For all the heroes of ancient poetry willed only what was possible to men, and from this arose that beautiful balance between Necessity, Will, and Accomplishment. Still their Necessity is a little too severe for it really to be able to please us, even though we may wonder at and admire it. A Necessity which more or less, or even completely, excludes human freedom does not chime with our views any longer. It is true that Shakespeare in his own way has approximated this, but in making this Necessity a moral necessity he has, to our pleasure and astonishment, united the spirit of the ancient and the modern worlds. If we are to learn anything from him, here is the point where we must study in his school. Instead of singing the praises of our Romanticism so exclusively, and sticking to it so uncritically—our Romanticism, which need not be chidden or rejected—and thus mistaking and obscuring its strong, solid practical aspect, we should rather attempt to make this great fusion between the old and the new, even though it does seem inconsistent and paradoxical; and all the more should we make the attempt, because a great and unique master, whom we value most highly, and, often without knowing why, give homage to above all others, has already most effectively accomplished this miracle. To be sure, he had the advantage of living in a true time of harvest, and of working in a vigorous Protestant country, where the madness of bigotry was silent for a time, so that freedom was given to a true child of nature, such as Shakespeare was, to develop religiously his own pure inner nature, without reference to any established religion.

The preceding words were written in the summer of 1813; I ask that the reader will not now find fault with me, but simply recall what was said above—that this is merely an individual attempt to show how different poetic geniuses have tried to reconcile and resolve that tremendous antithesis which has appeared in their works in so many forms. To say more would be superfluous, since interest has been centred in this question for the past few years, and excellent explanations have been given us. Above all I wish to mention Blümner's highly valuable treatise, *On the Idea of Fate in the Tragedies of Æschylus,* and the excellent criticism of it in the supplement of the *Jenaische Literaturzeitung.* Therefore, I come without further comment to my third point, which relates immediately to the German theatre and to Schiller's efforts to establish it for the future.

III. SHAKESPEARE AS PLAYWRIGHT

When lovers of art wish to enjoy any work, they contemplate and delight in it as a whole, that is, they try to feel and apprehend the unity which the artist can bring to them. Whoever, on the other hand, wishes to judge such works theoretically, to assert some judgment about them, or instruct some one about them, must use his discriminating and analytic faculty. This we attempted to carry out when we discussed Shakespeare, first as poet in general, and then compared him with the ancient and modern poets. Now we intend to close the matter by considering him as a playwright, or poet of the theatre.

Shakespeare's fame and excellence belong to the history of poetry; but it is an injustice towards all playwrights of earlier and more recent times to give him his entire merit in the annals of the theatre.

A universally recognized talent may make of its capacities some use which is problematical. Not everything which the great do is done in the best fashion. So Shakespeare belongs by necessity in the annals of poetry; in the annals of the theatre he appears only by accident. Since we can honor him so unreservedly in the first case, it behooves us in the second to explain the conditions to which he had to accommodate himself, but not therefore to extol these conditions as either admirable or worthy of imitation.

We must distinguish closely-related poetic *genres,* however often they may be confused and merged together in actual treatment—epic, dialogue, drama, play. *Epic* requires the verbal delivery to the crowd through the mouth of an individual; *dialogue,* conversation in a narrow circle, where the crowd may eventually listen; *drama,* conversation bound up with action, even if enacted only before the imagination; *play,* all three together, in so far as they appeal to the sense of vision, and can be embodied under certain conditions of personal presence and stage-setting.

Shakespeare's works are in this sense highly dramatic; by his treatment, his revelation of the inner life, he wins the reader; the theatrical demands appear to him unimportant, and so he takes it easy, and we, spiritually speaking, take it easy with him. We pass with him from place to place; our power of imagination provides all the episodes which he omits. We even feel grateful to him for arousing our imagination in so profitable a way. Since he exhibits everything in dramatic form, he renders easy the working of our imaginations; for with the "stage that signifies the world," we are more familiar than with the world itself, and we can read and hear the most fantastic things, and still imagine that they might pass before our eyes on the stage. This accounts for the frequently bungling dramatizations of favorite novels.

Strictly speaking, nothing is theatrical except what is immediately symbolical to the eye: an important action, that is, which signifies a still more important one. That Shakespeare knew how to attain this summit, that moment witnesses where the son and heir in *Henry IV* takes the crown from the side of the slumbering king, who lies sick unto death—takes the crown and marches proudly away with it. But these are only moments, scattered jewels, separated by much that is untheatrical. Shakespeare's whole method finds in the stage itself something unwieldy and hostile. His great talent is that of a universal interpreter, or "epitomizer" (*Epitomator*), and since the poet in essence appears as universal interpreter of Nature, so we must recognize Shakespeare's great genius as lying in this realm; it would be only falsehood—and in no sense is this to his dishonor—were we to say that the stage was a worthy field for his genius. These limitations of the stage, however, have forced upon him certain limitations of his own. But he does not, like other poets, pick out disconnected materials for his separate works, but puts an idea at the centre, and to it relates the world and the universe. As he works over and boils down ancient and modern history, he can often make use of the material of old chronicles; indeed, he often adapts them word for word. With romances he does not deal so conscientiously, as *Hamlet* shows us. *Romeo and Juliet* is truer to the original; still he almost destroys the tragic content of it by his two comic characters, Mercutio and the old nurse, played apparently by two favorite actors, the nurse perhaps originally by a male performer. If one examines the construction of the piece carefully, however, one notices that these two figures, and what surrounds them, come in only as farcical interludes, and must be as unbearable to the minds of the lovers on the stage as they are to us.

But Shakespeare appears most remarkable when he revises and pieces together already existing plays. In *King John* and *Lear* we can make this comparison, for the older plays are extant. But in these cases, too, he turns out to be more of a poet than playwright.

In closing, let us proceed to the solution of the riddle. The primitiveness of the English stage has been brought to our attention by scholars. There is no trace in it of that striving after realism, which we have developed with the improvement of machinery and the art of perspective and costuming, and from which we should find it hard to turn back to that childlike beginning of the stage—a scaffolding, where one saw little, where everything was *signified,* where the audience was content to assume a royal chamber behind a green curtain; and the trumpeter, who always blew his trumpet at a certain place, and all the rest of it. Who would be content to-day to put up with such a stage? But amid such surroundings, Shakespeare's plays were highly interesting stories, only told by several persons, who, in order to make somewhat more of an impression, had put on masks, and, when it

was necessary, moved back and forth, entered and left the stage;
but left to the spectator nevertheless the task of imagining at his
pleasure Paradise and palaces on the empty stage.

How else then did Schroeder acquire the great distinction of
bringing Shakespeare's plays to the German stage, except by the
fact that he was the "epitomizer" of the "epitomizer"!

Schroeder confined himself exclusively to effect; everything
else he discarded, even many necessary things, if they seemed to
injure the effect which he wanted to produce on his country and
his time. Thus by the omission, for instance, of the first scenes
of *King Lear,* he annulled the character of the play. And he was
right, for in this scene Lear seems so absurd that we are not able,
in what follows, to ascribe to his daughters the entire guilt. We
are sorry for the old man, but we do not feel real pity for him;
and it is pity that Schroeder wishes to arouse, as well as abhorrence for the daughters, who are indeed unnatural, but not
wholly blameworthy.

In the old play, which Shakespeare revised, this scene produces
in the course of the action the loveliest effect. Lear flees to France;
the daughters and the stepson, from romantic caprice, make a pilgrimage over the sea, and meet the old man, who does not recognize them. Here everything is sweet, where Shakespeare's
loftier tragic genius has embittered us. A comparison of these
plays will give the thoughtful reader ever fresh pleasure.

Many years ago the superstition crept into Germany that
Shakespeare must be given literally word for word, even if actors
and audience were murdered in the process. The attempts, occasioned by an excellent and exact translation, were nowhere
successful, of which fact the painstaking and repeated endeavors
of the stage at Weimar are the best witness. If we wish to see a
Shakespearean play, we must take up again Schroeder's version;
but the notion that in the staging of Shakespeare not an iota
may be omitted, senseless as it is, one hears constantly repeated.
If the defenders of this opinion maintain the upper hand, in a
few years Shakespeare will be quite driven from the stage, which
for that matter would be no great misfortune; for then the reader,
whether he be solitary or sociable, will be able to get so much the
purer pleasure out of him.

They have, however, with the idea of making an attempt along the lines of which we have spoken in detail above, revised *Romeo and Juliet* for the theatre at Weimar. The principles according to which this was done we shall develop before long, and it will perhaps become apparent why this version, whose staging is by no means difficult, although it must be handled artistically and carefully, did not take on the German stage. Attempts of a similar kind are going on, and perhaps something is preparing for the future, for frequent endeavors do not always show immediate effects.

1813–1816   Translated by
                                                RANDOLPH BOURNE

The Profitable Reading of Fiction

by THOMAS HARDY [1840-1928]

WHEN THE EDITOR of this review * courteously offered me space in his pages to formulate a few general notions upon the subject of novel reading, considered with a view to mental profit, I could not help being struck with the timeliness of the theme; for in these days the demand for novels has risen so high, in proportion to that for other kinds of literature, as to attract the attention of all persons interested in education. But I was by no means persuaded that one whose own writings have largely consisted in books of this class was in a position to say anything on the matter, even if he might be supposed to have anything to say. The field, however, is so wide and varied that there is plenty of room for impersonal points of regard; and I may as well premise that the remarks which follow, where not exclusively suggested by a consideration of the works of dead authors, are mere generalizations from a cursory survey, and no detailed analysis, of those of to-day.

* *The Forum* (New York).

If we speak of deriving good from a story, we usually mean something more than the gain of pleasure during the hours of its perusal. Nevertheless, to get pleasure out of a book is a beneficial and profitable thing, if the pleasure be of a kind which, while doing no moral injury, affords relaxation and relief when the mind is overstrained or sick of itself. The prime remedy in such cases is change of scene, by which change of the material scene is not necessarily implied. A sudden shifting of the mental perspective into a fictitious world, combined with rest, is well known to be often as efficacious for renovation as a corporeal journey afar.

In such a case the shifting of scene should manifestly be as complete as if the reader had taken the hind seat on a witch's broomstick. The town man finds what he seeks in novels of the country, the countryman in novels of society, the indoor class generally in outdoor novels, the villager in novels of the mansion, the aristocrat in novels of the cottage.

The narrative must be of a somewhat absorbing kind, if not absolutely fascinating. To discover a book or books which shall possess, in addition to the special scenery, the special action required, may be a matter of some difficulty, though not always of such difficulty as to be insuperable; and it may be asserted that after every variety of spiritual fatigue there is to be found refreshment, if not restoration, in some antithetic realm of ideas which lies waiting in the pages of romance.

In reading for such hygienic purposes it is, of course, of the first consequence that the reader be not too critical. In other words, his author should be swallowed whole, like any other alterative pill. He should be believed in slavishly, implicitly. However profusely he may pour out his coincidences, his marvelous juxtapositions, his catastrophes, his conversions of bad people into good people at a stroke, and *vice versa,* let him never be doubted for a moment. When he exhibits people going out of their way and spending their money on purpose to act consistently, or taking a great deal of trouble to move in a curious and roundabout manner when a plain, straight course lies open to them; when he shows that heroes are never faithless in love, and that the unheroic always are so, there should arise a conviction that this is precisely according to personal experience. Let the invalid reverse the attitude of a certain class of critics—now happily becoming less numerous—who only allow themselves to be interested in a novel by the defeat of every attempt to the contrary. The aim should be the exercise of a generous imaginativeness, which shall find in a tale not only all that was put there by the author, put he it never so awkwardly, but which shall find there what was never inserted by him, never foreseen, never contemplated. Sometimes these additions which are woven around a work of fiction by the intensitive power of the reader's own imagination are the finest parts of the scenery.

It is not altogether necessary to this tonic purpose that the stories chosen should be "of most disastrous chances, of moving accidents by flood and field." As stated above, the aim should be contrast. Directly the circumstances begin to resemble those of the reader, a personal connection, an interest other than an imaginative one, is set up, which results in an intellectual stir that is not in the present case to be desired. It sets his serious thoughts at work, and he does not want them stimulated just now; he wants to dream.

So much may be said initially upon alleviating the effects of over-work and carking care by a course of imaginative reading. But I will assume that benefit of this sort is not that which is primarily contemplated when we speak of getting good out of novels, but intellectual or moral profit to active and undulled spirits.

It is obvious that choice in this case, though more limited than in the former, is by no means limited to compositions which touch the highest level in the essential constituents of a novel—those without which it would be no novel at all—the plot and the characters. Not only may the book be read for these main features—the presentation, as they may collectively be called—but for the accidents and appendages of narrative; and such are of more kinds than one. Excursions into various philosophies, which vary or delay narrative proper, may have more attraction than the regular course of the enactment; the judicious inquirer may be on the look-out for didactic reflection, such as is found in large lumps in *Rasselas;* he may be a picker-up of trifles of useful knowledge, statistics, queer historic fact, such as sometimes occur in the pages of Hugo; he may search for specimens of the manners of good or bad society, such as are to be obtained from the fashionable writers; or he may even wish to brush up his knowledge of quotations from ancient and other authors by studying some chapters of *Pelham* and the disquisitions of Parson Adams in *Joseph Andrews.*

Many of the works which abound in appurtenances of this or a kindred sort are excellent as narrative, excellent as a portraiture, even if in spite rather than in consequence of their presence. But they are the exception. Directly we descend from the highest levels we find that the majority are not effectual in their ostensible undertaking, that of giving us a picture of life in action; they exhibit a machinery which often works awkwardly, and at the instigation of unlikely beings. Yet, being packed with thoughts of some solidity, or more probably sprinkled with smart observations on men and society, they may be read with advantage even by the critical, who, for what they bring, can forgive the audible working of the wheels and wires and carpentry, heard behind the performance, as the wires and trackers of a badly constructed organ are heard under its tones.

Novels of the latter class—formerly more numerous than now— are the product of cleverness rather than of intuition; and in taking them up—bearing in mind that profit, and not amusement, is the student's aim—his manifest course is to escape from the personages and their deeds, gathering the author's wit or wisdom nearly as it would have presented itself if he had cast his thoughts in the shape of an essay.

But though we are bound to consider by-motives like these for reading fiction as praiseworthy enough where practicable, they are by their nature of an illegitimate character, more or less, and apart from the ruling interest of the genuine investigator of this department of literature. Such ingredients can be had elsewhere in more convenient parcels. Our true object is a lesson in life, mental enlargement from elements essential to the narratives themselves and from the reflections they engender.

Among the qualities which appertain to representations of life, construed, though not distorted, by the light of imagination—qualities which are seldom shared by views *about* life, however profound—is that of self-proof or obviousness. A representation is less susceptible of error than a disquisition; the teaching, depending as it does upon intuitive conviction, and not upon logical reasoning, is not likely to lend itself to sophistry. If endowed with ordinary intelligence, the reader can discern, in delineative art professing to be natural, any stroke greatly at variance with nature, which, in the form of moral essay, *pensée,* may be so wrapped up as to escape him.

Good fiction may be defined here as that kind of imaginative writing which lies nearest to the epic, dramatic, or narrative masterpieces of the past. One fact is certain: in fiction there can be no intrinsically new thing at this stage of the world's history. New methods and plans may arise and come into fashion, as we see them do; but the general theme can neither be changed, nor (what is less obvious) can the relative importance of its various particulars be greatly interfered with. The higher passions must ever rank above the inferior—intellectual tendencies above animal, and moral above intellectual—whatever the treatment, realistic or ideal. Any system of inversion which should attach more importance to the delineation of man's appetites than to the delineation of his aspirations, affections, or humors, would condemn the old masters of imaginative creation from Æschylus to Shakespeare. Whether we hold the arts which depict mankind to be, in the words of Mr. Matthew Arnold, a criticism of life, or, in those of Mr. Addington Symonds, a revelation of life, the material remains the same, with its sublimities, its beauties, its uglinesses, as the case may be. The finer manifestations must precede in importance the meaner, without such a radical change in human nature as we can hardly conceive as pertaining to an even remote future of decline, and certainly do not recognize now.

In pursuance of his quest for a true exhibition of man, the reader will naturally consider whether he feels himself under the guidance of a mind who sees further into life than he himself has seen; or, at least, who can throw a stronger irradiation over subjects already within his ken than he has been able to do unaided. The new light needs not to be set off by a finish of phraseology or incisive sentences of subtle definition. The treatment may be baldly incidental, without inference or commentary. Many elaborate reflections, for example, have been composed by moralizing chroniclers on the effect of prosperity in blunting men's recollection of those to whom they have sworn friendship when they shared a hard lot in common. But the writer in Genesis who tells his legend of certain friends in such adverse circumstances, one of whom, a chief butler, afterward came to good fortune, and ends the account of this good fortune with the simple words, "Now the chief butler did not remember Joseph, but forgat him," brings out a dramatic sequence on ground prepared for assent, shows us the general principle in the particular case, and hence writes with a force beyond that of aphorism or argument. It is the force of an appeal to the emotional reason rather than to the logical reason; for by their emotions men are acted upon, and act upon others.

If it be true, as is frequently asserted, that young people nowadays go to novels for their sentiments, their religion, and their morals, the question as to the wisdom or folly of those young people hangs upon their methods of acquisition in each case. A deduction from what these works exemplify by action that bears evidence of being a counterpart of life, has a distinct educational value; but an imitation of what may be called the philosophy of the personages—the doctrines of the actors, as shown in their conversation—may lead to surprising results. They should be informed that a writer whose story is not a tract in disguise has as his main object that of characterizing the people of his little world. A philosophy which appears between the inverted commas of a dialogue may, with propriety, be as full of holes as a sieve if the person or persons who advance it gain any reality of humanity thereby.

These considerations only bring us back again to the vital question how to discriminate the best in fiction. Unfortunately the two hundred years or so of the modern novel's development have not left the world so full of fine examples as to make it particularly easy to light upon them when the first obvious list has been run through. The, at first sight, high-piled granary sifts down to a very small measure of genuine corn. The conclusion cannot be resisted, notwithstanding what has been stated to the contrary in so many places, that the scarcity of perfect novels in any language is because the art of writing them is as yet in its youth, if not in its infancy. Narrative art is neither mature in its artistic aspect, nor in its ethical or philosophical aspect; neither in form nor in substance. To me, at least, the difficulties of perfect presentation in both these kinds appear of such magnitude that the utmost which each generation can be expected to do is to add one or two strokes toward the selection and shaping of a possible ultimate perfection.

In this scarcity of excellence in novels as wholes the reader must content himself with excellence in parts; and his estimate of the degree to which any given modern instance approximates to greatness will, of course, depend not only upon the proportion that the finer characteristics bear to the mass, but upon the figure cut by those finer characteristics beside those of the admitted masterpieces as yet. In this process he will go with the professed critic so far as to inquire whether the story forms a regular structure of incident, accompanied by an equally regular development of character—a composition based on faithful imagination, less the transcript than the similitude of material fact. But the appreciative, perspicacious reader will do more than this. He will see what his author is aiming at, and by affording full scope to his own insight, catch the vision which the writer has in his eye, and is endeavoring to project upon the paper, even while it half eludes him.

He will almost invariably discover that, however numerous the writer's excellencies, he is what is called unequal; he has a specialty. This especial gift being discovered, he fixes his regard more particularly thereupon. It is frequently not that feature in an author's work which common repute has given him credit for; more often it is, while co-existent with his popular attribute, overshadowed by it, lurking like a violet in the shade of the more obvious, possibly more vulgar, talent, but for which it might have received high attention. Behind the broad humor of one popular

pen he discerns startling touches of weirdness; amid the colossal
fancies of another he sees strokes of the most exquisite tenderness;
and the unobtrusive quality may grow to have more charm for
him than the palpable one.

It must always be borne in mind, despite the claims of realism,
that the best fiction, like the highest artistic expression in other
modes, is more true, so to put it, than history or nature can be.
In history occur from time to time monstrosities of human action
and character explicable by no known law which appertains to
sane beings; hitches in the machinery of existence, wherein we
have not yet discovered a principle, which the artist is therefore
bound to regard as accidents, hinderances to clearness of presentation, and hence, weakeners of the effect. To take an example from
sculpture: no real gladiator ever died in such perfect harmony
with normal nature as is represented in the well-known Capito-
line marble. There was always a jar somewhere, a jot or tittle of
something foreign in the real death-scene, which did not essentially appertain to the situation, and tended toward neutralizing
its pathos; but this the sculptor omitted, and so consecrated his
theme. In drama likewise. Observe the characters of any sterling
play. No dozen persons who were capable of being animated by
the profound reasons and truths thrown broadcast over *Hamlet*
or *Othello,* of feeling the pulse of life so accurately, ever met together in one place in this world to shape an end. And, to come
to fiction, nobody ever met an Uncle Toby who was Uncle Toby
all round; no historian's Queen Elizabeth was ever so perfectly a
woman as the fictitious Elizabeth of *Kenilworth.* What is called
the idealization of characters is, in truth, the making of them
too real to be possible.

It may seem something of a paradox to assert that the novels
which most conduce to moral profit are likely to be among those
written without a moral purpose. But the truth of the statement
may be realized if we consider that the didactic novel is so generally devoid of *vraisemblance* as to teach nothing but the impossibility of tampering with natural truth to advance dogmatic opinions. Those, on the other hand, which impress the reader with
the inevitableness of character and environment in working out

destiny, whether that destiny be just or unjust, enviable or cruel, must have a sound effect, if not what is called a good effect, upon a healthy mind.

Of the effects of such sincere presentation on weak minds, when the courses of the characters are not exemplary, and the rewards and punishments ill adjusted to deserts, it is not our duty to consider too closely. A novel which does moral injury to a dozen imbeciles, and has bracing results upon a thousand intellects of normal vigor, can justify its existence; and probably a novel was never written by the purest-minded author for which there could not be found some moral invalid or other whom it was capable of harming.

To distinguish truths which are temporary from truths which are eternal, the accidental from the essential, accuracies as to custom and ceremony from accuracies as to the perennial procedure of humanity, is of vital importance in our attempts to read for something more than amusement. There are certain novels, both among the works of living and the works of deceased writers, which give convincing proof of much exceptional fidelity, and yet they do not rank as great productions; for what they are faithful in is life garniture and not life. You are fully persuaded that the personages are clothed precisely as you see them clothed in the street, in the drawing-room, at the assembly. Even the trifling accidents of their costume are rendered by the honest narrator. They use the phrases of the season, present or past, with absolute accuracy as to idiom, expletive, slang. They lift their tea-cups or fan themselves to date. But what of it, after our first sense of its photographic curiousness is past? In aiming at the trivial and the ephemeral they have almost surely missed better things. A living French critic goes even further concerning the novelists of social minutiæ. "They are far removed," says he, "from the great imaginations which create and transform. They renounce free invention; they narrow themselves to scrupulous exactness; they paint clothes and places with endless detail."

But we must not, as inquiring readers, fail to understand that attention to accessories has its virtues when the nature of its regard does not involve blindness to higher things; still more when it conduces to the elucidation of higher things. The writer who describes his type of a jeweled leader of society by saying baldly how much her diamonds cost at So-and-So's, what the largest of them weighed and measured, how it was cut and set, the particular style in which she wore her hair, cannot convey much profit to any class of readers save two—those bent on making a purchase of the like ornaments or of adorning themselves in the same fashion: and, a century hence, those who are studying the costumes and expenditure of the period. But, supposing the subject to be the same, let the writer be one who takes less of a broker's view of his heroine and her adornments; he may be worth listening to, though his simplicity be quite childlike. It is immaterial that our example is in verse:

> Be you not proud of that rich hair
> Which wantons with the love-sick air;
> Whenas that ruby which you wear,
> Sunk from the tip of your soft ear,
> Will last to be a precious stone
> When all your world of beauty's gone.—HERRICK

And thus we are led to the conclusion that, in respect of our present object, our concern is less with the subject treated than with its treatment. There have been writers of fiction, as of poetry, who can gather grapes of thorns and figs of thistles.

Closely connected with the humanizing education found in fictitious narrative which reaches to the level of an illuminant of life, is the æsthetic training insensibly given by familiarity with story which, presenting nothing exceptional in other respects, has the merit of being well and artistically constructed. To profit of this kind, from this especial source, very little attention has hitherto been paid, though volumes have been written upon the development of the æsthetic sense by the study of painting and sculpture, and thus adding to the means of enjoyment. Probably few of the general body denominated the reading public consider, in their hurried perusal of novel after novel, that, to a masterpiece in story there appertains a beauty of shape, no less than to a masterpiece in pictorial or plastic art, capable of giving to the trained mind an equal pleasure. To recognize this quality clearly when present, the construction of the plot, or fable, as it used to be called, is to be more particularly observed than either in a reading for sentiments and opinions, or in a reading merely to discover the fates of the chief characters. For however real the persons, however profound, witty, or humorous the observations, as soon as the book comes to be regarded as an exemplification of the art of story-telling, the story naturally takes the first place, and the example is not noteworthy as such unless the telling be artistically carried on.

The distinguishing feature of a well rounded tale has been defined in various ways, but the general reader need not be burdened with many definitions. Briefly, a story should be an organism. To use the words applied to the epic by Addison, whose artistic feeling in this kind was of the subtlest, "nothing should go before it, be intermixed with it, or follow after it, that is not related to it." Tested by such considerations as these there are obviously many volumes of fiction remarkable, and even great, in their character-drawing, their feeling, their philosophy, which are quite second-rate in their structural quality as narratives. Instances will occur to every one's mind; but instead of dwelling upon these it is more interesting to name some which most nearly fulfill the conditions. Their fewness is remarkable, and bears out the opinion expressed earlier in this essay, that the art of novel-writing is as yet in its tentative stage only. Among them *Tom Jones* is usually pointed out as a near approach to perfection in this as in some other characteristics; though, speaking for myself, I do not perceive its great superiority in artistic form over some other novels of lower reputation. The *Bride of Lammermoor* is an almost perfect specimen of form, which is the more remarkable in that Scott, as a rule, depends more upon episode, dialogue, and description, for exciting interest, than upon the well-knit interdependence of parts. And the first thirty chapters of *Vanity Fair* may be instanced as well-nigh complete in artistic presentation, along with their other magnificent qualities.

Herein lies Richardson's real if only claim to be placed on a level with Fielding: the artist spirit that he everywhere displays in the structural parts of his work and in the interaction of the personages, notably those of *Clarissa Harlowe*. However cold, even artificial, we may, at times, deem the heroine and her companions in the pages of that excellent tale, however numerous the twitches of unreality in their movements across the scene beside those in the figures animated by Fielding, we feel, nevertheless, that we are under the guidance of a hand which has consummate skill in evolving a graceful, well-balanced set of conjectures, forming altogether one of those circumstantial wholes which, when approached by events in real life, cause the observer to pause and reflect, and say, "What a striking history!" We should look generously upon his deficiency in the robuster touches of nature, for it is the deficiency of an author whose artistic sense of form was developed at the expense of his accuracy of observation as regards substance. No person who has a due perception of the constructive art shown in Greek tragic drama can be blind to the constructive art of Richardson.

I have dwelt the more particularly upon this species of excellence, not because I consider it to rank in quality beside truth of feeling and action, but because it is one which so few nonprofessional readers enjoy and appreciate without some kind of preliminary direction. It is usually the latest to be discerned by the novel consumer, and it is often never discerned by him or her at all. Every intelligent reader with a little experience of life can perceive truth to nature in some degree; but a great reduction must be made for those who can trace in narrative the quality which makes the Apollo and the Aphrodite a charm in marble. Thoughtful readers are continually met with who have no intuition that such an attribute can be claimed by fiction, except in so far as it is included in style.

The indefinite word style may be made to express almost any characteristic of story-telling other than subject and plot, and it is too commonly viewed as being some independent, extraneous virtue or varnish with which the substance of a narrative is artificially overlaid. Style, as far as the word is meant to express something more than literary finish, can only be treatment, and treatment depends upon the mental attitude of the novelist; thus entering into the very substance of a narrative, as into that of any other kind of literature. A writer who is not a mere imitator looks upon the world with his personal eyes, and in his peculiar moods; thence grows up his style, in the full sense of the term:

> Cui lecta potenter erit res,
> Nec facundia deseret hunc, nec lucidus ordo.*

Those who would profit from the study of style should formulate an opinion of what it consists in by the aid of their own educated understanding, their perception of natural fitness, true and high feeling, sincerity, unhampered by considerations of nice collocation and balance of sentences, still less by conventionally accepted examples. They will make the discovery that certain names have, by some accident or other, grown to be regarded as of high, if not of supreme merit in the catalogue of exemplars, which have no essential claims, in this respect, to be rated higher than hundreds of the rank and file of literature who are never mentioned by critic or considered by reader in that connection. An author who has once acquired a reputation for style may write English down to the depths of slovenliness if he choose, without losing his character as a master; and this probably because, as before observed, the quality of style is so vague and inapprehensible as a distinct ingredient that it may always be supposed to be something else than what the reader perceives to be indifferent.

Considerations as to the rank or station in life from which characters are drawn can have but little value in regulating the choice of novels for literary reasons, and the reader may thus leave much to the mood of the moment. I remember reading a lecture on novels by a young and ingenious, though not very profound, critic, some years ago, in which the theory was propounded that novels which depict life in the upper walks of society must, in the nature of things, be better reading than those which exhibit the life of any lower class, for the reason that the subjects of the former represent a higher stage of development than their less fortunate brethren. At the first blush this was a

* Hor. "De Arte Poetica," 40.

plausible theory; but when practically tested it is found to be based on such a totally erroneous conception of what a novel is, and where it comes from, as not to be worth a moment's consideration. It proceeds from the assumption that a novel is the thing, and not a view of the thing. It forgets that the characters, however they may differ, express mainly the author, his largeness of heart or otherwise, his culture, his insight, and very little of any other living person, except in such an inferior kind of procedure as might occasionally be applied to dialogue, and would take the narrative out of the category of fiction: *i.e.*, verbatim reporting without selective judgment.

But there is another reason, disconnected entirely from methods of construction, why the physical condition of the characters rules nothing of itself one way or the other. All persons who have thoughtfully compared class with class—and the wider their experience the more pronounced their opinion—are convinced that education has as yet but little broken or modified the waves of human impulse on which deeds and words depend. So that in the portraiture of scenes in any way emotional or dramatic—the highest province of fiction—the peer and the peasant stand on much the same level; the woman who makes the satin train and the woman who wears it. In the lapse of countless ages, no doubt, improved systems of moral education will considerably and appreciably elevate even the involuntary instincts of human nature; but at present culture has only affected the surface of those lives with which it has come in contact, binding down the passions of those predisposed to turmoil as by a silken thread only, which the first ebullition suffices to break. With regard to what may be termed the minor key of action and speech—the unemotional, every-day doings of men—social refinement operates upon character in a way which is oftener than not prejudicial to vigorous portraiture, by making the exteriors of men their screen rather than their index, as with untutored mankind. Contrasts are disguised by the crust of conventionality, picturesqueness obliterated, and a subjective system of description necessitated for the differentiation of character. In the one case the author's word has to be taken as to the nerves and muscles of his figures; in the other they can be seen as in an *écorché*.

The foregoing are a few imperfect indications how, to the best of my judgment, to discriminate fiction which will be the most desirable reading for the average man or woman of leisure, who does not wish the occupation to be wholly barren of results except in so far as it may administer to the pleasure of the hour. But, as with the horse and the stream in the proverb, no outside power can compel or even help a reader to gain good from such reading unless he has some natural eye for the finer qualities in the best productions of this class. It is unfortunately quite possible to read the most elevating works of imagination in our own or any language, and, by fixing the regard on the wrong sides of the subject, to gather not a grain of wisdom from them, nay, sometimes positive harm. What author has not had his experience of such readers?—the mentally and morally warped ones of both sexes, who will, where practicable, so twist plain and obvious meanings as to see in an honest picture of human nature an attack on religion, morals, or institutions. Truly has it been observed that "the eye sees that which it brings with it the means of seeing."

This essay first appeared in
The Forum (New York) in 1888.

Outside Glimpses of English Poverty

by NATHANIEL HAWTHORNE [1804–1864]

BECOMING an inhabitant of a great English town, I often turned aside from the prosperous thoroughfares (where the edifices, the shops, and the bustling crowd differed not so much from scenes with which I was familiar in my own country), and went designedly astray among precincts that reminded me of some of Dickens's grimiest pages. There I caught glimpses of a people and a mode of life that were comparatively new to my observation, a sort of sombre phantasmagoric spectacle, exceedingly undelightful to behold, yet involving a singular interest and even fascination in its ugliness.

Dirt, one would fancy, is plenty enough all over the world, being the symbolic accompaniment of the foul incrustation which began to settle over and bedim all earthly things as soon as Eve had bitten the apple; ever since which hapless epoch, her daughters have chiefly been engaged in a desperate and unavailing struggle to get rid of it. But the dirt of a poverty-stricken English street is a monstrosity unknown on our side of the Atlantic. It reigns supreme within its own limits, and is inconceivable everywhere beyond them. We enjoy the great advantage, that the brightness and dryness of our atmosphere keep everything clean that the sun shines upon, converting the larger portion of our impurities into transitory dust which the next wind can sweep away, in contrast with the damp, adhesive grime that incorporates itself with all surfaces (unless continually and painfully cleansed) in the chill moisture of the English air. Then the all-pervading smoke of the city, abundantly intermingled with the sable snow-flakes of bituminous coal, hovering overhead, descending, and alighting on pavements and rich architectural fronts, on the snowy muslin of the ladies, and the gentlemen's starched collars and shirt-bosoms, invests even the better streets in a half-mourning garb. It is beyond the resources of Wealth to keep the smut away from its premises or its own fingers' ends; and as for Poverty, it surrenders itself to the dark influence without a struggle. Along with disastrous circumstances, pinching need, adversity so lengthened out as to constitute the rule of life, there comes a certain chill depression of the spirits which seems especially to shudder at cold water. In view of so wretched a state of things, we accept the ancient Deluge not merely as an insulated phenomenon, but as a periodical necessity, and acknowledge that nothing less than such a general washing-day could suffice to cleanse the slovenly old world of its moral and material dirt.

Gin-shops, or what the English call spirit-vaults, are numerous in the vicinity of these poor streets, and are set off with the magnificence of gilded door-posts, tarnished by contact with the unclean customers who haunt there. Ragged children come thither with old shaving-mugs, or broken-nosed teapots, or any such makeshift receptacle, to get a little poison or madness for their parents, who deserve no better requital at their hands for having engendered them. Inconceivably sluttish women enter at noonday and stand at the counter among boon-companions of both sexes, stirring up misery and jollity in a bumper together, and quaffing off the mixture with a relish. As for the men, they lounge there continually, drinking till they are drunken—drinking as long as they have a halfpenny left, and then, as it seemed to me, waiting for a sixpenny miracle to be wrought in their pockets so as to enable them to be drunken again. Most of these establishments have a significant advertisement of "Beds," doubtless for the accommodation of their customers in the interval between one intoxication and the next. I never could find it in my heart, however, utterly to condemn these sad revellers, and should certainly wait till I had some better consolation to offer before depriving them of their dram of gin, though death itself were in the glass; for methought their poor souls needed such fiery stimulant to lift them a little way out of the smothering squalor of both their outward and interior life, giving them glimpses and suggestions, even if bewildering ones, of a spiritual existence that limited their present misery. The temperance-reformers unquestionably derive their commission from the Divine Beneficence, but have never been taken fully into its counsels. All may not be lost, though those good men fail.

Pawnbrokers' establishments, distinguished by the mystic symbol of the three golden balls, were conveniently accessible; though what personal property these wretched people could possess, capable of being estimated in silver or copper, so as to afford a basis for a loan, was a problem that still perplexes me. Old clothesmen, likewise, dwelt hard by, and hung out ancient garments to dangle in the wind. There were butchers' shops, too, of a class adapted to the neighborhood, presenting no such generously fattened carcasses as Englishmen love to gaze at in the market, no stupendous

halves of mighty beeves, no dead hogs, or muttons ornamented
with carved bas-reliefs of fat on their ribs and shoulders, in a peculiarly British style of art—not these, but bits and gobbets of
lean meat, selvages snipt off from steaks, tough and stringy mor-
sels, bare bones smitten away from joints by the cleaver; tripe,
liver, bullocks' feet, or whatever else was cheapest and divisible
into the smallest lots. I am afraid that even such delicacies came
to many of their tables hardly oftener than Christmas. In the
windows of other little shops you saw half a dozen wizened her-
rings; some eggs in a basket, looking so dingily antique that your
imagination smelt them; fly-speckled biscuits, segments of a
hungry cheese, pipes and papers of tobacco. Now and then a
sturdy milk-woman passed by with a wooden yoke over her shoulders, supporting a pail on either side, filled with a whitish fluid,
the composition of which was water and chalk and the milk of
a sickly cow, who gave the best she had, poor thing! but could
scarcely make it rich or wholesome, spending her life in some
close city-nook and pasturing on strange food. I have seen, once
or twice, a donkey coming into one of these streets with panniers
full of vegetables, and departing with a return cargo of what
looked like rubbish and street-sweepings. No other commerce
seemed to exist, except, possibly, a girl might offer you a pair of
stockings or a worked collar, or a man whisper something mysterious about wonderfully cheap cigars. And yet I remember seeing
female hucksters in those regions, with their wares on the edge
of the sidewalk and their own seats right in the carriage-way,
pretending to sell half-decayed oranges and apples, toffy, Orms-
kirk cakes, combs, and cheap jewelry, the coarsest kind of crock-
ery, and little plates of oysters—knitting patiently all day long,
and removing their undiminished stock in trade at nightfall. All
indispensable importations from other quarters of the town were
on a remarkably diminutive scale: for example, the wealthier inhabitants purchased their coal by the wheelbarrow-load, and the
poorer ones by the peck-measure. It was a curious and melancholy
spectacle, when an overladen coal-cart happened to pass through
the street and drop a handful or two of its burden in the mud, to
see half a dozen women and children scrambling for the treasure-

trove, like a flock of hens and chickens gobbling up some spilt corn. In this connection I may as well mention a commodity of boiled snails (for such they appeared to me, though probably a marine production) which used to be peddled from door to door, piping hot, as an article of cheap nutriment.

The population of these dismal abodes appeared to consider the sidewalks and middle of the street as their common hall. In a drama of low life, the unity of place might be arranged rigidly according to the classic rule, and the street be the one locality in which every scene and incident should occur. Courtship, quarrels, plot and counterplot, conspiracies for robbery and murder, family difficulties or agreements—all such matters, I doubt not, are constantly discussed or transacted in this sky-roofed saloon, so regally hung with its sombre canopy of coal-smoke. Whatever the disadvantages of the English climate, the only comfortable or wholesome part of life, for the city poor, must be spent in the open air. The stifled and squalid rooms where they lie down at night, whole families and neighborhoods together, or sulkily elbow one another in the daytime, when a settled rain drives them within doors, are worse horrors than it is worth while (without a practical object in view) to admit into one's imagination. No wonder that they creep forth from the foul mystery of their interiors, stumble down from their garrets, or scramble up out of their cellars, on the upper step of which you may see the grimy housewife, before the shower is ended, letting the raindrops gutter down her visage; while her children (an impish progeny of cavernous recesses below the common sphere of humanity) swarm into the daylight and attain all that they know of personal purification in the nearest mud-puddle. It might almost make a man doubt the existence of his own soul, to observe how Nature has flung these little wretches into the street and left them there, so evidently regarding them as nothing worth, and how all mankind acquiesce in the great mother's estimate of her offspring. For, if they are to have no immortality, what superior claim can I assert for mine? And how difficult to believe that anything so precious as a germ of immortal growth can have been buried under this dirt-heap, plunged into this cesspool of

misery and vice! As often as I beheld the scene, it affected me with
surprise and loathsome interest, much resembling, though in a
far intenser degree, the feeling with which, when a boy, I used
to turn over a plank or an old log that had long lain on the damp
ground, and found a vivacious multitude of unclean and devilish-
looking insects scampering to and fro beneath it. Without an infinite faith, there seemed as much prospect of a blessed futurity
for those hideous bugs and many-footed worms as for these brethren of our humanity and co-heirs of all our heavenly inheritance.
Ah, what a mystery! Slowly, slowly, as after groping at the bottom of a deep, noisome, stagnant pool, my hope struggles upward
to the surface, bearing the half-drowned body of a child along
with it, and heaving it aloft for its life, and my own life, and all
our lives. Unless these slime-clogged nostrils can be made capable
of inhaling celestial air, I know not how the purest and most intellectual of us can reasonably expect ever to taste a breath of it.
The whole question of eternity is staked there. If a single one
of those helpless little ones be lost, the world is lost!

The women and children greatly preponderate in such places;
the men probably wandering abroad in quest of that daily miracle,
a dinner and a drink, or perhaps slumbering in the daylight that
they may the better follow out their cat-like rambles through the
dark. Here are women with young figures, but old, wrinkled,
yellow faces, tanned and blear-eyed with the smoke which they
cannot spare from their scanty fires—it being too precious for its
warmth to be swallowed by the chimney. Some of them sit on the
doorsteps, nursing their unwashed babies at bosoms which we
will glance aside from, for the sake of our mothers and all wom-
anhood, because the fairest spectacle is here the foulest. Yet
motherhood, in these dark abodes, is strangely identical with
what we have all known it to be in the happiest homes. Nothing,
as I remember, smote me with more grief and pity (all the more
poignant because perplexingly entangled with an inclination to
smile) than to hear a gaunt and ragged mother priding herself on
the pretty ways of her ragged and skinny infant, just as a young
matron might, when she invites her lady friends to admire her
plump, white-robed darling in the nursery. Indeed, no womanly

characteristic seemed to have altogether perished out of these poor souls. It was the very same creature whose tender torments make the rapture of our young days, whom we love, cherish, and protect, and rely upon in life and death, and whom we delight to see beautify her beauty with rich robes and set it off with jewels, though now fantastically masquerading in a garb of tatters, wholly unfit for her to handle. I recognized her, over and over again, in the groups round a doorstep or in the descent of a cellar, chatting with prodigious earnestness about intangible trifles, laughing for a little jest, sympathizing at almost the same instant with one neighbor's sunshine and another's shadow; wise, simple, sly, and patient, yet easily perturbed, and breaking into small feminine ebullitions of spite, wrath, and jealousy, tornadoes of a moment, such as vary the social atmosphere of her silken-skirted sisters, though smothered into propriety by dint of a well-bred habit. Not that there was an absolute deficiency of good-breeding, even here. It often surprised me to witness a courtesy and deference among these ragged folks, which, having seen it, I did not thoroughly believe in, wondering whence it should have come. I am persuaded, however, that there were laws of intercourse which they never violated—a code of the cellar, the garret, the common staircase, the doorstep, and the pavement, which perhaps had as deep a foundation in natural fitness as the code of the drawing-room.

Yet again I doubt whether I may not have been uttering folly in the last two sentences, when I reflect how rude and rough these specimens of feminine character generally were. They had a readiness with their hands that reminded me of Molly Seagrim and other heroines in Fielding's novels. For example, I have seen a woman meet a man in the street, and, for no reason perceptible to me, suddenly clutch him by the hair and cuff his ears—an infliction which he bore with exemplary patience, only snatching the very earliest opportunity to take to his heels. Where a sharp tongue will not serve the purpose, they trust to the sharpness of their finger-nails, or incarnate a whole vocabulary of vituperative words in a resounding slap, or the downright blow of a doubled fist. All English people, I imagine, are influenced in a far greater degree than ourselves by this simple and honest tendency, in cases of disagreement, to batter one another's persons; and whoever has seen a crowd of English ladies (for instance, at the door of the Sistine Chapel, in Holy Week) will be satisfied that their belligerent propensities are kept in abeyance only by a merciless rigor on the part of society. It requires a vast deal of refinement to spiritualize their large physical endowments. Such being the case with the delicate ornaments of the drawing-room, it is less to be wondered at that women who live mostly in the open air, amid the coarsest kind of companionship and occupation, should carry on the intercourse of life with a freedom unknown to any class of American females, though still, I am resolved to think, compatible with a generous breadth of natural propriety. It shocked me, at first, to see them (of all ages, even elderly, as well as infants that could just toddle across the street alone) going about in the mud and mire, or through the dusky snow and slosh of a severe week in winter, with petticoats high uplifted above bare, red feet and legs; but I was comforted by observing that both shoes and stockings generally reappeared with better weather, having been thriftily kept out of the damp for the convenience of dry feet within doors. Their hardihood was wonderful, and their strength greater than could have been expected from such spare diet as they probably lived upon. I have seen them carrying on their heads great burdens under which they walked as freely as if they were fashionable bonnets; or sometimes the burden was huge enough almost to cover the whole person, looked at from behind—as in Tuscan villages you may see the girls coming in from the country with great bundles of green twigs upon their backs, so that they resemble locomotive masses of verdure and fragrance. But these poor English women seemed to be laden with rubbish, incongruous and indescribable, such as bones and rags, the sweepings of the house and of the street, a merchandise gathered up from what poverty itself had thrown away, a heap of filthy stuff analogous to Christian's bundle of sin.

Sometimes, though very seldom, I detected a certain gracefulness among the younger women that was altogether new to my observation. It was a charm proper to the lowest class. One girl

I particularly remember, in a garb none of the cleanest and nowise smart, and herself exceedingly coarse in all respects, but yet endowed with a sort of witchery, a native charm, a robe of simple beauty and suitable behavior that she was born in and had never been tempted to throw off, because she had really nothing else to put on. Eve herself could not have been more natural. Nothing was affected, nothing imitated; no proper grace was vulgarized by an effort to assume the manners or adornments of another sphere. This kind of beauty, arrayed in a fitness of its own, is probably vanishing out of the world, and will certainly never be found in America, where all the girls, whether daughters of the upper-tendom, the mediocrity, the cottage, or the kennel, aim at one standard of dress and deportment, seldom accomplishing a perfectly triumphant hit or an utterly absurd failure. Those words, "genteel" and "ladylike," are terrible ones, and do us infinite mischief, but it is because (at least, I hope so) we are in a transition state, and shall emerge into a higher mode of simplicity than has ever been known to past ages.

In such disastrous circumstances as I have been attempting to describe, it was beautiful to observe what a mysterious efficacy still asserted itself in character. A woman, evidently poor as the poorest of her neighbors, would be knitting or sewing on the doorstep, just as fifty other women were; but round about her skirts (though woefully patched) you would be sensible of a certain sphere of decency, which, it seemed to me, could not have been kept more impregnable in the cosiest little sitting-room, where the teakettle on the hob was humming its good old song of domestic peace. Maidenhood had a similar power. The evil habit that grows upon us in this harsh world makes me faithless to my own better perceptions; and yet I have seen girls in these wretched streets, on whose virgin purity, judging merely from their impression on my instincts as they passed by, I should have deemed it safe, at the moment, to stake my life. The next moment, however, as the surrounding flood of moral uncleanness surged over their footsteps, I would not have staked a spike of thistle-down on the same wager. Yet the miracle was within the scope of Providence, which is equally wise and equally beneficent (even to

those poor girls, though I acknowledge the fact without the re-
motest comprehension of the mode of it), whether they were
pure or what we fellow-sinners call vile. Unless your faith be
deep-rooted and of most vigorous growth, it is the safer way not
to turn aside into this region so suggestive of miserable doubt. It
was a place "with dreadful faces thronged," wrinkled and grim
with vice and wretchedness; and, thinking over the line of Mil-
ton here quoted, I come to the conclusion that those ugly lineaments which startled Adam and Eve, as they looked backward
to the closed gate of Paradise, were no fiends from the pit, but
the more terrible foreshadowings of what so many of their descendants were to be. God help them, and us likewise, their brethren and sisters! Let me add, that, forlorn, ragged, careworn, hopeless, dirty, haggard, hungry, as they were, the most pitiful thing of
all was to see the sort of patience with which they accepted their
lot, as if they had been born into the world for that and nothing
else. Even the little children had this characteristic in as perfect
development as their grandmothers.

The children, in truth, were the ill-omened blossoms from
which another harvest of precisely such dark fruitage as I saw
ripened around me was to be produced. Of course you would
imagine these to be lumps of crude iniquity, tiny vessels as full as
they could hold of naughtiness; nor can I say a great deal to the
contrary. Small proof of parental discipline could I discern, save
when a mother (drunken, I sincerely hope) snatched her own imp
out of a group of pale, half-naked, humor-eaten abortions that
were playing and squabbling together in the mud, turned up its
tatters, brought down her heavy hand on its poor little tenderest
part, and let it go again with a shake. If the child knew what the
punishment was for, it was wiser than I pretend to be. It yelled
and went back to its playmates in the mud. You let me bear
testimony to what was beautiful, and more touching than anything that I ever witnessed before in the intercourse of happier
children. I allude to the superintendence which some of these
small people (too small, one would think, to be sent into the street
alone, had there been any other nursery for them) exercised over
still smaller ones. Whence they derived such a sense of duty, un-

less immediately from God, I cannot tell; but it was wonderful to observe the expression of responsibility in their deportment, the anxious fidelity with which they discharged their unfit office, the tender patience with which they linked their less pliable impulses to the wayward footsteps of an infant, and let it guide them whithersoever it liked. In the hollow-cheeked, large-eyed girl of ten, whom I saw giving a cheerless oversight to her baby-brother, I did not so much marvel at it. She had merely come a little earlier than usual to the perception of what was to be her business in life. But I admired the sickly-looking little boy, who did violence to his boyish nature by making himself the servant of his little sister—she was too small to walk, and he too small to take her in his arms—and therefore working a kind of miracle to transport her from one dirt-heap to another. Beholding such works of love and duty, I took heart again, and deemed it not so impossible, after all, for these neglected children to find a path through the squalor and evil of their circumstances up to the gate of heaven. Perhaps there was this latent good in all of them, though generally they looked brutish, and dull even in their sports; there was little mirth among them, nor even a fully awakened spirit of blackguardism. Yet sometimes, again, I saw, with surprise and a sense as if I had been asleep and dreaming, the bright, intelligent, merry face of a child whose dark eyes gleamed with vivacious expression through the dirt that incrusted its skin, like sunshine struggling through a very dusty window-pane.

In these streets the belted and blue-coated policeman appears seldom in comparison with the frequency of his occurrence in more reputable thoroughfares. I used to think that the inhabitants would have ample time to murder one another, or any stranger, like myself, who might violate the filthy sanctities of the place, before the law could bring up its lumbering assistance. Nevertheless, there is a supervision; nor does the watchfulness of authority permit the populace to be tempted to any outbreak. Once, in a time of dearth, I noticed a ballad-singer going through the street hoarsely chanting some discordant strain in a provincial dialect, of which I could only make out that it addressed the sensibilities of the auditors on the score of starvation; but by his side stalked the policeman, offering no interference, but watchful to hear what this rough minstrel said or sang, and silence him, if his effusion threatened to prove too soul-stirring. In my judgment, however, there is little or no danger of that kind: they starve patiently, sicken patiently, die patiently, not through resignation, but a diseased flaccidity of hope. If ever they should do mischief to those above them, it will probably be by the communication of some destructive pestilence; for, so the medical men affirm, they suffer all the ordinary diseases with a degree of virulence elsewhere unknown, and keep among themselves traditionary plagues that have long ceased to afflict more fortunate societies. Charity herself gathers her robe about her to avoid their contact. It would be a dire revenge, indeed, if they were to prove their claims to be reckoned of one blood and nature with the noblest and wealthiest by compelling them to inhale death through the diffusion of their own poverty-poisoned atmosphere.

A true Englishman is a kind man at heart, but has an unconquerable dislike to poverty and beggary. Beggars have heretofore been so strange to an American that he is apt to become their prey, being recognized through his national peculiarities, and beset by them in the streets. The English smile at him, and say that there are ample public arrangements for every pauper's possible need, that street charity promotes idleness and vice, and that yonder personification of misery on the pavement will lay up a good day's profit, besides supping more luxuriously than the dupe who gives him a shilling. By and by the stranger adopts their theory and begins to practise upon it, much to his own temporary freedom from annoyance, but not entirely without moral detriment or sometimes a too late contrition. Years afterwards, it may be, his memory is still haunted by some vindictive wretch whose cheeks were pale and hunger-pinched, whose rags fluttered in the east-wind, whose right arm was paralyzed and his left leg shrivelled into a mere nerveless stick, but whom he passed by remorselessly because an Englishman chose to say that the fellow's misery looked too perfect, was too artistically got up, to be genuine. Even allowing this to be true (as, a hundred chances to one, it was), it would still have been a clear case of economy to buy him off with a little loose silver, so that his lamentable figure should not limp at the heels of your conscience all over the world. To own the truth, I provided myself with several such imaginary persecutors in England, and recruited their number with at least one sickly-looking wretch whose acquaintance I first made at Assisi, in Italy, and, taking a dislike to something sinister in his aspect, permitted him to beg early and late, and all day long, without getting a single baiocco. At my latest glimpse of him, the villain avenged himself, not by a volley of horrible curses as any other Italian beggar would, but by taking an expression so grief-stricken, want-wrung, hopeless, and withal resigned, that I could paint his lifelike portrait at this moment. Were I to go over the same ground again, I would listen to no man's theories, but buy the little luxury of beneficence at a cheap rate, instead of doing myself a moral mischief by exuding a stony incrustation over whatever natural sensibility I might possess.

On the other hand, there were some mendicants whose utmost efforts I even now felicitate myself on having understood. Such was a phenomenon abridged of his lower half, who beset me for two or three years together, and, in spite of his deficiency of locomotive members, had some supernatural method of transporting himself (simultaneously, I believe) to all quarters of the city. He wore a sailor's jacket (possibly, because skirts would have been a superfluity to his figure), and had a remarkably broad-shouldered and muscular frame, surmounted by a large, fresh-colored face, which was full of power and intelligence. His dress and linen were the perfection of neatness. Once a day, at least, wherever I went, I suddenly became aware of this trunk of a man on the path before me, resting on his base, and looking as if he had just sprouted out of the pavement, and would sink into it again and reappear at some other spot the instant you left him behind. The expression of his eye was perfectly respectful, but terribly fixed, holding your own as by fascination, never once winking, never wavering from its point-blank gaze right into your face, till you were completely beyond the range of his battery of one immense rifled cannon. This was his mode of soliciting alms; and he reminded me of the old beggar who appealed so touchingly to the charitable sympathies of Gil Blas, taking aim at him from the roadside with a long-barrelled musket. The intentness and directness of his silent appeal, his close and unrelenting attack upon your individuality, respectful as it seemed, was the very flower of insolence; or, if you give it a possibly truer interpretation, it was the tyrannical effort of a man endowed with great natural force of character to constrain your reluctant will to his purpose. Apparently, he had staked his salvation upon the ultimate success of a daily struggle between himself and me, the triumph of which would compel me to become a tributary to the hat that lay on the pavement beside him. Man or fiend, however, there was a stubbornness in his intended victim which this massive fragment of a mighty personality had not altogether reckoned upon, and by its aid I was enabled to pass him at my customary pace hundreds of times over, quietly meeting his terribly respectful eye, and allowing him the fair chance which I felt to be his due, to subjugate me, if he really had the strength for it. He never succeeded, but, on the other hand, never gave up the contest; and should I ever walk those streets again, I am certain that the truncated tyrant will sprout up through the pavement and look me fixedly in the eye, and perhaps get the victory.

I should think all the more highly of myself, if I had shown equal heroism in resisting another class of beggarly depredators, who assailed me on my weaker side and won an easy spoil. Such was the sanctimonious clergyman, with his white cravat, who visited me with a subscription-paper, which he himself had drawn up, in a case of heart-rending distress; the respectable and ruined tradesman, going from door to door, shy and silent in his own person, but accompanied by a sympathizing friend, who bore testimony to his integrity, and stated the unavoidable misfortunes that had crushed him down; or the delicate and prettily dressed lady, who had been bred in affluence, but was suddenly thrown upon the perilous charities of the world by the death of an indulgent, but secretly insolvent father, or the commercial catastrophe and simultaneous suicide of the best of husbands; or the gifted, but unsuccessful author, appealing to my fraternal sympathies, generously rejoicing in some small prosperities which he was kind enough to term my own triumphs in the field of letters, and claiming to have largely contributed to them by his unbought notices in the public journals. England is full of such people, and a hundred other varieties of peripatetic tricksters, higher than these, and lower, who act their parts tolerably well, but seldom with an absolutely illusive effect. I knew at once, raw Yankee as I was, that they were humbugs, almost without an exception—rats that nibble at the honest bread and cheese of the community, and grow fat by their petty pilferings—yet often gave them what they asked, and privately owned myself a simpleton. There is a decorum which restrains you (unless you happen to be a police-constable) from breaking through a crust of plausible respectability, even when you are certain that there is a knave beneath it.

After making myself as familiar as I decently could with the poor streets, I became curious to see what kind of a home was provided for the inhabitants at the public expense, fearing that it must needs be a most comfortless one, or else their choice (if choice it were) of so miserable a life outside was truly difficult to account for. Accordingly, I visited a great almshouse, and was glad to observe how unexceptionally all the parts of the establishment were carried on, and what an orderly life, full-fed, sufficiently reposeful, and undisturbed by the arbitrary exercise of authority, seemed to be led there. Possibly, indeed, it was that very orderliness, and the cruel necessity of being neat and clean, and even the comfort resulting from these and other Christian-like restraints and regulations, that constituted the principal grievance on the part of the poor, shiftless inmates, accustomed to a lifelong luxury of dirt and harum-scarumness. The wild life of the streets has perhaps as unforgetable a charm, to those who have once thoroughly imbibed it, as the life of the forest or the prairie. But I conceive rather that there must be insuperable difficulties, for the majority of the poor, in the way of getting admittance to the almshouse, than that a merely æsthetic preference for the street would incline the pauper class to fare scantily and precariously, and expose their raggedness to the rain and snow, when such a hospitable door stood wide open for their entrance. It might be that the roughest and darkest side of the matter was not shown me, there being persons of eminent station and of both sexes in the party which I accompanied; and, of course, a properly trained public functionary would have deemed it a monstrous rudeness, as well as a great shame, to exhibit anything to people of rank that might too painfully shock their sensibilities.

The women's ward was the portion of the establishment which we especially examined. It could not be questioned that they were treated with kindness as well as care. No doubt, as has been already suggested, some of them felt the irksomeness of submission to general rules of orderly behavior, after being accustomed to that perfect freedom from the minor proprieties, at least, which is one of the compensations of absolutely hopeless poverty, or of any circumstances that set us fairly below the decencies of life. I asked the governor of the house whether he met with any difficulty in keeping peace and order among his inmates; and he informed me that his troubles among the women were incomparably greater than with the men. They were freakish, and apt to be quarrelsome, inclined to plague and pester one another in ways that it was impossible to lay hold of, and to thwart his own authority by the like intangible methods. He said this with the utmost good-nature, and quite won my regard by so placidly resigning himself to the inevitable necessity of letting the women throw dust into his eyes. They certainly looked peaceable and sisterly enough as I saw them, though still it might be faintly perceptible that some of them were consciously playing their parts before the governor and his distinguished visitors.

This governor seemed to me a man thoroughly fit for his position. An American, in an office of similar responsibility, would doubtless be a much superior person, better educated, possessing a far wider range of thought, more naturally acute, with a quicker tact of external observation and a readier faculty of dealing with difficult cases. The women would not succeed in throwing half so much dust into his eyes. Moreover, his black coat, and thin, sallow visage, would make him look like a scholar, and his manners would indefinitely approximate to those of a gentleman. But I cannot help questioning whether, on the whole, these higher endowments would produce decidedly better results. The Englishman was thoroughly plebeian both in aspect and behavior, a bluff, ruddy-faced, hearty, kindly, yeoman-like personage, with no refinement whatever, nor any superfluous sensibility, but gifted with a native wholesomeness of character which must have been a very beneficial element in the atmosphere of the almshouse. He spoke to his pauper family in loud, good-humored, cheerful tones, and treated them with a healthy freedom that probably caused the forlorn wretches to feel as if they were free and healthy likewise. If he had understood them a little better, he would not have treated them half so wisely. We are apt to make sickly people more morbid, and unfortunate people more miserable, by endeavoring to adapt our deportment to their especial and individual needs. They eagerly accept our well-meant efforts; but it is like returning their own sick breath back upon themselves, to be breathed over and over again, intensifying the inward mischief at every reception. The sympathy that would really do them good is of a kind that recognizes their sound and healthy parts, and ignores the part affected by disease, which will thrive under the eye of a too close observer like a poisonous weed in the sunshine. My good friend the governor had no tendencies in the latter direction, and abundance of them in the former, and was consequently as wholesome and invigorating as the west-wind with a little spice of the north in it, brightening the dreary visages that encountered us as if he had carried a sunbeam in his hand. He expressed himself by his whole being and personality, and by works more than words, and had the not unusual English merit of knowing what to do much better than how to talk about it.

The women, I imagine, must have felt one imperfection in their state, however comfortable otherwise. They were forbidden, or, at all events, lacked the means, to follow out their natural instinct of adorning themselves; all were well dressed in one homely uniform of blue-checked gowns, with such caps upon their heads as English servants wear. Generally, too, they had one dowdy English aspect, and a vulgar type of features so nearly alike that they seemed literally to constitute a sisterhood. We have few of these absolutely unilluminated faces among our native American population, individuals of whom must be singularly unfortunate, if, mixing as we do, no drop of gentle blood has contributed to refine the turbid element, no gleam of hereditary intelligence has lighted up the stolid eyes, which their forefathers brought from the Old Country. Even in this English almshouse, however, there was at least one person who claimed to be intimately connected with rank and wealth. The governor, after suggesting that this person would probably be gratified by our visit, ushered us into a small parlor, which was furnished a little more like a room in a private dwelling than others that we entered, and had a row of religious books and fashionable novels on the mantel-piece. An old lady sat at a bright coal-fire, reading a romance, and rose to receive us with a certain pomp of manner and elaborate display of ceremonious courtesy, which, in spite of myself, made me inwardly question the genuineness of her aristocratic pretensions. But, at any rate, she looked like a respectable old soul, and was evidently gladdened to the very core of her frost-bitten heart by the awful punctiliousness with which we responded to her gracious and hospitable, though unfamiliar welcome. After a little polite conversation, we retired; and the governor, with a lowered voice and an air of deference, told us that she had been a lady of quality, and had ridden in her own equipage, not many years before, and now lived in continual expectation that some of her rich relatives would drive up in their carriages to take her away. Meanwhile, he added, she was treated with great respect by her fellow-paupers. I could not help thinking, from a few criticisable peculiarities in her talk and manner, that there might have been a mistake on the governor's part, and perhaps a venial exaggeration on the old lady's, concerning her former position in society; but what struck me was the forcible instance of that most prevalent of English vanities, the pretension to aristocratic connection, on one side, and the submission and reverence with which it was accepted by the governor and his household, on the other. Among ourselves, I think, when wealth and eminent position have taken their departure, they seldom leave a pallid ghost behind them—or, if it sometimes stalks abroad, few recognize it.

We went into several other rooms, at the doors of which, pausing on the outside, we could hear the volubility, and sometimes the wrangling, of the female inhabitants within, but invariably found silence and peace when we stepped over the threshold. The women were grouped together in their sitting-rooms, sometimes three or four, sometimes a larger number, classified by their spontaneous affinities, I suppose, and all busied, so far as I can remember, with the one occupation of knitting coarse yarn stockings. Hardly any of them, I am sorry to say, had a brisk or cheerful air, though it often stirred them up to a momentary vivacity to be accosted by the governor, and they seemed to like being noticed, however slightly, by the visitors. The happiest person whom I saw there (and running hastily through my experiences, I hardly recollect to have seen a happier one in my life, if you take a careless flow of spirits as happiness) was an old woman that lay in bed among ten or twelve heavy-looking females, who plied their knitting-work round about her. She laughed, when we entered, and immediately began to talk to us, in a thin, little, spirited quaver, claiming to be more than a century old; and the governor (in whatever way he happened to be cognizant of the fact) confirmed her age to be a hundred and four. Her jauntiness and cackling merriment were really wonderful. It was as if she had got through with all her actual business in life two or three generations ago, and now, freed from every responsibility for herself or others, had only to keep up a mirthful state of mind till the short time, or long time (and, happy as she was, she appeared not to care whether it were long or short), before Death, who had misplaced her name in his list, might remember to take her away. She had gone quite round the circle of human existence, and come back to the play-ground again. And so she had grown to be a kind of miraculous old pet, the plaything of people seventy or eighty years younger than her-

self, who talked and laughed with her as if she were a child, finding great delight in her wayward and strangely playful responses,
into some of which she cunningly conveyed a gibe that caused their
ears to tingle a little. She had done getting out of bed in this
world, and lay there to be waited upon like a queen or a baby.

In the same room sat a pauper who had once been an actress of
considerable repute, but was compelled to give up her profession
by a softening of the brain. The disease seemed to have stolen the
continuity out of her life, and disturbed all healthy relationship
between the thoughts within her and the world without. On our
first entrance, she looked cheerfully at us, and showed herself
ready to engage in conversation; but suddenly, while we were
talking with the century-old crone, the poor actress began to weep,
contorting her face with extravagant stage-grimaces, and wringing
her hands for some inscrutable sorrow. It might have been a remi-
niscence of actual calamity in her past life, or, quite as probably,
it was but a dramatic woe, beneath which she had staggered
and shrieked and wrung her hands with hundreds of repetitions
in the sight of crowded theatres, and been as often comforted
by thunders of applause. But my idea of the mystery was,
that she had a sense of wrong in seeing the aged woman (whose
empty vivacity was like the rattling of dry peas in a bladder)
chosen as the central object of interest to the visitors, while she
herself, who had agitated thousands of hearts with a breath, sat
starving for the admiration that was her natural food. I appeal to
the whole society of artists of the Beautiful and the Imaginative—
poets, romancers, painters, sculptors, actors—whether or no this
is a grief that may be felt even amid the torpor of a dissolving
brain!

We looked into a good many sleeping-chambers, where were
rows of beds, mostly calculated for two occupants, and provided
with sheets and pillow-cases that resembled sackcloth. It appeared
to me that the sense of beauty was insufficiently regarded in all the
arrangements of the almshouse; a little cheap luxury for the eye,
at least, might do the poor folks a substantial good. But, at all
events, there was the beauty of perfect neatness and orderliness,
which, being heretofore known to few of them, was perhaps as

much as they could well digest in the remnant of their lives. We were invited into the laundry, where a great washing and drying were in process, the whole atmosphere being hot and vaporous with the steam of wet garments and bedclothes. This atmosphere was the pauper-life of the past week or fortnight resolved into a gaseous state, and breathing it, however fastidiously, we were forced to inhale the strange element into our inmost being. Had the Queen been there, I know not how she could have escaped the necessity. What an intimate brotherhood is this in which we dwell, do what we may to put an artificial remoteness between the high creature and the low one! A poor man's breath, borne on the vehicle of tobacco-smoke, floats into a palace-window and reaches the nostrils of a monarch. It is but an example, obvious to the sense, of the innumerable and secret channels by which, at every moment of our lives, the flow and reflux of a common humanity pervade us all. How superficial are the niceties of such as pretend to keep aloof! Let the whole world be cleansed, or not a man or woman of us all can be clean.

By and by we came to the ward where the children were kept, on entering which, we saw, in the first place, several unlovely and unwholesome little people lazily playing together in a court-yard. And here a singular incommodity befell one member of our party. Among the children was a wretched, pale, half-torpid little thing (about six years old, perhaps, but I know not whether a girl or a boy), with a humor in its eyes and face, which the governor said was the scurvy, and which appeared to bedim its powers of vision, so that it toddled about gropingly, as if in quest of it did not precisely know what. This child—this sickly, wretched, humor-eaten infant, the offspring of unspeakable sin and sorrow, whom it must have required several generations of guilty progenitors to render so pitiable an object as we beheld it—immediately took an unaccountable fancy to the gentleman just hinted at. It prowled about him like a pet kitten, rubbing against his legs, following everywhere at his heels, pulling at his coat-tails, and, at last, exerting all the speed that its poor limbs were capable of, got directly before him and held forth its arms, mutely insisting on being taken up. It said not a word, being perhaps under-witted and incapable of prattle. But it smiled up in his face—a sort of woeful gleam was that smile, through the sickly blotches that covered its features—and found means to express such a perfect confidence that it was going to be fondled and made much of, that there was no possibility in a human heart of balking its expectation. It was as if God had promised the poor child this favor on behalf of that individual, and he was bound to fulfil the contract, or else no longer call himself a man among men. Nevertheless, it could be no easy thing for him to do, he being a person burdened with more than an Englishman's customary reserve, shy of actual contact with human beings, afflicted with a peculiar distaste for whatever was ugly, and, furthermore, accustomed to that habit of observation from an insulated standpoint which is said (but, I hope, erroneously) to have the tendency of putting ice into the blood.

So I watched the struggle in his mind with a good deal of interest, and am seriously of opinion that he did an heroic act, and effected more than he dreamed of towards his final salvation, when he took up the loathsome child and caressed it as tenderly as if he had been its father. To be sure, we all smiled at him, at the time, but doubtless would have acted pretty much the same in a similar stress of circumstances. The child, at any rate, appeared to be satisfied with his behavior; for when he had held it a considerable time, and set it down, it still favored him with its company, keeping fast hold of his forefinger till we reached the confines of the place. And on our return through the court-yard, after visiting another part of the establishment, here again was this same little Wretchedness waiting for its victim, with a smile of joyful, and yet dull recognition about its scabby mouth and in its rheumy eyes. No doubt, the child's mission in reference to our friend was to remind him that he was responsible, in his degree, for all the sufferings and misdemeanors of the world in which he lived, and was not entitled to look upon a particle of its dark calamity as if it were none of his concern: the offspring of a brother's iniquity being his own blood-relation, and the guilt, likewise, a burden on him, unless he expiated it by better deeds.

All the children in this ward seemed to be invalids, and, going up stairs, we found more of them in the same or a worse condition than the little creature just described, with their mothers (or more probably other women, for the infants were mostly foundlings) in attendance as nurses. The matron of the ward, a middle-aged woman, remarkably kind and motherly in aspect, was walking to and fro across the chamber—on that weary journey in which careful mothers and nurses travel so continually and so far, and gain never a step of progress—with an unquiet baby in her arms. She assured us that she enjoyed her occupation, being exceedingly fond of children; and, in fact, the absence of timidity in all the little people was a sufficient proof that they could have had no experience of harsh treatment, though, on the other hand, none of them appeared to be attracted to one individual more than another. In this point they differed widely from the poor child below stairs. They seemed to recognize a universal motherhood in womankind, and cared not which individual might be the mother of the moment. I found their tameness as shocking as did Alexander Selkirk that of the brute subjects of his else solitary kingdom. It was a sort of tame familiarity, a perfect indifference to the approach of strangers, such as I never noticed in other children. I accounted for it partly by their nerveless, unstrung state of body, incapable of the quick thrills of delight and fear which play upon the lively harpstrings of a healthy child's nature, and partly by their woeful lack of acquaintance with a private home, and their being therefore destitute of the sweet home-bred shyness, which is like the sanctity of heaven about a mother-petted child. Their condition was like that of chickens hatched in an oven, and growing up without the especial guardianship of a matron hen: both the chicken and the child, methinks, must needs want something that is essential to their respective characters.

In this chamber (which was spacious, containing a large number of beds) there was a clear fire burning on the hearth, as in all the other occupied rooms; and directly in front of the blaze sat a woman holding a baby, which, beyond all reach of comparison, was the most horrible object that ever afflicted my sight. Days afterwards—nay, even now, when I bring it up vividly before my mind's eye—it seemed to lie upon the floor of my heart, polluting my moral being with the sense of something grievously amiss in the entire conditions of humanity. The holiest man could not be otherwise than full of wickedness, the chastest virgin seemed impure, in a world where such a babe was possible. The governor whispered to me, apart, that, like nearly all the rest of them, it was the child of unhealthy parents. Ah, yes! There was the mischief. This spectral infant, a hideous mockery of the visible link which Love creates between man and woman, was born of disease and sin. Diseased Sin was its father, and Sinful Disease its mother, and their offspring lay in the woman's arms like a nursing Pestilence, which, could it live and grow up, would make the world a more accursed abode than ever heretofore. Thank Heaven, it could not live! This baby, if we must give it that sweet name, seemed to be three or four months old, but, being such an unthrifty changeling, might have been considerably older. It was all covered with blotches, and preternaturally dark and discolored; it was withered away, quite shrunken and fleshless; it breathed only amid pantings and gaspings, and moaned painfully at every gasp. The only comfort in reference to it was the evident impossibility of its surviving to draw many more of those miserable, moaning breaths; and it would have been infinitely less heart-depressing to see it die, right before my eyes, than to depart and carry it alive in my remembrance, still suffering the incalculable torture of its little life. I can by no means express how horrible this infant was, neither ought I to attempt it. And yet I must add one final touch. Young as the poor little creature was, its pain and misery had endowed it with a premature intelligence, insomuch that its eyes seemed to stare at the by-standers out of their sunken sockets knowingly and appealingly, as if summoning us one and all to witness the deadly wrong of its existence. At least, I so interpreted its look, when it positively met and responded to my own awe-stricken gaze, and therefore I lay the case, as far as I am able, before mankind, on whom God has imposed the necessity to suffer in soul and body till this dark and dreadful wrong be righted.

Thence we went to the school-rooms, which were underneath the chapel. The pupils, like the children whom we had just seen, were, in large proportion, foundlings. Almost without exception, they looked sickly, with marks of eruptive trouble in their doltish faces, and a general tendency to diseases of the eye. Moreover, the poor little wretches appeared to be uneasy within their skins, and screwed themselves about on the benches in a disagreeably suggestive way, as if they had inherited the evil habits of their parents as an innermost garment of the same texture and material as the shirt of Nessus, and must wear it with unspeakable discomfort as long as they lived. I saw only a single child that looked healthy; and on my pointing him out, the governor informed me that this little boy, the sole exception to the miserable aspect of his schoolfellows, was not a foundling, nor properly a work-house child, being born of respectable parentage, and his father one of the officers of the institution. As for the remainder—the hundred pale abortions to be counted against one rosy-cheeked boy—what shall we say or do? Depressed by the sight of so much misery, and uninventive of remedies for the evils that force themselves on my perception, I can do little more than recur to the idea already hinted at in the early part of this article, regarding the speedy necessity of a new deluge. So far as these children are concerned, at any rate, it would be a blessing to the human race, which they will contribute to enervate and corrupt—a greater blessing to themselves, who inherit no patrimony but disease and vice, and in whose souls, if there be a spark of God's life, this seems the only possible mode of keeping it aglow—if every one of them could be drowned to-night, by their best friends, instead of being put tenderly to bed. This heroic method of treating human maladies, moral and material, is certainly beyond the scope of man's discretionary rights, and probably will not be adopted by Divine Providence until the opportunity of milder reformation shall have been offered us again and again, through a series of future ages.

It may be fair to acknowledge that the humane and excellent governor, as well as other persons better acquainted with the subject than myself, took a less gloomy view of it, though still so dark a one as to involve scanty consolation. They remarked that individuals of the male sex, picked up in the streets and nurtured in the work-house, sometimes succeed tolerably well in life, because they are taught trades before being turned into the world, and, by dint of immaculate behavior and good luck, are not unlikely to get employment and earn a livelihood. The case is different with the girls. They can only go to service, and are invariably rejected by families of respectability on account of their origin, and for the better reason of their unfitness to fill satisfactorily even the meanest situations in a well-ordered English household. Their resource is to take service with people only a step or two above the poorest class, with whom they fare scantily, endure harsh treatment, lead shifting and precarious lives, and finally drop into the slough of evil, through which, in their best estate, they do but pick their slimy way on stepping-stones.

From the schools we went to the bake-house, and the brew-house (for such cruelty is not harbored in the heart of a true Englishman as to deny a pauper his daily allowance of beer), and through the kitchens, where we beheld an immense pot over the fire, surging and walloping with some kind of a savory stew that filled it up to its brim. We also visited a tailor's shop, and a shoe-maker's shop, in both of which a number of men, and pale, diminutive apprentices, were at work, diligently enough, though seemingly with small heart in the business. Finally, the governor ushered us into a shed, inside of which was piled up an immense quantity of new coffins. They were of the plainest description, made of pine boards, probably of American growth, not very nicely smoothed by the plane, neither painted nor stained with black, but provided with a loop of rope at either end for the convenience of lifting the rude box and its inmate into the cart that shall carry them to the burial-ground. There, in holes ten feet deep, the paupers are buried one above another, mingling their relics indistinguishably. In another world may they resume their individuality, and find it a happier one than here!

As we departed, a character came under our notice which I have met with in all almshouses, whether of the city or village, or in England or America. It was the familiar simpleton, who shuffled across the court-yard, clattering his wooden-soled shoes, to greet us with a howl or a laugh, I hardly know which, holding out his hand for a penny, and chuckling grossly when it was given him. All under-witted persons, so far as my experience goes, have this craving for copper coin, and appear to estimate its value by a miracu-

lous instinct, which is one of the earliest gleams of human intelligence while the nobler faculties are yet in abeyance. There may
come a time, even in this world, when we shall all understand
that our tendency to the individual appropriation of gold and
broad acres, fine houses, and such good and beautiful things as
are equally enjoyable by a multitude, is but a trait of imperfectly
developed intelligence, like the simpleton's cupidity of a penny.
When that day dawns—and probably not till then—I imagine
that there will be no more poor streets nor need of almshouses.

I was once present at the wedding of some poor English people,
and was deeply impressed by the spectacle, though by no means
with such proud and delightful emotions as seem to have affected
all England on the recent occasion of the marriage of its Prince. It
was in the Cathedral at Manchester, a particularly black and grim
old structure, into which I had stepped to examine some ancient
and curious wood-carvings within the choir. The woman in attendance greeted me with a smile (which always glimmers forth
on the feminine visage, I know not why, when a wedding is in
question), and asked me to take a seat in the nave till some poor
parties were married, it being the Easter holidays, and a good time
for them to marry, because no fees would be demanded by the
clergyman. I sat down accordingly, and soon the parson and his
clerk appeared at the altar, and a considerable crowd of people
made their entrance at a side-door, and ranged themselves in a
long, huddled line across the chancel. They were my acquaintances
of the poor streets, or persons in a precisely similar condition of
life, and were now come to their marriage-ceremony in just such
garbs as I had always seen them wear: the men in their loafer's
coats, out at elbows, or their laborer's jackets, defaced with grimy
toil; the women drawing their shabby shawls tighter about their
shoulders, to hide the raggedness beneath; all of them unbrushed,
unshaven, unwashed, uncombed, and wrinkled with penury and
care; nothing virgin-like in the brides, nor hopeful or energetic in
the bridegrooms—they were, in short, the mere rags and tatters of
the human race, whom some east-wind of evil omen, howling along
the streets, had chanced to sweep together into an unfragrant heap.
Each and all of them, conscious of his or her individual misery,

had blundered into the strange miscalculation of supposing that they could lessen the sum of it by multiplying it into the misery of another person. All the couples (and it was difficult, in such a confused crowd, to compute exactly their number) stood up at once, and had execution done upon them in the lump, the clergyman addressing only small parts of the service to each individual pair, but so managing the larger portion as to include the whole company without the trouble of repetition. By this compendious contrivance, one would apprehend, he came dangerously near making every man and woman the husband or wife of every other; nor, perhaps, would he have perpetrated much additional mischief by the mistake; but, after receiving a benediction in common, they assorted themselves in their own fashion, as they only knew how, and departed to the garrets, or the cellars, or the unsheltered street-corners, where their honeymoon and subsequent lives were to be spent. The parson smiled decorously, the clerk and the sexton grinned broadly, the female attendant tittered almost aloud, and even the married parties seemed to see something exceedingly funny in the affair; but for my part, though generally apt enough to be tickled by a joke, I laid it away in my memory as one of the saddest sights I ever looked upon.

Not very long afterwards, I happened to be passing the same venerable Cathedral, and heard a clang of joyful bells, and beheld a bridal party coming down the steps towards a carriage and four horses, with a portly coachman and two postilions, that waited at the gate. One parson and one service had amalgamated the wretchedness of a score of paupers; a Bishop and three or four clergymen had combined their spiritual might to forge the golden links of this other marriage-bond. The bridegroom's mien had a sort of careless and kindly English pride; the bride floated along in her white drapery, a creature so nice and delicate that it was a luxury to see her, and a pity that her silk slippers should touch anything so grimy as the old stones of the churchyard avenue. The crowd of ragged people, who always cluster to witness what they may of an aristocratic wedding, broke into audible admiration of the bride's beauty and the bridegroom's manliness, and uttered prayers and ejaculations (possibly paid for in alms) for the happiness of both. If the most favorable of earthly conditions could make them happy, they had every prospect of it. They were going to live on their abundance in one of those stately and delightful English homes, such as no other people ever created or inherited, a hall set far and safe within its own private grounds, and surrounded with venerable trees, shaven lawns, rich shrubbery, and trimmest pathways, the whole so artfully contrived and tended that summer rendered it a paradise, and even winter would hardly disrobe it of its beauty; and all this fair property seemed more exclusively and inalienably their own, because of its descent through many forefathers, each of whom had added an improvement or a charm, and thus transmitted it with a stronger stamp of rightful possession to his heir. And is it possible, after all, that there may be a flaw in the title-deeds? Is, or is not, the system wrong that gives one married pair so immense a superfluity of luxurious home, and shuts out a million others from any home whatever? One day or another, safe as they deem themselves, and safe as the hereditary temper of the people really tends to make them, the gentlemen of England will be compelled to face this question.

From *English Note-Books,* 1870.

London and the English

by HEINRICH HEINE [1797–1856]

I HAVE SEEN the greatest wonder which the world can show to the astonished spirit; I have seen it, and am still astonished; and still there remains fixed in my memory the stone forest of houses, and amid the rushing stream of faces of living men with all their motley passions, all their terrible impulses of love, of hunger, and of hatred—I mean London.

Send a *philosopher* to London, but, for your life, no poet! Send a philosopher there, and stand him at a corner of Cheapside, where he will learn more than from all the books of the last Leipzig fair; and as the billows of human life roar around him, so will a sea of new thoughts rise before him, and the Eternal Spirit which moves upon the face of the waters will breathe upon him; the most hidden secrets of social harmony will be suddenly revealed to him; he will hear the pulse of the world beat audibly, and see it visibly; for if London is the right hand of the world—its active, mighty right hand—then we may regard that route which leads from the Exchange to Downing Street as the world's pyloric artery.

But never send a poet to London! This downright earnestness of all things, this colossal uniformity, this machine-like movement, this troubled spirit in pleasure itself, this exaggerated London, smothers the imagination and rends the heart. And should you ever send a German poet thither—a dreamer, who stares at everything, even a ragged beggar-woman, or the shining wares of a goldsmith's shop—why, then, at least he will find things going right badly with him, and he will be hustled about on every side, or perhaps be knocked over with a mild *"God damn!" God damn!*— damn the knocking about and pushing! I see at a glance that these people have enough to do. They live on a grand scale, and though food and clothes are dearer with them than with us, they must still be better fed and clothed than we are—as gentility requires. Moreover, they have enormous debts, yet occasionally, in a vain-glorious mood, they make ducks and drakes of their guineas, pay other nations to box about for their pleasure, give their kings a handsome *douceur* into the bargain; and, therefore, John Bull must work to get the money for such expenditure. By day and by night he must tax his brain to discover new machines, and he sits and reckons in the sweat of his brow, and runs and rushes, without much looking around, from the Docks to the Exchange, and from the Exchange to the Strand; and therefore it is quite pardonable if he, when a poor German poet, gazing into a print-shop window, stands bolt in his way on the corner of Cheapside, should knock the latter sideways with a rather rough "God damn!"

But the picture at which I was gazing as I stood at Cheapside corner was that of the French crossing the Beresina.

And when I, jolted out of my gazing, looked again on the raging

street, where a parti-coloured coil of men, women, and children,
horses, stagecoaches, and with them a funeral, whirled groaning
and creaking along, it seemed to me as though all London were
such a Beresina Bridge, where every one presses on in mad haste
to save his scrap of life; where the daring rider stamps down the
poor pedestrian; where every one who falls is lost for ever; where
the best friends rush, without feeling, over each other's corpses;
and where thousands in the weakness of death, and bleeding,
grasp in vain at the planks of the bridge, and are shot down into
the icy grave of death.

How much more pleasant and home-like it is in our dear Germany! With what dreaming comfort, in what Sabbath-like repose,
all glides along here! Calmly the sentinels are changed, uniforms
and houses shine in the quiet sunshine, swallows flit over the flag-
stones, fat Court-councilloresses smile from the windows, while
along the echoing streets there is room enough for the dogs to sniff
at each other, and for men to stand at ease and chat about the
theatre, and bow deeply—oh, how deeply!—when some small
aristocratic scamp or vice-scamp, with coloured ribbons on his
shabby coat, or some Court-marshal-low-brain * struts along as if
in judgment, graciously returning salutations.

I had made up my mind in advance not to be astonished at that
immensity of London of which I had heard so much. But I had as
little success as the poor schoolboy who determined beforehand
not to feel the whipping which he was to receive. The facts of the
case were, that he expected to get the usual blows with the usual
stick in the usual way on the back, whereas he received a most unusually severe licking on an unusual place with a cutting switch.
I anticipated great palaces, and saw nothing but mere small houses.
But their very uniformity and their limitless extent impress the
soul wonderfully.

These houses of brick, owing to the damp atmosphere and coal
smoke, are all of an uniform colour, that is to say, of a brown olive-
green, and are all of the same style of building, generally two or
three windows wide, three storeys high, and finished above with
small red tiles, which remind one of newly extracted bleeding

* Hofmarschalkchen.

teeth; while the broad and accurately squared streets which these houses form seem to be bordered by endlessly long barracks. This has its reason in the fact that every English family, though it consist of only two persons, must still have a house to itself for its own castle, and rich speculators, to meet the demand, build wholesale entire streets of these dwellings, which they retail singly. In the principal streets of the city where the business of London is most at home, where old-fashioned buildings are mingled with the new, and where the fronts of the houses are covered with signs, yards in length, generally gilt, and in relief, this characteristic uniformity is less striking—the less so, indeed, because the eye of the stranger is incessantly caught by the new and brilliant wares exposed for sale in the windows. And these articles do not merely produce an effect, because the Englishman completes so perfectly everything which he manufactures, and because every article of luxury, every astral lamp and every boot, every tea-kettle and every woman's dress, shines out so invitingly and so *finished*. There is also a peculiar charm in the art of arrangement, in the contrast of colours, and in the variety of the English shops; even the most commonplace neces-saries of life appear in a startling magic light through this artistic power of setting forth everything to advantage. Ordinary articles of food attract us by the new light in which they are placed; even uncooked fish lie so delightfully dressed that the rainbow gleam of their scales attracts us; raw meat lies, as if painted, on neat and many-coloured porcelain plates, garlanded about with parsley—yes, everything seems painted, reminding us of the highly polished yet modest pictures of Franz Mieris. But the human beings whom we see are not so cheerful as in the Dutch paintings, for they sell the jolliest wares with the most serious faces, and the cut and colour of their clothes is as uniform as that of their houses.

On the opposite side of the town, which they call the West End—*"the west end of the town"*—and where the more aristo-cratic and less occupied world lives, the uniformity spoken of is still more dominant; yet here there are very long and very broad streets, where all the houses are large as palaces, though any-thing but remarkable as regards their exterior, unless we except the fact that in these, as in all the better class of houses in London, the windows of the first *étage* (or second storey) are adorned with iron-barred balconies, and also on the *rez de chaussée* there is a black railing protecting the entrance to certain subterranean apartments. In this part of the city there are also great "squares," where rows of houses like those already described form a quadrangle, in whose centre there is a garden, enclosed by an iron railing and containing some statue or other. In all of these places and streets the eye is never shocked by the dilapidated huts of misery. Everywhere we are stared down on by wealth and respectability, while crammed away in retired lanes and dark, damp alleys Poverty dwells with her rags and her tears.

The stranger who wanders through the great streets of London, and does not chance right into the regular quarters of the multitude, sees little or nothing of the fearful misery existing there. Only here and there at the mouth of some dark alley stands a ragged woman with a suckling babe at her weak breast, and begs with her eyes. Perhaps, if those eyes are still beautiful, we glance into them, and are shocked at the world of wretchedness visible within. The common beggars are old people, generally blacks, who stand at the corners of the streets cleaning pathways —a very necessary thing in muddy London—and ask for "coppers" in reward. It is in the dusky twilight that Poverty with her mates Vice and Crime glide forth from their lairs. They shun daylight the more anxiously since their wretchedness there contrasts more cruelly with the pride of wealth which glitters everywhere; only Hunger sometimes drives them at noonday from their dens, and then they stand with silent, speaking eyes, staring beseechingly at the rich merchant who hurries along, busy and jingling gold, or at the lazy lord who, like a surfeited god, rides by on his high horse, casting now and then an aristocratically indifferent glance at the mob below, as though they were swarming ants, or rather a mass of baser beings, whose joys and sorrows have nothing in common with his feelings. Yes—for over the vulgar multitude which sticks fast to the soil soar, like beings of a higher nature, England's nobility, to whom their little island is only a temporary resting-place, Italy their summer garden, Paris their social saloon, and the whole world their inheritance. They sweep along, knowing nothing of sorrow or suffering, and their gold is a talisman which conjures into fulfilment their wildest wish.

Poor Poverty! how agonising must thy hunger be, where others swell in scornful superfluity! And when some one casts with indifferent hand a crust into thy lap, how bitter must the tears be wherewith thou moistenest it! Thou poisonest thyself with thine own tears. Well art thou in the right when thou alliest thyself to Vice and Crime. Outlawed criminals often bear more humanity in their hearts than those cool, reproachless town burghers of virtue, in whose white hearts the power of evil, it is true, is quenched—but with it, too, the power of good. And even vice is not always vice. I have seen women on whose cheeks red vice was painted, and in whose hearts dwelt heavenly purity. I have seen women—I would that I saw them again!

Under the archways of the London Exchange every nation has its allotted place, and on high tablets we read the names of Russians, Spaniards, Swedes, Germans, Maltese, Jews, Hanseatics, Turks, &c. Now, however, you would seek them there in vain, for the men who have been jostled away; where Spaniards once stood Dutchmen now stand, the citizens of Hanse Towns have elbowed out the Jews, Russians are now where Turks once were, Italians on the ground formerly held by Frenchmen; even the Germans have advanced a little.

As in the London Exchange, so in the rest of the world the ancient tablets have remained, and men have been moved away while other people appear in their place, whose new heads agree very indifferently with the old inscriptions. The old stereotyped characteristics of races, as we find them in learned compendiums and ale-houses, are no longer profitable, and can only lead us into dreary errors. As we during the last ten years have observed a striking change in the character of our Western neighbours, just so has there been, since the continent was thrown open, a corresponding metamorphosis on the other side of the canal. Stiff, taciturn Englishmen go pilgrim-like in hordes to France, there to learn to speak and move their limbs; and on returning we observe with amazement that their tongues are loosened, they no longer have two left hands, and are no longer contented with beef-steak and plum-puddings. I myself have seen such an Englishman, who in Tavistock Tavern asked for some sugar with his cauliflowers—a heresy against the stern laws of the English *cuisine,* which nearly caused the waiter to fall flat on his back; for, certainly, since the days of the Roman invasion, cauliflower was never cooked otherwise than by simply boiling in water, nor was it ever eaten with sweet seasoning. It was the self-same Englishman who, although I had never seen him before, sat down opposite to me and began to converse so genially in French that I could not for my life help telling him how delighted I was to meet, for once, an Englishman who was not reserved towards strangers; whereupon he, without smiling, quite as candidly remarked that he merely talked with me for the sake of practice in French.

It is amazing how the French, day by day, become more reflecting, deeper, and more serious, while the English, on the other hand, strive to assume a light, superficial, and cheerful manner, not merely in life, but in literature. The London presses are fully busied with fashionable works, with romances which move in the glittering sphere of "high life," or mirror it; as, for instance, *Almacks,* or *Vivian Grey, Tremaine, The Guards,* and *Flirtation.* This last romance bears a name which would be most appropriate for the whole species, since it indicates that coquetry with foreign airs and phrases, that clumsy refinement, that heavy bumping lightness, that sour style of honeyed compliment, that ornamented coarseness; in a word, the entire lifeless life of those wooden butterflies who flutter in the saloons of West London.

But, on the contrary, what a literature is at present offered us by the French press—that real representative of French spirit and volition! When their great Emperor undertook, in the leisure of his captivity, to dictate his life, to reveal the most secret solutions of the enigmas of his divine soul, and to change the rocks of St. Helena to a chair of history, from whose height his contemporaries should be judged and latest posterity be taught, then the French themselves began to employ the days of their adversity and the period of their political inactivity as profitably as possible. They also are now writing the history of their deeds, the hands which once grasped the sword are again becoming a terror to their enemies by wielding the pen, the whole nation is busied in publishing its memoirs, and if it will follow my advice it will prepare a particular edition *ad usum Delphini,* with nicely coloured engravings of the taking of the Bastille and storming of the Tuileries.

If I have above remarked that the English of the present day are seeking to become light and frivolous, and endeavouring to creep into the monkey's skin which the French are gradually stripping off, I must also add that the tendency in question proceeds rather from the nobility and gentry, or aristocratic world, than from the citizens. On the contrary, the trading and working portion of the people, especially the merchants in the manufacturing towns, and nearly all the Scotch, bear the external marks of pietism—yes, I might almost say of Puritanism, so that this blessed portion of the people contrast with the worldly-minded aristocrats, like the cavaliers and Roundheads so truthfully set forth by Scott in his novels.

Those readers honour the Scottish bard too highly who believe that his genius imitated and penetrated the outer form and inner manner of feeling of those two historical parties, and that it is an indication of his poetic greatness that he, free from prejudice as a god in his judgment, does justice to both and treats them with equal love. Let any one cast a glance into the prayer-meetings of Liverpool and Manchester, and then into the fashionable saloons of the West End, and he will plainly see that Walter Scott has simply described his own times, and clothed forms which are altogether modern in dresses of the olden time. And if we remember that he himself from one side, as a Scotchman, sucked in by education and national influence a Puritan spirit, while on the other side, as a Tory who even regarded himself as a scion of the Stuarts, he must have been right royally and aristocratically inclined, and that therefore his feelings and thoughts must have embraced either tendency with equal love, and must also have been neutralised by their opposition, we can very readily understand his impartiality in describing the democrats and aristocrats of Cromwell's time, an impartiality which might well lead us into error if we hoped to find in his *History of Napoleon* an equally "fair-play" description of the heroes of the French Revolution.*

He who regards England attentively may now find daily opportunities of observing those two tendencies, the frivolous and the Puritanic, in their most repulsive vigour, and with them, of course, their mutual contest. Such an opportunity was recently manifested in the famous suit at law of Mr. Wakefield, a gay cavalier, who, in an off-hand manner eloped with the daughter of the rich Mr. Turner, a Liverpool merchant, and married her at Gretna Green, where a blacksmith lives who forges the strongest sort of fetters. The entire head-hanging community, the whole race of the elect of the Lord, screamed murder at such horrible conduct; in the conventicles of Liverpool the vengeance of Heaven was evoked on Wakefield and his brother who assisted; they prayed that the earth's abyss might swallow them as it once swallowed the host of Korah, Dathan, and Abiram; while, to make celestial anger more certain, they brought the thunders of the King's Bench, of the Lord Chancellor, and even of the Upper House to bear on this profaner of the holy sacrament; while in the fashionable saloons people merely laughed merrily and jested in the most liberal manner at the bold damsel-stealer. But the contrast of the two states of thought or feeling was recently shown me in the most delightful manner as I sat in the Grand Opera near two fat Manchester ladies who visited this *rendezvous* of the aristocratic world for the first time in their lives, and who could not find words strong enough to express the utter detestation and abhorrence which filled their hearts as the ballet began, and the short-skirted beautiful dancing-girls exhibited their lasciviously graceful movements, and fell passionately, like burning Bacchantes, into the arms of the male dancers who leaped towards them. The inspiring music, the

---

* With change of name and circumstance one might accept this as an accurate description of Heine himself.—*Translator.*

primitive clothing of flesh-coloured stockinet, the bounds so like the exuberance of nature, all united to force the sweat of agony from the poor ladies; their bosoms flushed with repugnance; they continually heaved out in chorus, *"Shocking! For shame! for shame!"* and were so benumbed with horror that they could not for an instant take their opera-glasses from their eyes, and consequently remained in that situation to the last instant when the curtain fell.

Despite these diametrically opposed tendencies of mind and of life, we still find in the English people an unity in their way of thinking, which comes from the very fact that they are always realising that they are a people by themselves; the modern cavaliers and Roundheads may hate and despise one another mutually and as much as they please; they do not, for all that, cease to be English; as such they are at union and together, like plants which have grown out of the same soil and are strangely interwoven with it. Hence the secret unity of the entire life and activity and intercourse of England, which at the first glance seems to us but a theatre of confusion and of contradiction. Excessive wealth and misery, orthodoxy and infidelity, freedom and serfdom, cruelty and mildness, honour and deceit—all of these incongruities in their maddest extremes; over all a grey misty heaven, on every side buzzing machines, reckoning, gas-lights, chimneys, pots of porter, closed mouths—all this hangs together in such-wise that we can hardly think of the one without the other; and that which singly, really ought to excite our astonishment or laughter appears to be, when taken as a part of the whole, quite commonplace and serious.

But I imagine that such would be the case everywhere, even in countries of which we have much more eccentric conceptions, and where we anticipate a much richer booty of merriment or amazement. Our earnest longing to travel, our desire to see foreign lands, particularly as we feel it in early youth, generally results from an erroneous anticipation of extraordinary contrasts, and from that spiritual pleasure in masquerades which makes us involuntarily expect to find the men and manner of thought of our own home, and to a certain degree our nearest friends and acquaintances, disguised in foreign dress and manners. If we think, for example, of the Hottentots, at once the ladies of our native town dance around in our imaginations, but painted black and endowed with the proper *a posteriori* developments, while our *beaux esprits* climb the palm-trees as bush-beaters; and if we think of the North Polanders, we see there also the well-known faces; our aunt glides in her dog-sleigh over the ice road; the dry Herr Conrector lies lazily on the bearskin and calmly sips his morning train-oil; Madame the inspector's wife, Madame the tax-gatherer's lady, and Madame the wife of the Councillor of Infibulation gossip together and munch candles. But when we are really in those countries, we at once observe that mankind has there grown up from infancy with its manners and modes; that people's faces harmonise with their thoughts and clothes to their needs—yes, that plants, animals, human beings, and the land itself form a harmonious whole.

From *English Fragments,* 1828.   Translated by
                                          CHARLES GODFREY LELAND

Death in the Afternoon

by ERNEST HEMINGWAY [1898–1961]

THE BULLFIGHT is not a sport in the Anglo-Saxon sense of the word, that is, it is not an equal contest or an attempt at an equal contest between a bull and a man. Rather it is a tragedy; the death of the bull, which is played, more or less well, by the bull and the man involved and in which there is danger for the man but certain death for the animal. This danger to the man can be increased by the bullfighter at will in the measure in which he works close to the bull's horns. Keeping within the rules for bullfighting on foot in a closed ring formulated by years of experience, which, if known and followed, permit a man to perform certain actions with a bull without being caught by the bull's horns, the bullfighter may, by decreasing his distance from the bull's horns, depend more and more on his own reflexes and judgment of that distance to protect him from the points. This danger of goring, which the man creates voluntarily, can be changed to certainty of being caught and tossed by the bull if the man, through ignorance, slowness, torpidity, blind folly or momentary grogginess breaks any of these fundamental rules for the execution of the different suertes. Everything that is done by the man in the ring is called a "suerte." It is the easiest term to use as it is short. It means act, but the word act has, in English, a connotation of the theatre that makes its use confusing.

People seeing their first bullfight say, "But the bulls are so stupid. They always go for the cape and not for the man."

The bull only goes for the percale of the cape or for the scarlet serge of the muleta if the man makes him and so handles the cloth that the bull sees it rather than the man. Therefore to really start to see bullfights a spectator should go to the novilladas or apprentice fights. There the bulls do not always go for the cloth because the bullfighters are learning before your eyes the rules of bullfighting and they do not always remember or know the proper terrain to take and how to keep the bull after the lure and away from the man. It is one thing to know the rules in principle and another to remember them as they are needed when facing an animal that is seeking to kill you, and the spectator who wants to see men tossed and gored rather than judge the manner in which the bulls are dominated should go to a novillada before he sees a corrida de toros or complete bullfight. It should be a good thing for him to see a novillada first anyway if he wants to learn about technique, since the employment of knowledge that we call by that bastard name is always most visible in its imperfection. At a novillada the spectator may see the mistakes of the bullfighters, and the penalties that these mistakes carry. He will learn something too about the state of training or lack of training of the men and the effect this has on their courage.

One time in Madrid I remember we went to a novillada in the middle of the summer on a very hot Sunday when every one who could afford it had left the city for the beaches of the north or the mountains and the bullfight was not advertised to start until six o'clock in the evening, to see six Tovar bulls killed by three aspirant matadors who have all since failed in their profession. We sat in the first row behind the wooden barrier and when the first bull came out it was clear that Domingo Hernandorena, a short, thick-ankled, graceless Basque with a pale face who looked nervous and incompletely fed in a cheap rented suit, if he was to kill this bull would either make a fool of himself or be gored. Hernandorena could not control the nervousness of his feet. He wanted to stand quietly and play the bull with the cape with a slow movement of his arms, but when he tried to stand still as the bull charged his feet jumped away in short, nervous jerks. His feet were obviously not under his personal control and his effort to be statuesque while his feet jittered him away out of danger was very funny to the crowd. It was funny to them because many of them knew that was how their own feet would behave if they saw the horns coming toward them, and as always, they resented any one else being in there in the ring, making money, who had the same physical defects which barred them, the spectators, from that supposedly highly paid way of making a living. In their turn the other two matadors were very fancy with the cape and Hernandorena's nervous jerking was even worse after their performance. He had not been in the ring with a bull for over a year and he was altogether unable to control his nervousness. When the banderillas were in and it was time for him to go out with the red cloth and the sword to prepare the bull for killing and to kill, the crowd which had applauded ironically at every nervous move he had made knew something very funny would happen. Below us, as he took the muleta and the sword and rinsed his mouth out with water I could see the muscles of his cheeks twitching. The bull stood against the barrier watching him. Hernandorena could not trust his legs to carry him slowly toward the bull. He knew there was only one way he could stay in one place in the ring. He ran out toward the bull, and ten yards in front of him dropped to both knees on the sand. In that position he was safe from ridicule. He spread the red cloth with his sword and jerked himself forward on his knees toward the bull. The bull was watching the man and the triangle of red cloth, his ears pointed, his eyes fixed, and Hernandorena knee-ed himself a yard closer and shook the cloth. The bull's tail rose, his head lowered and he charged and, as he reached the man, Hernandorena rose solidly from his knees into the air, swung over like a bundle, his legs in all directions now, and then dropped to the ground. The bull looked for him, found a wide-spread moving cape held by another bullfighter instead, charged it, and Hernandorena stood up with sand on his white face and looked for his sword and the cloth. As he stood up I saw the heavy, soiled gray silk of his rented trousers open cleanly and deeply to show the thigh bone from the hip almost to the knee. He saw it too and looked very surprised and put his hand on it while people jumped over the barrier and ran toward him to carry him to the infirmary. The technical error that he had committed was in not keeping the red cloth of the muleta between himself and the bull until the charge; then at the moment of jurisdiction as it is called, when the bull's lowered head reaches the cloth, swaying back while he held the cloth, spread by the stick and the sword, far enough forward so that the bull following it would be clear of his body. It was a simple technical error.

That night at the café I heard no word of sympathy for him. He was ignorant, he was torpid, and he was out of training. Why did he insist on being a bullfighter? Why did he go down on both knees? Because he was a coward, they said. The knees are for cowards. If he was a coward why did he insist on being a bullfighter? There was no natural sympathy for uncontrollable nervousness because he was a paid public performer. It was preferable that he be gored rather than run from the bull. To be gored was honorable; they would have sympathized with him had he been caught in one of his nervous uncontrollable jerky retreats, which, although they mocked, they knew were from lack of training, rather than for him to have gone down on his knees. Because the hardest thing when frightened by the bull is to control the feet and let the bull come, and any attempt to control the feet was honorable even though they jeered at it because it looked ridiculous. But when he went on both knees, without the technique to fight from that position; the technique that Marcial Lalanda, the most scientific of living bullfighters, has, and which alone makes that position honorable; then Hernandorena admitted his nervousness. To show his nervousness was not shameful; only to admit it. When, lacking the technique and thereby admitting his inability to control his feet, the matador went down on both knees before the bull the crowd had no more sympathy with him than with a suicide.

For myself, not being a bullfighter, and being much interested in suicides, the problem was one of depiction and waking in the night I tried to remember what it was that seemed just out of my remembering and that was the thing that I had really seen and, finally, remembering all around, I got it. When he stood up, his face white and dirty and the silk of his breeches opened from waist to knee, it was the dirtiness of the rented breeches, the dirtiness of his slit underwear and the clean, clean, unbearably clean whiteness of the thigh bone that I had seen, and it was that which was important.

At the novilladas, too, besides the study of technique, and the consequences of its lack you have a chance to learn about the manner of dealing with defective bulls since bulls which cannot be used in a formal bullfight because of some obvious defect are killed in the apprentice fights. Nearly all bulls develop defects in the course of any fight which must be corrected by the bullfighter, but in the novillada these defects, those of vision for instance, are many times obvious at the start and so the manner of their correcting, or the result of their not being corrected, is apparent.

The formal bullfight is a tragedy, not a sport, and the bull is certain to be killed. If the matador cannot kill him and, at the end of the allotted fifteen minutes for the preparation and killing, the bull is led and herded out of the ring alive by steers to dishonor the killer, he must, by law, be killed in the corrals. It

is one hundred to one against the matador de toros or formally
invested bullfighter being killed unless he is inexperienced, ignorant, out of training or too old and heavy on his feet. But
the matador, if he knows his profession, can increase the amount
of the danger of death that he runs exactly as much as he wishes.
He should, however, increase this danger, *within the rules provided for his protection*. In other words it is to his credit if he
does something that he knows how to do in a highly dangerous
but still geometrically possible manner. It is to his discredit if
he runs danger through ignorance, through disregard of the
fundamental rules, through physical or mental slowness, or
through blind folly.

The matador must dominate the bulls by knowledge and science. In the measure in which this domination is accomplished
with grace will it be beautiful to watch. Strength is of little use to
him except at the actual moment of killing. Once some one asked
Rafael Gomez, "El Gallo," nearing fifty years old, a gypsy, brother
of Jose Gomez, "Gallito," and the last living member of the great
family of gypsy bullfighters of that name, what physical exercise
he, Gallo, took to keep his strength up for bullfighting.

"Strength," Gallo said. "What do I want with strength, man?
The bull weighs half a ton. Should I take exercises for strength to
match him? Let the bull have the strength."

If the bulls were allowed to increase their knowledge as the bullfighter does and if those bulls which are not killed in the allotted
fifteen minutes in the ring were not afterwards killed in the corrals but were allowed to be fought again they would kill all the
bullfighters, if the bullfighters fought them according to the rules.
Bullfighting is based on the fact that it is the first meeting between
the wild animal and a dismounted man. This is the fundamental
premise of modern bullfighting; that the bull has never been in
the ring before. In the early days of bullfighting bulls were allowed
to be fought which had been in the ring before and so many men
were killed in the bull ring that on November 20, 1567, Pope Pius
the Fifth issued a Papal edict excommunicating all Christian
princes who should permit bullfights in their countries and denying Christian burial to any person killed in the bull ring. The
Church only agreed to tolerate bullfighting, which continued stead-

ily in Spain in spite of the edict, when it was agreed that the bulls should only appear once in the ring.

You would think then that it would make of bullfighting a true sport, rather than merely a tragic spectacle, if bulls that had been in the ring were allowed to reappear. I have seen such bulls fought, in violation of the law, in provincial towns in improvised arenas made by blocking the entrances to the public square with piled-up carts in the illegal capeas, or town-square bullfights with used bulls. The aspirant bullfighters, who have no financial backing, get their first experience in capeas. It is a sport, a very savage and primitive sport, and for the most part a truly amateur one. I am afraid however due to the danger of death it involves it would never have much success among the amateur sportsmen of America and England who play games. We, in games, are not fascinated by death, its nearness and its avoidance. We are fascinated by victory and we replace the avoidance of death by the avoidance of defeat. It is a very nice symbolism but it takes more cojones to be a sportsman when death is a closer party to the game. The bull in the capeas is rarely killed. This should appeal to sportsmen who are lovers of animals. The town is usually too poor to afford to pay for the killing of the bull and none of the aspirant bullfighters has enough money to buy a sword or he would not have chosen to serve his apprenticeship in the capeas. This would afford an opportunity for the man who is a wealthy sportsman, for he could afford to pay for the bull and buy himself a sword as well.

However, due to the mechanics of a bull's mental development the used bull does not make a brilliant spectacle. After his first charge or so he will stand quite still and will only charge if he is certain of getting the man or boy who is tempting him with a cape. When there is a crowd and the bull charges into it he will pick one man out and follow him, no matter how he may dodge, run and twist until he gets him and tosses him. If the tips of the bull's horns have been blunted this chasing and tossing is good fun to see for a little while. No one has to go in with the bull who does not want to, although of course many who want to very little go in to show their courage. It is very exciting for those who are down in the square, that is one test of a true amateur sport, whether it is more enjoyable to player than to spectator (as soon as it becomes enjoyable enough to the spectator for the charging of admission to be profitable the sport contains the germ of professionalism), and the smallest evidence of coolness or composure brings immediate applause. But when the bull's horns are sharp-pointed it is a disturbing spectacle. The men and boys try cape work with sacks, blouses and old capes on the bull just as they do when his horns have been blunted; the only difference is that when the bull catches them and tosses them they are liable to come off the horn with wounds no local surgeon can cope with. One bull which was a great favorite in the capeas of the province of Valencia killed sixteen men and boys and badly wounded over sixty in a career of five years. The people who go into these capeas do so sometimes as aspirant professionals to get free experience with bulls but most often as amateurs, purely for sport, for the immediate excitement, and it is very great excitement; and for the retrospective pleasure, of having shown their contempt for death on a hot day in their own town square. Many go in from pride, hoping that they will be brave. Many find they are not brave at all; but at least they went in. There is absolutely nothing for them to gain except the inner satisfaction of having been in the ring with a bull; itself a thing that any one who has done it will always remember. It is a strange feeling to have an animal come toward you consciously seeking to kill you, his eyes open looking at you, and see the oncoming of the lowered horn that he intends to kill you with. It gives enough of a sensation so that there are always men willing to go into the capeas for the pride of having experienced it and the pleasure of having tried some bullfighting maneuver with a real bull although the actual pleasure at the time may not be great. Sometimes the bull is killed if the town has the money to afford it, or if the populace gets out of control; every one swarming on him at once with knives, daggers, butcher knives and rocks; a man perhaps between his horns, being swung up and down, another flying through the air, surely several holding his tail, a swarm of choppers, thrusters and stabbers pushing into him, laying on him or cutting up at him until he sways and goes down. All amateur or group killing is a very barbarous, messy, though exciting business and is a long way from the ritual of the formal bullfight.

The bull which killed the sixteen and wounded the sixty was killed in a very odd way. One of those he had killed was a gypsy boy of about fourteen. Afterward the boy's brother and sister followed the bull around hoping perhaps to have a chance to assassinate him when he was loaded in his cage after a capea. That was difficult since, being a very highly valued performer, the bull was carefully taken care of. They followed him around for two years, not attempting anything, simply turning up wherever the bull was used. When the capeas were again abolished, they are always being abolished and re-abolished, by government order, the bull's owner decided to send him to the slaughterhouse in Valencia, for the bull was getting on in years anyway. The two gypsies were at the slaughterhouse and the young man asked permission, since the bull had killed his brother, to kill the bull. This was granted and he started in by digging out both the bull's eyes while the bull was in his cage, and spitting carefully into the sockets, then after killing him by severing the spinal marrow between the neck vertebrae with a dagger, he experienced some difficulty in this, he asked permission to cut off the bull's testicles, which being granted, he and his sister built a small fire at the edge of the dusty street outside the slaughterhouse and roasted the two glands on sticks and when they were done, ate them. They then turned their backs on the slaughterhouse and went away along the road and out of town.

1932

Ivan Turgénieff

by HENRY JAMES [1843-1916]

WHEN THE mortal remains of Ivan Turgénieff were about to be transported from Paris for interment in his own country, a short commemorative service was held at the Gare du Nord. Ernest

Renan and Edmond About, standing beside the train in which his coffin had been placed, bade farewell in the name of the French people to the illustrious stranger who for so many years had been their honoured and grateful guest. M. Renan made a beautiful speech, and M. About a very clever one, and each of them characterized, with ingenuity, the genius and the moral nature of the most touching of writers, the most lovable of men. "Turgénieff," said M. Renan, "received by the mysterious decree which marks out human vocations the gift which is noble beyond all others: he was born essentially impersonal." The passage is so eloquent that one must repeat the whole of it.

> His conscience was not that of an individual to whom nature had been more or less generous: it was in some sort the conscience of a people. Before he was born he had lived for thousands of years; infinite successions of reveries had amassed themselves in the depths of his heart. No man has been as much as he the incarnation of a whole race: generations of ancestors, lost in the sleep of centuries, speechless, came through him to life and utterance.

I quote these lines for the pleasure of quoting them; for while I see what M. Renan means by calling Turgénieff impersonal, it has been my wish to devote to his delightful memory a few pages written under the impression of contact and intercourse. He seems to us impersonal, because it is from his writings almost alone that we of English, French and German speech have derived our notions—even yet, I fear, rather meagre and erroneous—of the Russian people. His genius for us is the Slav genius; his voice the voice of those vaguely imagined multitudes whom we think of more and more to-day as waiting their turn, in the arena of civilization, in the grey expanses of the North. There is much in his writings to encourage this view, and it is certain that he interpreted with wonderful vividness the temperament of his fellow-countrymen. Cosmopolite that he had become by the force of circumstances, his roots had never been loosened in his native soil. The ignorance with regard to Russia and the Russians which he found in abundance in the rest of Europe—and not least in the country he inhabited for ten years before his death—had indeed the effect, to a certain degree, to throw him back upon the deep feelings which so many of his companions were unable to share with him, the memories of his early years, the sense of wide Russian horizons, the joy and pride of his mother-tongue. In the collection of short pieces, so deeply interesting, written during the last few years of his life, and translated into German under the name of *Senilia,* I find a passage—it is the last in the little book— which illustrates perfectly this reactionary impulse:

> In days of doubt, in days of anxious thought on the destiny of my native land, thou alone art my support and my staff, O great powerful Russian tongue, truthful and free! If it were not for thee how should man not despair at the sight of what is going on at home? But it is inconceivable that such a language has not been given to a great people.

This Muscovite, home-loving note pervades his productions, though it is between the lines, as it were, that we must listen for it. None the less does it remain true that he was not a simple conduit or mouthpiece; the inspiration was his own as well as the voice. He was an individual, in other words, of the most unmistakable kind, and those who had the happiness to know him have no difficulty to-day in thinking of him as an eminent, responsible figure. This pleasure, for the writer of these lines, was as great as the pleasure of reading the admirable tales into which he put such a world of life and feeling: it was perhaps even greater, for it was not only with the pen that nature had given Turgénieff the power to express himself. He was the richest, the most delightful, of talkers, and his face, his person, his temper, the thoroughness with which he had been equipped for human intercourse, make in the memory of his friends an image which is completed, but not thrown into the shade, by his literary distinction. The whole image is tinted with sadness: partly because the element of melancholy in his nature was deep and constant—readers of his novels have no need to be told of that; and partly because, during the last years of his life, he had been condemned to suffer atrociously. Intolerable pain had been his portion for too many months before he died; his end was not a soft decline, but a deepening distress. But of brightness, of the faculty of enjoyment, he had also the large allowance usually made to first-rate men, and he was a singularly complete human being. The author of these pages had greatly admired his writings before having the fortune to make his acquaintance, and this privilege, when it presented itself, was highly illuminating. The man and the writer together occupied from that moment a very high place in his affection. Some time before knowing him I committed to print certain reflections which his tales had led me to make; and I may perhaps, therefore, without impropriety give them a supplement which shall have a more vivifying reference. It is almost irresistible to attempt to say, from one's own point of view, what manner of man he was.

It was in consequence of the article I just mentioned that I found reason to meet him, in Paris, where he was then living, in 1875. I shall never forget the impression he made upon me at that first interview. I found him adorable; I could scarcely believe that he would prove—that any man could prove—on nearer acquaintance so delightful as that. Nearer acquaintance only confirmed my hope, and he remained the most approachable, the most practicable, the least unsafe man of genius it has been my fortune to meet. He was so simple, so natural, so modest, so destitute of personal pretension and of what is called the consciousness of powers, that one almost doubted at moments whether he were a man of genius after all. Everything good and fruitful lay near to him; he was interested in everything; and he was absolutely without that eagerness of self-reference which sometimes accompanies great, and even small, reputations. He had not a particle of vanity; nothing whatever of the air of having a part to play or a reputation to keep up. His humour exercised itself as freely upon himself as upon other subjects, and he told stories at his own expense with a sweetness of hilarity which made his peculiarities really sacred in the eyes of a friend. I remember vividly the smile and tone of voice with which he once repeated to me a figurative epithet which Gustave Flaubert (of whom he was extremely fond) had applied to him—an epithet intended to characterize a certain expansive softness, a comprehensive indecision, which pervaded his nature, just as it pervades so many of the characters he has painted. He enjoyed Flaubert's use of this term, good-naturedly opprobrious, more even than Flaubert himself, and recognized perfectly the element of truth in it. He was natural to an extraordinary degree; I do not think I have ever seen his match in this respect, certainly not among people who bear, as he did, at the same time, the stamp of the highest cultivation. Like all men of a large pattern, he was composed of many different pieces; and what was always striking in him was the mixture of simplicity with the fruit of the most various observation. In the little article in which I had attempted to express my admiration for his works, I had been moved to say of him that he had the aristocratic temperament: a remark which in the light of further knowledge seemed to me singularly innane. He was not subject to any definition of that sort, and to say that he was democratic would be (though his political ideal was a democracy) to give an equally superficial account of him. He felt and understood the opposite sides of life; he was imaginative, speculative, anything but literal. He had not in his mind a grain of prejudice as large as the point of a needle, and people (there are many) who think this a defect would have missed it immensely in Ivan Serguéitch. (I give his name, without attempting the Russian orthography, as it was uttered by his friends when they addressed him in French.) Our Anglo-Saxon, Protestant, moralistic, conventional standards were far away from him, and he judged things with a freedom and spontaneity in which I found a perpetual refreshment. His sense of beauty, his love of truth and right, were the foundation of his nature; but half the charm of conversation with him was that one breathed an air in which cant phrases and arbitrary measurements simply sounded ridiculous.

I may add that it was not because I had written a laudatory article about his books that he gave me a friendly welcome; for in the first place my article could have very little importance for him, and in the second it had never been either his habit or his hope to bask in the light of criticism. Supremely modest as he was, I think he attached no great weight to what might happen to be said about him; for he felt that he was destined to encounter a very small amount of intelligent appreciation, especially in foreign countries.

I never heard him even allude to any judgment which might have been passed upon his productions in England. In France he knew that he was read very moderately; the "demand" for his volumes was small, and he had no illusions whatever on the subject of his popularity. He had heard with pleasure that many intelligent persons in the United States were impatient for everything that might come from his pen; but I think he was never convinced, as one or two of the more zealous of these persons had endeavoured to convince him, that he could boast of a "public" in America. He gave me the impression of thinking of criticism as most serious workers think of it—that it is the amusement, the exercise, the subsistence of the critic (and, so far as this goes, of immense use); but that though it may often concern other readers, it does not much concern the artist himself. In comparison with all those things which the production of a considered work forces the artist little by little to say to himself, the remarks of the critic are vague and of the moment; and yet, owing to the large publicity of the proceeding, they have a power to irritate or discourage which is quite out of proportion to their use to the person criticized. It was not, moreover (if this explanation be not more gross than the spectre it is meant to conjure away), on account of any esteem which he accorded to my own productions (I used regularly to send them to him) that I found him so agreeable, for to the best of my belief he was unable to read them. As regards one of the first that I had offered him he wrote me a little note to tell me that a distinguished friend, who was his constant companion, had read three or four chapters aloud to him the evening before and that one of them was written *de main de maître!* This gave me great pleasure, but it was my first and last pleasure of the kind. I continued, as I say, to send him my fictions, because they were the only thing I had to give; but he never alluded to the rest of the work in question, which he evidently did not finish, and never gave any sign of having read its successors. Presently I quite ceased to expect this, and saw why it was (it interested me much) that my writings could not appeal to him. He cared, more than anything else, for the air of reality, and my reality was not to the purpose. I do not think my stories struck him as quite meat for men. The manner was more apparent than the matter; they were too *tarabiscoté,* as I once heard him say of the style of a book —had on the surface too many little flowers and knots of ribbon. He had read a great deal of English, and knew the language remarkably well—too well, I used often to think, for he liked to speak it with those to whom it was native, and, successful as the effort always was, it deprived him of the facility and raciness with which he expressed himself in French.

I have said that he had no prejudices, but perhaps after all he had one. I think he imagined it to be impossible to a person of English speech to converse in French with complete correctness. He knew Shakespeare thoroughly, and at one time had wandered far and wide in English literature. His opportunities for speaking English were not at all frequent, so that when the necessity (or at least the occasion) presented itself, he remembered the phrases he had encountered in books. This often gave a charming quaintness and an unexpected literary turn to what he said. "In Russia, in spring, if you enter a beechen grove"—those words come back to me from the last time I saw him. He continued to read English books and was not incapable of attacking the usual Tauchnitz novel. The English writer (of our day) of whom I remember to have heard him speak with most admiration was Dickens, of whose faults he was conscious, but whose power of presenting to the eye a vivid, salient figure he rated very high. In the young French school he was much interested; I mean, in the new votaries of realism, the grandsons of Balzac. He was a good friend of most of them, and with Gustave Flaubert, the most singular and most original of the group, he was altogether intimate. He had his reservations and discriminations, and he had, above all, the great back-garden of his Slav imagination and his Germanic culture, into which the door constantly stood open, and the grandsons of Balzac were not, I think, particularly free to accompany him. But he had much sympathy with their experiment, their general movement, and it was on the side of the careful study of life as the best line of the novelist that, as may easily be supposed, he ranged himself. For some of the manifestations of the opposite tradition he had a great contempt. This was a kind

of emotion he rarely expresed, save in regard to certain public
wrongs and iniquities; bitterness and denunciation seldom passed
his mild lips. But I remember well the little flush of conviction,
the seriousness, with which he once said, in allusion to a novel
which had just been running through the *Revue des Deux Mondes,*
"If I had written anything so bad as that, I should blush for it all
my life."

His was not, I should say, predominantly, or even in a high degree, the artistic nature, though it was deeply, if I may make the
distinction, the poetic. But during the last twelve years of his life
he lived much with artists and men of letters, and he was eminently capable of kindling in the glow of discussion. He cared
for questions of form, though not in the degree in which Flaubert
and Edmond de Goncourt cared for them, and he had very lively
sympathies. He had a great regard for Madame George Sand, the
head and front of the old romantic tradition; but this was on
general grounds, quite independent of her novels, which he never
read, and which she never expected him, or apparently any one
else, to read. He thought her character remarkably noble and
sincere. He had, as I have said, a great affection for Gustave Flaubert, who returned it; and he was much interested in Flaubert's
extraordinary attempts at bravery of form and of matter, knowing
perfectly well when they failed. During those months which it was
Flaubert's habit to spend in Paris, Turgénieff went almost regularly to see him on Sunday afternoon, and was so good as to introduce me to the author of *Madame Bovary,* in whom I saw many
reasons for Turgénieff's regard. It was on these Sundays, in Flaubert's little salon, which, at the top of a house at the end of the
Faubourg Saint-Honoré, looked rather bare and provisional, that,
in the company of the other familiars of the spot, more than one
of whom * have commemorated these occasions, Turgénieff's beautiful faculty of talk showed at its best. He was easy, natural, abundant, more than I can describe, and everything that he said was
touched with the exquisite quality of his imagination. What was
discussed in that little smoke-clouded room was chiefly questions
of taste, questions of art and form; and the speakers, for the most

* Maxime Du Camp, Alphonse Daudet, Emile Zola.

part, were in æsthetic matters, radicals of the deepest dye. It would have been late in the day to propose among them any discussion of the relation of art to morality, any question as to the degree in which a novel might or might not concern itself with the teaching of a lesson. They had settled these preliminaries long ago, and it would have been primitive and incongruous to recur to them. The conviction that held them together was the conviction that art and morality are two perfectly different things, and that the former has no more to do with the latter than it has with astronomy or embryology. The only duty of a novel was to be well written; that merit included every other of which it was capable. This state of mind was never more apparent than one afternoon when *ces messieurs* delivered themselves on the subject of an incident which had just befallen one of them. *L'Assommoir* of Emile Zola had been discontinued in the journal through which it was running as a serial, in consequence of repeated protests from the subscribers. The subscriber, as a type of human imbecility, received a wonderful dressing, and the Philistine in general was roughly handled. There were gulfs of difference between Turgénieff and Zola, but Turgénieff, who, as I say, understood everything, understood Zola too, and rendered perfect justice to the high solidity of much of his work. His attitude, at such times, was admirable, and I could imagine nothing more genial or more fitted to give an idea of light, easy, human intelligence. No one could desire more than he that art should be art; always, ever, incorruptibly, art. To him this proposition would have seemed as little in need of proof, or susceptible of refutation, as the axiom that law should always be law or medicine always medicine. As much as any one he was prepared to take note of the fact that the demand for abdications and concessions never comes from artists themselves, but always from purchasers, editors, subscribers. I am pretty sure that his word about all this would have been that he could not quite see what was meant by the talk about novels being moral or the reverse; that a novel could no more propose to itself to be moral than a painting or a symphony, and that it was arbitrary to lay down a distinction between the numerous forms of art. He was the last man to be blind to the unity. I suspect that he would have said, in short, that distinctions were demanded in the interest of the moralists, and that the demand was indelicate, owing to their want of jurisdiction. Yet at the same time that I make this suggestion as to his state of mind I remember how little he struck me as bound by mere neatness of formula, how little there was in him of the partisan or the pleader. What he thought of the relation of art to life his stories, after all, show better than anything else. The immense variety of life was ever present to his mind, and he would never have argued the question I have just hinted at in the interest of particular liberties—the liberties that were apparently the dearest to his French *confrères*. It was this air that he carried about with him of feeling all the variety of life, of knowing strange and far-off things, of having an horizon in which the Parisian horizon —so familiar, so wanting in mystery, so perpetually *exploité*— easily lost itself, that distinguished him from these companions. He was not all there, as the phrase is; he had something behind, in reserve. It was Russia, of course, in a large measure; and, especially before the spectacle of what is going on there to-day, that was a large quantity. But so far as he was on the spot, he was an element of pure sociability.

I did not intend to go into these details immediately, for I had only begun to say what an impression of magnificent manhood he made upon me when I first knew him. That impression, indeed, always remained with me, even after it had been brought home to me how much there was in him of the quality of genius. He was a beautiful intellect, of course, but above all he was a delightful, mild, masculine figure. The combination of his deep, soft, lovable spirit, in which one felt all the tender parts of genius, with his immense, fair Russian physique, was one of the most attractive things conceivable. He had a frame which would have made it perfectly lawful, and even becoming, for him to be brutal; but there was not a grain of brutality in his composition. He had always been a passionate sportsman; to wander in the woods or the steppes, with his dog and gun, was the pleasure of his heart. Late in life he continued to shoot, and he had a friend in Cambridgeshire for the sake of whose partridges, which were famous, he used sometimes to cross the Channel. It would have been impossible to imagine a better representation of a Nimrod of the north. He was exceedingly tall, and broad and robust in proportion. His head was one of the finest, and though the line of his features was irregular, there was a great deal of beauty in his face. It was eminently of the Russian type—almost everything in it was wide. His expression had a singular sweetness, with a touch of Slav languor, and his eye, the kindest of eyes, was deep and melancholy. His hair, abundant and straight, was as white as silver, and his beard, which he wore trimmed rather short, was of the colour of his hair. In all his tall person, which was very striking wherever it appeared, there was an air of neglected strength, as if it had been a part of his modesty never to remind himself that he was strong. He used sometimes to blush like a boy of sixteen. He had very few forms and ceremonies, and almost as little manner as was possible to a man of his natural *prestance*. His noble appearance was in itself a manner; but whatever he did he did very simply, and he had not the slightest pretension to not being subject to rectification. I never saw any one receive it with less irritation. Friendly, candid, unaffectedly benignant, the impression that he produced most strongly and most generally was, I think, simply that of goodness.

When I made his acquaintance he had been living, since his removal from Baden-Baden, which took place in consequence of the Franco-Prussian war, in a large detached house on the hill of Montmartre, with his friends of many years, Madame Pauline Viardot and her husband, as his fellow-tenants. He occupied the upper floor, and I like to recall, for the sake of certain delightful talks, the aspect of his little green sitting-room, which has, in memory, the consecration of irrecoverable hours. It was almost entirely green, and the walls were not covered with paper, but draped in stuff. The *portières* were green, and there was one of those immense divans, so indispensable to Russians, which had apparently been fashioned for the great person of the master, so that smaller folk had to lie upon it rather than sit. I remember the white light of the Paris street, which came in through windows more or less blinded in their lower part, like those of a studio. It rested, during the first years that I went to see Turgénieff, upon

several choice pictures of the modern French school, especially
upon a very fine specimen of Théodore Rousseau, which he valued exceedingly. He had a great love of painting, and was an excellent critic of a picture. The last time I saw him—it was at his house
in the country—he showed me half a dozen large copies of Italian
works, made by a young Russian in whom he was interested, which
he had, with characteristic kindness, taken into his own apartments in order that he might bring them to the knowledge of his
friends. He thought them, as copies, remarkable; and they were
so, indeed, especially when one perceived that the original work of
the artist had little value. Turgénieff warmed to the work of praising them, as he was very apt to do; like all men of imagination he
had frequent and zealous admirations. As a matter of course there
was almost always some young Russian in whom he was interested,
and refugees and pilgrims of both sexes were his natural clients. I
have heard it said by persons who had known him long and well
that these enthusiasms sometimes led him into error, that he was
apt to *se monter la tête* on behalf of his protégés. He was prone to
believe that he had discovered the coming Russian genius; he
talked about his discovery for a month, and then suddenly one
heard no more of it. I remember his once telling me of a young
woman who had come to see him on her return from America,
where she had been studying obstetrics at some medical college,
and who, without means and without friends, was in want of help
and of work. He accidentally learned that she had written something, and asked her to let him see it. She sent it to him, and it
proved to be a tale in which certain phases of rural life were described with striking truthfulness. He perceived in the young lady
a great natural talent; he sent her story off to Russia to be printed,
with the conviction that it would make a great impression, and he
expressed the hope of being able to introduce her to French
readers. When I mentioned this to an old friend of Turgénieff he
smiled, and said that we should not hear of her again, that Ivan
Serguéitch had already discovered a great many surprising talents,
which, as a general thing, had not borne the test. There was apparently some truth in this, and Turgénieff's liability to be deceived was too generous a weakness for me to hesitate to allude

to it, even after I have insisted on the usual certainty of his taste. He was deeply interested in his young Russians; they were what interested him most in the world. They were almost always unhappy, in want and in rebellion against an order of things which he himself detested. The study of the Russian character absorbed and fascinated him, as all readers of his stories know. Rich, unformed, undeveloped, with all sorts of adumbrations, of qualities in a state of fusion, it stretched itself out as a mysterious expanse in which it was impossible as yet to perceive the relation between gifts and weaknesses. Of its weaknesses he was keenly conscious, and I once heard him express himself with an energy that did him honour and a frankness that even surprised me (considering that it was of his countrymen that he spoke), in regard to a weakness which he deemed the greatest of all—a weakness for which a man whose love of veracity was his strongest feeling would have least toleration. His young compatriots, seeking their fortune in foreign lands, touched his imagination and his pity, and it is easy to conceive that under the circumstances the impression they often made upon him may have had great intensity. The Parisian background, with its brilliant sameness, its absence of surprises (for those who have known it long), threw them into relief and made him see them as he saw the figures in his tales, in relations, in situations which brought them out. There passed before him in the course of time many wonderful Russian types. He told me once of his having been visited by a religious sect. The sect consisted of but two persons, one of whom was the object of worship and the other the worshipper. The divinity apparently was travelling about Europe in company with his prophet. They were intensely serious but it was very handy, as the term is, for each. The god had always his altar and the altar had (unlike some altars) always its god.

In his little green salon nothing was out of place; there were none of the odds and ends of the usual man of letters, which indeed Turgénieff was not; and the case was the same in his library at Bougival, of which I shall presently speak. Few books even were visible; it was as if everything had been put away. The traces of work had been carefully removed. An air of great comfort, an immeasurable divan and several valuable pictures—that was the effect of the place. I know not exactly at what hours Turgénieff did his work; I think he had no regular times and seasons, being in this respect as different as possible from Anthony Trollope, whose autobiography, with its candid revelation of intellectual economies, is so curious. It is my impression that in Paris Turgénieff wrote little; his times of production being rather those weeks of the summer that he spent at Bougival, and the period of that visit to Russia which he supposed himself to make every year. I say "supposed himself," because it was impossible to see much of him without discovering that he was a man of delays. As on the part of some other Russians whom I have known, there was something Asiatic in his faculty of procrastination. But even if one suffered from it a little one thought of it with kindness, as a part of his general mildness and want of rigidity. He went to Russia, at any rate, at intervals not infrequent, and he spoke of these visits as his best time for production. He had an estate far in the interior, and here, amid the stillness of the country and the scenes and figures which give such a charm to the *Memoirs of a Sportsman,* he drove his pen without interruption.

It is not out of place to allude to the fact that he possessed considerable fortune; this is too important in the life of a man of letters. It had been of great value to Turgénieff, and I think that much of the fine quality of his work is owing to it. He could write according to his taste and his mood; he was never pressed nor checked (putting the Russian censorship aside) by considerations foreign to his plan, and never was in danger of becoming a hack. Indeed, taking into consideration the absence of a pecuniary spur and that complicated indolence from which he was not exempt, his industry is surprising, for his tales are a long list. In Paris, at all events, he was always open to proposals for the midday breakfast. He liked to breakfast *au cabaret,* and freely consented to an appointment. It is not unkind to add that, at first, he never kept it. I may mention without reserve this idiosyncrasy of Turgénieff's, because in the first place it was so inveterate as to be very amusing—it amused not only his friends but himself; and in the second, he was as sure to come in the end as he was sure not to come in the beginning. After the appointment had been made or the invitation accepted, when the occasion was at hand, there arrived a note or a telegram in which Ivan Serguéitch excused himself, and begged that the meeting might be deferred to another date, which he usually himself proposed. For this second date still another was sometimes substituted; but if I remember no appointment that he exactly kept, I remember none that he completely missed. His friends waited for him frequently, but they never lost him. He was very fond of that wonderful Parisian *déjeûner*—fond of it I mean as a feast of reason. He was extremely temperate, and often ate no breakfast at all; but he found it a good hour for talk, and little, on general grounds, as one might be prepared to agree with him, if he was at the table one was speedily convinced. I call it wonderful, the *déjeûner* of Paris, on account of the assurance with which it plants itself in the very middle of the morning. It divides the day between rising and dinner so unequally, and opposes such barriers of repletion to any prospect of ulterior labours, that the unacclimated stranger wonders when the fertile French people do their work. Not the least wonderful part of it is that the stranger himself likes it, at last, and manages to piece together his day with the shattered fragments that survive. It was not, at any rate, when one had the good fortune to breakfast at twelve o'clock with Turgénieff that one was struck with its being an inconvenient hour. Any hour was convenient for meeting a human being who conformed so completely to one's idea of the best that human nature is capable of. There are places in Paris which I can think of only in relation to some occasion on which he was present, and when I pass them the particular things I heard him say there come back to me. There is a café in the Avenue de l'Opéra—a new, sumptuous establishment, with very deep settees, on the right as you leave the Boulevard—where I once had a talk with him, over an order singularly moderate, which was prolonged far into the afternoon, and in the course of which he was extraordinarily suggestive and interesting, so that my memory now reverts affectionately to all the circumstances. It evokes the grey damp of a Parisian December, which made the dark interior of the café look more and more rich and hospitable, while the light faded, the lamps

were lit, the habitués came in to drink absinthe and play their
afternoon game of dominoes, and we still lingered over our
morning meal. Turgénieff talked almost exclusively about Russia, the nihilists, the remarkable figures that came to light
among them, the curious visits he received, the dark prospects
of his native land. When he was in the vein, no man could speak
more to the imagination of his auditor. For myself, at least, at
such times, there was something extraordinarily vivifying and
stimulating in his talk, and I always left him in a state of "intimate" excitement, with a feeling that all sorts of valuable things
had been suggested to me; the condition in which a man swings
his cane as he walks, leaps lightly over gutters, and then stops,
for no reason at all, to look, with an air of being struck, into
a shop window where he sees nothing. I remember another
symposium, at a restaurant on one of the corners of the little
place in front of the Opéra Comique, where we were four, including Ivan Serguéitch, and the two other guests were also
Russian, one of them uniting to the charm of this nationality the
merit of a sex that makes the combination irresistible. The establishment had been a discovery of Turgénieff's—a discovery, at
least, as far as our particular needs were concerned—and I remember that we hardly congratulated him on it. The dinner, in
a low entresol, was not what it had been intended to be, but the
talk was better even than our expectations. It was not about
nihilism but about some more agreeable features of life, and I
have no recollection of Turgénieff in a mood more spontaneous
and charming. One of our friends had, when he spoke French,
a peculiar way of sounding the word *adorable,* which was frequently on his lips, and I remember well his expressive prolonga-
tion of the *a* when, in speaking of the occasion afterwards, he
applied this term to Ivan Serguéitch. I scarcely know, however,
why I should drop into the detail of such reminiscences, and
my excuse is but the desire that we all have, when a human relationship is closed, to save a little of it from the past—to make a
mark which may stand for some of the happy moments of it.

Nothing that Turgénieff had to say could be more interesting
than his talk about his own work, his manner of writing. What

I have heard him tell of these things was worthy of the beautiful results he produced; of the deep purpose, pervading them all, to show us life itself. The germ of a story, with him, was never an affair of plot—that was the last thing he thought of: it was the representation of certain persons. The first form in which a tale appeared to him was as the figure of an individual, or a combination of individuals, whom he wished to see in action, being sure that such people must do something very special and interesting. They stood before him definite, vivid, and he wished to know, and to show, as much as possible of their nature. The first thing was to make clear to himself what he did know, to begin with; and to this end, he wrote out a sort of biography of each of his characters, and everything that they had done and that had happened to them up to the opening of the story. He had their *dossier,* as the French say, and as the police has of that of every conspicuous criminal. With this material in his hand he was able to proceed; the story all lay in the question, What shall I make them do? He always made them do things that showed them completely; but, as he said, the defect of his manner and the reproach that was made him was his want of "architecture"—in other words, of composition. The great thing, of course, is to have architecture as well as precious material, as Walter Scott had them, as Balzac had them. If one reads Turgénieff's stories with the knowledge that they were composed—or rather that they came into being— in this way, one can trace the process in every line. Story, in the conventional sense of the word—a fable constructed, like Wordsworth's phantom, "to startle and waylay"—there is as little as possible. The thing consists of the motions of a group of selected creatures, which are not the result of a preconceived action, but a consequence of the qualities of the actors. Works of art are produced from every possible point of view, and stories, and very good ones, will continue to be written in which the evolution is that of a dance—a series of steps the more complicated and lively the better, of course, determined from without and forming a figure. This figure will always, probably, find favour with many readers, because it reminds them enough, without reminding them too much, of life. On this opposition many young talents in France are ready to rend each other, for there is a numerous school on either side. We have not yet in England and America arrived at the point of treating such questions with passion, for we have not yet arrived at the point of feeling them intensely, or indeed, for that matter, of understanding them very well. It is not open to us as yet to discuss whether a novel had better be an excision from life or a structure built up of picture-cards, for we have not made up our mind as to whether life in general may be described. There is evidence of a good deal of shyness on this point— a tendency rather to put up fences than to jump over them. Among us, therefore, even a certain ridicule attaches to the consideration of such alternatives. But individuals may feel their way, and perhaps even pass unchallenged, if they remark that for them the manner in which Turgénieff worked will always seem the most fruitful. It has the immense recommendation that in relation to any human occurrence it begins, as it were, further back. It lies in its power to tell us the most about men and women. Of course it will but slenderly satisfy those numerous readers among whom the answer to this would be, "Hang it, we don't care a straw about men and women: we want a good story!"

And yet, after all, *Elena* is a good story, and *Lisa* and *Virgin Soil* are good stories. Reading over lately several of Turgénieff's novels and tales, I was struck afresh with their combination of beauty and reality. One must never forget, in speaking of him, that he was both an observer and a poet. The poetic element was constant, and it had great strangeness and power. It inspired most of the short things that he wrote during the last few years of his life, since the publication of *Virgin Soil,* things that are in the highest degree fanciful and exotic. It pervades the frequent little reveries, visions, epigrams of the *Senilia.* It was no part of my intention, here, to criticize his writings, having said my say about them, so far as possible, some years ago. But I may mention that in rereading them I find in them all that I formerly found of two other elements—their richness and their sadness. They give one the impression of life itself, and not of an arrangement, a *réchauffé* of life. I remember Turgénieff's once saying in regard to Homais, the little Norman country apothecary, with his pedantry of "enlightened opinions," in *Madame Bovary,* that the great strength of such a portrait consisted in its being at once an individual, of the most concrete sort, and a type. This is the great strength of his own representations of character; they are so strangely, fascinatingly particular, and yet they are so recognizably general. Such a remark as that about Homais makes me wonder why it was that Turgénieff should have rated Dickens so high, the weakness of Dickens being in regard to just that point. If Dickens fails to live long, it will be because his figures are particular without being general; because they are individuals without being types; because we do not feel their continuity with the rest of humanity—see the matching of the pattern with the piece out of which all the creations of the novelist and the dramatist are cut. I often meant, but accidentally neglected, to put Turgénieff on the subject of Dickens again, and ask him to explain his opinion. I suspect that his opinion was in a large measure merely that Dickens diverted him, as well he might. That complexity of the pattern was in itself fascinating. I have mentioned Flaubert, and I will return to him simply to say that there was something very touching in the nature of the friendship that united these two men. It is much to the honour of Flaubert, to my sense, that he appreciated Ivan Turgénieff. There was a partial similarity between them. Both were large, massive men, though the Russian reached to a greater height than the Norman; both were completely honest and sincere, and both had the pessimistic element in their composition. Each had a tender regard for the other, and I think that I am neither incorrect nor indiscreet in saying that on Turgénieff's part this regard had in it a strain of compassion. There was something in Gustave Flaubert that appealed to such a feeling. He had failed, on the whole, more than he had succeeded, and the great machinery of erudition—the great polishing process—which he brought to bear upon his productions, was not accompanied with proportionate results. He had talent without having cleverness, and imagination without having fancy. His effort was heroic, but except in the case of *Madame Bovary,* a masterpiece, he imparted something to his works (it was as if he had covered them with metallic plates) which made

them sink rather than sail. He had a passion for perfection of form
and for a certain splendid suggestiveness of style. He wished to
produce perfect phrases, perfectly interrelated, and as closely
woven together as a suit of chain-mail. He looked at life altogether as an artist, and took his work with a seriousness that
never belied itself. To write an admirable page—and his idea of
what constituted an admirable page was transcendent—seemed
to him something to live for. He tried it again and again, and
he came very near it; more than once he touched it, for *Madame
Bovary* surely will live. But there was something ungenerous in
his genius. He was cold, and he would have given everything he
had to be able to glow. There is nothing in his novels like the passion of Elena for Inssaroff, like the purity of Lisa, like the anguish
of the parents of Bazaroff, like the hidden wound of Tatiana; and
yet Flaubert yearned, with all the accumulations of his vocabulary,
to touch the chord of pathos. There were some parts of his mind
that did not "give," that did not render a sound. He had had too
much of some sorts of experience and not enough of others. And
yet this failure of an organ, as I may call it, inspired those who
knew him with a kindness. If Flaubert was powerful and limited,
there is something human, after all, and even rather august in a
strong man who has not been able completely to express himself.

After the first year of my acquaintance with Turgénieff I saw
him much less often. I was seldom in Paris, and sometimes when
I was there he was absent. But I neglected no opportunity of seeing him, and fortune frequently assisted me. He came two or
three times to London, for visits provokingly brief. He went to
shoot in Cambridgeshire, and he passed through town in arriving
and departing. He liked the English, but I am not sure that he
liked London, where he had passed a lugubrious winter in 1870–71.
I remember some of his impressions of that period, especially
a visit that he had paid to a "bishopess" surrounded by her
daughters, and a description of the cookery at the lodgings which
he occupied. After 1876 I frequently saw him as an invalid. He
was tormented by gout, and sometimes terribly besieged; but his
account of what he suffered was as charming—I can apply no
other word to it—as his description of everything else. He had so

the habit of observation, that he perceived in excruciating sensations all sorts of curious images and analogies, and analysed them to an extraordinary fineness. Several times I found him at Bougival, above the Seine, in a very spacious and handsome chalet—a little unsunned, it is true—which he had built alongside of the villa occupied by the family to which, for years, his life had been devoted. The place is delightful; the two houses are midway up a long slope, which descends, with the softest inclination, to the river, and behind them the hill rises to a wooded crest. On the left, in the distance, high up and above an horizon of woods, stretches the romantic aqueduct of Marly. It is a very pretty domain. The last time I saw him, in November 1882, it was at Bougival. He had been very ill, with strange, intolerable symptoms, but he was better, and he had good hopes. They were not justified by the event. He got worse again, and the months that followed were cruel. His beautiful serene mind should not have been darkened and made acquainted with violence; it should have been able to the last to take part, as it had always done, in the decrees and mysteries of fate. At the moment I saw him, however, he was, as they say in London, in very good form, and my last impression of him was almost bright. He was to drive into Paris, not being able to bear the railway, and he gave me a seat in the carriage. For an hour and a half he constantly talked, and never better. When we got into the city I alighted on the boulevard extérieur, as we were to go in different directions. I bade him good-bye at the carriage window and never saw him again. There was a kind of fair going on, near by, in the chill November air, beneath the denuded little trees of the Boulevard, and a Punch and Judy show, from which nasal sounds proceeded. I almost regret having accidentally to mix up so much of Paris with this perhaps too complacent enumeration of occasions, for the effect of it may be to suggest that Ivan Turgénieff had been Gallicized. But this was not the case; the French capital was an accident for him, not a necessity. It touched him at many points, but it let him alone at many others, and he had, with that great tradition of ventilation of the Russian mind, windows open into distances which stretched far beyond the *banlieue*. I have spoken of him from the limited point of view of my own acquaintance with him, and unfortunately left myself little space to allude to a matter which filled his existence a good deal more than the consideration of how a story should be written —his hopes and fears on behalf of his native land. He wrote fictions and dramas, but the great drama of his life was the struggle for a better state of things in Russia. In this drama he played a distinguished part, and the splendid obsequies that, simple and modest as he was, have unfolded themselves over his grave, sufficiently attest the recognition of it by his countrymen. His funeral, restricted and officialized, was none the less a magnificent "manifestation." I have read the accounts of it, however, with a kind of chill, a feeling in which assent to the honours paid him bore less part than it ought. All this pomp and ceremony seemed to lift him out of the range of familiar recollection, of valued reciprocity, into the majestic position of a national glory. And yet it is in the presence of this obstacle to social contact that those who knew and loved him must address their farewell to him now. After all, it is difficult to see how the obstacle can be removed. He was the most generous, the most tender, the most delightful, of men; his large nature overflowed with the love of justice: but he also was of the stuff of which glories are made.

From *Partial Portraits*, 1888.

The Aeroplanes at Brescia

by FRANZ KAFKA [1883-1924]

LA SENTINELLA BRESCIANA of September 9, 1909, announces with delight: "In Brescia we have a throng of people such as we have never had before, not even at the time of the great automobile races; visitors from Venice, Liguria, Piedmont, Tuscany, Rome, even from as far away as Naples; indeed, the big men of France, England, and America are crowding our squares, our hotels, every nook and corner of our private houses: all prices are rising splendidly; the means of transport are insufficient to carry the crowds to the *'circuito aerio';* the restaurants at the aerodrome can serve two thousand people excellently, confronted with several thousand they could not but break down. The militia was needed to protect the buffets. In the cheap places fifty thousand people are standing the whole day."

As my two friends and I read this news we were filled with courage and fear simultaneously. Courage, because where there are such fearful crowds, things are generally done in a beautifully democratic way, and where there is no room, one needn't look for it. Fear—fear of the way Italians organize such undertakings; fear of the committee that will take us in hand; fear of the journey by trains of which the *Sentinella* proudly boasts that they are four hours late. All expectations are false, all one's memories of Italy get completely mixed up with each other as soon as we get back home; they fade, and we cannot rely on them.

As we drive into the black hole of the station at Brescia, where people are screaming as if the ground were on fire under their feet, we are still earnestly warning each other that whatever happens we must stick together. Aren't we going with a kind of hostility?

We get out; a carriage that hardly manages to stay on its wheels accepts us; the driver is in a very good temper; we drive through almost empty streets up to the palace of the committee, where they overlook our inward wickedness, as if it were not there; we find out everything we need to know. The inn we are directed to seems to us at first sight to be the dirtiest we have ever seen, but after a while it is not at all so exaggeratedly bad. It is dirt which is just there, that's all, and about which no more is said; dirt which will never change any more, which has made itself at home, which in a certain sense makes life more tangible, more earthly; dirt out of which our host hurries forth, proud towards himself, humble towards us, continually stroking his elbows, and casting new and ever new shadows on his face with his hands—every finger is a compliment—bowing from the waist all the time in a way we recognize later at the aerodrome, in Gabriele d'Annunzio, for instance. Who, one must ask, could still have anything on his mind against this dirt?

The aerodrome is at Montechiari, and can be reached in a bare hour by the local line that goes to Mantua. This local line has reserved itself a length of rail along the general highway, on which it lets its trains travel with all modesty neither higher nor lower than the rest of the traffic, between the cyclists who ride into the dust with their eyes almost closed, between the completely unusable carriages from the whole province—which pick up as many passengers as you like, and are besides so quick, you can't believe it —and between the motorcars which are often huge, and which, given their head, are deliberately trying to run into each other at every moment, with their manifold hootings which, at the speed, have become one noise. At times one gives up hope altogether of ever coming to the *circuito* with this wretched train. But people are laughing all around you, and to the right and to the left people are laughing into the train. I am standing on a platform, squeezed up against an enormous man who is standing with his legs stretched wide apart over the buffers of two carriages, in a shower of soot and dust that falls from the roofs of the gently shaking carriages. Twice the train stops and waits for a train coming in the opposite direction, as long and as patiently as if it were waiting only for a chance meeting. A few villages pass slowly by, wild posters announcing the last automobile race appear on the walls here and there, all growth on the side of the road is unrecognizable under the olive-leaf color of the white dust. At last the train stops, because it can't go any farther. A group of cars put their brakes on at the same moment, through the clouds of dust that arise we see not far away a lot of little flags; a herd of cattle which has got out of all control, swaying on the bumpy ground and deliberately charging the automobiles, holds us up still.

We have arrived. In front of the aerodrome lies a great square with suspicious-looking little wooden houses, on which we should have expected to see quite different things written up than, "Garage," "Grand Buffet International" and so on. Enormous beggars grown fat in their little gocarts stretch their arms out across one's path, one is tempted in one's haste to leap over them. We catch up with a lot of people, a lot of people catch up with us. We look up, at the sky, which is, after all, the thing that matters here. Thank God, nobody is flying! We refuse to get out of the way and yet we are not run over. Between and behind, and advancing to meet the thousands of vehicles, plunges the Italian cavalry. Order and accidents seem equally impossible.

Once, in Brescia, late in the evening, we wanted to get to a certain street in a hurry and we thought it was rather far. A cab driver wanted three liras, we offered two. The driver wouldn't take us, and only out of friendliness, described to us how frightfully far this street really was. We began to be ashamed of our offer. All right, three liras. We got in, the cab made three turns through short streets; we were there. Otto, more energetic than we two, explained that he had no intention, of course, of paying three liras for a journey that took one minute. One lira was more than enough. There was a lira. It was already night, the little street was empty, the cabby was strong. He flew into a passion immediately, as though the quarrel had been going on for an hour already. What?—That was swindling. What were we thinking of, then? Three liras was the bargain, three liras we must pay. Out with the three liras, or we should be surprised. . . . OTTO: "The tariff or the police!" Tariff? There wasn't any tariff. How should there be a tariff for things like that! It was a special price for a night fare, but if we would give him two liras he would let us go. OTTO, enough to scare anybody: "The tariff or the police!" A little more shouting and searching, then a tariff was produced, on which nothing was to be seen but dirt. So we agreed on one lira fifty, and the cabby went off down the narrow street in which he could not turn, not only raging, but also saddened as I can't help thinking. For our behavior was, alas, not the right behavior; one doesn't behave that way in Italy. In other countries that may be all right, but not here. Well, who thinks of all that when he is in a hurry! There is nothing to complain about in that, one can't become an Italian in a short week's holiday tour.

But repentance shall not spoil our pleasure at the aerodrome, that would only give ground for fresh repentance, and we jump into the aerodrome rather than walk, in this enthusiasm of all our limbs which sometimes suddenly seizes us, one after the other, in this country, under this sun.

We pass the hangars, which, with their curtains drawn, look like the closed-up stages of a touring dramatic company. On their pediments are written the names of the aviators whose machines they house, and over that fly the colors of their countries. We read the names of Cobianchi, Cagno, Rougier, Curtiss, Moucher (a "Tridentiner" flying Italian colors, he trusts them more than he does ours), Anzani, the Club of Roman Aviators. *And Blériot?* we ask. Blériot, of whom we have been thinking all the time, where is Blériot?

In the fenced-in ground in front of his hangar, Rougier, a little man with a conspicuous nose, is dashing about in his shirt sleeves. He is extremely, if somewhat obscurely, busy, he waves his arms about, his hands in violent gesticulation, feels himself all over as he walks, sends his workmen behind the curtain of his hangar, calls them back, goes in himself, thrusting them all on one side, while his wife stands to one side in a tight, white dress, a little black hat pressed firmly into her hair, her legs under a short skirt, gently outstretched, she is gazing into the empty heat, a business woman, with all the cares of business in her little head.

In front of the next hangar Curtiss is sitting all alone. Through the curtains, slightly drawn back, his machine can be seen; it is bigger than we had heard. As we were passing, Curtiss was holding up the *New York Herald* in front of him, and reading a line on the top of a page. After half an hour we pass him again, he has already got to the middle of this page; another half an hour and he has finished the page and begun another. Obviously he is not going to fly today. We turn and look at the broad field. It is so big that everything on it looks forlorn: the guide posts near us, the signaling mast in the distance, the catapult for starting somewhere to the right, a committee car, that, with little yellow flags fluttering in the wind, describes a curve about the field, stops in its own dust, and then goes on again. An artificial desert has been created here in an almost tropical land, and the aristocracy of Italy, sparkling ladies from Paris, and all the other thousands of people are here to look at this sunny desert with harrowed eyes for many hours. In this place there is none of the distractions that are otherwise provided on other sports fields. One misses the beautiful hurdles of the racecourse, the white lines of the tennis court, the fresh green meadow of the football ground, the stony up-and-down of the automobile and cycle tracks. Only two or three times during the afternoon a troop of colorful horsemen rides straight across the plain. The horses' hoofs are invisible in the dust, the steady light of the sun doesn't change until about five o'clock in the afternoon. And, that nothing may disturb the view of this plain, there is also no music at all, only the whistling of the crowds in the cheap places tries to meet the demands of the ear and of impatience. From the expensive, tall grandstands which stand behind us, all this crowd, it is true, probably melts into the empty plain without any difference.

On one side of the wooden fence a lot of people are standing together. "How tiny," a group of Frenchmen cries, like a sigh. What's the matter then? We push our way through. But look, here there is indeed, on the field, quite near, with real yellow coloring, a small flying machine that they are getting ready for flight. Now, too, we see Blériot's hangar, and next it that of his pupil Leblanc; they have been built on the flying ground itself. Standing, leaning against one of the two wings of his machine is Blériot, whom we immediately recognize, with his head set firmly on his shoulders, watching the fingers of his mechanics as they work at the engine.

Is he going to go up in the air in this tiny thing? Then people on the water, for instance, have an easier job after all. They can practice in puddles first, then in ponds, and not venture out to sea until much later, for this man there is only the sea.

Blériot is in his seat already, holding some kind of lever in his hand, but he lets his mechanics do their best, as if they were over-diligent children. He looks slowly over in our direction, looks away from us and again in another direction, but keeps his look to himself always. He is going to fly now, nothing is more natural. This feeling of naturalness, with the simultaneous, general feeling of the extraordinary that cannot be withheld from him, lends him this attitude.

A workman grasps one of the blades of the screw, in order to
turn it, tugs at it, it gives a jerk, too; one hears something like the
gasp of a strong man in his sleep, but the screw doesn't move any
farther. Once again they try, ten times they try, sometimes the
screw stops immediately, sometimes it lets itself go round for a few
turns. It's the fault of the engine. Work is begun on it afresh, the
onlookers get more tired than those who are taking close part.
The engine is oiled on every side, hidden screws are loosened and
tightened up; one man runs into the hangar and brings out a spare
part; that doesn't fit again; he hurries back, and sitting on his
haunches on the floor of the hangar, he holds it between his knees,
and hammers away at it. Blériot changes his seat with a mechanic,
the mechanic with Leblanc. Now this man, now that, tugs away
at the screw. But the engine is intractable. Like a schoolboy one
always helps, the whole class prompts him; no, he doesn't know it,
he stops again and again, he breaks down. For a while Blériot sits
quite still in his seat: his six assistant workers stand round him
without moving, they all seem to be dreaming.

The onlookers can breathe again, and look around. The young
Mrs. Blériot passes by with a motherly face, two children behind
her. If her husband can't fly, that does not suit her, and if he flies,
she is afraid; moreover her lovely dress is a little heavy for this
temperature.

Once again the screw is given a turn, perhaps a better one than
before, perhaps just the same. The engine comes to life with a
roar, as if it were a different thing; four men hold the machine
from behind and in the middle of the complete calm all around,
the gusts from the swinging screw go in thrusts through the over-
alls of these men. One doesn't hear a word, only the noise of the
screw seems to give orders, eight hands release the machine, which
rolls a long way over the waving ground like a clumsy man on
a polished floor.

Many such attempts are made, and all of them end without result. Each one sends the public rushing up to the bundles of hay
on which one stretches one's arms out partly to keep one's balance,
and partly to express hope, fear, and joy. In the intervals, however,

the Italian aristocracy walks along the grandstands. They say good day to each other, bow, recognize each other once again, they embrace each other, they walk up and down the gangways of the grandstand. People point out to each other Princess Laetitia Savoia Bonaparte, Princess Borghese, an elderly woman whose face is the color of dark yellow grapes, Countess Morosini. Marcello Borghese is in every lady's company and no lady's company; from a distance he seems to have an understanding face, but when you get close to him, his cheeks overlap the corners of his mouth in the oddest way. Gabriele d'Annunzio, short and weakly, dances attendance, apparently shyly, before Count Oldofredi, one of the most important men on the committee. Over the railings of the stand peers the strong face of Puccini, with a nose that one might well call a drinker's nose.

But you see these people only if you look for them. Otherwise one sees everywhere, depreciating everything, the tall ladies of the present fashion! They prefer walking to sitting, in their clothes sitting doesn't go very easily. All their faces, veiled like Asiatics, are borne in a faint twilight; the dress, loose on the bust, gives the whole figure a kind of fainthearted appearance; a kind of mixed, restless feeling overcomes one when such ladies look fainthearted. The bodice is low-cut, one can hardly reach it; the waist seems broader than usual because everything else is narrow; these women want to be embraced lower down.

It was only Leblanc's machine that had been shown so far. But now comes the machine in which Blériot flew over the Channel; nobody says so, everybody knows it. A long pause, and Blériot is in the air. One sees his straight body over the wings, his legs are stretched down like a part of the engine. The sun is sinking, and under the baldachin of the grandstands, throws its light on the hovering wings. Devotedly everybody looks up to him, there is no room in anybody's heart for anyone else. And everybody looks with outstretched neck at the monoplane, as it falls, is seized by Blériot, and even climbs. What is happening? Here, above us, there is a man twenty meters above the earth, imprisoned in a wooden box, and pitting his strength against an invisible danger which he has taken on of his own free will. But we are standing below, thrust right back out of the way, without existence, and looking at this man.

Everything goes well, the signaling mast at the same time shows that the wind has got more favorable, and that Curtiss is going to fly for the Grand Prix of Brescia. Is he really going to, after all? One has hardly finished finding out whether he is or not when Curtiss's engine roars, and one has hardly had time to look at it before he is flying away from us, flying over the plains that widen in front of him, towards the woods in the distance that seem to be rising out of the ground for the first time. His flight extends far over these woods; he disappears from sight; we are gazing at the woods, not at him. From behind some houses, God knows where, he comes out at the same height as before, and races towards us; when he climbs, you can see the undersurfaces of his biplane dipping darkly; when he descends, the upper surfaces glisten in the sun. He makes a turn round the signal mast and, indifferent to the roars of welcome, turns straight back to where he has come from, only to become speedily tiny and lonely again. He does five rounds like this, flies fifty kilometers in forty-nine minutes twenty-four seconds, and so wins the Grand Prix of Brescia—30,000 liras. It is a perfect achievement; but perfect achievements cannot be appreciated; everyone, when you come to think of it, thinks he is capable of a perfect achievement, no courage seems to be needed for perfect achievements. And while Curtiss is working all on his own there above the woods, while his wife, whom everybody knows, is worried about him the crowd has almost forgotten him. All one hears on every side is complaining because Calderara is not going to fly—his machine was smashed; Rougier has been tinkering about with his Voisin for two whole days without letting go of it; and *Zodiac,* the Italian navigable balloon, has not yet arrived. The rumors running around about Calderara's accident are so full of his glory that one is ready to believe the love of the nation would raise him into the air more securely than his Wright.

Curtiss had not yet finished his flight before the engines in three hangars were tuning up, as if out of enthusiasm. Wind and dust are driven together from opposite directions. One pair of eyes is not enough. One twists and turns in one's seat, loses one's balance, clutches somebody or other firmly, apologizes; somebody or other loses his balance, drags somebody else after him, is thanked. The early evening of the Italian autumn is beginning; it is impossible to see everything clearly in the field any longer.

Just as Curtiss passes over us after his winning flight, and takes his cap off with a slight smile without looking at us, Blériot begins a little round trip which everybody is immediately confident will be successful. Now, one doesn't know whether one is applauding Curtiss or Blériot, whose big heavy machine is now hurling itself into the air. Rougier sits at his levers like a great man at a writing desk which one climbs up to by a couple of steps behind his back. He climbs in small circles, flies above Blériot, turns him into an onlooker, and continues to climb without stopping.

If we want to get a carriage back again, it is high time to get going; there are already a lot of people pushing past us. One knows, of course, that this is only a trial flight; as it is already getting on to seven, it would not be counted officially any longer. In the approach to the aerodrome the chauffeurs and attendants are standing on their seats and pointing to Rougier; on Rougier's account three trains crowded to the last buffers refuse to move. We are lucky enough to get a carriage; the coachman squats down in front of us—there is no box—and, having at last become independent existences once more, we set off. Max very rightly remarks that one could and should arrange something of this kind in Prague too. It wouldn't have to be a prize race, he thought, although that would also be worth while, but to invite an airman would certainly be an easy matter after all, and none of the participants would have any grounds for regrets. The thing would be so simple, in fact; Wright was now flying in Berlin; all you would have to do, then, would be to persuade the people to come a little out of their way. We two others didn't answer a word, first of all because we were tired, and secondly because we had no objections anyway. The road turned, and Rougier appeared, so high in the air that one thought that soon his course would have to be determined only by the stars that were soon about to shine in the sky, which had already grown dark. We couldn't stop turning round; Rougier was still climbing straight up, but our way led with finality deeper into the Campagna.

First appeared in a Prague   Translated by
newspaper, *Bohemia*, 1909.   G. HUMPHREYS ROBERTS

Chicago

by RUDYARD KIPLING [1865-1936]

> I know thy cunning and thy greed,
> Thy hard high lust and wilful deed,
> And all thy glory loves to tell
> Of specious gifts material.

I HAVE STRUCK a city—a real city—and they call it Chicago.

The other places do not count. San Francisco was a pleasure-resort as well as a city, and Salt Lake was a phenomenon.

This place is the first American city I have encountered. It holds rather more than a million of people with bodies, and stands on the same sort of soil as Calcutta. Having seen it, I urgently desire never to see it again. It is inhabited by savages. Its water is the water of the Hooghly, and its air is dirt. Also it says that it is the "boss" town of America.

I do not believe that it has anything to do with this country. They told me to go to the Palmer House, which is overmuch gilded and mirrored, and there I found a huge hall of tessellated marble crammed with people talking about money, and spitting about everywhere. Other barbarians charged in and out of this inferno with letters and telegrams in their hands, and yet others shouted at each other. A man who had drunk quite as much as was good for him told me that this was "the finest hotel in the finest city on God Almighty's earth." By the way, when an American wishes to indicate the next country or state, he says, "God A'mighty's earth." This prevents discussion and flatters his vanity.

Then I went out into the streets, which are long and flat and without end. And verily it is not a good thing to live in the East for any length of time. Your ideas grow to clash with those held by every right-thinking man. I looked down interminable vistas flanked with nine, ten, and fifteen-storied houses, and crowded with men and women, and the show impressed me with a great horror.

Except in London—and I have forgotten what London was like—I had never seen so many white people together, and never such a collection of miserables. There was no color in the street and no beauty—only a maze of wire ropes overhead and dirty stone flagging under foot.

A cab-driver volunteered to show me the glory of the town for so much an hour, and with him I wandered far. He conceived that all this turmoil and squash was a thing to be reverently admired, that it was good to huddle men together in fifteen layers, one atop of the other, and to dig holes in the ground for offices.

He said that Chicago was a live town, and that all the creatures hurrying by me were engaged in business. That is to say they were trying to make some money that they might not die through lack of food to put into their bellies. He took me to canals as black as ink, and filled with untold abominations, and bid me watch the stream of traffic across the bridges.

He then took me into a saloon, and while I drank made me note that the floor was covered with coins sunk in cement. A Hottentot would not have been guilty of this sort of barbarism. The coins made an effect pretty enough, but the man who put them there had no thought of beauty, and, therefore, he was a savage.

Then my cab-driver showed me business blocks gay with signs and studded with fantastic and absurd advertisements of goods, and looking down the long street so adorned, it was as though each vender stood at his door howling:

"For the sake of money, employ or buy of me, and me only!"

Have you ever seen a crowd at a famine-relief distribution? You know then how the men leap into the air, stretching out their arms above the crowd in the hope of being seen, while the women dolorously slap the stomachs of their children and whimper. I had sooner watch famine relief than the white man engaged in what he calls legitimate competition. The one I understand. The other makes me ill.

And the cabman said that these things were the proof of progress, and by that I knew he had been reading his newspaper, as every intelligent American should. The papers tell their *clientèle* in language fitted to their comprehension that the snarling together of telegraph-wires, the heaving up of houses, and the making of money is progress.

I spent ten hours in that huge wilderness, wandering through scores of miles of these terrible streets and jostling some few hundred thousand of these terrible people who talked *paisa bat* through their noses.

The cabman left me; but after awhile I picked up another man, who was full of figures, and into my ears he poured them as occasion required or the big blank factories suggested. Here they turned out so many hundred thousand dollars' worth of such and such an article; there so many million other things; this house was worth so many million dollars; that one so many million, more or less. It was like listening to a child babbling of its hoard of shells. It was like watching a fool playing with buttons. But I was expected to do more than listen or watch. He demanded that I should admire; and the utmost that I could say was:

"Are these things so? Then I am very sorry for you."

That made him angry, and he said that insular envy made me unresponsive. So, you see, I could not make him understand.

About four and a half hours after Adam was turned out of the Garden of Eden he felt hungry, and so, bidding Eve take care that her head was not broken by the descending fruit, shinned up a cocoanut-palm. That hurt his legs, cut his breast, and made him breathe heavily, and Eve was tormented with fear lest her lord should miss his footing, and so bring the tragedy of this world to an end ere the curtain had fairly risen. Had I met Adam then, I should have been sorry for him. To-day I find eleven hundred thousand of his sons just as far advanced as their father in the art of getting food, and immeasurably inferior to him in that they think that their palm-trees lead straight to the skies. Consequently, I am sorry in rather more than a million different ways.

In the East bread comes naturally, even to the poorest, by a little scratching or the gift of a friend not quite so poor. In less favored countries one is apt to forget. Then I went to bed. And that was on a Saturday night.

Sunday brought me the queerest experiences of all—a revelation of barbarism complete. I found a place that was officially described as a church. It was a circus really, but that the worshippers did not know. There were flowers all about the building, which was fitted up with plush and stained oak and much luxury, including twisted brass candlesticks of severest Gothic design.

To these things and a congregation of savages entered suddenly a wonderful man, completely in the confidence of their God, whom he treated colloquially and exploited very much as a newspaper reporter would exploit a foreign potentate. But, unlike the newspaper reporter, he never allowed his listeners to forget that he, and not He, was the centre of attraction. With a voice of silver and with imagery borrowed from the auction-room, he built up for his hearers a heaven on the lines of the Palmer House (but with all the gilding real gold, and all the plate-glass diamond), and set in the centre of it a loud-voiced, argumentative, very shrewd creation that he called God. One sentence at this point caught my delighted ear. It was apropos of some question of the Judgment, and ran:

"No! I tell you God doesn't do business that way."

He was giving them a deity whom they could comprehend, and a gold and jewelled heaven in which they could take a natural interest. He interlarded his performance with the slang of the streets, the counter, and the exchange, and he said that religion ought to enter into daily life. Consequently, I presume he introduced it as daily life—his own and the life of his friends.

Then I escaped before the blessing, desiring no benediction

at such hands. But the persons who listened seemed to enjoy themselves, and I understood that I had met with a popular preacher.

Later on, when I had perused the sermons of a gentleman called Talmage and some others, I perceived that I had been listening to a very mild specimen. Yet that man, with his brutal gold and silver idols, his hands-in-pocket, cigar-in-mouth, and hat-on-the-back-of-the-head style of dealing with the sacred vessels, would count himself, spiritually, quite competent to send a mission to convert the Indians.

All that Sunday I listened to people who said that the mere fact of spiking down strips of iron to wood, and getting a steam and iron thing to run along them was progress, that the telephone was progress, and the net-work of wires overhead was progress. They repeated their statements again and again.

One of them took me to their City Hall and Board of Trade works, and pointed it out with pride. It was very ugly, but very big, and the streets in front of it were narrow and unclean. When I saw the faces of the men who did business in that building, I felt that there had been a mistake in their billeting.

By the way, 'tis a consolation to feel that I am not writing to an English audience. Then I should have to fall into feigned ecstasies over the marvellous progress of Chicago since the days of the great fire, to allude casually to the raising of the entire city so many feet above the level of the lake which it faces, and generally to grovel before the golden calf. But you, who are desperately poor, and therefore by these standards of no account, know things, will understand when I write that they have managed to get a million of men together on flat land, and that the bulk of these men together appear to be lower than Mahajans and not so companionable as a Punjabi Jat after harvest.

But I don't think it was the blind hurry of the people, their *argot,* and their grand ignorance of things beyond their immediate interests that displeased me so much as a study of the daily papers of Chicago.

Imprimis, there was some sort of a dispute between New York and Chicago as to which town should give an exhibition of products to be hereafter holden, and through the medium of their more dignified journals the two cities were yahooing and hi-yi-ing at each other like opposition newsboys. They called it humor, but it sounded like something quite different.

That was only the first trouble. The second lay in the tone of the productions. Leading articles which include gems such as "Back of such and such a place," or, "We noticed, Tuesday, such an event," or, "don't" for "does not," are things to be accepted with thankfulness. All that made me want to cry was that in these papers were faithfully reproduced all the war-cries and "back-talk" of the Palmer House bar, the slang of the barber-shops, the mental elevation and integrity of the Pullman car porter, the dignity of the dime museum, and the accuracy of the excited fish-wife. I am sternly forbidden to believe that the paper educates the public. Then I am compelled to believe that the public educate the paper; yet suicides on the press are rare.

Just when the sense of unreality and oppression was strongest upon me, and when I most wanted to help, a man sat at my side and began to talk what he called politics.

I had chanced to pay about six shillings for a travelling-cap worth eighteen-pence, and he made of the fact a text for a sermon. He said that this was a rich country, and that the people liked to pay two hundred per cent on the value of a thing. They could afford it. He said that the government imposed a protective duty of from ten to seventy per cent on foreign-made articles, and that the American manufacturer consequently could sell his goods for a healthy sum. Thus an imported hat would, with duty, cost two guineas. The American manufacturer would make a hat for seventeen shillings, and sell it for one pound fifteen. In these things, he said, lay the greatness of America and the effeteness of England. Competition between factory and factory kept the prices down to decent limits, but I was never to forget that this people were a rich people, not like the pauper Continentals, and that they enjoyed paying duties.

To my weak intellect this seemed rather like juggling with

counters. Everything that I have yet purchased costs about twice as much as it would in England, and when native made is of inferior quality.

Moreover, since these lines were first thought of, I have visited a gentleman who owned a factory which used to produce things. He owned the factory still. Not a man was in it, but he was drawing a handsome income from a syndicate of firms for keeping it closed, in order that it might not produce things. This man said that if protection were abandoned, a tide of pauper labor would flood the country, and as I looked at his factory I thought how entirely better it was to have no labor of any kind whatever rather than face so horrible a future.

Meantime, do you remember that this peculiar country enjoys paying money for value not received? I am an alien, and for the life of me I cannot see why six shillings should be paid for eighteen-penny caps, or eight shillings for half-crown cigar-cases. When the country fills up to a decently populated level a few million people who are not aliens will be smitten with the same sort of blindness.

But my friend's assertion somehow thoroughly suited the grotesque ferocity of Chicago.

See now and judge! In the village of Isser Jang, on the road to Montgomery, there be four Changar women who winnow corn —some seventy bushels a year. Beyond their hut lives Purun Dass, the money-lender, who on good security lends as much as five thousand rupees in a year. Jowala Singh, the smith, mends the village plows—some thirty, broken at the share, in three hundred and sixty-five days; and Hukm Chund, who is letter-writer and head of the little club under the travellers' tree, generally keeps the village posted in such gossip as the barber and the midwife have not yet made public property.

Chicago husks and winnows her wheat by the million bushels, a hundred banks lend hundreds of millions of dollars in the year, and scores of factories turn out plow-gear and machinery by steam. Scores of daily papers do work which Hukm Chund and the barber and the midwife perform, with due regard for public opinion, in the village of Isser Jang. So far as manufactories go, the difference between Chicago on the lake, and Isser Jang on the Montgomery road, is one of degree only, and not of kind. As far as the understanding of the uses of life goes, Isser Jang, for all its seasonal cholers, has the advantage over Chicago.

Jowala Singh knows and takes care to avoid the three or four ghoul-haunted fields on the outskirts of the village; but he is not urged by millions of devils to run about all day in the sun and swear that his plowshares are the best in the Punjab; nor does Purun Dass fly forth in an ekka more than once or twice a year, and he knows, on a pinch, how to use the railway and the telegraph as well as any son of Israel in Chicago. But this is absurd.

The East is not the West, and these men must continue to deal with the machinery of life, and to call it progress. Their very preachers dare not rebuke them. They gloss over the hunting for money and the thrice-sharpened bitterness of Adam's curse, by saying that such things dower a man with a larger range of thoughts and higher aspirations. They do not say, "Free yourselves from your own slavery," but rather, "If you can possibly manage it, do not set quite so much store on the things of this world."

And they do not know what the things of this world are!

I went off to see cattle killed, by way of clearing my head, which, as you will perceive, was getting muddled. They say every Englishman goes to the Chicago stock-yards. You shall find them about six miles from the city; and once having seen them, you will never forget the sight.

As far as the eye can reach stretches a township of cattle-pens, cunningly divided into blocks, so that the animals of any pen can be speedily driven out close to an inclined timber path which leads to an elevated covered way straddling high above the pens. These viaducts are two-storied. On the upper story tramp the doomed cattle, stolidly for the most part. On the lower, with a scuffling of sharp hoofs and multitudinous yells, run the pigs, the same end being appointed for each. Thus you will see the gangs of cattle waiting their turn—as they wait sometimes for days; and they need not be distressed by the sight of their fellows running about in the fear of death. All they know is that a man on horseback causes their next-door neighbors to move by means of a whip. Certain bars and fences are unshipped, and behold! that crowd have gone up the mouth of a sloping tunnel and return no more.

It is different with the pigs. They shriek back the news of the exodus to their friends, and a hundred pens skirl responsive.

It was to the pigs I first addressed myself. Selecting a viaduct which was full of them, as I could hear, though I could not see, I marked a sombre building whereto it ran, and went there, not unalarmed by stray cattle who had managed to escape from their proper quarters. A pleasant smell of brine warned me of what was coming. I entered the factory and found it full of pork in barrels, and on another story more pork unbarrelled, and in a huge room the halves of swine, for whose behoof great lumps of ice were being pitched in at the window. That room was the mortuary chamber where the pigs lay for a little while in state ere they began their progress through such passages as kings may sometimes travel.

Turning a corner, and not noting an overhead arrangement of greased rail, wheel, and pulley, I ran into the arms of four eviscerated carcasses, all pure white and of a human aspect, pushed by a man clad in vehement red. When I leaped aside, the floor was slippery under me. Also there was a flavor of farm-yard in my nostrils and the shouting of a multitude in my ears. But there was no joy in that shouting. Twelve men stood in two lines six a side. Between them and overhead ran the railway of death that had nearly shunted me through the window. Each man carried a knife, the sleeves of his shirt were cut off at the elbows, and from bosom to heel he was blood-red.

Beyond this perspective was a column of steam, and beyond that was where I worked my awe-struck way, unwilling to touch beam or wall. The atmosphere was stifling as a night in the rains by reason of the steam and the crowd. I climbed to the beginning of things and, perched upon a narrow beam, overlooked very nearly all the pigs ever bred in Wisconsin. They had just been shot out of the mouth of the viaduct and huddled together in a large pen. Thence they were flicked persuasively, a few at a time, into a smaller chamber, and there a man fixed tackle on their hinder legs, so that they rose in the air, suspended from the railway of death.

Oh! it was then they shrieked and called on their mothers, and made promises of amendment, till the tackle-man punted them in their backs and they slid head down into a brick-floored passage, very like a big kitchen sink, that was blood-red. There awaited them a red man with a knife, which he passed jauntily through their throats, and the full-voiced shriek became a splutter, and then a fall as of heavy tropical rain, and the red man, who was backed against the passage-wall, you will understand, stood clear of the wildly kicking hoofs and passed his hand over his eyes, not from any feeling of compassion, but because the spurted blood was in his eyes, and he had barely time to stick the next arrival. Then that first stuck swine dropped, still kicking, into a great vat of boiling water, and spoke no more words, but wallowed in obedience to some unseen machinery, and presently came forth at the lower end of the vat, and was heaved on the blades of a blunt paddle-wheel, things which said "Hough, hough, hough!" and skelped all the hair off him, except what little a couple of men with knives could remove.

Then he was again hitched by the heels to that said railway, and passed down the line of the twelve men, each man with a knife—losing with each man a certain amount of his individuality, which was taken away in a wheel-barrow, and when he reached the last man he was very beautiful to behold, but excessively unstuffed and limp. Preponderance of individuality was ever a bar to foreign travel. That pig could have been in case to visit you in India had he not parted with some of his most cherished notions.

The dissecting part impressed me not so much as the slaying. They were so excessively alive, these pigs. And then, they were so excessively dead, and the man in the dripping, clammy, hot passage did not seem to care, and ere the blood of such a one had ceased to foam on the floor, such another and four friends with him had shrieked and died. But a pig is only the unclean animal—the forbidden of the prophet.

From *American Notes,* 1891.

Market Day

by D. H. LAWRENCE [1885-1930]

THIS IS THE LAST Saturday before Christmas. The next year will be momentous, one feels. This year is nearly gone. Dawn was windy, shaking the leaves, and the rising sun shone under a gap of yellow cloud. But at once it touched the yellow flowers that rise above the *patio* wall, and the swaying, glowing magenta of the bougain-villea, and the fierce red outbursts of the poinsettia. The poinsettia is very splendid, the flowers very big, and of a sure stainless red. They call them Noche Buenas, flowers of Christmas Eve. These tufts throw out their scarlet sharply, like red birds ruffling in the wind of dawn as if going to bathe, all their feathers alert. This for Christmas, instead of holly-berries. Christmas seems to need a red herald.

The yucca is tall, higher than the house. It is, too, in flower, hang-ing an arm's-length of soft creamy bells, like a yard-long grape-cluster of foam. And the waxy bells break on their stems in the wind, fall noiselessly from the long creamy bunch, that hardly sways.

The coffee-berries are turning red. The hibiscus flowers, rose-coloured, sway at the tips of the thin branches, in rosettes of soft red.

In the second *patio,* there is a tall tree of the flimsy acacia sort. Above itself it puts up whitish fingers of flowers, naked on the blue sky. And in the wind these fingers of flowers in the bare blue sky, sway, sway with the reeling, roundward motion of tree-tips in a wind.

A restless morning, with clouds lower down, moving also with a larger roundward motion. Everything moving. Best to go out in motion too, the slow roundward motion like the hawks.

Everything seems slowly to circle and hover towards a central point, the clouds, the mountains round the valley, the dust that rises, the big, beautiful, white-barred hawks, *gabilanes,* and even the snow-white flakes of flowers upon the dim *palo-blanco* tree. Even the organ cactus, rising in stock-straight clumps, and the candelabrum cactus, seem to be slowly wheeling and pivoting upon a centre, close upon it.

Strange that we should think in straight lines, when there are none, and talk of straight courses, when every course, sooner or later, is seen to be making the sweep round, swooping upon the centre. When space is curved, and the cosmos is sphere within sphere, and the way from any one point to any other point is round the bend of the inevitable, that turns as the tips of the broad wings of the hawk turn upwards, leaning upon the air like the invisible half of the ellipse. If I have a way to go, it will be round the swoop of a bend impinging centripetal towards the centre. The straight course is hacked out in wounds, against the will of the world.

Yet the dust advances like a ghost along the road, down the valley plain. The dry turf of the valley-bed gleams like soft skin, sunlit and pinkish ochre, spreading wide between the mountains that seem to emit their own darkness, a dark-blue vapor translucent, sombring them from the humped crests downwards. The many-pleated, noiseless mountains of Mexico.

And away on the footslope lie the white specks of Huayapa, among its lake of trees. It is Saturday, and the white dots of men are threading down the trail over the bare humps to the plain, following the dark twinkle-movement of asses, the dark nodding of the woman's head as she rides between the baskets. Saturday and market-day, and morning, so the white specks of men, like sea-gulls on plough-land, come ebbing like sparks from the *palo-blanco,* over the fawn undulating of the valley slope.

They are dressed in snow-white cotton, and they lift their knees in the Indian trot, following the ass where the woman sits perched between the huge baskets, her child tight in the *rebozo,* at the brown breast. And girls in long, full, soiled cotton skirts running, trotting, ebbing along after the twinkle-movement of the ass. Down they come in families, in clusters, in solitary ones, threading with ebbing, running, barefoot movement noiseless towards the town, that blows the bubbles of its church-domes above the stagnant green of trees, away under the opposite fawn-skin hills.

But down the valley middle comes the big road, almost straight. You will know it by the tall walking of the dust, that hastens also towards the town, overtaking, overpassing everybody. Overpassing all the dark little figures and the white specks that thread tinily, in a sort of underworld, to the town.

From the valley villages and from the mountains the peasants and the Indians are coming in with supplies, the road is like a pilgrimage, with the dust in greatest haste, dashing for town. Dark-eared asses and running men, running women, running girls, running lads, twinkling donkeys ambling on fine little feet, under twin great baskets with tomatoes and gourds, twin great nets of bubble-shaped jars, twin bundles of neat-cut faggots of wood, neat as bunches of cigarettes, and twin net-sacks of charcoal. Donkeys, mules, on they come, great pannier baskets making a rhythm under the perched woman, great bundles bouncing against the sides of the slim-footed animals. A baby donkey trotting naked after its piled-up dam, a white, sandal-footed man following with the silent Indian haste, and a girl running again on light feet.

Onwards, on a strange current of haste. And slowly rowing among the foot-travel, the ox-wagons rolling solid wheels below the high net of the body. Slow oxen, with heads pressed down nosing to the earth, swaying, swaying their great horns as a snake sways itself, the shovel-shaped collar of solid wood pressing down on their necks like a scoop. On, on between the burnt-up turf and the solid, monumental green of the organ cactus. Past the rocks and the floating *palo-blanco* flowers, past the towsled dust of the *mesquite* bushes. While the dust once more, in a greater haste than anyone, comes tall and rapid down the road, overpowering and obscuring all the little people, as in a cataclysm.

They are mostly small people, of the Zapotec race: small men with lifted chests and quick, lifted knees, advancing with heavy energy in the midst of dust. And quiet, small, round-headed women running barefoot, tightening their blue *rebozos* round their shoulders, so often with a baby in the fold. The white cotton clothes of the men so white that their faces are invisible places of darkness under their big hats. Clothed darkness, faces of night, quickly, silently, with inexhaustible energy advancing to the town.

And many of the serranos, the Indians from the hills, wearing their little conical black felt hats, seem capped with night, above the straight white shoulders. Some have come far, walking all yesterday in their little black hats and black-sheathed sandals. Tomorrow they will walk back. And their eyes will be just the same, black and bright and wild, in the dark faces. They have no goal, any more than the hawks in the air, and no course to run, any more than the clouds.

The market is a huge roofed-in place. Most extraordinary is the noise that comes out, as you pass along the adjacent street. It is a huge noise, yet you may never notice it. It sounds as if all the ghosts in the world were talking to one another, in ghost-voices, within the darkness of the market structure. It is a noise something like rain, or banana leaves in a wind. The market, full of Indians, dark-faced, silent-footed, hush-spoken, but pressing in in countless numbers. The queer hissing murmurs of the Zapotec *idioma,* among the sounds of Spanish, the quiet, aside-voices of the Mixtecas.

To buy and to sell, but above all, to commingle. In the old world, men make themselves two great excuses for coming together to a centre, and commingling freely in a mixed, unsuspicious host. Market and religion. These alone bring men, unarmed, together since time began. A little load of firewood, a woven blanket, a few eggs and tomatoes are excuse enough for men, women, and children to cross the foot-weary miles of valley and mountain. To buy, to sell, to barter, to exchange. To exchange, above all things, human contact.

That is why they like you to bargain, even if it's only the difference of a centavo. Round the centre of the covered market, where there is a basin of water, are the flowers: red, white, pink roses in heaps, many-coloured little carnations, poppies, bits of larkspur, lemon and orange marigolds, buds of madonna lilies, pansies, a few forget-me-nots. They don't bring the tropical flowers. Only the lilies come wild from the hills, and the mauve red orchids.

"How much this bunch of cherry-pie heliotrope?"

"Fifteen centavos."

"Ten."

"Fifteen."

You put back the cherry-pie, and depart. But the woman is quite content. The contact, so short even, brisked her up.

"Pinks?"

"The red ones, Señorita? Thirty centavos."

"No. I don't want red ones. The mixed."

"Ah!" The woman seizes a handful of little carnations of all colours, carefully puts them together. "Look, Señorita! No more?"

"No, no more. How much?"

"The same. Thirty centavos."

"It is much."

"No, Señorita, it is not much. Look at this little bunch. It is eight centavos."—Displays a scrappy little bunch. "Come then, twenty-five."

"No! Twenty-two."

"Look!" She gathers up three or four more flowers, and claps them to the bunch. "Two *reales*, Señorita."

It is a bargain. Off you go with multicoloured pinks, and the woman has had one more moment of contact, with a stranger, a perfect stranger. An intermingling of voices, a threading together of different wills. It is life. The centavos are an excuse.

The stalls go off in straight lines, to the right, brilliant vegetables, to the left, bread and sweet buns. Away at the one end, cheese, butter, eggs, chickens, turkeys, meat. At the other, the native-woven blankets and *rebozos,* skirts, shirts, handkerchiefs. Down the far-side, sandals and leather things.

The *sarape* men spy you, and whistle to you like ferocious birds, and call "Señor! Señor! Look!" Then with violence one flings open a dazzling blanket, while another whistles more ear-piercingly still, to make you look at *his* blanket. It is the veritable den of lions and tigers, that spot where the *sarape* men have their blankets piled on the ground. You shake your head, and flee.

To find yourself in the leather avenue.

"Señor! Señor! Look! Huaraches! Very fine, very finely made! Look, Señor!"

The fat leather man jumps up and holds a pair of sandals at one's breast. They are of narrow woven strips of leather, in the newest Paris style, but a style ancient to these natives. You take them in your hand, and look at them quizzically, while the fat wife of the huarache man reiterates, "Very fine work. Very fine. Much work!"

Leather men usually seem to have their wives with them.

"How much?"

"Twenty reales."

"Twenty!"—in a voice of surprise and pained indignation.

"How much do you give?"

You refuse to answer. Instead you put the huaraches to your nose. The huarache man looks at his wife, and they laugh aloud.

"They smell," you say.

"No, Señor, they don't smell!"—and the two go off into fits of laughter.

"Yes, they smell. It is not American leather."

"Yes, Señor, it is American leather. They don't smell, Señor. No, they don't smell." He coaxes you till you wouldn't believe your own nose.

"Yes, they smell."

"How much do you give?"

"Nothing, because they smell."

And you give another sniff, though it is painfully unnecessary. And in spite of your refusal to bid, the man and wife go into fits of laughter to see you painfully sniffing.

You lay down the sandals and shake your head.

"How much do you offer?" reiterates the man, gaily.

You shake your head mournfully, and move away. The leather man and his wife look at one another and go off into another fit of laughter, because you smelt the huaraches, and said they stank.

They did. The natives use human excrement for tanning leather. When Bernal Diaz came with Cortes to the great market-place of Mexico City, in Montezuma's day, he saw the little pots of human excrement in rows for sale, and the leather-makers going round sniffing to see which was the best, before they paid for it. It staggered even a fifteenth-century Spaniard. Yet my leather

man and his wife think it screamingly funny that I smell the
huaraches before buying them. Everything has its own smell, and
the natural smell of huaraches is what it is. You might as well
quarrel with an onion for smelling like an onion.

The great press of the quiet natives, some of them bright and
clean, many in old rags, the brown flesh showing through the
rents in the dirty cotton. Many wild hillmen, in their little hats
of conical black felt, with their wild, staring eyes. And as they
cluster round the hat-stall, in a long, long suspense of indecision
before they can commit themselves, trying on a new hat, their
black hair gleams blue-black, and falls thick and rich over their
foreheads, like gleaming bluey-black feathers. And one is reminded again of the blue-haired Buddha, with the lotus at his
navel.

But already the fleas are travelling under one's clothing.

Market lasts all day. The native inns are great dreary yards
with little sheds, and little rooms around. Some men and families
who have come from far, will sleep in one or other of the little
stall-like rooms. Many will sleep on the stones, on the earth,
round the market, anywhere. But the asses are there by the hundred, crowded in the inn-yards, drooping their ears with the
eternal patience of the beast that knows better than any other
beast that every road curves round to the same centre of rest,
and hither and thither means nothing.

And towards nightfall the dusty road will be thronged with
shadowy people and unladen asses and new-laden mules, urging
silently into the country again, their backs to the town, glad to get
away from the town, to see the cactus and the pleated hills, and
the trees that mean a village. In some village they will lie under a
tree, or under a wall, and sleep. Then the next day, home.

It is fulfilled, what they came to market for. They have sold and
bought. But more than that, they have had their moment of contact and centripetal flow. They have been part of a great stream
of men flowing to a centre, to the vortex of the market-place. And
here they have felt life concentrate upon them, they have been
jammed between the soft hot bodies of strange men come from
afar, they have had the sound of stranger's voices in their ears,
they have asked and been answered in unaccustomed ways.

There is no goal, and no abiding-place, and nothing is fixed, not even the cathedral towers. The cathedral towers are slowly leaning, seeking the curve of return. As the natives curved in a strong swirl, towards the vortex of the market. Then on a strong swerve of repulsion, curved out and away again, into space.

Nothing but the touch, the spark of contact. That, no more. That, which is most elusive, still the only treasure. Come, and gone, and yet the clue itself.

True, folded up in the handkerchief inside the shirt, are the copper centavos, and maybe a few silver pesos. But these too will disappear as the stars disappear at daybreak, as they are meant to disappear. Everything is meant to disappear. Every curve plunges into the vortex and is lost, re-emerges with a certain relief and takes to the open, and there is lost again.

Only that which is utterly intangible, matters. The contact, the spark of exchange. That which can never be fastened upon, forever gone, forever coming, never to be detained: the spark of contact.

Like the evening star, when it is neither night nor day. Like the evening star, between the sun and the moon, and swayed by neither of them. The flashing intermediary, the evening star that is seen only at the dividing of the day and night, but then is more wonderful than either.

From *Mornings in Mexico*, 1927.

Chrysanthemums

by MAURICE MAETERLINCK [1862-1949]

I

EVERY YEAR, in November, at the season that follows on the hour of the dead, the crowning and majestic hour of Autumn, reverently I go to visit the chrysanthemums in the places where chance offers them to my sight. For the rest, it matters little where they are shown to me by the good will of travel or of sojourn. They are, indeed, the most universal, the most diverse of flowers; but their diversity and surprises are, so to speak, concerted, like those of fashion, in arbitrary Edens. At the same moment, even as with silks, laces, jewels and curls, a voice composed of sky and light gives the password in time and space; and, docile as the most beautiful of women, simultaneously, in every country, in every latitude, the flowers obey the sacred decree.

It is enough, then, to enter at random one of those crystal museums in which their somewhat funereal riches are displayed under the harmonious veil of a November day. We at once grasp the dominant idea, the obtrusive beauty, the conscious effort of the year in this special world, strange and privileged even in the midst of the strange and privileged world of flowers. And we ask ourselves if this new idea is a profound and really necessary idea on the part of the sun, the earth, life, Autumn, or man.

2

Yesterday, then, I went to admire the year's gentle and gorgeous floral feast, the last which the snows of December and January, like a broad belt of peace, sleep, silence and oblivion, separate from the delicious festivals that commence again with the germination, powerful already, though hardly visible, that seeks the light in February.

They are there, under the immense transparent domes, the noble flowers of the month of fogs; they are there, at the royal meeting-place, all the grave autumn fairies, whose dances and attitudes seem to have been struck motionless with a magic word. The eye that recognizes them and has learned to love them perceives, at the first pleased glance, that they have actively and dutifully continued to evolve towards their uncertain ideal. Go back for a moment to their modest origin: recall the poor buttercup of not so long ago, the humble little blush-red or damask rose that still smiles sadly in the scanty garden-patches of our villages, beside the roads filled with dead leaves; compare with them these enormous masses and fleeces of snow, these disks and globes of red copper, these spheres of old silver, these trophies of alabaster and amethyst, this delirious prodigy of petals which seems to be trying to exhaust to its last riddle the world of autumnal shapes and shades which Winter entrusts to the bosom of the sleeping woods; let the unwonted and unexpected varieties pass before your eyes; admire and appraise them.

Here, for instance, is the marvellous family of the stars: flat stars, bursting stars, diaphanous stars, solid and fleshy stars, milky ways and constellations of the earth that correspond with those of the firmament. Here are the proud egret-plumes that await the diamonds of the dew; here, to put our dreams to shame, the fascinating poem of unreal tresses: mad and miraculous tresses; honeyed moonbeams, golden bushes, and flaming whirlpools; curls of fair and smiling maidens, of fleeing nymphs, of passionate bacchantes, of swooning sirens, of cold virgins, of frolicsome children, which angels, mothers, fauns, lovers have caressed with their calm or quivering hands. And then here, pell-mell, are the monsters that cannot be classed: hedgehogs, spiders, frizzles, curly endives, pine-apples, pompons, rosettes, shells, vapours, breaths, stalactites of ice and falling snow, a throbbing hail of sparks, wings, chips, fluffy, pulpy, fleshy things, wattles, bristles, funeral piles and skyrockets, bursts of light, a stream of fire and sulphur. . . .

3

Now that the shapes have capitulated comes the question of conquering the region of the proscribed colours, of the reserved shades, which Autumn, it would seem, denies to the flowers that represent it. Lavishly it bestows on them all the wealth of the twilight and the night, all the riches of the vintage-time: it gives them all the mud-brown work of the rain in the woods, all the silvery fashionings of the mist in the plains, of the frost and snow in the gardens. It permits them, above all, to draw at will upon the inexhaustible treasures of the dead leaves and the expiring forest. It allows them to deck themselves with the golden sequins, the bronze medals, the silver buckles, the copper spangles, the fairy feathers, the powdered amber, the burnt topazes, the neglected pearls, the smoked amethysts, the calcined garnets, all the dead but still resplendent jewellery which the north wind heaps up in the hollow of ravines and ruts; but it insists that they shall remain faithful to their old masters and wear the livery of the drab and weary months that give them birth. It does not permit them to betray those masters and to don the princely shot garments of Spring and sunrise; and, if, sometimes, it suffers a pink, this is only on condition that it be borrowed from the cold lips, the pale brow of the veiled and afflicted virgin praying on a tomb. It forbids most strictly the tints of Summer, of too youthful, ardent and serene a life, of a health too joyous and exuberant. In no case will it consent to hilarious vermilions, impetuous scarlets, imperious and dazzling purples. As for the blues, from the azure of the dawn to the indigo of the sea and the deep lakes, from the periwinkle to the borage and the larkspur, they are banished under pain of death.

4

Nevertheless, thanks to some inadvertence on the part of nature, the most unusual colour in the world of flowers and the most severely forbidden, the colour which the corolla of the poisonous spurge is almost alone in wearing in the city of umbels, petals and calyces, green, the colour exclusively reserved for the servile and nutrient leaves, has penetrated within the jealously-guarded precincts. True, it has slipped in only by favour of a lie, as a traitor, a spy, a livid deserter. It is a forsworn yellow, cowardly steeped in the trembling azure of a moonbeam. It is still of the night and false, like the opal depths of the sea; it shows itself only in shifting patches at the tip of the petals; it is elusive and anxious, frail and deceptive, but undeniable. It has made its entrance, it exists, it asserts itself; it will be daily more fixed and more decided; and, through the breach which it has contrived in the citadels of light, all the joys and all the splendours of the banned prism will hurl themselves into the virgin domain, there to prepare unwonted feasts for our eyes. This is a great tidings and a memorable conquest in the land of flowers.

5

We must not think that it is childish thus to interest one's self in the capricious forms, the unwritten shades of a flower that bears no fruit; nor must we treat those who seek to make it more beauti-

ful or more strange as La Bruyère, in his day, treated the lover of
the tulip or the plum. Do you remember the charming page?

The lover of flowers has a garden in the suburbs, where he
spends all his time from sunrise to sunset. You see him standing there and would think that he had taken root in the midst
of his tulips before his "Solitaire"; he opens his eyes wide, rubs
his hands, stoops down and looks closer at it; it never before
seemed to him so handsome; he is in an ecstasy of joy and
leaves it to go to the "Orient," then to the "Widow," from
thence to the "Cloth of Gold," on to the "Agatha," and at last
returns to the "Solitaire," where he remains, is tired out, sits
down and forgets his dinner; he looks at the tulip and admires
its shade, shape, colour, sheen and edges, its beautiful form
and calyx; but God and nature are not in his thoughts, for
they do not go beyond the bulb of his tulip, which he would
not sell for a thousand crowns, though he will give it to you
for nothing when tulips are no longer in fashion and carnations are all the rage. This rational being, who has a soul
and professes some religion, comes home tired and half
starved, but very pleased with his day's work; he has seen
some tulips.

Talk to another of the healthy look of the crops, of a plentiful harvest, of a good vintage, and you will find that he cares
only for fruit and understands not a single word that you say;
then turn to figs and melons; tell him that this year the pear-
trees are so heavily laden with fruit that the branches almost
break, that there is abundance of peaches, and you address
him in a language which he completely ignores; and he will
not answer you, for his sole hobby is plum-trees. Do not
even speak to him of your plum-trees, for he is fond only of
a certain kind and laughs and sneers at the mention of any
others; he takes you to his tree and cautiously gathers this exquisite plum, divides it, gives you one half, keeps the other
himself and exclaims, "How delicious! Do you like it? Is it
not heavenly? You cannot find its equal anywhere"; and
then his nostrils dilate, and he can hardly contain his joy

and pride under an appearance of modesty. What a wonderful person, never enough praised and admired, whose name will be handed down to future ages! Let me look at his mien and shape, while he is still in the land of the living, that I may study the features and the countenance of a man who, alone among mortals, is the happy possessor of such a plum.

Well, La Bruyère is wrong. We readily forgive him his mistake, for the sake of the pleasant window which he, alone among the authors of his time, opens upon the unexpected gardens of the seventeenth century. The fact none the less remains that it is to his somewhat bigoted florist, to his somewhat frenzied horticulturist that we owe our exquisite flower-beds, our more varied, more abundant, more luscious vegetables, our ever more delicious fruits. Contemplate, for instance, around the chrysanthemums, the marvels that ripen nowadays in the humblest gardens, among the long branches wisely restrained by the patient, spreading espaliers. Less than a century ago, they were unknown; and we owe them to the innumerable and infinitesimal exertions of a legion of small seekers, all more or less hampered, all more or less absurd.

It is thus that man acquires nearly all his riches. There is nothing trivial in nature; and he who becomes impassioned of a flower, a blade of grass, a butterfly's wing, a nest, a shell, wraps his passion around a small thing that always contains a great truth. To succeed in modifying the appearance of a flower is an insignificant act in itself, if you will; but reflect upon it, for however short a while, and it becomes gigantic. In thus succeeding, do we not violate or divert profound, perhaps essential and, in any case, time-honoured laws? Do we not exceed too-easily-accepted limits? Do we not directly intrude our ephemeral will on that of the eternal forces? Does not this suggest our possession of a singular power, an almost supernatural power? And, although it is wise to guard against over-ambitious dreams, does not this allow us to hope that we may perhaps learn to elude or to transgress other laws no less time-honoured, more akin to our own life and far more important? For, in the end, all things hold together; all things go hand to hand; all things obey the same unseen principles; all things share the same spirit, the same substance in the terrifying and wonderful problem; and the most modest victory gained in the matter of a flower may one day disclose to us an infinity of the untold. . . .

6

That is why I love the chrysanthemum; that is why I follow its evolution with a brotherly interest. It is, among familiar plants, the most submissive, the most docile, the most tractable and the most attentive of all that we meet on life's long way. It bears flowers impregnated with the thought and will of man: flowers already human, so to speak. And, if the vegetable world is some day to reveal to us one of the messages that we are awaiting, perhaps it will be through this flower of the dead that we shall learn the first secret of existence, even as, in another kingdom, it is probably through the dog, the almost thinking guardian of our homes, that we shall discover the mystery of animal life. . . .

1907   Translated by
                          ALEXANDER TEIXEIRA DE MATTOS

Anna Karenina

by THOMAS MANN [1875-1955]

TODAY high tide is at ten. The waters rush up the narrowing strand, carrying foam-bubbles and jelly-fish—primitive children of an unnatural mother, who will abandon them on the sands to death by evaporation. The waves run up, almost to the foot of my beach-chair; sometimes I must lift away my plaid-wrapped legs as the waters encroach and threaten to cover them. My heart responds blithely, though also with utter respect, to these sportive little tricks the mighty ocean plays me; my sympathy, a deep and tender, primitive, soul-extending stirring, is far indeed from any annoyance.

No bathers yet. They await the midday warmth to wade out into the ebbing tide, little flutters and shrieks escaping them as they begin their pert yet fearful toying with the vast. Coast-guards in cork jackets, lynx-eyed, tooting their horns, watch over all this amateurish frivolity. My "workshop" here surpasses any I know. It is lonely; but even were it livelier, the tumultuous surf so shuts me in, and the sides of my admirable beach-chair, seat and cabin in one, familiar from my youth up, is so peculiarly protective that there can be no distraction. Beloved, incomparably soothing and suitable situation—it recurs in my life again and again, as by a law. Beneath a sky where gently shifting continents of cloud link the blue depths, rolls the sea, a darkening green against the clear horizon, oncoming in seven or eight foaming white rows of surf that reach out of sight in both directions. There is superb activity farther out, where the advancing waves hurl themselves first and highest against the bar. The bottle-green wall gleams metallic as it mounts and halts and curls over, then shatters with a roar and an explosion of foam down, down, in ever recurrent crash, whose dull thunder forms the deep ground-bass to the higher key of the boiling and hissing waves as they break nearer in. Never does the eye tire of this sight nor the ear of this music.

A more fitting spot could not be for my purpose: which is to recall and to reflect upon the great book whose title stands at the head of my paper. And here by the sea there comes to mind inevitably an old, I might almost say an innate association of ideas: the spiritual identity of two elementary experiences, one of which is a parable of the other. I mean the ocean and the epic. The epic, with its rolling breadth, its breath of the beginnings and the roots of life, its broad and sweeping rhythm, its all-consuming monotony—how like it is to the sea, how like to it is the sea! It is the Homeric element I mean, the story going on and on, art and nature at once, naïve, magnificent, material, objective, immortally healthy, immortally realistic! All this was strong in Tolstoy, stronger than in any other modern creator of epic art; it distinguishes his genius, if not in rank, yet in essence, from the morbid manifestation, the ecstatic and highly distorted phenomenon, that was Dostoyevsky. Tolstoy himself said of his early work *Childhood* and *Boyhood:* "Without false modesty, it is something like the Iliad." That is the merest statement of fact; only on exterior grounds does it fit still better the giant work of his maturity, *War and Peace.* It fits everything he wrote. The pure narrative power of his work is unequalled. Every contact with it, even when he wished no longer to be an artist, when he scorned and reviled art and only employed it as a means of communicating moral lessons; every contact with it, I say, rewards the talent that knows how to receive (for there is no other) with rich streams of power and refreshment, of creative primeval lustiness and health. Seldom did art work so much like nature; its immediate, natural power is only another manifestation of nature itself; and to read him again, to be played upon by the animal keenness of this eye, the sheer power of this creative attack, the entirely clear and true greatness, unclouded by any mysticism, of this epic, is to find one's way home, safe from every danger of affectation and morbid trifling; home to originality and health, to everything within us that is fundamental and sane.

Turgenyev once said: "We have all come out from under Gogol's *Mantle*"—a fiendishly clever pun which puts in a phrase the extraordinary uniformity and unity, the thick traditionalism of Russian literature as a whole. Actually, they are all there simultaneously, its masters and geniuses, they can put out their hands to each other, their life-spans in great part overlap. Nikolai Gogol read aloud some of *Dead Souls* to the great Pushkin, and the author of *Yevgeny Onyegin* shook with laughter—and then suddenly grew sad. Lermontov was the contemporary of both. Turgenyev, as one may easily forget, for his fame, like Dostoyevsky's, Lieskov's, and Tolstoy's, belongs to the second half of the nineteenth century, came only four years later than Lermontov into the world and ten before Tolstoy, whom he adjured in a touching letter expressing his faith in humanistic art, "to go back to literature." What I mean by thick traditionalism is illustrated by an anecdote that most significantly connects Tolstoy's artistically finest work, *Anna Karenina,* with Pushkin.

One evening in the spring of 1873, Count Leo Nikolayevich en-

tered the room of his eldest son, who was reading aloud to his old
aunt Pushkin's *Stories of Byelkin;* the father took the book and
read: "The guests assembled in the country house." "That's the
way to begin," he said; went into his study and wrote: "In the
Oblonsky house great confusion reigned." That was the original
first sentence from *Anna Karenina.* The present beginning, the
aperçu about happy and unhappy families, was introduced later.
That is a marvellously pretty little anecdote. He had already begun
much and brought much to triumphant conclusion. He was the
fêted creator of the Russian national epos, in the form of a modern
novel, the giant panorama *War and Peace.* And he was about to
excel both formally and artistically this chef-d'œuvre of his thirty-
five years in the work he had now in hand, which one may with an
easy mind pronounce the greatest society novel of world literature.
And here he was, restlessly prowling about the house, searching,
searching, not knowing how to begin. Pushkin taught him, tradition taught him, Pushkin the classic master, from whose world his
own was so remote, both personally and generally speaking. Pushkin rescued him, as he hesitated on the brink; showed him how
one sets to, takes a firm grip, and plumps the reader *in medias res.*
Unity is achieved, the continuity of that astonishing family of
intellects which one calls Russian literature is preserved in this little
piece of historical evidence.

Merezhkovsky points out that historically and pre-modernly
only Pushkin among these writers really possesses charm. He in-
habits a sphere by himself, a sensuously radiant, naïve, and blithely
poetic one. But with Gogol there begins what Merezhkovsky calls
critique: "the transition from unconscious creation to creative
consciousness"; for him that means the end of poetry in the Pushkin sense, but at the same time the beginning of something new.
The remark is true and perceptive. Thus did Heine speak of the
age of Goethe, an æsthetic age, an epoch of art, an objective-ironic
point of view. Its representative and dominant figure had been the
Olympian; it died with his death. What then began was a time of
taking sides, of conflicting opinions, of social consolidation, yes,
of politics and, in short, of morals—a morality that branded as
frivolous every purely æsthetic and universal point of view.

In Heine's comments, as in Merezhkovsky's, there is feeling for temporal change, together with feeling for its opposite, the timeless and perpetual. Schiller, in his immortal essay, reduced it to the formula of the sentimental and the naïve. What Merezhkovsky calls "critique" or "creative consciousness," what seems to him like contrast with the unconscious creation of Pushkin, as the more modern element, the future on the way, is precisely what Schiller means by the sentimental in contrast to the naïve. He too brings in the temporal, the evolutional, and—*"pro domo,"* as we know—declares the sentimental, the creativeness of conscious critique, in short the moralistic, to be the newer, more modern stage of development.

There are now two things to say: first, Tolstoy's original convictions were definitely on the side of the æsthetic, of pure art, the objectively shaping, anti-moralistic principle; and second, in him took place that very cultural and historical change which Merezhkovsky speaks of, that move away from Pushkin's simplicity towards critical responsibility and morality. Within his own being it took such a radical and tragic form that he went through the severest crises and much anguish and even so could not utterly repudiate his own mighty creativeness. What he finally arrived at was a rejection and negation of art itself as an idle, voluptuous, and immoral luxury, admissible only in order to make moral teachings acceptable to men, even though dressed in the mantle of art.

But to return to the first position: we have his own unequivocal declarations to the effect that a purely artistic gift stands higher than one with social significance. In 1859, when he was thirty-one years old, he gave, as a member of the Moscow society of Friends of Russian Literature, an address in which he so sharply emphasized the advantages of the purely art element in literature over all the fashions of the day that the president of the society, Khomyakov, felt constrained to rejoin that a servant of pure art might quite easily become a social reformer even without knowing or willing it. Contemporary criticism saw in the author of *Anna Karenina* the protagonist of the art for art's sake position, the representative of free creativeness apart from all tendentiousness or doctrine. Indeed, it considered this naturalism the characteristi-

cally new thing; the public must in time grow up to it, though
at present they had got used, in the works of others, to the presentation of political and social ideas in the form of art. In point of
fact, all this was only one side of the business. As an artist and son
of his time, the nineteenth century, Tolstoy was a naturalist, and
in this connection he represented—in the sense of a trend—the
new. But as an intellectual he was beyond (or rather, he struggled
amid torments to arrive beyond) the new, to something further
still, on the other side of his, the naturalistic century. He was reaching after conceptions of art which approached much nearer to
"mind" (*Geist*), to knowledge, to "critique" than to nature. The
commentators of 1875, impressed by the first chapters of *Anna
Karenina* as they appeared in a Russian magazine, the *Messenger*,
seeking benevolently to prepare the way with the public for the
naturalism of the work, did not dream that the author was in full
flight towards an anti-art position, which was already hampering
his work on his masterpiece and even endangering its completion.

This development was to go very far, the vehemence of its consistency shrank from nothing: neither from the anti-cultural nor
even from the absurd. Before long, he was to regret in public having written *Childhood* and *Youth,* the work of his freshest youthful hours—so poor, so insincere, so literary, so sinful was this
book. He was to condemn root and branch the "artist twaddle"
with which the twelve volumes of his works were filled, to which
"the people of our day ascribe an undeserved significance." It was
the same undeserved significance that they ascribed to art itself—
for instance, to Shakespeare's plays. He went so far—one must
set it down with respect and a sober face, or at least with the smallest, most non-committal smile—as to put Mrs. Harriet Beecher
Stowe, the author of *Uncle Tom's Cabin,* far above Shakespeare.

We must be at pains to understand this. Tolstoy's hatred for
Shakespeare dated from much earlier than is usually supposed. It
signified rebellion against nature, the universal, the all-affirming.
It was jealousy of the morally tormented for the irony of the absolute creator, it meant the straining away from nature, naïveté,
moral indifference, towards *"Geist"* in the moralistically critical
sense of the word; towards moral valuations and edifying doctrine.

Tolstoy hated himself in Shakespeare, hated his own vital bearish strength, which was originally like Shakespeare's, natural and creatively a-moral; though his struggles for the good, the true and right, the meaning of life, the doctrine of salvation, were after all only the same thing in another and self-denying form. The immensity of his writings sometimes resulted in a gigantic clumsiness which forces a respectful smile. And yet it is precisely the paradoxically ascetic application of a titanic helplessness arising from a primeval force that, viewed as art, gives his work that huge moral *élan,* that Atlas-like moral muscle-tensing and flexing which reminds one of the agonized figures of Michelangelo's sculpture.

I said that Tolstoy's hatred of Shakespeare belongs to an earlier period than is generally thought. But all that which later made his friends and admirers like Turgenyev weep, his denial of art and culture, his radical moralism, his highly questionable pose of prophet and confessor in his last period—all that begins much further back, it is quite wrong to imagine this process as something suddenly occurring in a crisis of conversion in later life, coincident with Tolstoy's old age. The same kind of mistake occurs in the popular opinion that Richard Wagner suddenly got religion— whereas the matter was one of a development vastly and fatally consistent and inevitable, the direction of which is clearly and unmistakably traceable in *The Flying Dutchman* and in *Tannhäuser.* The judgment of the Frenchman, Vogüé, was entirely correct when, on the news that the great Russian writer was now "as though paralysed by a sort of mystic madness," Vogüé declared that he had long ago seen it coming. The course of Tolstoy's intellectual development had been present in the seed in *Childhood* and *Boyhood* and the psychology of Levin in *Anna Karenina* had marked out the path it would take.

So much is true, that Levin is Tolstoy, the real hero of the mighty novel, which is a glorious, indestructible signpost on the woeful Way of the Cross the poet was taking; a monument of an elemental and creative bear-strength, which was first heightened and then destroyed by the inner ferment of his subtilizing conscience and his fear of God. Yes, Levin is Tolstoy—almost altogether Tolstoy, this side Tolstoy the artist. To this character Tolstoy transferred not only the important facts and dates of his own life: his experiences as a farmer, his romance and betrothal (which are completely autobiographic), the sacred, beautiful, and awe-full experiences of the birth of his first child, and the death of his brother—which forms a pendant of equal and boundless significance—not only there but in this whole inner life, his crises of conscience, his groping after the whole duty of man and the meaning of life, his painful wrestling over the good life, which so decisively estranged him from the doings of urban society; his gnawing doubts about culture itself or that which his society called culture, doubts of all this brought him close to the anchorite and nihilist type. What Levin lacks of Tolstoy is only just that he is not a great artist besides. But to estimate *Anna Karenina* not only artistically but also humanly, the reader must saturate himself with the thesis that Constantin Levin himself wrote the novel. Instead of being the man with the pointer, indicating the incomparable beauty of the painting as a whole, I shall do better to speak of the conditions of difficulty and stress under which the work came to birth.

That is the right word: it came to birth; but there did not lack much for it not to be born. A work of this kind, so all of one piece and that piece so absorbing, so complete in the large and in the small, makes us suppose that its creator gave himself utterly to it with entire and devoted heart and, like one driven to self-expression, committed it, so to speak, in one gush to paper. That is a misapprehension; although, even so, the origin of *Anna Karenina* does in fact lie in the happiest, most harmonious period of Tolstoy's life. The years in which he worked on it belong to the first decade and a half of his marriage with the woman whose literary image is Kitty Shtcherbatsky and who later suffered so much from her Lievotshka—until at last just before his death the old man broke away and ran. It is she who, in addition to her constant pregnancies, and her abundant activities as mistress of the farm, as mother and housewife, copies *War and Peace* seven times with her own hand—that first colossal intellectual harvest of the period that brought the doubting, brooding man relative peace in the patriarchal animalism of marriage and family life in the country. It was the period at which the poor Countess looked so yearningly back when Leochen had become "the prophet of Yasnaya Polyana" and succeeded under self-torture, and even so up to the end never quite succeeded, in brooding to death all his sensual and instinctive passions: family, nation, state, church, club, and chase, at bottom the whole life of the body, but most particularly art, which for him quite essentially meant sensuality and the body's life.

Well, those fifteen years were a good, happy time, though from a later, higher point of view, good only in a low and animal sense. *War and Peace* had made Tolstoy the "great writer of Russia," and as such he went to work to write a new historical and national epos. He had in mind a novel about Peter the Great and his times. And for months he carried on conscientious and comprehensive studies for it in the libraries and archives of Moscow. "Lievotshka reads and reads," it says in the Countess's letters. Did he read too much? Did he take in too much, did he spoil his appetite? Oddly enough, it turned out that the Czar reformer, the imperial compeller of civilization, was at bottom an unsympathetic figure to Tolstoy. To hold the position he had achieved as the national epic-writer, he had wanted to repeat his performance in *War and Peace*. It would not come off; the material unexpectedly resisted him. After endless preparatory labour he flung the whole thing away, sacrificed his whole investment of time and study, and turned to something quite different: the passion and stumbling of *Anna Karenina*, the modern novel of St. Petersburg and Moscow high society.

The first onset, by dint of Pushkin's help, was fresh and blithe. But before long Tolstoy got stuck, though the reader in his untrammelled enjoyment would never guess it. For weeks and months the work only dragged on or did not go at all. What was the trouble? Household cares, children's illnesses, fluctuations in his own health—oh, no, these were all nothing compared with a piece of work like *Anna Karenina*—or they ought to be. What is really disturbing is doubt of the importance and personal urgency of what we are doing. Might we not do better to learn Greek, to get some fundamental knowledge of the New Testament? Then the schools for the children of peasants we have founded. Should they not claim more of our time and thought? Is not the whole of belles-lettres folly? And is it not our duty or even much more consistent with our deepest need to bury ourselves in theological and philosophical studies in order to find at last the meaning of life? That contact with the mystery of death which he had had when his older brother died had made a strong impression on Tolstoy's own vitality, powerful to the point of mysticism, which demanded spiritual wrestling, not in a literary way but in something confessional on the pattern of Saint Augustine and Rousseau. Such a book, sincere as far as human power could make it, weighed on his mind and gave him increasing distaste for writing novels. Actually, he would never have finished *Anna Karenina* if it had not begun appearing in the *Rusky Vyestnik* (*Russian Messenger*) of Katkov. The fact made him responsible to the publisher and the reading public. In January 1875 and the following three months successive numbers of the novel appeared in the magazine. Then they left off, because the author had no more to deliver. The first months of the next year produced a few fragments, then seven months' pause. Then in December one more number. What we find simply enchanting, what we cannot imagine as originating in anything except a state of prolonged inspiration—Tolstoy groaned over. "My tiresome, horrible *Anna Karenina*," he wrote from Samara, where he was drinking mares' milk. *Sic!* Literally. "At last," he wrote in March 1876, "I was driven to finish my novel, of which I am sick to death." Of course in the process the enthusiasm and eagerness came back by fits and starts. But it was just at such times that the writing was prone to go more slowly—owing to fastidious artistry that caused endless filing and remodelling and improving out of a stylistic perfectionism which still shows through the most inadequate translation. This amazing saint took his art the more seriously the less he believed in it.

The publication dragged on, with constant interruptions, as far as the eighth book. Then it stopped, for now the thing had become political and the national epic-writer of Russia had in the latest number expressed himself so heretically about Slavophilism, the current enthusiasm for the Bulgarian, Serbian, Bosnian brothers in their fight for freedom against the Turks, the much ado over the volunteers and the patriotic nonsense uttered by Russian society, that Katkov dared not print it. He demanded cuts and changes, which the author in high dudgeon refused to make. Tolstoy had the final numbers printed separately with a note on the disagreement.

What I have boldly called the greatest society novel in all literature is an anti-society novel. The Bible text: "Vengeance is mine, I will repay, saith the Lord," stands at its head. The moral momentum of the work was certainly the desire to lash society for the cold, cruel rebuff inflicted by it on a woman who goes astray through passion but is fundamentally proud and high-minded, instead of leaving to God the punishment for her sins. Indeed, society might well do just that, for after all it is society and its irrevocable laws that God too avails Himself of to exact the payment. It shows the fatal and inevitable character of Anna's doom that it proceeds inscrutably, step by step, up to the frightful end out of her affront to the moral law. So there is a certain contradiction in the author's original moral motive, in the complaint he lodges against society. One asks oneself in what way would God punish if society did not behave as it does? Custom and morality, how far are they distinguishable, how far are they—in effect—one and the same, how far do they coincide in the heart of the socially circumscribed human being? The question hovers unanswered over the whole novel. But such a work is not compelled to answer questions. Its task is to bring them out, to enrich the emotions, to give them the highest and most painful degree of questionableness. Thus it will have performed its task, and in this case the storyteller's love for his creature leaves no doubt at all, no matter how much suffering he painfully and relentlessly visits on her.

Tolstoy loves Anna very much, one feels that. The book bears her name; it could bear no other. But its hero is not Anna's lover, the strong, decent, chivalrous, and somewhat limited officer of the Guards, Count Vronsky. Nor is it Alexander Alexandrovich, Anna's husband, with whatever profound skill Tolstoy has modelled this incomparable, at once repellent and superior, comic and touching cuckold. No, the hero is another person altogether, who has as good as nothing to do with Anna's lot, and whose intro-

duction in a way twists the theme of the novel and almost pushes
its first motive into second place. It is Constantin Levin, the in-
trospective man, the author's image—he, no other, with his brooding and scrutinizing, with the peculiar force and obstinate resistance of his critical conscience, that makes the great society novel
into an anti-society novel.

What an extraordinary fellow he is, this surrogate of the author!
What in the French *pièce à thèse* is called the *raisonneur*—Levin
is that in Tolstoy's society world. Yet how un-French! To amount
to something as a critic of society, one must, I suppose, be in society oneself; but precisely that he is not in the least, this tortured,
radically remote *raisonneur,* despite his native right to move in
the highest circles. Strong and shy, defiant and dubious, with an
intelligence of great anti-logical, natural, even helpless abundance,
Levin is at bottom convinced that decency, uprightness, seriousness, and sincerity are possible only in singleness, in dumb isolation, each for himself; and that all social life turns him into a chat-
terer, a liar, and a fool. Observe him in the salons of Moscow, or on
cultural occasions when he has to make conversation, play a
social part, express "views." Such a coming-together of people
seems to him banal, he sees himself a blushing fool, a prattler, a
parrot. This Rousseauian quite sincerely considers all urban civilization, with the intellectual and cultural goings-on bound up in it,
a sink of iniquity. Only life in the country is worthy of a man—
though not the country life that the city man in sentimental relaxation finds "charming." Levin's learned brother, for instance,
even boasts in a way that he enjoyed such an unintellectual occupation as fishing. No, what Levin means is the real, serious life on the
land, where you have to work hard, where the human being dwells
truly and perforce at the heart of that nature whose "beauty" the
guest from civilization sentimentally admires from outside.

Levin's morality and conscientiousness are strongly physical,
having reference to the body and bound up with it. "I need physical exercise," he says to himself, "otherwise my character suffers."
He resolves to help the peasants with the mowing and it gives him
the highest moral and physical pleasure (a splendid and Tolstoyan

chapter). His scorn of the "intellectual" or, better, his disbelief in it, estranging him as a product of civilization, involving him in contradictions, is radical. It leads him, when he has to come right down to it, into paradoxes, into opinions hard to express among civilized beings. Take for instance popular education—or, worse still, any education at all. Levin's position towards it is the same as his position towards nature: "The same people whom you say you love."—"I never said that," thought Constantin Levin.—"Why should I bother my head about schools where I shall never send my own children and where the peasants will never send theirs either? And on top of that, I am not even convinced that it is necessary to send them!"—"You can make better use of a peasant and labourer who can read and write than of one who cannot."—"No, ask anybody you like," countered Constantin Levin decisively; "a worker with some schooling is distinctly worse."—"Do you admit that education is a blessing for the people?"—"Yes, that I admit," responded Levin thoughtlessly, and saw at once that what he had said was not really just what he thought.—Very bad! A difficult, dangerous case! He recognizes the blessings of "education," because what he "really" thinks about it, in the nineteenth century, cannot be put into words and for that reason may even be unthinkable.

Of course he moves in the thought-channels of his century, and they in a certain way are scientific. He "observes humanity, not as something standing outside of zoological law but as something dependent on its environment, and he proceeds from this dependence in order to discover the laws lying at the base of its development." So at least the scholar understands him; and it is no other than Taine to whom he there makes acknowledgment, good, great nineteenth century. But there is something in him that either goes back behind the scientific spirit of his epoch or goes on beyond it, something desperately bold, inadmissible, impossible in conversation. He lies on his back and looks up at the high and cloudless sky. "Do I not know that that is infinite space and not a round vault? But however I screw up my eyes and strain my sight I cannot see it not round and not bounded; and in spite of my knowl-

edge about infinite space I am incontestably right when I see a solid
blue dome, and more right than when I strain my eyes to see beyond it. . . . Can this be faith?"

But whether faith or the new realism, it is no longer the scientific spirit of the nineteenth century. In a sort of way it recalls
Goethe. And Levin-Tolstoy's sceptical, realistic, rebellious attitude towards patriotism, towards the Slavic brethren and the war
volunteers, does the same. He declines to share in the enthusiasm,
he is solitary in the midst of it, precisely as Goethe was at the time
of the Freiheitskrieg—although in both cases something new, the
democratic, joined the national movement and for the first time
the popular will conditioned the conduct of the government. That
too is nineteenth-century; and Levin, or Lievotshka, as the poor
Countess called him, could simply not do with the truths of his
time. He called them comfortless. He is a step further on; I cannot help calling it a very dangerous step, which, if not safeguarded
by the profoundest love of truth and human sympathy, can quite
easily lead to black reaction and barbarism. Today it takes no forlorn, single-handed courage to throw overboard the scientific discipline of the nineteenth century and surrender to the "mythus,"
the "faith"—in other words, to a paltry and culture-destroying
vulgarity. Masses of people do it today; but it is not a step forward,
it is a hundred miles backwards. Such a step will be in a forward
direction only when it is taken for humanity's sake, only if another step follows it straightway, moving from the new realism
of the solid blue vault to the neither old nor new but humanly
eternal idealism of truth, freedom, and knowledge. Today there are
some desperately stupid ideas about reaction in the air.

A digression—but a necessary one. Levin, then, cannot do with
the ideals of his epoch, he cannnot live with them. What I call his
physical morality and conscientiousness is shaken to the depths by
the experience of the physically transcendent and transparent mysteries of birth and death; and all that the times teach him about
organisms and their destruction, about the indestructibility of
matter and the laws of conservation of energy, about evolution,
and so forth, all that looks to him not only like utter ignorance of
the whole problem of the meaning of life but also like a kind of

thinking that makes it impossible for him to get the knowledge he needs. That in infinite time, infinite space, infinite matter, and organism, a cell frees itself; that it persists for a while and then bursts and that this bubble is he himself, Levin; that seems to him like the malicious mockery of some demon. It cannot indeed be refuted; it must be overcome some other way, that one may not be driven to shoot oneself.

What to his profounder necessities looks like a mortal lie and a kind of thinking which is no sort of instrument for the apprehension of truth—that actually is the naturalistic materialism of the nineteenth century, whose inspiration is honest love of truth, despite the comfortless pessimism that is its necessary aura. The honesty must be preserved; but a little illumination is required in order to do justice to life and its deeper concerns. So there is real humour in the fact that in *Anna Karenina* a simple little peasant shows the brooding man the way out of his despair. This little peasant teaches him, or recalls to his mind, something he has always known: true, he says, living for our physical well-being and in order to fill our bellies is natural and inborn and laid upon us all. But even so, it is not righteous or even important. What we have to do is to live for the "truth," "for our souls," "as God wills," for "the Good." How wonderful that this necessity is laid upon us just as naturally inborn and imposed as the need to fill our bellies! Wonderful indeed; for the sure conviction common to all men that it is shameful to live only for the belly, and that one must rather live for God, for the true and the good, has nothing to do with reason, but quite the contrary. It is reason that makes us care for the body and in its interest to exploit our neighbours all we can. Knowledge of the good, asserts Levin, does not lie in the realm of reason; the good stands outside the scientific chain of cause and effect. The good is a miracle, because it is contrary to reason and yet everyone understands it.

There is something outside of and beyond the melancholy science of the nineteenth century, which resigned all attempt to give meaning to life. There is a spiritual factor, a spiritual need. And Levin is enchanted and soothed by this absurdly simple statement of the human being's supra-reasonable obligation to be good.

In his joy he forgets that also that melancholy materialistic naturalistic science of the nineteenth century had, after all, as motive power, human striving for the good. He forgot that it was stern and bitter love of truth that made it deny meaning to life. It too, denying God, lived for God. That, too, is possible, and Levin forgets it. Art he does not need even to forget; he knows, it seems, nothing about it, obviously thinking of it only as the society prattle of the "cultured" about painting, the Luccas, Wagner, and so on. Here is the difference between him and Leo Tolstoy. Tolstoy knew art; he has suffered frightfully from and for it, achieved mightier things in it than the rest of us can hope to achieve. Perhaps it was just the violence of his artist personality that made him fail to see that knowledge of the good is just the opposite of a reason to deny art. Art is the most beautiful, austerest, blithest, most sacred symbol of all supra-reasonable human striving for good above and beyond reason, for truth and fullness. The breath of the rolling sea of epic would not so expand our lungs with living air if it did not bring with it the astringent quickening spice of the spiritual and the divine.

1939
Translated by
H. T. LOWE-PORTER

A Summing Up

by W. SOMERSET MAUGHAM [1874–1965]

FROM TIME TO TIME I have asked myself whether I should have been a better writer if I had devoted my whole life to literature. Somewhat early, but at what age I cannot remember, I made up my mind that, having but one life, I should like to get the most I could out of it. It did not seem to me enough merely to write. I wanted to make a pattern of my life, in which writing would be an essential element, but which would include all the other activities proper to man, and which death would in the end round off in complete fulfilment. I had many disabilities. I was small; I had endurance but little physical strength; I stammered; I was shy; I had poor health. I had not facility for games, which play so great a part in the normal life of Englishmen; and I had, whether for any of these reasons or from nature I do not know, an instinctive shrinking from my fellow men that has made it difficult for me to enter into any familiarity with them. I have loved individuals; I have never much cared for men in the mass. I have none of that engaging come-hitherness that makes people take to one another on first acquaintance. Though in the course of years I have learnt to assume an air of heartiness when forced into contact with a stranger, I have never liked anyone at first sight. I do not think I have ever addressed someone I did not know in a railway carriage or spoken to a fellow-passenger on board ship unless he first spoke to me. The weakness of my flesh has prevented me from enjoying that communion with the human race that is engendered by alcohol; long before I could reach the state of intoxication that enables so many, more happily constituted, to look upon all men as their brothers, my stomach has turned upon me and I have been as sick as a dog. These are grave disadvantages both to the writer and the man. I have had to make the best of them. I have followed the pattern I made with persistence. I do not claim that it was a perfect one. I think it was the best that I could hope for in the circumstances and with the very limited powers that were granted to me by nature.

Looking for the special function of man Aristotle decided that since he shares growth with the plants and perception with the beasts, and alone has a rational element, his function is the activity of the soul. From this he concluded, not as you would have thought sensible, that man should cultivate the three forms of activity which he ascribed to him, but that he should pursue only that which is especial to him. Philosophers and moralists have looked at the body with misgiving. They have pointed out that its satisfactions are brief. But a pleasure is none the less a pleasure because it does not please forever. It is delightful to plunge into cold water on a hot day even though in a moment your skin is no longer sensitive to the coldness. White is no whiter if it lasts for a year or a day. I looked upon it then as a part of the pattern I was attempting to draw to experience all the pleasures of sense. I have not been afraid of excess: excess on occasion is exhilarating. It prevents moderation from acquiring the deadening effect of a habit. It tonifies the system and rests the nerves. The spirit is often most free when the body is satiated with pleasure; indeed, sometimes the stars shine more brightly seen from the gutter than from the hilltop. The keenest pleasure to which the body is susceptible is that of sexual congress. I have known men who gave up their whole lives to this; they are grown old now, but I have noticed, not without surprise, that they look upon them as well spent. It has been my misfortune that a native fastidiousness has prevented me from indulging as much in this particular delight as I might have. I have exercised moderation because I was hard to please. When from time to time I have seen the persons with whom the great lovers satisfied their desires I have been more often astonished by the robustness of their appetites than envious of their successes. It is obvious that you need not often go hungry if you are willing to dine off mutton hash and turnip tops.

Most people live haphazard lives subject to the varying winds of fortune. Many are forced by the situation in which they were born and the necessity of earning a living to keep to a straight and narrow road in which there is no possibility of turning to the right or to the left. Upon these the pattern is imposed. Life itself has forced it on them. There is no reason why such a pattern should not be as complete as that which anyone has tried self-consciously to make. But the artist is in a privileged position. I use the word artist, not meaning to attach any measure of value to what he produces, but merely to signify someone who is occupied with the arts. I wish I could find a better word. Creator is pretentious and seems to make a claim to originality that can seldom be justified. Craftsman is not enough. A carpenter is a craftsman, and though he may be in the narrower sense an artist, he has not as a rule the freedom of action which the most incompetent scribbler, the poorest dauber, possesses. The artist can within certain limits make what he likes of his life. In other callings, in medicine for instance or the law, you are free to choose whether you will adopt them or not, but having chosen, you are free no longer. You are bound by the rules of your profession; a standard of conduct is imposed upon you. The pattern is predetermined. It is only the artist, and maybe the criminal, who can make his own.

Perhaps it was a natural sense of tidiness that engaged me, when still so young, to design a pattern for my life; perhaps it was due to something I discovered in myself about which I shall have a little to say later. The defect of such an undertaking is that it may kill spontaneity. One great difference between the persons of real life and the persons of fiction is that the persons of real life are creatures of impulse. It has been said that metaphysics is the finding of bad reasons for what we believe upon instinct; and it might be said also that in the conduct of life we make use of deliberation to justify ourselves in doing what we want to do. And to surrender to impulse is part of the pattern. I think a greater defect is that it leads you to live too much in the future. I have long known that this was a fault of mine and have in vain tried to correct it. I have never, except by an effort of will, wished that the passing moment might linger so that I could get more enjoyment from it, for even when it has brought me something I had immensely looked forward to, my imagination in the very moment of fulfilment has been busy with the problematical delight of whatever was to come. I have never walked down the south side of Piccadilly without being all in a dither about what was happening on the north. This is folly. The passing moment is all we can be sure of; it is only common sense to extract its utmost value from it; the future will one day be the present and will seem as unimportant as the present does now. But common sense avails me little. I do not find the present unsatisfactory; I merely take it for granted. It is interwoven in the pattern and what interests me is what remains to come.

I have made a great many mistakes. I have at times fallen victim to a snare to which the writer is peculiarly liable, the desire to carry out in my own life certain actions which I made the characters of my invention do. I have attempted things that were foreign to my nature and obstinately persevered in them because in my vanity I would not confess myself beaten. I have paid too much attention to the opinion of others. I have made sacrifices to unworthy objects because I had not the courage to inflict pain. I have committed follies. I have a sensitive conscience, and I have done certain things in my life that I am unable entirely to forget; if I had been fortunate enough to be a Catholic I could have delivered myself of them at confession and after performing the penance imposed received absolution and put them out of my mind forever. I have had to deal with them as my common sense suggested. I do not regret them, for I think it is because of my own grave faults that I have learnt indulgence for others. It took me a long time. In youth I was harshly intolerant. I remember my indignation upon hearing someone make the remark, not an original one, but new to me then, that hypocrisy was the tribute that vice paid to virtue. I thought that one should have the courage of one's vices. I had ideals of honesty, uprightness, truth; I was impatient not of human weakness, but of cowardice, and I would make no allowances for those who hedged and temporized. It never occurred to me that no one stood in greater need of indulgence than I.

At first sight it is curious that our own offences should seem to us so much less heinous than the offences of others. I suppose the reason is that we know all the circumstances that have occasioned them and so manage to excuse in ourselves what we cannot excuse in others. We turn our attention away from our own defects, and when we are forced by untoward events to consider them find it easy to condone them. For all I know we are right to do this; they are part of us and we must accept the good and the bad in ourselves together. But when we come to judge others it is not by ourselves as we really are that we judge them, but by an image that we have formed of ourselves from which we have left out everything that offends our vanity or would discredit us in the eyes of the world. To take a trivial instance: how scornful we are when we catch someone out telling a lie; but who can say that he has never told not one, but a hundred? We are shocked when we discover that great men were weak and petty, dishonest or selfish, sexually vicious, vain or intemperate; and many people think it disgraceful to disclose to the public its heroes' failings. There is not much to choose between men. They are all a hotchpotch of greatness and littleness, of virtue and vice, of nobility and baseness. Some have more strength of character, or more opportunity, and so in one direction or another give their instincts freer play, but potentially they are the same. For my part I do not think I am any better or any worse than most people, but I know that if I set down every action in my life and every thought that has crossed my mind the world would consider me a monster of depravity.

I wonder how anyone can have the face to condemn others when he reflects upon his own thoughts. A great part of our lives is occupied in reverie, and the more imaginative we are, the more varied and vivid this will be. How many of us could face having our reveries automatically registered and set before us? We should be overcome with shame. We should cry that we could not really be as mean, as wicked, as petty, as selfish, as obscene, as snobbish, as vain, as sentimental, as that. Yet surely our reveries are as much part of us as our actions, and if there were a being to whom our inmost thoughts were known we might just as well be held responsible for them as for our deeds. Men forget the horrible thoughts that wander through their own minds, and are indignant when they discover them in others. In Goethe's *Wahrheit und Dichtung* he relates how in his youth he could not bear the idea that his father was a middle-class lawyer in Frankfurt. He felt that noble blood must flow in his veins. So he sought to persuade himself that some prince travelling through the city had met and loved his mother, and that he was the offspring of the union. The editor of the copy I read wrote an indignant footnote on the subject. It seemed to him unworthy of so great a poet that he should impugn the undoubted virtue of his mother in order snobbishly to plume himself on his bastard aristocracy. Of course it was disgraceful, but it was not unnatural and I venture to say not uncommon. There must be few romantic, rebellious and imaginative boys who

have not toyed with the idea that they could not be the son of
their dull and respectable father, but ascribe the superiority they
feel in themselves, according to their own idiosyncrasies, to an
unknown poet, great statesman or ruling prince. The Olympian
attitude of Goethe's later years inspires me with esteem; this confession arouses in me a warmer feeling. Because a man can write
great works he is none the less a man.

It is, I suppose, these lewd, ugly, base and selfish thoughts,
dwelling in their minds against their will, that have tormented
the saints when their lives were devoted to good works and repentance had redeemed the sins of their past. St Ignatius Loyola,
as we know, when he went to Monserrat made a general confession and received absolution; but he continued to be obsessed by
a sense of sin so that he was on the point of killing himself. Till
his conversion he had led the ordinary life of the young man of
good birth at that time; he was somewhat vain of his appearance,
he had wenched and gambled; but at least on one occasion he
had shown rare magnanimity and he had always been honoura-
ble, loyal, generous and brave. If peace was still denied him it
looks as though it was his thoughts that he could not forgive
himself. It would be a comfort to know that even the saints
were thus afflicted. When I have seen the great ones of the earth,
so upright and dignified, sitting in state I have often asked myself whether at such moments they ever remembered how their
minds in solitude were sometimes occupied and whether it ever
made them uneasy to think of the secrets that their subliminal self
harboured. It seems to me that the knowledge that these reveries
are common to all men should inspire one with tolerance to
oneself as well as to others. It is well also if they enable us to
look upon our fellows, even the most eminent and respectable,
with humour and if they lead us to take ourselves not too seriously. When I have heard judges on the bench moralizing with
unction I have asked myself whether it was possible for them to
have forgotten their humanity so completely as their words suggested. I have wished that beside his bunch of flowers at the Old
Bailey, his lordship had a packet of toilet paper. It would remind him that he was a man like any other.

I have been called cynical. I have been accused of making men out worse than they are. I do not think I have done this. All I have done is to bring into prominence certain traits that many writers shut their eyes to. I think what has chiefly struck me in human beings is their lack of consistency. I have never seen people all of a piece. It has amazed me that the most incongruous traits should exist in the same person and for all that yield a plausible harmony. I have often asked myself how characteristics, seemingly irreconcilable, can exist in the same person. I have known crooks who were capable of self-sacrifice, sneak-thieves who were sweet-natured and harlots for whom it was a point of honour to give good value for money. The only explanation I can offer is that so instinctive is each one's conviction that he is unique in the world, and privileged, that he feels that, however wrong it might be for others, what he for his part does, if not natural and right, is at least venial. The contrast that I have found in people has interested me, but I do not think I have unduly emphasized it. The censure that has from time to time been passed on me is due perhaps to the fact that I have not expressly condemned what was bad in the characters of my invention and praised what was good. It must be a fault in me that I am not gravely shocked at the sins of others unless they personally affect me, and even when they do I have learnt at last generally to excuse them. It is meet not to expect too much of others. You should be grateful when they treat you well, but unperturbed when they treat you ill. "For every one of us," as the Athenian Stranger said, "is made pretty much what he is by the bent of his desires and the nature of his soul." It is want of imagination that prevents people from seeing things from any point of view but their own, and it is unreasonable to be angry with them because they lack this faculty.

I think I could be justly blamed if I saw only people's faults and were blind to their virtues. I am not conscious that this is the case. There is nothing more beautiful than goodness and it has pleased me very often to show how much of it there is in persons who by common standards would be relentlessly condemned. I have shown it because I have seen it. It has seemed to me sometimes to shine more brightly in them because it was surrounded

by the darkness of sin. I take the goodness of the good for granted
and I am amused when I discover their defects or their vices; I
am touched when I see the goodness of the wicked and I am
willing enough to shrug a tolerant shoulder at their wickedness.
I am not my brother's keeper. I cannot bring myself to judge
my fellows; I am content to observe them. My observation has
led me to believe that, all in all, there is not so much difference
between the good and the bad as the moralists would have us
believe.

I have not on the whole taken people at their face value. I do
not know if this coolness of scrutiny has been inherited from my
fathers; they could hardly have been successful lawyers if they
had not possessed a shrewdness that prevented them from being
deceived by appearances; or if I owe it to the lack in me of that
joyful uprush of emotion on meeting people that makes many,
as the saying is, take their geese for swans. It was certainly encouraged by my training as a medical student. I did not want to
be a doctor. I did not want to be anything but a writer, but I
was much too shy to say so, and in any case at that time it was
unheard of that a boy of eighteen, belonging to a respectable
family, should adopt literature as a profession. The notion was so
preposterous that I never even dreamt of imparting it to anybody.
I had always supposed that I should enter the law, but my three
brothers, much older than I, were practising it and there did not
seem room for me too.

From *The Summing Up*, 1938.

Hawthorne and His Mosses

by HERMAN MELVILLE [1819–1891]

A PAPERED CHAMBER in a fine old farmhouse, a mile from any
other dwelling, and dipped to the eaves in foliage—surrounded
by mountains, old woods, and Indian pools—this surely, is the

place to write of Hawthorne. Some charm is in this northern
air, for love and duty seem both impelling to the task. A man of
a deep and noble nature has seized me in this seclusion. His
wild, witch-voice rings through me; or, in softer cadences, I
seem to hear it in the songs of the hillside birds that sing in the
larch trees at my window.

Would that all excellent books were foundlings, without
father or mother, that so it might be we could glorify them, without including their ostensible authors! Nor would any true man
take exception to this; least of all, he who writes, "When the
artist rises high enough to achieve the beautiful, the symbol by
which he makes it perceptible to mortal senses becomes of little
value in his eyes, while his spirit possesses itself in the enjoyment
of the reality."

But more than this. I know not what would be the right name
to put on the title-page of an excellent book; but this I feel, that
the names of all fine authors are fictitious ones, far more so than
that of Junius; simply standing, as they do, for the mystical ever-
eluding spirit of all beauty, which ubiquitously possesses men
of genius. Purely imaginative as this fancy may appear, it nevertheless seems to receive some warranty from the fact, that on a
personal interview no great author has every come up to the idea
of his reader. But that dust of which our bodies are composed,
how can it fitly express the nobler intelligences among us? With
reverence be it spoken, that not even in the case of one deemed
more than man, not even in our Saviour, did his visible frame be-
token anything of the augustness of the nature within. Else, how
could those Jewish eyewitnesses fail to see heaven in his glance!

It is curious how a man may travel along a country road, and
yet miss the grandest or sweetest of prospects by reason of an
intervening hedge, so like all other hedges, as in no way to hint
of the wide landscape beyond. So has it been with me concerning
the enchanting landscape in the soul of this Hawthorne, this
most excellent Man of Mosses. His Old Manse has been written
now four years, but I never read it till a day or two since. I had
seen it in the book-stores—heard of it often—even had it recommended to me by a tasteful friend, as a rare, quiet book, per-

haps too deserving of popularity to be popular. But there are
so many books called "excellent," and so much unpopular merit,
that amid the thick stir of other things, the hint of my tasteful
friend was disregarded and for four years the Mosses on the
Old Manse never refreshed me with their perennial green. It
may be, however, that all this while the book, likewise, was
only improving in flavor and body. At any rate, it so chanced
that this long procrastination eventuated in a happy result. At
breakfast the other day, a mountain girl, a cousin of mine, who
for the last two weeks has every morning helped me to straw-
berries and raspberries, which, like the roses and pearls in the fairy
tale, seemed to fall into the saucer from those strawberry-beds,
her cheeks—this delightful creature, this charming Cherry says
to me—"I see you spend your mornings in the haymow; and
yesterday I found there Dwight's *Travels in New England*.
Now I have something far better than that, something more congenial to our summer on these hills. Take these raspberries, and
then I will give you some moss." "Moss!" said I. "Yes, and you
must take it to the barn with you, and good-by to Dwight."

With that she left me, and soon returned with a volume,
verdently bound, and garnished with a curious frontispiece in
green; nothing less than a fragment of real moss, cunningly
pressed to a fly-leaf. "Why, this," said I, spilling my raspberries,
"this is the *Mosses from an Old Manse*." "Yes," said cousin
Cherry, "yes, it is that flowery Hawthorne." "Hawthorne and
Mosses," said I, "no more it is morning: it is July in the country:
and I am off for the barn."

Stretched on that new mown clover, the hillside breeze blowing over me through the wide barn door, and soothed by the hum
of the bees in the meadows around, how magically stole over
me this Mossy Man! and how amply, how bountifully, did he
redeem that delicious promise to his guests in the Old Manse, of
whom it is written: "Others could give them pleasure, or amusement, or instruction—these could be picked up anywhere; but
it was for me to give them rest—rest, in a life of trouble! What
better could be done for those weary and world-worn spirits?
. . . what better could be done for anybody who came within

our magic circle than to throw the spell of a tranquil spirit over him?" So all that day, half-buried in the new clover, I watched this Hawthorne's "Assyrian dawn, and Paphian sunset and moonrise from the summit of our eastern hill."

The soft ravishments of the man spun me round about in a web of dreams, and when the book was closed, when the spell was over, this wizard "dismissed me with but misty reminiscences, as if I had been dreaming of him."

What a wild moonlight of contemplative humor bathes that Old Manse! the rich and rare distilment of a spicy and slowly-oozing heart. No rollicking rudeness, no gross fun fed on fat dinners, and bred in the lees of wine—but a humor so spiritually gentle, so high, so deep, and yet so richly relishable, that it were hardly inappropriate in an angel. It is the very religion of mirth; for nothing so human but it may be advanced to that. The orchard of the Old Manse seems the visible type of the fine mind that has described it—those twisted and contorted old trees, "they stretch out their crooked branches, and take such hold of the imagination that we remember them as humorists and odd-fellows." And then, as surrounded by these grotesque forms, and hushed in the noonday repose of this Hawthorne's spell, how aptly might the still fall of his ruddy thoughts into your soul be symbolized by: "In the stillest afternoon, if I listened, the thump of a great apple was audible, falling without a breath of wind, from the mere necessity of perfect ripeness." For no less ripe than ruddy are the apples of the thoughts and fancies in this sweet Man of Mosses.

Buds and Bird Voices. What a delicious thing is that! "Will the world ever be so decayed, that spring may not renew its greenness?" And the *Fire Worship.* Was ever the hearth so glorified into an altar before? The mere title of that piece is better than any common work in fifty folio volumes. How exquisite is this:

> Nor did it lessen the charm of his soft, familiar courtesy and helpfulness that the mighty spirit, were opportunity offered him, would run riot through the peaceful house, wrap its inmates in his terrible embrace, and leave nothing of them

save their whitened bones. This possibility of mad destruction
only made his domestic kindness the more beautiful and
touching. It was so sweet of him, being endowed with such
power, to dwell day after day, and one long lonesome night
after another, on the dusky hearth, only now and then betraying his wild nature by thrusting his red tongue out of
the chimney-top! True, he had done much mischief in the
world, and was pretty certain to do more; but his warm heart
atoned for all. He was kindly to the race of man; and they
pardoned his characteristic imperfections.

But he has still other apples, not quite so ruddy, though full
as ripe: apples, that have been left to wither on the tree, after
the pleasant autumn gathering is past. The sketch of *The Old
Apple Dealer* is conceived in the subtlest spirit of sadness; he
whose "subdued and nerveless boyhood prefigured his abortive
prime, which likewise contained within itself the prophecy and
image of his lean and torpid age." Such touches as are in this
piece cannot proceed from any common heart. They argue such
a depth of tenderness, such a boundless sympathy with all forms
of being, such an omnipresent love, that we must needs say that
this Hawthorne is here almost alone in his generation—at least,
in the artistic manifestation of these things. Still more. Such
touches as these—and many, very many similar ones, all through
his chapters—furnish clues whereby we enter a little way into
the intricate, profound heart where they originated. And we see
that suffering, some time or other and in some shape or other—
this only can enable any man to depict it in others. All over him,
Hawthorne's melancholy rests like an Indian-summer, which,
though bathing a whole country in one softness, still reveals the
distinctive hue of every towering hill and each far-winding vale.
But it is the least part of genius that attracts admiration. Where
Hawthorne is known, he seems to be deemed a pleasant writer,
with a pleasant style—a sequestered, harmless man, from whom
any deep and weighty thing would hardly be anticipated—a man
who means no meanings. But there is no man, in whom humor
and love, like mountain peaks, soar to such a rapt height as to

receive the irradiations of the upper skies; there is no man in whom humor and love are developed in that high form called genius; no such man can exist without also possessing, as the indispensable complement of these, a great, deep intellect, which drops down into the universe like a plummet. Or, love and humor are only the eyes through which such an intellect views this world. The great beauty in such a mind is but the product of its strength. What, to all readers, can be more charming than the piece entitled *Monsieur du Miroir;* and to a reader at all capable of fully fathoming it, what, at the same time, can possess more mystical depth of meaning? yes, there he sits and looks at me—this "shape of mystery," this "identical MONSIEUR DU MIROIR!" "Methinks I should tremble now were his wizard power of gliding through all impediments in search of me to place him suddenly before my eyes."

How profound, nay, appalling, is the moral evolved by the *Earth's Holocaust;* where—beginning with the hollow follies and affectations of the world—all vanities and empty theories and forms are, one after another, and by an admirably graduated, growing comprehensiveness, thrown into the allegorical fire, till, at length, nothing is left but the all-engendering heart of man; which remaining still unconsumed, the great conflagration is naught.

Of a piece with this, is the *Intelligence Office,* a wondrous symbolizing of the secret workings in men's souls. There are other sketches still more charged with ponderous import.

The Christmas Banquet, and *The Bosom Serpent,* would be fine subjects for a curious and elaborate analysis, touching the conjectural parts of the mind that produced them. For spite of all the Indian-summer sunlight on the hither side of Hawthorne's soul, the other side—like the dark half of the physical sphere—is shrouded in a blackness, ten times black. But this darkness but gives more effect to the ever-moving dawn, that forever advances through it, and circumnavigates his world. Whether Hawthorne has simply availed himself of this mystical blackness as a means to the wondrous effects he makes it to produce in his lights and shades; or whether there really lurks in him, perhaps unknown to himself, a touch of Puritanic gloom—this, I cannot altogether tell. Certain it is, however, that this great power of blackness in him derives its force from its appeals to that Calvinistic sense of Innate Depravity and Original Sin, from whose visitations, in some shape or other, no deeply thinking mind is always and wholly free. For, in certain moods, no man can weigh this world without throwing in something, somehow like Original Sin, to strike the uneven balance. At all events, perhaps no writer has ever wielded this terrific thought with greater terror than this same harmless Hawthorne. Still more: this black conceit pervades him through and through. You may be witched by his sunlight—transported by the bright gildings in the skies he builds over you; but there is the blackness of darkness beyond; and even his bright gildings but fringe and play upon the edges of thunder-clouds. In one word, the world is mistaken in this Nathaniel Hawthorne. He himself must often have smiled at its absurd misconception of him. He is immeasurably deeper than the plummet of the mere critic. For it is not the brain that can test such a man; it is only the heart. You cannot come to know greatness by inspecting it; there is no glimpse to be caught of it, except by intuition; you need not ring it, you but touch it, and you find it is gold.

Now, it is that blackness in Hawthorne, of which I have spoken that so fixes and fascinates me. It may be, nevertheless, that it is too largely developed in him. Perhaps he does not give us a ray of light for every shade of his dark. But however this may be, this blackness it is that furnishes the infinite obscure of his background—that background, against which Shakspeare plays his grandest conceits, the things that have made for Shakspeare his loftiest but most circumscribed renown, as the profoundest of thinkers. For by philosophers Shakspeare is not adored, as the great man of tragedy and comedy: "Off with his head; so much for Buckingham!" This sort of rant interlined by another hand, brings down the house—those mistaken souls, who dream of Shakspeare as a mere man of Richard the Third humps and Macbeth daggers. But it is those deep far-away things in him; those occasional flashings-forth of the intuitive Truth in him;

those short, quick probings at the very axis of reality—these are the things that make Shakspeare, Shakspeare. Through the mouths of the dark characters of Hamlet, Timon, Lear, and Iago, he craftily says, or sometimes insinuates the things which we feel to be so terrifically true, that it were all but madness for any good man, in his own proper character, to utter, or even hint of them. Tormented into desperation, Lear, the frantic king, tears off the mask, and speaks the same madness of vital truth. But, as I before said, it is the least part of genius that attracts admiration. And so, much of the blind, unbridled admiration that has been heaped upon Shakspeare, has been lavished upon the least part of him. And few of his endless commentators and critics seem to have remembered, or even perceived, that the immediate products of a great mind are not so great as that undeveloped and sometimes undevelopable yet dimly-discernible greatness, to which those immediate products are but the infallible indices. In Shakspeare's tomb lies infinitely more than Shakspeare ever wrote. And if I magnify Shakspeare, it is not so much for what he did do as for what he did not do, or refrained from doing. For in this world of lies, Truth is forced to fly like a scared white doe in the woodlands; and only by cunning glimpses will she reveal herself, as in Shakspeare and other masters of the great Art of Telling the Truth—even though it be covertly and by snatches.

But if this view of the all-popular Shakspeare be seldom taken by his readers, and if very few who extol him have ever read him deeply, or perhaps, only have seen him on tricky stage (which alone made, and is still making him his mere mob renown)— if few men have time, or patience, or palate, for the spiritual truth as it is in that great genius—it is then no matter of surprise, that in a contemporaneous age, Nathaniel Hawthorne is a man as yet almost utterly mistaken among men. Here and there, in some quiet armchair in the noisy town, or some deep nook among the noiseless mountains, he may be appreciated for something of what he is. But unlike Shakspeare, who was forced to the contrary course by circumstances, Hawthorne (either from simple disinclination, or else from inaptitude) refrains from all the popularizing noise and show of broad farce and blood-besmeared tragedy; content with the still, rich utterance of a great intellect in respose, and which sends few thoughts into circulation, except they be arterialized at his large warm lungs, and expanded in his honest heart.

Nor need you fix upon that blackness in him, if it suit you not. Nor, indeed, will all readers discern it; for it is, mostly, insinuated to those who may best understand it, and account for it; it is not obtruded upon every one alike.

Some may start to read of Shakspeare and Hawthorne on the same page. They may say, that if an illustration were needed, a lesser light might have sufficed to elucidate this Hawthorne, this small man of yesterday. But I am not willingly one of those who, as touching Shakspeare at least, exemplify the maxim of Rochefoucauld, that "we exalt the reputation of some, in order to depress that of others"—who, teach all noble-souled aspirants that there is no hope for them, pronounce Shakspeare absolutely unapproachable. But Shakspeare has been approached. There are minds that have gone as far as Shakspeare into the universe. And hardly a mortal man, who, at some time or other, has not felt as great thoughts in him as any you will find in Hamlet. We must not inferentially malign mankind for the sake of any one man, whoever he may be. This is too cheap a purchase of contentment for conscious mediocrity to make. Besides, this absolute and unconditional adoration of Shakspeare has grown to be a part of our Anglo-Saxon superstitions. The Thirty-Nine Articles are now Forty. Intolerance has come to exist in this matter. You must believe in Shakspeare's unapproachability, or quit the country. But what sort of a belief is this for an American, a man who is bound to carry republican progressiveness into Literature as well as into Life? Believe me, my friends, that men, not very much inferior to Shakspeare are this day being born on the banks of the Ohio. And the day will come when you shall say, Who reads a book by an Englishman that is a modern? The great mistake seems to be, that even with those Americans who look forward to the coming of a great literary genius among us, they somehow fancy he will come in the costume of Queen

Elizabeth's day; be a writer of dramas founded upon old English history or the tales of Boccaccio. Whereas, great geniuses are parts of the times, they themselves are the times, and possess a corresponding coloring. It is of a piece with the Jews, who, while their Shiloh was meekly walking in their streets, were still praying for his magnificent coming; looking for him in a chariot, who was already among them on an ass. Nor must we forget that, in his own lifetime, Shakspeare was not Shakspeare, but only Master William Shakspeare of the shrewd, thriving, business firm of Condell, Shakspeare and Co., proprietors of the Globe Theatre in London; and by a courtly author, of the name of Chettle, was looked at as an "upstart crow," beautified "with other birds' feathers." For, mark it well, imitation is often the first charge brought against originality. Why this is so, there is not space to set forth here. You must have plenty of sea-room to tell the Truth in; especially when it seems to have an aspect of newness, as America did in 1492, though it was then just as old, and perhaps older than Asia, only those sagacious philosophers, the common sailors, had never seen it before, swearing it was all water and moonshine there.

Now I do not say that Nathaniel of Salem is a greater man than William of Avon, or as great. But the difference between the two men is by no means immeasurable. Not a very great deal more, and Nathaniel were verily William.

This, too, I mean, that if Shakspeare has not been equalled, give the world time, and he is sure to be surpassed in one hemisphere or the other. Nor will it at all do to say that the world is getting grey and grizzled now, and has lost that fresh charm which she wore of old, and by virtue of which the great poets of past times made themselves what we esteem them to be. Not so. The world is as young to-day as when it was created; and this Vermont morning dew is as wet to my feet, as Eden's dew to Adam's. Nor has nature been all over ransacked by our progenitors, so that no new charms and mysteries remain for this latter generation to find. Far from it. The trillionth part has not yet been said; and all that has been said, but multiplies the avenues to what remains to be said. It is not so much paucity as superabundance of material that seems to incapacitate modern authors.

Let America, then, prize and cherish her writers; yea, let her glorify them. They are not so many in number as to exhaust her goodwill. And while she has good kith and kin of her own, to take to her bosom, let her not lavish her embraces upon the household of an alien. For believe it or not, England after all, is in many things an alien to us. China has more bonds of real love for us than she. But even were there no strong literary individualities among us, as there are some dozens at least, nevertheless, let America first praise mediocrity even, in her children, before she praises (for everywhere, merit demands acknowledgment from every one) the best excellence in the children of any other land. Let her own authors, I say, have the priority of appreciation. I was much pleased with a hot-headed Carolina cousin of mine, who once said, "If there were no other American to stand by, in literature, why, then, I would stand by Pop Emmons and his *Fredoniad,* and till a better epic came along, swear it was not very far behind the *Iliad.*" Take away the words, and in spirit he was sound.

Not that American genius needs patronage in order to expand. For that explosive sort of stuff will expand though screwed up in a vice, and burst it, though it were triple steel. It is for the nation's sake, and not for her authors' sake, that I would have America be heedful of the increasing greatness among her writers. For how great the shame, if other nations should be before her, in crowning her heroes of the pen! But this is almost the case now. American authors have received more just and discriminating praise (however loftily and ridiculously given, in certain cases) even from some Englishmen, than from their own countrymen. There are hardly five critics in America; and several of them are asleep. As for patronage, it is the American author who now patronizes his country, and not his country him. And if at times some among them appeal to the people for more recognition, it is not always with selfish motives, but patriotic ones.

It is true, that but few of them as yet have evinced that decided originality which merits great praise. But that graceful writer, who perhaps of all Americans has received the most plaudits from his own country for his productions—that very popular and amiable writer, however good and self-reliant in many things, perhaps owes his chief reputation to the self-acknowledged imitation of a foreign model, and to the studied avoidance of all topics but smooth ones. But it is better to fail in originality, than to succeed in imitation. He who has never failed somewhere, that man cannot be great. Failure is the true test of greatness. And if it be said, that continual success is a proof that a man wisely knows his powers—it is only to be added, that, in that case, he knows them to be small. Let us believe it, then, once for all, that there is no hope for us in these smooth, pleasing writers that know their powers. Without malice, but to speak the plain fact, they but furnish an appendix to Goldsmith, and other English authors. And we want no American Goldsmiths, nay, we want no American Miltons. It were the vilest thing you could say of a true American author, that he were an American Tompkins. Call him an American and have done, for you cannot say a nobler thing of him. But it is not meant that all American writers should studiously cleave to nationality in their writings; only this, no American writer should write like an Englishman or a Frenchman; let him write like a man, for then he will be sure to write like an Ameriman. Let us away with this leaven of literary flunkeyism towards England. If either must play the flunkey in this thing, let England do it, not us. While we are rapidly preparing for that political supremacy among the nations which prophetically awaits us at the close of the present century, in a literary point of view, we are deplorably unprepared for it; and we seem studious to remain so. Hitherto, reasons might have existed why this should be; but no good reason exists now. And all that is requisite to amendment in this matter, is simply this; that while fully acknowledging all excellence everywhere, we should refrain from unduly lauding foreign writers, and, at the same time, duly recognize the meritorious writers that are our own—those writers who breathe that unshackled, democratic spirit of Christianity in all things, which now takes the practical lead in this world, though at the same time led by ourselves—us Americans. Let us boldly condemn all imitation, though it comes to us graceful and fragrant as the morning; and foster all originality though at first it be crabbed and ugly as our own pine knots. And if any of our authors fail, or seem to fail, then, in the words of my Carolina cousin, let us clap him on the shoulder and back him against all Europe for his second round. The truth is, that in one point of view this matter of a national literature has come to pass with us, that in some sense we must turn bullies, else the day is lost, or superiority so far beyond us, that we can hardly say it will ever be ours.

And now, my countrymen, as an excellent author of your own flesh and blood—an unimitating, and, perhaps, in his way, an inimitable man—whom better can I commend to you, in the first place, than Nathaniel Hawthorne. He is one of the new, and far better generation of your writers. The smell of young beeches and hemlocks is upon him; your own broad praises are in his soul; and if you travel away inland into his deep and noble nature, you will hear the far roar of his Niagara. Give not over to future generations the glad duty of acknowledging him for what he is. Take that joy to yourself, in your own generation; and so shall he feel those grateful impulses on him, that may possibly prompt him to the full flower of some still greater achievement in your eyes. And by confessing him you thereby confess others; you brace the whole brotherhood. For genius, all over the world, stands hand in hand, and one shock of recognition runs the whole circle round.

In treating of Hawthorne, or rather of Hawthorne in his writings (for I never saw the man; and in the chances of a quiet plantation life, remote from his haunts, perhaps never shall); in treating of his works, I say, I have thus far omitted all mention of his *Twice Told Tales,* and *Scarlet Letter.* Both are excellent, but full of such manifold, strange, and diffusive beauties, that time would all but fail me to point the half of them out. But there are things in those two books, which, had they been written in England a century ago, Nathaniel Hawthrone had utterly displaced many of the bright names we now revere on authority. But I am content to leave Hawthorne to himself, and to the infallible finding of posterity; and however great may be the praise I have bestowed upon him, I feel that in so doing I have served and honored myself, than him. For, at bottom, great excellence is praise enough to itself; but the feeling of a sincere and appreciative love and admiration towards it, this is relieved by utterance, and warm, honest praise ever leaves a pleasant flavor in the mouth; and it is an honorable thing to confess to what is honorable in others.

But I cannot leave my subject yet. No man can read a fine author, and relish him to his very bones while he reads, without subsequently fancying to himself some ideal image of the man and his mind. And if you rightly look for it, you will almost always find that the author himself has somewhere furnished you with his own picture. For poets (whether in prose or verse), being painters by nature, are like their brethern of the pencil, the true portrait-painters, who, in the multitude of likenesses to be sketched, do not invariably omit their own; and in all high instances, they paint them without any vanity, though at times with a lurking something that would take several pages to properly define.

I submit it, then, to those best acquainted with the man personally, whether the following is not Nathaniel Hawthorne; and to himself, whether something involved in it does not express the temper of his mind—that lasting temper of all true, candid men—a seeker, not a finder yet:

A man now entered, in neglected attire, with the aspect of a thinker, but somewhat too roughhewn and brawny for a scholar. His face was full of sturdy vigor, with some finer and keener attribute beneath; though harsh at first, it was tempered with the glow of a large, warm heart, which had force enough to heat his powerful intellect through and through. He advanced to the Intelligencer, and looked at him with a glance of such stern sincerity, that perhaps few secrets were beyond its scope.

"I seek for Truth," said he.

Twenty-four hours have elapsed since writing the foregoing. I have just returned from the haymow, charged more and more with love and admiration of Hawthorne. For I have just been gleaning through the Mosses, picking up many things here and there that had previously escaped me. And I found that but to glean after this man, is better than to be in at the harvest of others. To be frank (though, perhaps, rather foolish) notwithstanding what I wrote yesterday of these Mosses, I had not then culled them all; but had, nevertheless, been sufficiently sensible of the subtle essence in them, as to write as I did. To what infinite height of loving wonder and admiration I may yet be borne, when by repeatedly banqueting on these Mosses I shall have thoroughly incorporated their whole stuff into my being— that, I cannot tell. But already I feel that this Hawthorne has dropped germinous seeds into my soul. He expands and deepens down, the more I contemplate him; and further and further, shoots his strong New England roots into the hot soil in my Southern soul.

By careful reference to the table of contents, I now find that I have gone through all the sketches; but that when I yesterday wrote, I had not at all read two particular pieces, to which I now desire to call special attention—*A Select Party* and *Young Goodman Brown*. Here, be it said to all those whom this poor fugitive scrawl of mine may tempt to the perusal of the Mosses, that they must on no account suffer themselves to be trifled with, disappointed, or deceived by the triviality of many of the titles to these sketches. For in more than one instance, the title utterly belies the piece. It is as if rustic demijohns containing the very best and costliest of Falernian and Tokay, were labelled "Cider," "Perry," and "Elderberry wine." The truth seems to be, that like many other geniuses, this Man of Mosses takes great delight in hoodwinking the world—at least, with respect to himself. Personally, I doubt not that he rather prefers to be generally esteemed but a so-so sort of author; being willing to reserve the thorough and acute appreciation of what he is, to that party most qualified to judge—that is, to himself. Besides, at the bottom of their natures, men like Hawthorne, in many things, deem the plaudits of the public such strong presumptive evidence of mediocrity in the object of them, that it would in some degree render them doubtful of their own powers, did they hear much and vociferous braying concerning them in the public pastures. True, I have been braying myself (if you please to be witty enough to have it so), but then I claim to be the first that has so brayed in this particular matter; and, therefore, while pleading guilty to the charge, still claim all the merit due to originality.

But with whatever motive, playful or profound, Nathaniel Hawthorne has chosen to entitle his pieces in the manner he has, it is certain that some of them are directly calculated to deceive— egregiously deceive, the superficial skimmer of pages. To be downright and candid once more, let me cheerfully say, that two of these titles did dolefully dupe no less an eager-eyed reader than myself; and that, too, after I had been impressed with a sense of the great depth and breadth of this American man. "Who in the name of thunder" (as the country people say in this neighborhood), "who in the name of thunder, would anticipate any marvel in a piece entitled *Young Goodman Brown?*" You would of course suppose that it was a simple little tale, intended as a supplement to *Goody Two Shoes*. Whereas, it is deep as Dante; nor can you finish it, without addressing the author in his own words—"It shall be yours to penetrate, in every bosom, the deep mystery of sin". . . . And with Young Goodman, too, in allegorical pursuit of his Puritan wife, you cry out in your anguish:

> "Faith!" shouted Goodman Brown, in a voice of agony and desperation; and the echoes of the forest mocked him, crying, "Faith! Faith!" as if bewildered wretches were seeking her all through the wilderness.

Now this same piece entitled *Young Goodman Brown,* is one of the two that I had not all read yesterday; and I allude to it now, because it is, in itself, such a strong positive illustration of the blackness in Hawthorne, which I had assumed from the mere occasional shadows of it; as revealed in several of the other sketches. But had I previously perused *Young Goodman Brown,*

I should have been at no pains to draw the conclusion, which I came to at a time when I was ignorant that the book contained one such direct and unqualified manifestation of it.

The other piece of the two referred to, is entitled *A Select Party,* which, in my first simplicity upon originally taking hold of the book, I fancied must treat of some pumpkin-pie party in old Salem; or some chowder party on Cape Cod. Whereas, by all the gods of Peedee, it is the sweetest and sublimest thing that has been written since Spenser wrote. Nay, there is nothing in Spenser that surpasses it, perhaps nothing that equals it. And the test is this. Read any canto in *The Faerie Queene* and then read *A Select Party,* and decide which pleases you most—that is, if you are qualified to judge. Do not be frightened at this; for when Spenser was alive, he was thought of very much as Hawthorne is now—was generally accounted just such a "gentle" harmless man. It may be, that to common eyes, the sublimity of Hawthorne seems lost in his sweetness—as perhaps in that same *Select Party* of his; for whom he has builded so august a dome of sunset clouds, and served them on richer plate than Belshazzar when he banqueted his lords in Babylon.

But my chief business now, is to point out a particular page in this piece, having reference to an honored guest, who under the name of the Master Genius, but in the guise "of a young man of poor attire, with no insignia of rank or acknowledged eminence," is introduced to the Man of Fancy, who is the giver of the feast. Now, the page having reference to this Master Genius, so happily expresses much of what I yesterday wrote, touching the coming of the literary Shiloh of America, that I cannot but be charmed by the coincidence; especially, when it shows such a parity of ideas, at least in this one point, between a man like Hawthorne and a man like me.

And here, let me throw out another conceit of mine touching this American Shiloh, or Master Genius, as Hawthorne calls him. May it not be, that this commanding mind has not been, is not, and never will be, individually developed in any one man? And would it, indeed, appear so unreasonable to suppose that this great fulness and overflowing may be, or may be destined to be, shared by a plurality of men of genius? Surely, to take the very greatest example on record, Shakspeare cannot be regarded as in himself the concretion of all the genius of his time; nor as so immeasurably beyond Marlowe, Webster, Ford, Beaumont, Jonson, that these great men can be said to share none of his power? For one, I conceive that there were dramatists in Elizabeth's day, between whom and Shakspeare the distance was by no means great. Let any one, hitherto little acquainted with those neglected old authors, for the first time read them thoroughly, or even read Charles Lamb's *Specimens* of them, and he will be amazed at the wondrous ability of those Anaks of men, and shocked at this renewed example of the fact, that Fortune has more to do with fame than merit—though, without merit, lasting fame there can be none.

Nevertheless, it would argue too ill of my country were this maxim to hold good concerning Nathaniel Hawthorne, a man, who already, in some few minds has shed "such a light as never illuminates the earth save when a great heart burns as the household fire of a grand intellect."

The words are his—in the *Select Party;* and they are a magnificent setting to a coincident sentiment of my own, but ramblingly expressed yesterday, in reference to himself. Gainsay it who will, as I now write, I am Posterity speaking by proxy—and after times will make it more than good, when I declare, that the American, who up to the present day has evinced, in literature, the largest brain with the largest heart, that man is Nathaniel Hawthorne. Moreover, that whatever Nathaniel Hawthorne may hereafter write, *Mosses from an Old Manse* will be ultimately accounted his masterpiece. For there is a sure, though secret sign in some works which proves the culmination of the powers (only the developable ones, however) that produced them. But I am by no means desirous of the glory of a prophet. I pray Heaven that Hawthorne may yet prove me an imposter in this prediction. Especially, as I somehow cling to the strange fancy, that, in all men, hiddenly reside certain wondrous, occult properties—as in some plants and minerals—which by some happy but very rare accident (as bronze was discovered by the melting

of the iron and brass at the burning of Corinth) may chance to
be called forth here on earth; not entirely waiting for their better
discovery in the more congenial, blessed atmosphere of heaven.

Once more—for it is hard to be finite upon an infinite subject, and all subjects are infinite. By some people this entire
scrawl of mine may be esteemed altogether unnecessary, inasmuch "as years ago" (they may say) "we found out the rich
and rare stuff in this Hawthorne, who you now parade forth, as if
only you *yourself* were the discoverer of this Portuguese diamond
in your literature." But even granting all this—and adding to it,
the assumption that the books of Hawthorne have sold by the
five thousand—what does that signify? They should be sold
by the hundred thousand; and read by the million; and admired by every one who is capable of admiration.

This essay first appeared
in *The Literary World*, 1850.

Tangiers

by MARTIN ANDERSEN NEXÖ [1869–1954]

HOW NEAR is Tangiers—and yet how far and strange! From the
summit of Gibraltar I can distinguish its houses, and from the
minaret in Tangiers the Meuzzin was able to observe the great
naval battle of Trafalgar; it is possible for a bee to fly from
continent to continent, from Europe to Africa. And how remote
are the characteristics of the two places! A living oriental bazaar,
a motley fairy tale from the Arabian Nights, taken bodily out of
the book and populated with fabulous characters of all kinds, with
dervishes and pashas, eunuchs and ladies of the harem. There
lies the city on its hills, house against house, whitewashed and
dazzling in the sun of Africa, without windows, but with flat
oriental roofs. The towers of azulejos show you where the

mosque stands; the zig-zag Moorish fortress-walls indicate the limits of the city on the desert side.

Yet how old and familiar it all is! Who is there that has not dreamed through all this in his soul, that has not built for himself curiously colored fantasies that become all the richer because it was impossible for them to assume definite form.

Pilgrims come singing all the way from Mecca, with sacred relics on their bosoms and cholera in the folds of their mantles. Bedouins and Berbers cross the strait armed with long-barreled carbines or crescent; camels float down from the hills and the wind blows dry and stifling off the desert; one swears by Allah on the market place; one prays to Allah in the mosque.

I crossed the straits in the little steamer, anchored a bit up along the shore, got into a smaller boat, from which I transferred to straddle the back of a naked negro who carried me ashore.

My official entrance into Tangiers was the one familiar in all southern cities. A band of burnous-clad bandits tugged at my garments from all sides and fastened themselves on my hand baggage. I dragged my body from the landing-dock up through the gloomy crevice in the walls where the customs agent was nodding sleepily, his lance in his lap, and then on through the strange streets. Each of the bandits was trying to drag me to his own hotel, promising me gold and the ownership of earth if I should go with him. "Come with me, sir, take no notice of these loafers; I shall lead you to the best hotel in the whole town," said an elderly one-eyed rascal. "It's easy for him to make such promises; he has just been to the market and bought potatoes!" grins another. "See for yourself, sir, how he still has the skins in his beard!" "Filthy dog," the first screams back, "I suppose you eat of a roast to-night! Did I not see you myself bearing home a dead dog from the riverside!" Their poor English leaves them in the lurch. They drop back into their native Arabic, and I can pursue their quarrels no further. Suddenly one of them spits in the other's eyes, and is answered by his adversary in the same coin, and when this harmless ammunition had been used up, they turned to fistic blows and kicks. I took my advantage, disappeared into a side street and turned at every corner, in order that

they might not be able to follow my trail. I had not gone far
when the one-eyed fellow overtook me; his nose was bleeding;
he looked like a fugitive but he snatched my bag and it came to
pass, this time, that the vanquished won the spoils, a form of
justice which is as reasonable as it is rare in history. Hadji abd
Islam—for such was the name of my one-eyed conqueror—delivered me to the hotel keeper with much ceremony and com-
mended himself to me as a guide. I used him so for two weeks;
and though at first he seemed to me a bandit, he turned out to
be an excellent fellow. He would go about with me all day long,
from morning to night, asking but little in return, never sparing
himself, never making any attempt to cheat me, and never permitting any one else to cheat me either. May Allah reward him
for his kindness and preserve him from cholera and from the
yellow snakes of the swamps.

I had an unusual feeling of delight as I stepped out on my
balcony after Hadji had left me. The hotel was built in the
Spanish style with balcony windows. Around it lay the Arab
city, white-stuccoed, windowless, with flat roofs on which white-
veiled women walked up and down.

It was evening; bay and street were silent; far off lay Spain
and Gibraltar, like a distant wall of clouds. The moon cast a
magical brightness over the white city before me with its deep
shadows in the background, and the green air floating over it.
Minarets and towers of azulejos seemed to come nearer in this
nocturnal light. From my veranda, I could look down over the
roofs into Moorish courtyards; under the pillared loggia in one
of the courts an Arab sat on the stone flags, his legs drawn up
under him, saying his evening prayers by the light of the red
lamp. I could hear his assiduous mumbling. Then he ceased, pros-
trated his brow, which he struck thrice against the stones, and
went on mumbling again. Later, as I sat bent over a letter to
my native land, I could hear the Muezzin summoning the faithful to midnight prayers, in a soft but powerful voice, which
came down from the slender minaret and bathed all the houses in
its melody: God is great and all-powerful! Come to prayer! God
the Lord Calls!

In the night I was awakened by loud calls, guttural voices and hasty steps in the alley. I jumped out of bed and dashed out on the balcony, whence I could see two white-clad policemen running along the railing of the bluff, pointing with the long barrels of their carbines in the direction of the beach. They disappeared in the misty light; I heard a shot. Then everything was still, I went back to bed, and lay, wide awake, listening for more.

The night was marked by the familiar sing-song hum that is characteristic of a still night at all times and in all places— it is silence audible. This silence was suddenly broken for a second time by the deep-chested call to prayers which came from the mouth of the Meuzzin like a calm but strong swell of the sea. It was two o'clock. When I was about to sleep again, I heard loud but undistinguishable conversation going on under my balcony, and a shower of pebbles was cast into my room. Again I got up, and below on the railing, now covered by shadows, sat two guards, staring at my windows. When they caught sight of me, they broke out in Arabic and made signs with their hands. I understood nothing. But began to feel quite nervous. I thought of everything: the street fight I had seen in the afternoon—no doubt they would arrest me—and I had not filed my papers yet—they would probably kick me out of the place—one of them suddenly called out to me in English: "Mind your pockets!" It suddenly dawned on me that the guard was merely giving me a general warning to beware of thieves. I answered him again in English, hoping to find out what he meant, but the sentence he had spoken must have contained all the English words he knew, and he kept on calling, "Mind your pockets, mind your pockets!" I took hold of the doors of my balcony to close them, at which the guards laughed loudly and clapped their hands with joy at being understood. Next day I told Hadji what had happened. He consoled me by saying there was nothing to be afraid of, still I had better lock my balcony doors and look under my bed at night.

I slept until long past the hour I had set for my next excursion. When I woke up Hadji abd Islam was sitting on a chair at the end of the room, legs crossed under him, his head at an angle, staring at me with his single eye, like an inquisitive hen. When I rose from bed, he removed—contrary to the custom of all good Moroccans—the red fez from his head, revealing a cranium that was entirely smooth-shaven, excepting a little patch at the crown, no bigger than a penny piece, from which grew a clump of long hairs. His skull, shining like polished bone, was covered with a criss-cross of old scars extending all the way from hair patch to forehead. "Souvenirs of old brawls," I thought, but later I found the explanation. I saw the same isolated bundles of hair frequently during the following days among members of a Berber tribe, tall slender marauders wearing sandals of vine-wood and a *gehab* of camel's or goat's hair, hoods thrown over the back. In place of turbans, they often had rope strands or fibers of bast wound about their foreheads, which made them look very bold as they stood in large groups about the streets, haggling for carbines which they carelessly discharged at the white walls, so that plaster and lead fell in showers. They are said to come from the hills of Oran, and they believe that when they die Allah will draw them up into Paradise by the single strand of hair on their crowns.

After telling this yarn, Hadji sets forth to show me all the things which he likes to see himself, and this he does day after day. If the sun is not too high in the heavens and the *sirocco* not too hot, I am as zealous as he is, although my admiration is not always as undisguised as his. Hadji knows what is worth seeing, for he has traveled much. Once he went on a pilgrimage to Mecca, where he had the attack of smallpox which cost him an eye and spotted his skin. He has crossed the straits often to the Rock of Gibraltar, and once he took the train as far as Granada, where from the battlements of the Alhambra he gazed over the Vega, promised land from which his people had once been driven forth and to which Allah will again lead back his faithful ones. In the Alhambra, he tells me, the halls are larger and the vaulting more beautiful—in short all things are lovelier—than even in Mecca; it is the most fruitful land of the whole world, for the Heaven of the Faithful is arched over it. . . . He becomes so interested that he stops short in his tracks, crouching on the ground before me, and demands whether I too have seen Granada. For now the Spaniards hold it and they are the people who stick out their tongues at all nations that are different from themselves.

Hadji hates the Spaniards—did they not even try to get Morocco too? Fortunately Allah did not permit them to gain their end—Hadji clenches his fists and waves his hands wildly—as he tells of the bloody predatory campaign waged by Spain in 1859 and 1860. He himself as a child saw the men of his tribe dash westward over the desert in the direction of Tetuan, in order to drive out the great enemy; he saw them rushing back faster than they had come—broken and in despair.

At times, he forgets himself and me and his murder of the English language and relapses into incomprehensible Maghreb, his own speech. His English is poor in words but his narrations are rich in illustrative gesture. As he tells me of the Moroccan heroes Akhmed and Abbas and the cruel Spanish General Prim, he leads me out over the sun-dried, sandy, desolate heights and venomous swamps, which he loves so much.

On these hills are tall dry grasses which no animal will eat; there are rows of aloe, whose fibers are worked into textiles, as well as a few lone palms; and you enjoy wide panoramas of curved roads that lead through sand and nothing but sand. Down below in the swamps, there are dense jungles with poisonous snakes and acrid stagnant water that supply drink and pestilence to the city, and herds of little short-haired buffaloes that are served as food to the garrison at Gibraltar across the straits. The Moroccan himself eats no meat.

The dense under-growth of these jungles is the place of refuge for slaves that have fled from the hinterland. Tangiers has become a free city for them—the only such city in the whole country —although the city is subject to the same laws as the rest of the country.

For, the ambassadors of the powers to Tangiers do not live in the capital, but in Tangiers itself—there are times when it is a pleasant feeling to know you are as near Europe as possible—

and the ambassadors have strongly fortified villas, which lie close together, as well as a numerous retinue of servants, most of them negroes.

These negroes are in many cases run-away slaves; the ambassadors take them under their protection and have made the slave trade impossible in Tandja—"the city protected by God"—owing to their energetic intervention.

There are probably great numbers of slaves still in the city, but these slaves are practically on the footing of servants, and the conditions of their lives are so favorable that they seem to have no desire to run away and expose themselves to the competition of free men.

In this respect at least, therefore, a few European settlers have inculcated the rudiments of European civilization—by reason of their superior authority—in this outpost of the Moroccan sultanate.

Tangiers is quite as taboo to European civilization as is all the rest of Morocco. Southern Europe is not particularly eager for conquest, and the current of water that flows through the narrow Straits of Gibraltar has too vehement a flow. On this southern side of the Straits, the number of wives a man keeps is in direct proportion to his money. A Pasha has only eight wives; he cannot afford to support more; and if there are so many men who have to get along with only one wife and some with none at all, Hadji says this is due entirely to the hard times. Hadji himself is not married and has not the slightest intention to marry until he can keep two wives. In fact, he would be in a position to do this now if there were more English women visiting the town, for the English women pay their guides very well. But since the bridge-head was finished down by the beach, enabling boats to moor instead of anchoring out in the bay, which obliged passengers to ride ashore on the backs of naked negroes except at high tide, the English women do not cross the Straits as much as they used to. For this reason, Hadji does not want to get married; it would be too boring to have to get along with one wife only; only "these niggers" could do such a thing.

Again and again he reverts to the subject of Pasha's harem,

telling me all sorts of improbable things concerning the edifice and its inmates. But he has no hair-raising tales of romantic incidents, of faithless women of the harem stuck into bags and sunk in the Straits by night where the current is strongest. Pasha's women are proud of their station, which they have chosen of their own free will, says Hadji, and do not wish to go in for silly adventures. However, there are guards with long spears and plenty of eunuchs around the harem so that things hardly give the appearance of a Pasha as sure of his women as Hadji says he is. Men are not permitted to enter. But one day as I was going by, I caught a glimpse of a thick-skirted eunuch who was opening the door for an English woman to pass out. This woman told me that all the women inside sat in a beautiful apartment in semidarkness stitching little objects intended for sale. Pasha's favorite wife, who distinguished herself from the others by doing nothing, had kissed the English lady's hand as she left and begged her for a franc for coffee.

These creatures so low in the social scale that each one of them is entitled only to a small fraction of the favor of the great Mussulman are of course considered objects unworthy of his glances at any moment at which he himself does not voluntarily come to visit them. Therefore they are not permitted to show themselves in the streets except when clad in a very plain white bag, their faces completely veiled; they may not enter the main street, but are required to keep to the small narrow alleys and, wherever there are large congregations of men, to make a wide detour around such groups. They remind you of perambulating flour-bags clinging as close to the walls as possible, and the constant repetition of veiled women and nothing but veiled women has the effect of an enigma, finally leading one into fabulous imaginings, not imaginings of wondrous beauties, but visions of old women of such unusual ugliness that they do not dare appear in the streets except with their faces covered.

However much these women may be crushed, they yet have something of the innate fearlessness of their sex. If you meet them in remote spots with no Mohammedan anywhere around, they will push aside their veils and smile at you, revealing features that are quite presentable. And you feel a desire to attempt the impossible, namely, to speak to these outcast creatures face to face and ask them whether they believe in Allah—although they have no souls of their own—and whether they do not feel it a deprivation to be forbidden to pray to him in the mosque. Or whether they do not know, perchance, that it will be possible for them to attain the Paradise of the faithful if their husbands are willing to dispense with a few of their celestial spouses to the advantage of their terrestrial brides? Perhaps they know all this and are nevertheless confident of securing admission to Heaven, because they are women, and because, being women, they have faith in men. Could it be any particular hardship for Pasha, for example, if he should renounce eight out of the seventy-two beauties which are destined for him after death, in order by this generous act to secure admission to Paradise for his eight wives on earth? Even if he should have had more than enough of them here below and should be no longer capable of tolerating the sight of them he might nevertheless take so generous a step, for he would still have sixty-four new wives. Yet, it is hard to say what Pasha will do about it. And besides, do women set any great store on getting into Heaven, anyway?

Not much has been done in the way of instruction in the school-room in Morocco, but there are a few schools. One I found in Tangiers in one of the narrowest little streets of the city. Here were eight or ten little mites from the most wealthy Moorish families crouching on the stone floor, rattling off their Koran. They are dressed like grown-ups, in a red fez, white burnous, and yellow slippers. Their slight limbs seem to be drowning in their voluminous garments as they babble away at the sacred verses, their eyes closed, their bodies swaying to and fro. The school-room is without any windows, and reminds you of nothing so much as an empty wagon-shed. There are no torn maps and charts on the walls, no school benches and desks for the boys to carve their names on, no inkwells to be upset for the general amusement. In fact, there is no trace of any of the paraphernalia of teaching; there is nothing but an old white-bearded Moor, who sits in front of the boys holding a lash in his hand

and playing schoolmaster, with an open Koran on his knees. He smiles and nods and I smile and nod; he politely invites me to have a seat and I seat myself on the soiled floor and make an effort to stow my feet Arab-fashion under my body. I now have an opportunity to hear the littlest one of the boys rattle off, without any interruption, a whole chapter out of the Koran, apparently without making the slightest mistake. A conversation ensues beween the two of us, with Hadji serving as an interpreter—although the schoolmaster can speak "all the languages on earth"—and I compliment him dutifully on his pupils. Then I make a few attempts to test his prowess, but he is too clever for me and I am obliged to content myself with the knowledge that he is at least able to read. I rise, brush the dirt from the seat of my trousers, attracting as little attention as possible in the process, in order not to give offense, and take my leave. Hadji winks at me with his big eye from the doorway; I grasp the significance of the signal at once and give the old white-bearded "professor" a one-franc coin for coffee.

It cannot be said that the machinery of government is very complicated. Twice a week Pasha sits on his heels outside the great gate of his splendid palace and administers justice according to the good Old Testament method. The adversaries in litigation approach, each from his own side of the road, and depart side by side, conciliated, along the center of the thoroughfare. If the case is particularly complicated, Pasha will angrily pull his long white beard, "and then the question is always cleared up."

If you are willing to pay a small gratuity for the guard, you may secure permission to view, from the outside, the treasure-chamber of the province, a massive stone structure with a solid door guarded by seven great padlocks. The seven keys to these seven locks are held by seven different men of excellent reputation in the city, and thus it is possible to feel secure from any theft of public funds. Not even Pasha himself may hold these keys, for his monthly salary amounts to barely more than twenty-five dollars.

One day Hadji and I undertook to visit all the public institutions, one after the other, on which occasion we also had a view of the municipal hospital and the prison. The former is in a narrow street with houses built over it, running along the rear wall of the mosque. After going for some distance along this street, Hadji himself poked open a door and we entered a dark space from which I was driven out forthwith by a stifling stench. But I had seen enough. It was a long apartment, one side of which was divided into sections resembling stable stalls. In each stall there was a bundle of straw or of ragged matting—it was too dark to distinguish which—and lying on this heap I could make out the shapes of naked human bodies writhing and moaning. From one a pair of yellowish-gray legs stuck out; a naked child with scales all over its body was crawling out of another. The old woman who had charge of the place swept the child back into its section with the aid of her cane, and with a countenance as angry as if she herself were a neat chambermaid and the little one a toad that had crawled over the threshold. The principal duty of the old woman is to see to it that the patients do not run away and that each dies in his own section. There is no doubt that they will all die—what other reason could have induced them to resort to the hospital? They receive no food but what is brought them by their relatives; and it is also obvious that once one has brought one's dear ones to this institution and thus made it possible for them to die in its conventional surroundings, there is no particular reason for supplying them with too much food. Such a procedure would be equivalent to throwing Allah's gifts out of the window. They will have things enough to eat in the place they are going to, at least so Hadji says. But suppose they are slow in going? "Then they send for the medicine man, and he helps them to die," is Hadji's simple answer. Perhaps this is the reason why I never saw a single cripple (and cripples are the curse of southern European countries)—anywhere in Tangiers.

The prison is based on like principles. It is situated far above the city, next to Kasbah—the fort—and reminds you of a church built in the rotunda form. It has no windows and no doors; light is admitted from above through the rickety roof, and when new prisoners arrive to be incarcerated, a hole is made in the wall, which is bricked up again after they are inside. There is no chance of the prisoner's ever getting out unless a certain sum is paid for his dismissal, but this sum has to be raised very quickly, since no one could live very long in this place. Nor are such liberations frequent. There is a little extension built on by the side of the circular wall; in this lodge the guards sleep on stone benches, surrounded by rifles and spears.

The sentinel opens the peep-hole, about one foot square, and you may look into the prison. If the stench in the hospital was intolerable, it is ten times worse here; you hold your nose and draw back your head every moment to get a breath of air. The floor inside is a morass of manure and reeds; some of the prisoners are lying down, others crouch; others slink about in a circular orbit dictated by the length of their chains. They are chained either to the circular wall or to the pillar that supports the roof.

As soon as they discover me at the peep-hole, they move slowly in my direction, as far as their chains will permit them. Lean scraggy necks and long thin trembling arms stretch out toward me; their eyes, their open mouths, seem to voice a consuming demand. They take hold of each other as a means of crawling forward themselves, forgetting that it is the chain that is holding them back. Matted beards and shaggy hair, naked backs covered with a thick crust of human excrement mingled with straw, a few rags swinging about their loins loose and wet and slapping over their naked legs whenever they tug at their chains to get closer to me.

They are never allowed to go out in the open air; they receive no water to wash with and obtain food only when their relatives and friends bring them some. Or, when they are able to earn some for themselves! Necessity has made them inventive and stimulated their energies. Although they may never have followed a calling while they were at liberty—here they sit surrounded by dirt and filth, engaged in turning out the neatest little baskets and purses of gayly colored reeds and Moroccan leather, which they sell to the tourists who come to see and enjoy this wretched spectacle. And the inhuman treatment they receive has made them more humane to each other; what other consideration would impel those who stand nearer to us and who are themselves offering objects they are eager to sell at any price, to pass on the output of the prisoners who stand behind them and offer them for sale together with their own? They would hardly do as much if they were trading under free conditions; in fact, society does not even deal so well by them, for society has locked them up here and exposed them to the certain fate of death by starvation and filth. Nor would any human society treat them much better.

This society, whose practice accords with the prescriptions of the Mosaic Code, and which dooms to destruction its diseased or demoralized members, by no means consists of barbarians who would find it a difficult task to acquire civilization step by step. In numbers, the Moors embrace but one-third of the population of Morocco, but they constitute the entire upper class, the official stratum—from the sultan down to the night watchman—as well as the merchant class and the higher artisans; they make up practically the entire population of the city. And they are the descendants of a race of high culture, remnants of which they still retain in the interior splendor of their buildings, in the gorgeousness of their raiment, and in the dazzling cleanliness of their outer garments, in their outward behavior and in their aristocratic bearing. You will look in vain in the streets of Tangiers for that "animal-like simplicity" and that frank and open conversation that is so characteristic of the cities of southern Europe; a lady can walk alone through these streets without hearing rude observations spoken behind her back or witnessing any sight that might cause her to blush. The Moors are well acquainted with the forms of good breeding, and observe them furthermore; for the rest, however, they have got far beyond these forms. They have freed themselves from the contents and requirements of these forms, because they had become a burden; and their feeling them a burden was due to the fact that they themselves had become degenerated and fatigued.

In their manners and their deeds they remind one vividly of a late scion of some great family. They are extremely blasé and incapable of feeling interest or compassion; in fact, of being carried away by any emotion. In southern Europe, the presence of a stranger may be the cause of a riot, yet, though strangers are far less frequent in Morocco than in some other regions, the Moor does not dignify him with even a fraction of a glance.

As for nerves, the Moor seems to have none; nor has he any evident desire for life and activity. He does as little as possible, hates to talk to you, prefers to walk by himself; he will stand leaning against a wall for hours, staring absent-mindedly in front of him without budging and without permitting any sound to awaken him; he will sit with his feet resting in the gutter, with his chin on his hands, day-dreaming, trying to fixate the tip of his own nose with his eyes. If you talk to the most wretched of these philosophers and ask him the way, or express some kindly polite thought, or offer him a profitable errand to run—you can interpret his expression and his inapt answers as meaning only one thing: his desire for repose.

That is what he has: repose. Excepting the Jewish quarter, the whole city is as dreamily silent as the castle of the Sleeping Beauty, except when the Berbers come to town. Life glides along with mechanical uniformity, with a sort of somnambulistic lethargy. The Moor sits by the gate of his little shop, at shop after shop, one right next to the other, and he reads in his Koran or ponders, indifferent as to whether purchasers come or not. He has made things comfortable for himself, has drawn his legs up under him completely, and his posture is such as to enable him to reach with his hands any object in the shop, as well as to take your money, without being obliged to rise. He has by his side everything he needs: a jug of water and a piece of bread. He can barely make the effort of speech when the black water-carrier comes by and he needs to have his jug refilled.

If there is a customer, the shopkeeper will hand him the required article silently and without raising his eyes, whereupon he slips the money into another jug and continues reading or idling. He will not consent to engage in haggling, nor will he take the pains to submit a number of articles, so that the purchaser may select what he wants. After the customer has received his article and finds that it is too large or too small, or at any rate not the right thing, and asks for another instead, the shop-keeper will silently put it back in its place, return the man's money, and drop back into metaphysical speculations. This done, no amount of entreaty or beseeching can induce him to continue to serve the customer.

There are some signs of life only in the market place above the city wall; but the traders here are for the most part Jews, and the half-savage charcoal-burners from the mountains. Food will cook all by itself in this heat, and there is not much demand for their charcoal. They stretch themselves out in the sunlight, converse or amble down to the inns under the half-roofs and drink green tea with a honey-bread that is black with flies. Whenever one of them lifts his bread to his mouth, the flies dis-perse, with a sound like the rustling of reeds in a jungle. After a piece has been bitten off, the swarm again gathers on the bread. It is for the fly to take care that it does not become part of his meal; he does not care; he leaves that to them.

Under the awning sits the teller of fairy tales. He has no listeners at this moment, but he continues reciting his tales, for all that, swaying to and fro the while—it sounds like the ceaseless croaking of frogs on a summer evening. Now and again a passer-by throws a shilling into his jug. The snake charmer sitting near him attracts more attention. Two ugly negresses—slaves—and a few gypsy children are his whole audi-ence and for their edification he takes out snake after snake from his leather pouch, with the utmost seriousness, and permits them to twine about his neck and arms to the accompaniment of a most diverting musical melody. When he is through and has consigned the snakes to his pouch again, the onlookers depart without making any payment; he does not care.

From the market-place I can view through the horseshoe of the city gate the main street in all its length straight down to-ward the white beach-walls and a patch of blue ocean. It re-minds you of a river bed that has run dry; in fact, in the rainy season it really is a river bed; you can see the marks left by the water along the wall and in the middle of its course great bowlders and sandy furrows bear witness to the latest rain. In all the shops all the way down the street salesmen sit in immutable postures, like the puppets of a marionette theater when the play is over. At the end of the street the ocean has a bluish shimmer. The houses gleam white on either side; petrified human forms, their legs crossed under them, lean against the walls; muscular artisans sleep under their tents, naked legs sticking out from under the canvas. A Moor in precious garments is sitting on the naked ground, his face pressed close to the wall; he is eating grapes, as silent and dream-lorn as a child.

For a moment there is life in the street. Three ragged men walk along singing and screaming. They strike a rattling instrument, causing it to sound, and wriggle about to the accompaniment of their howling melody, and there is delirious frenzy in their eyes and faces. These religious fanatics wander about with their host of admirers; they go and the street is again silent.

One hot August afternoon I was strolling in the market-place. The salesmen had disappeared, so had the teller of fairy tales, the snake charmer too; well-dressed Moors were standing in the sunny space, looking toward the city gate, expectantly. At the uppermost end of the market-place was a house whose flat roof was crowded with people, European settlers most of them. There was to be a parade I was told and accordingly purchased a ticket of admission to the grand stand on the roof.

An orange yellow banner came out from under the market gate. I could see the crowd milling in the gateway and hear a confused and distant racket. The market-place rises to the point which we occupied; the gate is about a thousand feet away.

The sun burned hotly and the heat of the flat asphalt roof seered your feet through the soles of your shoes; an hour had passed and I was beginning to think of going home. Suddenly the music emerged more distinctly—it was a deep boom! boom! which pounded away with a dense pertinacity as a clarinet shrilly embroidered it with a long irritating wail that rose and faintly fell, with no pauses for breath. It drilled its way into your ear monotonously and ceaselessly like the zoom of an importunate gnat.

The noise became more distinct; it seemed to me there was dancing with savage gestures and that I could see the onlookers being dispersed on one side or the other, retreating with yells.

The crowd would advance, then halt, then dance for a long time. Now and again I could see something dart forth and gleam in the air as a naked, smooth-shaven cranium rose high above the swarm and disappeared again.

Again an advance and again a stop. An ivory yellow skull rose in the air, disappeared; a gleaming flash had darted across it as the skull was at its highest point in the air. My eyes saw something red, like blood, a faint purple glow seemed to hover above the spot where the head had been.

I was speechless with astonishment, my blood was banging away in my veins. Explanations swarmed through my brain.

The bloody speck had just disappeared from my eyes when I beheld the great crowd parting on one side of the street while a fanatical figure in crouching posture, like that of the traditional American Indian, darted out of the circle with an ax in its hand. A veiled Moorish woman was fleeing from this creature in great panic. The woman became entangled in her long head-cloth and fell to the ground with a scream. Two men armed with heavy canes seized her pursuer just as he was raising his ax over her head; they took away his ax and pushed him back into the crowd. He permitted himself to be led by them without opposition and walked along as stiffly and inanimately as a sleep-walker. His close-shorn head hung down over his breast and bobbed up and down with each step he took, as if it was but loosely attached to his body; he was covered with dark red patches: coagulated blood.

Two hours have already passed since this crowd began flowing in through the market gate, so slow is its advance; now the crowd is directly in front of the house on which I stand, and I can see every detail of it. At the head of the multitude there dance a few savage figures with open wounds on their heads, their faces covered with blood, and blood also is on their chests and garments. They have thin-bladed axes in their hands, which they clash together over their heads with the beat of the music.

A few sedate—almost indifferent-looking—men with long beards, holding great armfuls of axes, walk behind the dancers.

Then there follows a great circular train—perhaps half a hundred—who, holding each other by the hand and darting up and down like Cartesian divers, keep step with the leader of the dance, a gigantic negro who occupies the center of the circle.

At the very end comes the band of music, the instruments of which consist of a few sounding-boards covered with membranes stretched over them, and the cursed clarinet, which still wails out its lamentation like an endless thread. The whole procession is in motion, dancing either as it halts, or as it moves slowly forward, and the dance has not ceased now for two hours. Even those who prostrate themselves and beat their brows upon the ground do not cease their measured swayings for a single moment—the rhythm of the music has hypnotized them.

The procession moves through thousands of onlookers—men and children; and above, on the high banks under the aloe hedges, there are rows of sitting women, resembling white sea-birds in their curious costumes. At times a dancing fanatic will make for them with his ax raised, whereupon they will dart to their feet with screams and escape into the jungle-like brushwood of the swamps.

As I stand there and look on, Hadji joins me; I ask him what this thing means.

"They are religious fanatics who are dancing in honor of Sedi Ali," he says. "They are genuine idiots who hop around and disfigure themselves." He assumes the expression of one who would say he is superior to all supernatural phenomena, but I recall the scars on his polished skull and am now able to guess their origin.

Fatigue seems to be making itself felt—after two hours of uninterrupted dancing uphill and two hours of ceaseless music. The dancer seems to be moving with effort, the music has lost its vigor; so have the fakirs; their axes are dropping, the men look as if they are about to collapse in their own blood.

Then, the sacred loaves, from Fez. The leader of the dance lays a loaf on the flat of his head and resorts to a new

rhythm as he leaps high in the air. The whole circle acquires
new energy. The spirit suddenly moves one of the dancers; he
leaves the circle, which closes again behind him. As he dances,
he kisses the bread borne by the leader of the dance. Then he
jumps over the joined hands of the circle, seizes an ax and attaches himself, still dancing, to the other fakirs—a new fakir. He
dances alone, like them, swinging his ax in a challenging manner, then he stops and jumps high into the air, as the edge of the
ax cuts its way into his shorn pate. Three bounds executed to
the musical accompaniment, and three blows of the ax—one at
each leap; and the blood comes pouring down from three open
cuts. The man collapses, but leaps to his feet again and continues
to dance—he has not broken the rhythm of the performance.
And the effect of his act is incendiary; each fakir, swinging his
ax, leaps in the air and strikes the ax into his skull three times.

The slow procession has passed the house. I leave my place on
the roof and follow it, crawling along the slopes, repeatedly
warned by good-natured Moors not to get too near the fakirs.
The monotonous music no longer tires me; it stimulates me; my
enervation has been succeeded by excitement, my excitement
passes into delirium. Some of the fakirs are completely bathed
in blood, and the two men who distribute the axes have had to
take them away from the fakirs. Some of them have not one
ax only, but three axes tied in a bundle, which clashes in the
air and strikes three wounds at once. The axes have very thin
blades and are very light; they do not fall with great impact;
but they are sharp and can leave an ugly wound. Occasionally a
fakir will fall and find it difficult to rise again. The sacred loaf is
placed over his head, and he at once gets to his feet; then he
prostrates himself, beating his forehead against the ground.

The cursed wail of the clarinet continues to pierce my brain
incessantly; I have the sensation of being about to perform some
insane act in order to liberate myself from this sound. These
mad wretches with their naked torsos, sullied with blood, sweat
and dust, and their bald heads covered with a profusion of red
wounds, are no longer repulsive to me, not even the wretch who
delicately caresses his own cheek with three ax edges, cutting

triple scars. The color of blood is no longer the color of blood, but simply a fiery red, voluptuously splendid in the sunlight.

I am unable to tear myself away; I cannot do otherwise than follow the procession through the outer gate and on over the flat hills of the road toward Fez. The crowd is left behind, and returns to the city; the axes are taken from the wild fakirs, one after the other; the spectacle draws to an end. The last thing I see is the figure of a man who will not give up his ax. He struggles with the other men and kisses the edge of his weapon; the blood spurts from his lips. He even embraces their knees, imploring them to leave him his ax. And the host passes out in the desert. To-morrow morning they will be in Fez, where—according to Hadji—Sedi Ali's sacred grave is situated, which works such great wonders that a single prayer pronounced at that spot will cure all the fakir's wounds.

The sun is setting, pouring its purple glow over the lowlands and crowning the heights with gold.

Out of the Straits of Gibraltar float the blue smoky trails of hundreds of steamers. But Tangiers is not concerned with steamers; they steam eastward, westward, to the Orient and to America, with their cargoes. But inland, across the flat hills of the desert, a caravan emerges, and slowly glides toward the market-place. The caravan brings grain from the fruitful country around Fez. Each animal carries on its back five or six big bags. They stagger awkwardly under their burdens, their small malignant heads perched on their long necks, moving up and down with a sinuous snakelike motion which reminds me of the groping progress of the gondolas on the canals of Venice. This is the commercial fleet of Tangiers. And as the darkness falls from a verdigris sky I hear the drivers struggling furiously with their camels, as they command them to lie down for unloading. The cries of pain emitted by the camels who bend down with their loads and whose knees strike hard against the ground, are mingled with the soft, all-embracing cry of the Muezzin: "God is great! Come to prayer! God the Lord calls!"

1903   Translated by
                                        JACOB WITTMER HARTMANN

Eleanora Duse: Actress Supreme

by LUIGI PIRANDELLO [1867–1936]

FROM THE VERY beginning of her long career Eleanora Duse had one controlling thought—the ambition to disappear, to merge herself, as a real person, in the character she brought to life on the stage.

Only by a hasty judgment could such an attitude be mistaken for an abdication of personality on an artist's part. As understood by Duse, it is her greatest title to glory, since this attitude implies obedience to the first duty of the actor—that supreme renunciation of self, which carries as its reward the realization not of one life only, but of as many lives as the actor succeeds in creating. And we shall see, too, that this attitude implies not, as some people conclude, an almost mechanical passiveness on the part of the actor, who must think of himself simply as an instrument for communicating an author's thought, but a spiritual creative activity of the rarest kind.

I remember that some years ago, an Italian newspaper conducted a referendum on this point among authors, actors, and dramatic critics of European distinction. The question proposed was whether or not actors have the right to judge the works which are given them for production; whether, in other words, they should or should not be regarded as more or less adequate vehicles of communication between writer and audience, which latter remains the only competent and legitimate judge. As I read the many answers to the question proposed, it seemed to me that people fail generally in appreciating the importance of one consideration which is really much more fundamental and comprehensive. It is commonly observed that, on the one hand, an author is never a good appraiser of his own work, and, on the other, that an actor is unable to recognize the artistic merits of the drama he acts; for, in a play, an actor looks only for a *good part:* if he finds it, the play is good; if he fails, it is bad.

The fact is that "feeling," as opposed to "thinking," plays a large part in the criticism which a writer makes of his own work. To be sure, a writer studies his creation as it is built up under his hand; but he cannot study it coldly, as an impartial critic would do, analyzing it point by point. Rather he views it all at once and as a whole through the total impression which he receives of it. On its author, that is, a work of art produces an impression quite analogous to the one it arouses in reader or spectator: it is *experienced* rather than *judged.*

It is the same way with the actor, and for this reason the actor can never be considered as a mechanical or passive instrument of communication. Indeed, if an actor examined the work he is to create coolly and coldly, studying it, analyzing it after the manner of a critic, and if he then tried to move on from this detached and dispassionate analysis to the interpretation of his own rôle, he would never succeed in giving life to an impersonation; any more than a writer could ever produce a piece of living literature if he did not start from a first feeling or inspiration, a first vision of his work as a whole, but tried to construct his book part by part, detail by detail, ultimately assembling all the separate elements in a work of deliberate composition built up as a mathematical proposition or as a theorem in logic.

The actor, in a word, also *experiences.* He does not *judge.* When a writer looks at a situation in life, or at an episode in history which for other people may be meaningless or commonplace, he must feel suddenly, by a spontaneous sympathy or emotion, that here is a subject which he must treat. In the same way, by a similar sympathy and emotion, the actor must recognize the part that is suitable for him. He must, that is, have an instantaneous experience within himself of the character he is to impersonate.

However, the actor is usually a professional artist living in the theater and on the theater, in contact, therefore, with what is most conventional and fictitious about the drama. That is why he

is very likely to see in a work of art those qualities which are
most specifically theatrical; just as the illustrator in looking
over a book for which he is to make the pictures will be most
impressed by the parts in it which best lend themselves to illustration. I mean to say that the professional actor is inclined to overlook the deeper meaning of a play and view it as so much stage
material. He will tend to subordinate the higher truth of the
artistic expression before him to the fictitious reality of its stage
effects.

Now, in this respect Eleanora Duse is the exact opposite of the
professional actor; because, if she exaggerates in any sense, it
is in her peculiar determination to see these higher meanings in
a play far beyond any *experience* she can possibly have of the
parts she has created or is to create—an exaggeration on her
part which may be of an artistic, ethical, sentimental, or "ideal"
character. The influence this tendency has had on her career
is an interesting one. It does not in any way diminish, as I feel,
her prodigious power as an actress on the stage; but it does do
her considerable harm otherwise, since it prevents her at times
from surrendering herself wholly to the *experience* of this or
that character, which, were she a less complex soul, she would
be able to do admirably. As it is, she is moved to limit her repertory unduly, while at the same time she is impelled, by very
praiseworthy consideration, doubtless, to favor works which
have an intellectual and moral rather than an artistic significance.

The point is this: Eleanora Duse is not, and never could be,
a mere actress. Gradually improving and elevating her innate
artistic taste, continuously developing and ripening her mind by
faithful study and by a deep meditation on life which has been
prompted by a variety of fortunes good and bad, Eleanora Duse
has eventually become a real personality on the wider stage of
our world at large. Now, a mere actress can impersonate almost
any character that is proposed to her, but a personality can live
only itself, and it rebels when any one attempts to impose upon
it rôles not in harmony with its own clearly asserted traits.
Eleanora Duse has built up a life of her own; as I like to put
it, she has selected a "form of being" which naturally excludes

all those other possibilities of being which once were in her—possibilities numerous indeed, because few creatures surely have ever lived to boast vital resources as rich and varied as those of Eleanora Duse. But venerable, noble, and worthy as any "form" may be, and as this particular "form" of Eleanora Duse certainly is, it nevertheless represents an unshakable will on her part to be just what she is, and nothing else; to be what she is, and to exclude every other personality that is different. This exclusiveness may be a merit, a virtue, an attainment, in the life of a woman; but it can only be a drawback in the professional career of an actress, since it limits—I might say wastes—all those possibilities of being which constitute the greatest wealth and the greatest glory of a dramatic artist. In the case of Eleanora Duse we see that, in proportion as her artistic, moral, and intellectual demands have become more exacting, rigid, jealous, her range has grown narrower and narrower. Her career on the stage has been the sequence of one exclusion after another.

Years ago she began by disdainfully throwing aside the repertory which had brought her her first successes, placing her at the forefront among Italian actresses, and giving her a world fame through her tours abroad.

Those who had, as I had, the fortune of seeing her as Marguerite in *Camille,* in her youthful days indeed, but in the full maturity of her art, can never forget the romantic charm, the anguished tenderness, the fervent emotion which she, and only she, was able to arouse in such great measure in that rôle. At that time she seemed born, natively predisposed, to become the most perfect interpreter of that theater which flourished in Europe, and more especially in France, in the last thirty years of the last century, and which was adorned with such names as Augier, Dumas *fils,* Sardou, Porto-Riche, Donney, and, with method and outlook somewhat changed, Henri Becque. It was a romantic, sentimental, psychological theater—a theater of manners, with some tendencies toward social satire. In its various aspects, it had echoes in Italy as well, and there also acquired distinguished names: Ferrari, Giacosa, Rovetta, Praga, Bracco, along with three unquestioned masterpieces to be credited to the name of Gio-

vanni Verga, *Cavalleria Rusticana, The Wolf, Mine and Thine.*
To this theater Eleanora Duse brought all the richness of her
temperament, which, as we looked at it in those days, seemed
to have been made for the express purpose of revealing not so
much the anxieties of mind as the torments and travails of the
passions: an exquisitely feminine sensibility which, at one bound,
as it were, and with the most agile directness, always arrived at
a wholly genuine expression of the state of the mind involved,
clarifying it with a light that shone from every line and fiber
of the actress's beautiful person—muscles vibrant, nerves tense,
a facial expression free from every conventional device, and changing only in direct correspondence with real inner transformations
of the soul; hands, divine hands, that seemed to talk, and a
voice such as may never again be heard on the stage—a voice
miraculous not so much for its musical quality, as for its plas-
ticity, its spontaneous sensitiveness to every subtle shading of
thought or sentiment. Duse's acting, at every moment of a production, was like the surface of a deep, still water, momentarily
responsive to the subtlest tremors of light and shadow.

And what variety! From one evening to another we used to see
her pass from the heroic passion of Marguerite Gautier to the
treachery of the *Femme de Claude;* from the sharp, shrewd,
rollicking gaiety of Goldoni's Mirandolina to the desperation of
Fedora; from the frivolous dissoluteness of Frou Frou to the
taciturn, rancorous sensuality of *The Wolf,* or to the exasperated
humility of Santuzza; from the spiteful, challenging obstinacy of
Francillon to the light, sarcastic capriciousness of Cypriana in
Divorçons.

For, at that time, Eleanora Duse was just an actress, a marvelous
actress, and, to conclude from the manner in which she could give
life to the separate and distinct personages of her first repertory,
we have no right to doubt that she felt these women, each and one
by one, alive in her, alive with her own life, with the vibration
of all her own sensations, feelings, and impulses.

How was it, then, that at a certain moment she suddenly
seemed to feel them no longer and actually, in some cases to
have a haughty disdain for them, almost a physical revulsion

at having incorporated them in her own being, endowing them with theatrical life from the substance of her own soul and in the form of her own body? Certainly, to have created them with such power, she must have experienced them with that experience which, as I said a moment ago, is the only legitimate judgment that an actress may pass upon one of her creations.

This happened. The esthetic criticism which Eleanora Duse had been forming on all that theater, after her wonderful reliving of the many characters it had offered her, had so seriously disconcerted her in her professional outlook that she simply was unable to go on working with those plays. This judgment corresponded to a change, a development, that had taken place in her own personality; and Duse seemed to feel that it was somehow incompatible with her sincerity as an artist to lend this changed personality of hers to the characters of a theater which she had come for the most part to despise. Crises of passion, tricks and artifices of female wile, needs of the flesh, petty cares and humdrum trials of daily life—in a word, the things which formed the principal content of the European theater between 1870 and 1900, were no longer enough for Eleanora Duse. Her spirit was athirst for something else, for something less commonplace, something less matter-of-fact, something more heroic—a nobler expression of life, in short.

In Italy, meantime, people were beginning to talk of Henrik Ibsen, who was arousing great interest in most of the nations of Europe, and even in France, where importations from abroad are not readily welcome. Ibsen's theater met both warm support and bitter hostility in the Italian public and among Italian men of letters. Luigi Capuana, the Sicilian novelist and dramatist, who had for many years been living in Rome, made a first translation (not from the Norwegian, but from the French) of *The Doll's House*. Eleanora Duse was much impressed, but her first approaches to Ibsen were timid ones. The perfect and complete understanding on her part of all the heroic spirituality contained in Ibsen's theater—qualities, which would fully have satisfied this thirst for the ideal in Eleanora Duse, at that time in the full possession of her powers—was made impossible by the distracting

influence she now began to feel through contact with the spectacular and refined, but only fictitiously heroic, art of Gabriele
D'Annunzio. To my way of thinking—an opinion that I have
reason to believe is shared by many people in Italy—the atmosphere of D'Annunzio's theater did harm rather than good to
Eleanora Duse, and great harm, indeed. Perhaps, from the esthetic demands of her inner life this experience was necessary
to her; but it wrought a violent distortion on her art, which had
once been so intimate and so profound, throwing her into false
attitudes which only time, and too tardily, has been able to correct.

To make clear just what I mean, I need only put in contrast
the most evident characteristics of the acting of Eleanora Duse
as that acting used to be, and as it has again become in these later
years, though now on a somewhat loftier plane.

D'Annunzio's art is wholly external. It relies on a sumptuous
display of forms, on a marvelous opulence of vocabulary. It is a
truly miraculous art, but it remains almost wholly superficial,
since in it everything that is expressed has value not so much in
itself as for the ingenuity with which it is expressed. It is an
art woven entirely of sensations, but of sensations that flourish
only when fed on imagery, and this imagery, if it would not
cloy, must have an ever more ample development, must become
ever more and more musical, ever more and more exciting to
the senses. It is a sluggish art, with a very scant interior agita-
tion, and even with a very scant external movement, since every
individual state of mind, no matter how subtle, needs to be rendered explicit in all its minute shadings, so that, rather than true
movement, we have a series of progressive attitudes, each one
made definite and precise in its particular esthetic value, pictorial, musical, or sculpturesque, as the case may be.

Whereas the art of Eleanora Duse is intrinsically and peculiarly opposite to all this. In her everything is internal, simple,
unadorned, almost naked. Her art is a quintessential distilla-
tion of pure truth, an art that works from within outward, which
shrinks from ingenious artifice, and scorns the applause of won-
derment that mere brilliancy seeks. With her to feel a thing is

to express it, and not to parade it; to express it in direct and immediate terms, without circumlocutions, without sonorous or
sculptured or painted imagery. Imagery, in fact, was a challenge
to Duse. She is natively lacking in that roundness of diction
which is a price requisite for the full elaboration of a word picture. And if she finds it by sheer effort, the effort in the end ex-
hausts her. For her art is wholly and always an art of movement.
It is a continuous, restless, momentary flow, which has neither
time nor power to stop and fix itself in any given attitude, even
for the pleasure of showing for a moment the beauty that a pose
may have in the truth of its expression. Here is a shy and retiring art, which at a tragic moment in her career she suddenly
put at the service of the least shy and the most assertive poet that
ever lived. That is why I ventured to use the word "distortion"
for the effects that D'Annunzio had upon the art of Eleanora
Duse.

I doubt whether I ever suffered so much inside a theater as I
suffered at the first production that Duse gave at the "Costanzi"
in Rome of D'Annunzio's *Francesca da Rimini.* The art of the
great actress seemed hampered, oppressed; crushed even, by the
gorgeous trappings of D'Annunzio's heroine; just as the action of
the tragedy itself is hampered, oppressed, crushed by the tremendous panoply of rhetoric that D'Annunzio's ponderous
erudition thrusts upon it. Poor Francesca! What a futile and
vacuous waster of precious words she seemed to be! To me, and
I think to everybody else, she gave a deep and almost bitter regret for the Marguerite Gautier whom Duse, only a short time
before, had been endowing with life on our Italian stage. And I
confess that I felt the same sorrow for many other commonplace
and mediocre persons of the old theater which Duse had abandoned, when I listened, later on, to her acting of two other
tragedies of D'Annunzio, *La Gioconda,* and *La Città Morta.* No
one will suppose that I am saying this out of any tenderness I
feel toward the old theater. I say it, rather, in view of an opinion
I have always held about the value that a work of dramatic art
may have in itself and of itself, and the value it may acquire or
lose in the scenic translation made of it by an actor.

As a play passes from the mind of an author through the mind of an actor, it must inevitably undergo some modification. No matter how hard the actor tries to grasp the intention of the writer, he will never quite succeed in seeing a character just as the author saw it, in feeling it just as the author felt it, in recreating it just as the author willed that it should be. How many times does the unhappy playwright, present at a rehearsal of his work, feel like exclaiming to the actor, "Oh, no! No! Not that way!" writhing in torment, disappointment, grief, or even rage, at seeing a character of his translated into a material reality which must perforce be something else! But in the presence of such a protest on the author's part, the actor will be just as much disturbed. He sees and feels the character in his own way and he has a right to regard the attempted imposition of the author's will as an act of gratuitous violence cruelly inflicted on him. For the actor is not a mere phonograph, grinding out through a megaphone words that have been written on a sheet of paper. He must see the character in his own way and feel it in his own way. All that the author has expressed must become an organic part of the actor, and produce in the actor's being a new life sufficiently forceful to make the character a real person on the stage. An actor's interpretation must, in other words, spring palpitating and alive from the actor's own conception of his part—a conception so intimately lived by him that it is soul of his soul, body of his body. Now, since the personality the actor now assumes is not an original creation of his own, but one suggested to him by the author, how can there possibly be a perfect correspondence between the character as the author sees it, and the character as the actor sees it? There may be a more or less close approximation, a more or less exact similarity, but nothing more. The actor may repeat the lines precisely as they are written, but the very same words will express sentiments which the actor, and not the author, feels; and these sentiments will find their own peculiar manifestation in the actor's tone of voice, temper of gesture, attitude of body.

It may happen, it not infrequently does happen, that the actor improves rather than not on the drama intrusted to him. But in such cases the drama is a bad one, and all the credit belongs to the actor. He has taken from the author a piece of canvas, as it were, and given it a life which the author failed to confer upon it.

It was just this miracle that Duse performed in her work with the old theater. In her repertory there may be some plays which do have a life of their own, and which will live as literature even if no actor ever again produces them. But the grandeur of Duse, in the eyes of her early audience, was the power she had of breathing the breath of life into many characters that had been barely outlined by their authors through various situations in which they were made to appear. And it was a true life that Duse thus created, holding the stage with its vivid, engrossing reality, laying hold upon every spectator witnessing the play. Duse gave a perfect form, that is, to the crude unmolded clay her old repertory offered her. She could do this, because in the various people she came to impersonate, however commonplace and insignificant they may have been in themselves, she found a certain potentiality of humanness which she could bring to full expression; and, having done so, she rejoiced in her own creation, leaving to others the task of passing judgment on the plays as a whole.

Why could she not perform the same miracle with the works of Gabriele D'Annunzio? The answer is already implicit in what we said about the conflicting characteristics of the respective arts of D'Annunzio and of herself.

In D'Annunzio's plays Duse met a form that was artistically complete, and had to be respected in every minute particular. And this put a fatal restriction upon her own art, which is so wholly spontaneous and genuine. D'Annunzio gave her a series of beautiful, elegant, literary masks, to which she must not supply a single detail, and to which she had to fit herself much as molten metal might be poured into a mold for a statue, to harden in the attitude of that statue—attitudes, moreover, which in this case were wholly foreign to Duse's native temperament. And, in addition, behind these masks of D'Annunzio there was none of those real fundamental human elements which Duse had met even in the worst plays of her repertory; no germ of life to bring to fruition, no formless clay to endow with perfection of form.

I should not risk asserting that the physical collapse of Eleanora Duse, and especially her growing weariness with stage life, should be attributed to the futile effort she made to adapt her own art to the art of D'Annunzio. But I am willing to state that the D'Annunzio episode was not without effect upon her career as an actress. There can be no doubt that Duse, at the peak of her development, was distracted by the D'Annunzio theater from the one real dramatic grandeur that her time might have offered her—the theater of Ibsen, I mean, which was surely far more harmonious with Duse's artistic temperament and with the need she has always felt of breathing a clear and rarefied atmosphere in the most lofty altitudes of the spirit.

What she was really looking for—the state of exaltation to which she had attained in her own inner life—we have been able to see from her recent return to the stage after a long retirement. She came back to us, it is true, with her old authors—Praga, D'Annunzio, Ibsen, as though to exemplify the three periods of her life. But there was a new author there—Gallarati-Scotti—significant not so much for the intrinsic merits of his *Così Sia,* as for the ethical qualities of that play and the spiritual air it breathes. The repertory exploited in this new appearance of Duse shows quite beyond the intention of the actress, as I believe, the truth of what I have said above. *La Porta Chiusa* of Praga is a mediocre work of the old theater, but it showed us to what extent Duse was able to vitalize such amount of living material as the play contained within itself. In *La Città Morta* we have again been able to see her struggling with all the resources of her genius, but failing in the end to adapt herself to the poses required by the static exterior art of Gabriele D'Annunzio. Her *Lady of the Sea* brings back to us the sense of all that we lost in not having seen Duse approach Ibsen in full possession of her youth. A gray-haired Ellida could only awaken in us, along with a deep regret, a profound admiration for the success with which Eleanora Duse was able to give this character the incomparable freshness of a spirit that literally basks in sunshine. And if we turn to her *Ghosts,* we have the full sense of what Duse might have been at her best: a more and more lucid, a more and more direct and immediate art, which concentrates more and more intensely the essences of truth, and which has been attained by a long travail of the spirit.

Eleanora Duse is a supreme actress in whose life the real tragedy has been this, that her age did not succeed in supplying her with her author.

1924   Translator unidentified

Philosophy of Furniture

by EDGAR ALLAN POE [1809-1849]

IN THE INTERNAL decoration, if not in the external architecture of their residences, the English are supreme. The Italians have but little sentiment beyond marbles and colors. In France, *meliora probant, deteriora sequuntur*—the people are too much a race of gad-abouts to maintain those household proprieties of which, indeed, they have a delicate appreciation, or at least the elements of a proper sense. The Chinese and most of the Eastern races have a warm but inappropriate fancy. The Scotch are poor decorists. The Dutch have, perhaps, an indeterminate idea that a curtain is not a cabbage. In Spain they are *all* curtains—a nation of hangmen. The Russians do not furnish. The Hottentots and Kickapoos are very well in their way. The Yankees alone are preposterous.

How this happens, it is not difficult to see. We have no aristocracy of blood, and having therefore, as a natural, and indeed as an inevitable thing, fashioned for ourselves an aristocracy of dollars, the *display of wealth* has here to take the place and perform the office of the heraldic display in monarchical countries. By a transition readily understood, and which might have been as readily foreseen, we have been brought to merge in simple *show* our notions of taste itself.

To speak less abstractly. In England, for example, no mere parade of costly appurtenances would be so likely as with us to create an impression of the beautiful in respect to the appurtenances themselves, or of taste as regards the proprietor; this for the reason, first, that wealth is not, in England, the loftiest of ambition as constituting a nobility; and secondly, that there the true nobility of blood, confining itself within the strict limits of legitimate taste, rather avoids than affects that mere costliness in which a *parvenu* rivalry may at any time be successfully attempted. The people *will* imitate the nobles, and the result is a thorough diffusion of the proper feeling. But in America, the coins current being the sole arms of the aristocracy, their display may be said, in general, to be the sole means of aristocratic distinction; and the populace, looking always upward for models, are insensibly led to confound the two entirely separate ideas of magnificence and beauty. In short, the cost of an article of furniture has at length come to be, with us, nearly the sole test of its merit in a decorative point of view; and this test, once established, has led the way to many analogous errors, readily traceable to the one primitive folly.

There could be nothing more directly offensive to the eye of an artist than the interior of what is termed in the United States—that is to say, in Appalachia—a well-furnished apartment. Its most usual defect is a want of keeping. We speak of the keeping of a room as we would of the keeping of a picture; for both the picture and the room are amenable to those undeviating principles which regulate all varieties of art; and very nearly the same laws, by which we decide on the higher merits of a painting, suffice for decision on the adjustment of a chamber.

A want of keeping is observable sometimes in the character of the several pieces of furniture, but generally in their colors or modes of adaptation to use. *Very* often the eye is offended by their inartistical arrangement. Straight lines are too prevalent, too uninterruptedly continued, or clumsily interrupted at right angles. If curved lines occur, they are repeated into unpleasant uniformity. By undue precision, the appearance of many a fine apartment is utterly spoiled.

Curtains are rarely well disposed, or well chosen in respect to other decorations. With formal furniture, curtains are out of place; and an extensive volume of drapery of any kind is, under any circumstances, irreconcilable with good taste—the proper quantum, as well as the proper adjustment, depending upon the character of the general effect.

Carpets are better understood of late than of ancient days, but we still very frequently err in their patterns and colors. The soul of the apartment is the carpet. From it are deduced not only the hues but the forms of all objects incumbent. A judge at common law may be an ordinary man; a good judge of a carpet *must be* a genius. Yet we have heard discoursing of carpets, with the air *"d'un mouton qui rêve,"* fellows who should not and who could not be intrusted with the management of their own mustaches. Every one knows that a large floor *may* have a covering of large figures, and that a small one *must* have a covering of small—yet this is not all the knowledge in the world. As regards texture, the Saxony is alone admissible. Brussels is the preter-pluperfect tense of fashion, and Turkey is taste in its dying agonies. Touching pattern, a carpet should *not* be bedizened out like a Riccaree Indian—all red chalk, yellow ochre, and cock's feathers. In brief—distinct grounds, and vivid circular or cycloid figures, *of no meaning,* are here Median laws. The abomination of flowers, or representations of well-known objects of any kind, should not be endured within the limits of Christendom. Indeed, whether on carpets, or curtains, or tapestry, or ottoman coverings, all upholstery of this nature should be rigidly arabesque. As for those antique floor-cloths still occasionally seen in the dwellings of the rabble—cloths of huge, sprawling, and radiating devices, stripe-interspersed, and glorious with all hues, among which no ground is intelligible—these are but the wicked invention of a race of time-servers and money-lovers, children of Baal and worshippers of Mammon; Benthams, who, to spare thought and economize fancy, first cruelly invented the kaleidoscope, and then established joint-stock companies to twirl it by steam.

Glare is a leading error in the philosophy of American household decoration, an error easily recognized as deduced from the perversion of taste just specified. We are violently enamoured of gas and of glass. The former is totally inadmissible within doors. Its harsh and unsteady light offends. No one having both brains and eyes will use it. A mild or what artists term a cool light, with its consequent warm shadows, will do wonders for even an ill-furnished apartment. Never was a more lovely thought than that of the astral lamp. We mean, of course, the astral lamp proper—the lamp of Argand, with its original plain ground-glass shade, and its tempered and uniform moonlight rays. The cut-glass shade is a weak invention of the enemy. The eagerness with which we have adopted it, partly on account of its flashiness, but principally on account of its greater cost, is a good commentary on the proposition with which we began. It is not too much to say that the deliberate employer of a cut-glass shade is either radically deficient in taste or blindly subservient to the caprices of fashion. The light proceeding from one of these gaudy abominations is unequal, broken, and painful. It alone is sufficient to mar a world of good effect in the furniture subjected to its influence. Female loveliness, in especial, is more than one-half disenchanted beneath its evil eye.

In the matter of glass, generally, we proceed upon false principles. Its leading feature is *glitter*—and in that one word how much of all that is detestable do we express! Flickering, unquiet lights are sometimes pleasing—to children and idiots always so—but in the embellishment of a room they should be scrupulously avoided. In truth, even strong *steady* lights are inadmissible. The huge and unmeaning glass chandeliers, prism-cut, gas-lighted, and without shade, which dangle in our most fashionable drawing-rooms, may be cited as the quintessence of all that is false in taste or preposterous in folly.

The rage for glitter—because its idea has become, as we before observed, confounded with that of magnificence in the abstract— has led us, also, to the exaggerated employment of mirrors. We line our dwellings with great British plates, and then imagine we have done a fine thing. Now, the slightest thought will be sufficient to convince any one, who has an eye at all, of the ill effect of numerous looking-glasses, and especially of large ones. Regarded apart from its reflection, the mirror presents a continuous, flat, colorless, unrelieved surface—a thing always and obviously unpleasant. Considered as a reflector, it is potent in producing a monstrous and odious uniformity; and the evil is here aggravated, not in merely direct proportion with the augmentation of its sources, but in a ratio constantly increasing. In fact, a room with four or five mirrors arranged at random is, for all purposes of artistic show, a room of no shape at all. If we add to this evil the attendant glitter upon glitter, we have a perfect farrago of discordant and displeasing effects. The veriest bumpkin, on entering an apartment so bedizened, would be instantly aware of something wrong, although he might be altogether unable to assign a cause for his dissatisfaction. But let the same person be led into a room tastefully furnished, and he would be startled into an exclamation of pleasure and surprise.

It is an evil growing out of our republican institutions, that here a man of large purse has usually a very little soul which he keeps in it. The corruption of taste is a portion or a pendant of the dollar-manufacture. As we grow rich, our ideas grow rusty. It is, therefore, not among *our* aristocracy that we must look (if at all, in Appalachia) for the spirituality of a British *boudoir*. But we have seen apartments in the tenure of Americans of moderate means, which, in negative merit at least, might vie with any of the *ormolu'd* cabinets of our friends across the water. Even *now,* there is present to our mind's eye a small and not ostentatious chamber with whose decorations no fault can be found. The proprietor lies asleep on a sofa—the weather is cool—the time is near midnight: we will make a sketch of the room during his slumber.

It is oblong—some thirty feet in length and twenty-five in breadth—a shape affording the best (ordinary) opportunities for the adjustment of furniture. It has but one door—by no means a wide one—which is at one end of the parallelogram, and but two windows, which are at the other. These latter are large, reaching down to the floor; have deep recesses, and open on an

Italian veranda. Their panes are of a crimson-tinted glass, set in
rosewood framings, more massive than usual. They are curtained
within the recess by a thick silver tissue adapted to the shape of
the window and hanging loosely in small volumes. Without the
recess are curtains of an exceedingly rich crimson silk, fringed
with a deep network of gold, and lined with the silver tissue,
which is the material of the exterior blind. There are no cornices;
but the folds of the whole fabric (which are sharp rather than
massive, and have an airy appearance) issue from beneath a
broad entablature of rich giltwork, which enriches the room at
the junction of the ceiling and walls. The drapery is thrown
open also, or closed, by means of a thick rope of gold loosely
enveloping it, and resolving itself readily into a knot; no pins
or other such devices are apparent. The colors of the curtains and
their fringe—the tints of crimson and gold—appear everywhere
in profusion, and determine the *character* of the room. The carpet
—of Saxony material—is quite half an inch thick, and is of the
same crimson ground, relieved simply by the appearance of a
bold cord (like that festooning the curtains) slightly relieved
above the surface of the ground, and thrown upon it in such a
manner as to form a succession of short irregular curves, one
occasionally overlaying the other. The walls are prepared with a
glossy paper of a silver-gray tint, spotted with small arabesque
devices of a fainter hue of the prevalent crimson. Many paintings relieve the expanse of the paper. These are chiefly landscapes
of an imaginative cast; such as the fairy grottos of Stanfield, or
the Lake of the Dismal Swamp of Chapman. There are, nevertheless, three or four female heads, of an ethereal beauty—portraits in the manner of Sully. The tone of each picture is warm,
but dark. There are no "brilliant effects." *Repose* speaks in all.
Not one is of small size. Diminutive paintings give that *spotty*
look to a room, which is the blemish of so many a fine work of
Art overtouched. The frames are broad but not deep, and richly
carved, without being *dulled* or filagreed. They have the whole
lustre of burnished gold. They lie flat on the walls, and do not
hang off with cords. The designs themselves are often seen to
better advantage in this latter position, but the general appear-

ance of the chamber is injured. But one mirror, and this not a very large one, is visible. In shape it is nearly circular, and it is hung so that a reflection of the person can be obtained from it in none of the ordinary sitting-places of the room. Two large low sofas of rosewood and crimson silk, gold-flowered, form the only seats, with the exception of two light conversation chairs, also of rosewood. There is a pianoforte (rosewood, also), without cover, and thrown open. An octagonal table, formed altogether of the richest, gold-threaded marble, is placed near one of the sofas. This is also without cover; the drapery of the curtains has been thought sufficient. Four large and gorgeous Sèvres vases, in which bloom a profusion of sweet and vivid flowers, occupy the slightly rounded angles of the room. A tall candelabrum, bearing a small antique lamp with highly perfumed oil, is standing near the head of my sleeping friend. Some light and graceful hanging shelves, with golden edges and crimson silk cords with gold tassels, sustain two or three hundred magnificently bound books. Beyond these things, there is no furniture, if we except an Argand lamp, with a plain, crimson-tinted ground-glass shade, which depends from the lofty vaulted ceiling by a single slender gold chain, and throws a tranquil but magical radiance over all.

First appeared in Burton's
Gentleman's Magazine, 1840.

Waking Dreams

by MARCEL PROUST [1871-1922]

FOR A LONG TIME I used to go to bed early. Sometimes, when I had put out my candle, my eyes would close so quickly that I had not even time to say "I'm going to sleep." And half an hour later the thought that it was time to go to sleep would awaken me; I would try to put away the book which, I imagined, was still in my hands, and to blow out the light; I had been thinking all the time, while I was asleep, of what I had just been reading, but my thoughts had run into a channel of their own, until I myself seemed actually to have become the subject of my book: a church, a quartet, the rivalry between François I and Charles V. This impression would persist for some moments after I was awake; it did not disturb my mind, but it lay like scales upon my eyes and prevented them from registering the fact that the candle was no longer burning. Then it would begin to seem unintelligible, as the thoughts of a former existence must be to a reincarnate spirit; the subject of my book would separate itself from me, leaving me free to choose whether I would form part of it or no; and at the same time my sight would return and I would be astonished to find myself in a state of darkness, pleasant and restful enough for the eyes, and even more, perhaps for my mind, to which it appeared incomprehensible, without a cause, a matter dark indeed.

I would ask myself what o'clock it could be; I could hear the whistling of trains, which, now nearer and now farther off, punctuating the distance like the note of a bird in a forest, shewed me in perspective the deserted countryside through which a traveller would be hurrying towards the nearest station: the path that he followed being fixed for ever in his memory by the general excitement due to being in a strange place, to doing unusual things, to the last words of conversation, to farewells exchanged beneath an unfamiliar lamp which echoed still in his ears amid the silence of the night; and to the delightful prospect of being once again at home.

I would lay my cheeks gently against the comfortable cheeks of my pillow, as plump and blooming as the cheeks of babyhood. Or I would strike a match to look at my watch. Nearly midnight. The hour when an invalid, who has been obliged to start on a journey and to sleep in a strange hotel, awakens in a moment of illness and sees with glad relief a streak of daylight shewing under his bedroom door. Oh, joy of joys! it is morning. The servants will be about in a minute: he can ring, and some one will come to look after him. The thought of being made comfortable gives him strength to endure his pain. He is certain he heard foot-steps: they come nearer, and then they die away. The ray of light beneath his door is extinguished. It is midnight; some one has turned out the gas; the last servant has gone to bed, and he must lie all night in agony with no one to bring him any help.

I would fall asleep, and often I would be awake again for short snatches only, just long enough to hear the regular creaking of the wainscot, or to open my eyes to settle the shifting kaleidoscope of the darkness, to savour, in an instantaneous flash of percep-tion, the sleep which lay heavy upon the furniture, the room, the whole surroundings of which I formed but an insignificant part and whose unconsciousness I should very soon return to share. Or, perhaps, while I was asleep I had returned without the least effort to an earlier stage in my life, now for ever outgrown; and had come under the thrall of one of my childish terrors, such as that old terror of my great-uncle's pulling my curls, which was effectually dispelled on the day—the dawn of a new era to me—on which they were finally cropped from my head. I had for-gotten that event during my sleep; I remembered it again im-mediately I had succeeded in making myself wake up to escape my great-uncle's fingers; still, as a measure of precaution, I would bury the whole of my head in the pillow before returning to the world of dreams.

Sometimes, too, just as Eve was created from a rib of Adam, so a woman would come into existence while I was sleeping, conceived from some strain in the position of my limbs. Formed by the appetite that I was on the point of gratifying, she it was, I imagined, who offered me that gratification. My body, con-scious that its own warmth was permeating hers, would strive to become one with her, and I would awake. The rest of humanity seemed very remote in comparison with this woman whose com-pany I had left but a moment ago: my cheek was still warm with her kiss, my body bent beneath the weight of her. If, as would sometimes happen, she had the appearance of some woman whom I had known in waking hours, I would abandon myself alto-gether to the sole quest of her, like people who set out on a journey to see with their own eyes some city that they have al-

ways longed to visit, and imagine that they can taste in reality
what has charmed their fancy. And then, gradually, the memory
of her would dissolve and vanish, until I had forgotten the maiden
of my dream.

When a man is asleep, he has in a circle round him the chain
of the hours, the sequence of the years, the order of the heavenly
host. Instinctively, when he awakes, he looks to these, and in
an instant reads off his own position on the earth's surface and
the amount of time that has elapsed during his slumbers; but
this ordered procession is apt to grow confused, and to break
its ranks. Suppose that, towards morning, after a night of in-
somnia, sleep descends upon him while he is reading, in quite
a different position from that in which he normally goes to
sleep, he has only to lift his arm to arrest the sun and turn it
back in its course, and, at the moment of waking, he will have
no idea of the time, but will conclude that he has just gone to
bed. Or suppose that he gets drowsy in some even more abnormal
position; sitting in an armchair, say, after dinner: then the world
will fall topsy-turvy from its orbit, the magic chair will carry him
at full speed through time and space, and when he opens his
eyes again he will imagine that he went to sleep months earlier
and in some far distant country. But for me it was enough if,
in my own bed, my sleep was so heavy as completely to relax
my consciousness; for then I lost all sense of the place in which I
had gone to sleep, and when I awoke at midnight, not knowing
where I was, I could not be sure at first who I was; I had only
the most rudimentary sense of existence, such as may lurk and
flicker in the depths of an animal's consciousness; I was more
destitute of human qualities than the cave-dweller; but then the
memory, not yet of the place in which I was, but of various other
places where I had lived, and might now very possibly be, would
come like a rope let down from heaven to draw me up out of the
abyss of not-being, from which I could never have escaped by
myself: in a flash I would traverse and surmount centuries of
civilisation, and out of a half-visualised succession of oil-lamps,
followed by shirts with turned-down collars, would put together
by degrees the component parts of my ego.

Perhaps the immobility of the things that surround us is forced upon them by our conviction that they are themselves, and not anything else, and by the immobility of our conceptions of them. For it always happened that when I awoke like this, and my mind struggled in an unsuccessful attempt to discover where I was, everything would be moving round me through the darkness: things, places, years. My body, still too heavy with sleep to move, would make an effort to construe the form which its tiredness took as an orientation of its various members, so as to induce from that where the wall lay and the furniture stood, to piece together and to give a name to the house in which it must be living. Its memory, the composite memory of its ribs, knees, and shoulder-blades offered it a whole series of rooms in which it had at one time or another slept; while the unseen walls kept changing, adapting themselves to the shape of each successive room that it remembered, whirling madly through the darkness. And even before my brain, lingering in consideration of when things had happened and of what they had looked like, had collected sufficient impressions to enable it to identify the room, it, my body, would recall from each room in succession what the bed was like, where doors were, how daylight came in at the windows, whether there was a passage outside, what I had had in my mind when I went to sleep, and had found there when I awoke. The stiffened side underneath my body would, for instance, in trying to fix its position, imagine itself to be lying, face to the wall, in a big bed with a canopy; and at once I would say to myself, "Why, I must have gone to sleep after all, and Mamma never came to say good night!" for I was in the country with my grandfather, who died years ago; and my body, the side upon which I was lying, loyally preserving from the past an impression which my mind should never have forgotten brought back before my eyes the glimmering flame of the night-light in its bowl of Bohemian glass, shaped like an urn and hung by chains from the ceiling, and the chimney-piece of Siena marble in my bedroom at Combray, in my great-aunt's house, in those far distant days which, at the moment of waking, seemed present without being clearly defined, but would become plainer in a little while when I was properly awake.

Then would come up the memory of a fresh position; the wall

slid away in another direction; I was in my room in Mme. de
Saint-Loup's house in the country; good heavens, it must be ten
o'clock, they will have finished dinner! I must have overslept
myself, in the little nap which I always take when I come in
from my walk with Mme. de Saint-Loup, before dressing for the
evening. For many years have now elapsed since the Combray
days, when, coming in from the longest and latest walks, I would
still be in time to see the reflection of the sunset glowing in the
panes of my bedroom window. It is a very different kind of
existence at Tansonville now with Mme. de Saint-Loup, and a
different kind of pleasure that I now derive from taking walks
only in the evenings, from visiting by moonlight the roads on
which I used to play, as a child, in the sunshine; while the bedroom, in which I shall presently fall asleep instead of dressing for
dinner, from afar off I can see it, as we return from our walk,
with its lamp shining through the window, a solitary beacon
in the night.

These shifting and confused gusts of memory never lasted for
more than a few seconds; it often happened that, in my spell
of uncertainty as to where I was, I did not distinguish the successive theories of which that uncertainty was composed any
more than, when we watch a horse running, we isolate the successive positions of its body as they appear upon a bioscope. But I
had seen first one and then another of the rooms in which I
had slept during my life, and in the end I would revisit them all
in the long course of my waking dream: rooms in winter, where
on going to bed I would at once bury my head in a nest, built up
out of the most diverse materials, the corner of my pillow, the
top of my blankets, a piece of a shawl, the edge of my bed, and a
copy of an evening paper, all of which things I would contrive,
with the infinite patience of birds building their nests, to cement
into one whole; rooms where, in a keen frost, I would feel the satisfaction of being shut in from the outer world (like the sea-swallow
which builds at the end of a dark tunnel and is kept warm by the
surrounding earth), and where, the fire keeping in all night, I
would sleep wrapped up, as it were, in a great cloak of snug
and savoury air, shot with the glow of the logs which would

break out again in flame: in a sort of alcove without walls, a cave
of warmth dug out of the heart of the room itself, a zone of
heat whose boundaries were constantly shifting and altering in
temperature as gusts of air ran across them to strike freshly upon
my face, from the corners of the room, or from parts near the window or far from the fireplace which had therefore remained cold
—or rooms in summer, where I would delight to feel myself a
part of the warm evening, where the moonlight striking upon
the half-opened shutters would throw down to the foot of my
bed its enchanted ladder; where I would fall asleep, as it might
be in the open air, like a titmouse which the breeze keeps poised
in the focus of a sunbeam—or sometimes the Louis XVI room,
so cheerful that I could never feel really unhappy, even on my
first night in it: that room where the slender columns which
lightly supported its ceiling would part, ever so gracefully, to
indicate where the bed was and to keep it separate; sometimes
again that little room with the high ceiling, hollowed in the form
of a pyramid out of two separate storeys, and partly walled with
mahogany, in which from the first moment my mind was drugged
by the unfamiliar scent of flowering grasses, convinced of the
hostility of the violet curtains and of the insolent indifference of
a clock that chattered on at the top of its voice as though I were
not there; while a strange and pitiless mirror with square feet,
which stood across one corner of the room, cleared for itself a
site I had not looked to find tenanted in the quiet surroundings
of my normal field of vision: that room in which my mind,
forcing itself for hours on end to leave its moorings, to elongate
itself upwards so as to take on the exact shape of the room, and to
reach to the summit of that monstrous funnel, had passed so many
anxious nights while my body lay stretched out in bed, my eyes
staring upwards, my ears straining, my nostrils sniffing uneasily,
and my heart beating; until custom had changed the colour of
the curtains, made the clock keep quiet, brought an expression
of pity to the cruel, slanting face of the glass, disguised or even
completely dispelled the scent of flowering grasses, and distinctly
reduced the apparent loftiness of the ceiling. Custom! that skilful
but unhurrying manager who begins by torturing the mind for

weeks on end with her provisional arrangements; whom the
mind, for all that, is fortunate in discovering, for without the help
of custom it would never contrive, by its own efforts, to make any
room seem habitable.

Certainly I was not well awake; my body had turned about for
the last time and the good angel of certainty had made all the
surrounding objects stand still, had set me down under my bedclothes, in my bedroom, and had fixed, approximately in their
right places in the uncertain light, my chest of drawers, my writ-
ing-table, my fireplace, the window overlooking the street, and
both the doors. But it was no good my knowing that I was not
in any of those houses of which, in the stupid moment of waking,
if I had not caught sight exactly, I could still believe in their
possible presence; for memory was now set in motion; as a rule
I did not attempt to go to sleep again at once, but used to spend
the greater part of the night recalling our life in the old days
at Combray with my great-aunt, at Balbec, Paris, Doncières,
Venice, and the rest; remembering again all the places and people
that I had known, what I had actually seen of them, and what
others had told me.

At Combray, as every afternoon ended, long before the time
when I should have to go up to bed, and to lie there, unsleeping,
far from my mother and grandmother, my bedroom became the
fixed point on which my melancholy and anxious thoughts were
centred. Some one had had the happy idea of giving me, to
distract me on evenings when I seemed abnormally wretched,
a magic lantern, which used to be set on top of my lamp while
we waited for dinner-time to come: in the manner of the master-
builders and glass-painters of gothic days it substituted for the
opaqueness of my walls an inpalpable iridescence, supernatural
phenomena of many colours, in which legends were depicted, as
on a shifting and transitory window. But my sorrows were only
increased, because this change of lighting destroyed, as nothing
else could have done, the customary impression I had formed of
my room, thanks to which the room itself, but for the torture
of having to go to bed in it, had become quite endurable. For
now I no longer recognised it, and I became uneasy, as though

I were in a room in some hotel or furnished lodging, in a place where I had just arrived, by train, for the first time.

Riding at a jerky trot, Golo, his mind filled with an infamous design, issued from the little three-cornered forest which dyed dark-green the slope of a convenient hill, and advanced by leaps and bounds towards the castle of poor Geneviève de Brabant. This castle was cut off short by a curved line which was in fact the circumference of one of the transparent ovals in the slides which were pushed into position through a slot in the lantern. It was only the wing of a castle, and in front of it stretched a moor on which Geneviève stood, lost in contemplation, wearing a blue girdle. The castle and the moor were yellow, but I could tell their colour without waiting to see them, for before the slides made their appearance the old-gold sonorous name of Brabant had given me an unmistakable clue. Golo stopped for a moment and listened sadly to the little speech read aloud by my great-aunt, which he seemed perfectly to understand, for he modified his attitude with a docility not devoid of a degree of majesty, so as to conform to the indications given in the text; then he rode away at the same jerky trot. And nothing could arrest his slow progress. If the lantern were moved I could still distinguish Golo's horse advancing across the window-curtains, swelling out with their curves and diving into their folds. The body of Golo himself, being of the same super-natural substance as his steed's, overcame all material obstacles— everything that seemed to bar his way—by taking each as it might be a skeleton and embodying it in himself: the door-handle, for instance, over which, adapting itself at once, would float invincibly his red cloak or his pale face, never losing its nobility or its melancholy, never shewing any sign of trouble at such a tran-substantiation.

And, indeed, I found plenty of charm in these bright projections, which seemed to have come straight out of a Merovingian past, and to shed around me the reflections of such ancient history. But I cannot express the discomfort I felt at such an intrusion of mystery and beauty into a room which I had succeeded in filling with my own personality until I thought no more of the room than of myself. The anaesthetic effect of custom being destroyed, I would begin to think and to feel very melancholy things. The door-handle of my room, which was different to me from all the other door-handles in the world, inasmuch as it seemed to open of its own accord and without my having to turn it, so unconscious had its manipulation become; lo and behold, it was now an astral body for Golo. And as soon as the dinner-bell rang I would run down to the dining-room, where the big hanging lamp, ignorant of Golo and Bluebeard but well acquainted with my family and the dish of stewed beef, shed the same light as on every other evening; and I would fall into the arms of my mother, whom the misfortunes of Geneviève de Brabant had made all the dearer to me, just as the crimes of Golo had driven me to a more than ordinarily scrupulous examination of my own conscience.

This essay constitutes the opening pages of *Swann's Way,* 1913.

Translated by
C. K. SCOTT-MONCRIEFF

Manhattan: The Great American Desert

by JEAN-PAUL SARTRE [1905–1980]

I KNEW VERY WELL that I would like New York. But I thought that I would be able to like it immediately, as I had immediately liked the red bricks of Venice and the sombre, massive houses of London. I did not know that for the newly arrived European there is a "New York sickness," just as there are seasickness, airsickness, and mountain sickness.

An official car took me from La Guardia Field at midnight to the Plaza Hotel. I pressed my forehead against the window but could see only red and green lights and dark buildings. The next day I found myself, without any transition, at the corner of 58th

Street and Fifth Avenue. I walked a long time under the icy sky. It was a Sunday in January, 1945—a deserted Sunday. I looked for New York and I could not find it. It seemed to retreat before me, like a phantom city, as I walked down an avenue that appeared coldly formal and without distinction. I was undoubtedly looking for a European city.

We Europeans live on the myth of the large city we constructed during the nineteenth century. The myths of the Americans are not the same, and the American city is not the same. It has neither the same nature nor the same functions. In Spain, Italy, Germany, France, we find *round* cities, formerly encircled by ramparts which served not only to protect the inhabitants from enemy invasion but also to hide from them the inexorable presence of Nature. The cities in turn are divided into districts equally round and closed upon themselves, where buildings piled up and tightly clustered weigh heavily upon the earth. They seem to have a natural tendency to draw close together—to such an extent that from time to time we must hack out new paths with the ax as we do in a virgin forest. Streets bump into other streets; sealed at both ends, they give no sign of leading out of the city. They are more than just thoroughfares, they are social milieus; you pause there, meet others, drink, eat, and live there. Sunday you dress up and go for a walk for the pleasure of greeting friends, to see and be seen. These are the streets that inspired Jules Romains with his "unanimism." They are infused with a collective spirit which varies with each hour of the day.

Thus my European, my myopic glance, advancing slowly and prying into everything, tried in vain to find something in New York to arrest it—anything, no matter what—a row of houses suddenly barring the way, the turning of a street, some house weathered and tanned by time. For New York is a city for the farsighted: there is nothing to focus upon except the vanishing point. My glance encountered only space. It slid over blocks of houses, all alike, and passed unchecked to the misty horizon.

Céline said New York was a "standing" city. True; but it seemed to me from the very first a *lengthwise* city. All priorities are given to length. Traffic stands still in the side streets but rolls tirelessly on the avenues. How often do cab drivers, who willingly take passengers north and south, refuse flatly to drive them east and west! The side streets are hardly more than the outlines of the buildings between the avenues. The avenues pierce them, tear them apart, and speed toward the north. It was because of this that, a naïve tourist, I sought for *quartiers,* a long time and in vain. In France these neighborhoods encircle and protect us: the rich neighborhood protects us from the envy of the poor; the poor neighborhood protects us from the disdain of the rich, just as the entire city protects us from Nature.

In New York, where the great axes are the parallel avenues, I could not find these neighborhoods, but only atmospheres—gaseous masses extending longitudinally without well-defined beginnings or endings. Gradually I learned to recognize the atmosphere of Third Avenue, where people meet, smile, talk together in the shadow of the noisy elevated without ever knowing each other, or where a German, passing near my table in an Irish bar, stopped a moment to ask, "Are you French? As for me, I am a Boche"; the reassuring comfort of the stores on Lexington; the sad elegance of Park Avenue; the cold luxury and stucco impassibility of Fifth; the gay frivolity of Sixth and Seventh; the food fairs of Ninth; the no-man's-land of Tenth. Each avenue draws the neighboring streets into its atmosphere but a block further away you are suddenly plunged into another world. Not far from the palpitating silence of Park Avenue, where private cars pass, I am on First, where the earth trembles perpetually as the trucks go by. How can I feel secure on one of those endless north-south trajectories when a few steps away, to east or west, other longitudinal worlds await me? Behind the Waldorf-Astoria and the white-and-blue awnings of fashionable buildings I see the elevated, still reeking of the Bowery.

All New York is thus striped with parallel, uncommunicable meanings. The long lines, drawn as if with a ruler, gave me suddenly the feeling of space. Our cities in Europe are built as a protection *against* space; the houses huddle like sheep. But space traverses New York, animates it, stretches it. Space, the great empty space of the Russian steppes and the pampas, flows through the streets like a cold draught, separating the inhabitants of one side from those of the other. An American friend who went for a walk with me in Boston on one of the fashionable streets said, pointing to the left side, "The best people live there"; and he added ironically, indicating the right, "No one has ever known who lives on this side." Similarly in New York, no one knows who lives across the street. All space is between them. When I flew above the great American desert of Texas, New Mexico, and Arizona, I was not astonished, for I had already seen the whole American desert in New York, where space, the great factor of separation between people and between things, has crept in. While I was in Los Angeles an acquaintance said, "Come see me tomorrow. I live very near you—only ten miles away." And when I went for a walk along the Cienega, beside a road lined with autos, I was the only pedestrian to be seen for miles. I don't mean to imply that New York is like that; it is halfway between the city for pedestrians and the city for autos. You do not go for a walk in New York; you either loiter at a drugstore or travel by express subway.

Your streets and avenues have not the same meanings as ours. You go *through* them. New York is a city of movement. If I walk rapidly I feel at ease, but if I stop for a moment I am troubled, and I wonder: Why am I in this street rather than in one of the hundred other streets that resemble it, why near this particular drugstore, Schrafft's, or Woolworth's, rather than any other drugstore, Schrafft's, or Woolworth's from among the thousands just like it? Pure space suddenly appears. I imagine that if a triangle were to become aware of its position in space it would be frightened at seeing how accurately it was defined and yet how, at the same time, it was simply *any* triangle. In New York you never get lost; a glance suffices to show you that you are on the East Side, at the corner of Fifty-second Street and Lexington. But this spatial precision is not accompanied by any sentimental precision. In the numerical anonymity of the streets and avenues I am simply *anyone*—as defined and as indefinite as the triangle—I am anyone who is lost and conscious of being unjustifiable, without valid reason for being in one place rather than another, because one place and another look so much alike. Am I lost in a city, or in Nature? New York is no protection from the violence of Nature. It is a city of open sky. The storms overflow its streets, which are so wide and long to cross when it rains. Blizzards shake the brick houses and sway the skyscrapers. In summer the air trembles between the houses, in winter the city is flooded, so that you might think you were in the suburbs of Paris when the Seine had overflowed, though it is only the snow melting. Nature's weight is so heavy on it that this most modern of cities is also the dirtiest. From my window I watch the wind playing with thick, muddy papers that flutter over the pavement. When I go out I walk in blackish snow, a sort of crusted swelling the same color as the sidewalk, as if the sidewalk itself were warped. Even in the depths of my apartment a hostile, deaf, mysterious nature assails me. I seem to be camping in the heart of a jungle swarming with insects. There is the moaning of the wind, there are the electric shocks I receive when I touch the doorknob or shake hands with a friend; there are the roaches that run through my kitchen, the elevators that make my heart contract, the unquenchable thirst that burns me from morning till night.

New York is a colonial city, a camping ground. All the hostility, all the cruelty of the world are present in this most prodigious monument man has ever raised to himself. It is a *light* city; its apparent lack of weight amazes most Europeans. In this immense, malevolent space, in this desert of rock that supports no vegetation, they have constructed thousands of houses in brick, wood, or reinforced concrete which give the appearance of being on the point of flying away.

I like New York. I have learned to like it. I have accustomed myself to looking at it in massive ensembles and great perspectives. My glance no longer lingers on façades seeking a house which, impossibly, would not be like every other house. It goes at once to the horizon and looks for the buildings which, hidden in mist, are nothing but volumes, nothing but the austere framework of the sky. If you know how to look at the two uneven rows of buildings that line the thoroughfare like cliffs, you are rewarded: they achieve their fulfillment below, at the end of the avenue, in simple harmonious lines, and a patch of sky flows between them. New York is revealed only from a certain height, from a certain distance, from a certain speed; they are not the height, distance, and speed of the pedestrian. The city very closely resembles the great Andalusian plains: it is monotonous if you pass through on foot, superb and ever-changing if you motor.

I learned to love its sky. In European cities, with their low roofs, the sky drags to the earth's level and seems tame. The New York sky is beautiful because the skyscrapers push it high above our heads. Solitary and pure, like a wild animal, it keeps watch over the city. It is not only the local covering; you feel that it reaches far out over all America. It is the sky of all the world.

I learned to love the avenues of Manhattan. They are not staid little promenades enclosed between houses; they are national highways. As soon as you set foot on one of them, you can see that it must run to Boston or Chicago. It vanishes outside the city, and the eye can almost follow it into the country. A savage sky above parallel highways: that is what New York is, first of all. In the heart of the city you are in the heart of Nature.

I had to become accustomed to this, and now that I am acclimated I can say that nowhere have I felt more free than in the midst of its crowds. This light, temporary city, which the sun's glancing rays reduce morning and evening to an arrangement of rectangular parallelepipeds, never stifles or depresses. Here you may suffer the anguish of loneliness, but not that of crushing defeat. In Europe we love a particular neighborhood in a city, become attached to a cluster of houses, are captivated by a little corner of a street; and we are no longer free. But hardly have you plunged into New York than you are living completely in the dimensions of New York. It is possible to admire it in the evening from the Queensborough Bridge, in the morning from New Jersey, at noon from the fifty-seventh floor of Rockefeller Center; but you will never be held by any of its streets, for none of them is distinguished by beauty peculiar to itself. The beauty is present in all of them, just as all Nature and the sky of all America are

present. Nowhere more than here can you feel the simulta-
neity of human lives.

In spite of its austerity, New York moves Europeans. Certainly we have learned to love our own ancient cities; but
what touches us in them is a Roman wall forming part of the
façade of an inn, or a house that Cervantes has lived in, or the
Place des Vosges, or the Hôtel de Ville in Rouen. We love our
museum-cities—and all our cities are a little like museums,
where we wander casually around among the dwellings of
our forefathers. New York is not a museum-city; nevertheless,
for Frenchmen of my generation, it has already acquired the
melancholy of the past. When we were twenty, back in 1925, we
were hearing about skyscrapers. They symbolized for us the
fabulous American prosperity. We beheld them with stupefaction in the moving pictures. They were the architecture of the
future, just as the movie was the art of the future and jazz the
music of the future. Today we know about jazz. We know there
is more past than future in it. It is a music of popular Negro
inspiration, capable of but limited development; it carries on by
slowly degenerating. Perhaps it has outlived its time. The talking
films also have not fulfilled the promise of the silent films. Holly-
wood walks in the old ruts. Undoubtedly, during the war,
America established herself as the mightiest power in the world.
But the era of easy living has passed. She was profoundly shaken
by the war, and many economists fear another crisis. So, they are
no longer building skyscrapers; it seems they are "too difficult
to rent." The man walking in New York before 1930 saw in the
tall buildings that dominated the city the first signs of an architecture that would spread over the entire country. In their thrust
toward the sky he saw a living symbol of the American urge
toward a peaceful conquest of the world. The skyscrapers were
alive. But today, for a Frenchman just come from Europe, they
are no longer alive. They are already historical monuments,
witnesses of a past epoch. They still rise toward the sky but my
spirit no longer follows them, and New Yorkers pass at their
feet without looking at them. I cannot view them without sadness:
they speak of a time when we thought the last war had been
fought, when we believed in peace. Already they are slightly

neglected; tomorrow, perhaps, they will be demolished. In any event, to build them in the first place required a faith we no longer feel.

I walk among the small brick houses, the color of dried blood. They are younger than European houses, but because of their fragility they seem much older. I see in the distance the Empire State Building or the Chrysler Building pointing vainly toward the sky, and it occurs to me that New York is about to acquire a history, that it already has its ruins. This is enough to adorn with a little softness the harshest city in the world.

1946   Translator unidentified

Chesterton on Shaw *

by BERNARD SHAW [1856-1950]

THIS BOOK is what everybody expected it to be: the best work of literary art I have yet provoked. It is a fascinating portrait study; and I am proud to have been the painter's model. It is in the great tradition of literary portraiture: it gives not only the figure, but the epoch. It makes the figure interesting and memorable by giving it the greatness and spaciousness of an epoch, and it makes it attractive by giving it the handsomest and friendliest personal qualities of the painter himself.

I have been asked whether the portrait resembles me. The question interests me no more than whether Velasquez's Philip was like Philip or Titian's Charles like Charles. No doubt some mean person will presently write a disparaging volume called The Real Shaw, which will be as true in its way as Mr. Chesterton's book. Perhaps some total stranger to the Irish-British environment may produce a study as unexpected, and as unflattering, as the very interesting picture of Nelson by a Turkish miniaturist which hangs in the National Portrait Gallery. Like all

* This essay is a review of G. K. Chesterton's study of Shaw.

men, I play many parts; and none of them is more or less real than another. To one audience I am the occupier of a house in Adelphi Terrace; to another I am "one of those damned Socialists." A discussion in a club of very young ladies as to whether I could be more appropriately described as an old josser or an old geezer ended in the carrying of an amendment in favor of an old bromide. I am also a soul of infinite worth. I am, in short, not only what I can make of myself, which varies greatly from hour to hour and emergency to no-emergency, but what you can see in me. And the whole difference between an observer of genius and a common man is not a difference in the number of objects they perceive, but in their estimate of the importance of the objects. Put one man into Fleet Street and ask him what he sees there; and he may give you an accurate description of the color of the buses, the sex of the horses, the numbers of the motor-cars, the signs of the public-houses, and the complexions and probable ages of the people. Another man, who could not answer a single question on these points, may tell you that what he sees is a Jacob's ladder with angels moving up and down between heaven and earth. Both descriptions are true. The first man, demurring to the other's description, would say that a cabman is not an angel. But the second man, the Jacob's ladder man, would never dream of saying that an angel is not a cabman. Call the taxi a chariot of fire (which it literally is) and the verbal difficulty is half smoothed. But the real difficulty is that the Jacob's ladder man is a man of genius and the other is not; and that difficulty is not to be got over. Mr. Chesterton is the Jacob's ladder man. He perceives that I am an angel; and he is quite right. But he will never convince those who cannot see my wings; and for them his portrait will never be a good likeness. Fortunately lots of other people will take his word for it, and some will rub their eyes and look a little more carefully; so his book will be of signal service to me.

All the same, it is in some respects quite a misleading book, not so much because it is here and there incautious, as because its only distinctive English quality is its fundamental madness. First, as to the incaution. Everything about me which Mr Chesterton had to divine, he has divined miraculously. But everything that he could have ascertained easily by reading my own plain directions on the bottle, as it were, remains for him a muddled and painful problem solved by a comically wrong guess. Let me give a screaming example. Here is Mr Chesterton on Major Barbara:

> Sometimes, especially in his later plays, he [Shaw] allows his clear conviction to spoil even his admirable dialogue, making one side entirely weak, as in an Evangelical tract. I do not know whether in Major Barbara the young Greek professor was supposed to be a fool. As popular tradition (which I trust more than anything else) declared that he is drawn from a real professor of my acquaintance, who is anything but a fool, I should imagine not. But in that case I am all the more mystified by the incredibly weak fight which he makes in the play in answer to the elephantine sophistries of Undershaft. It is really a disgraceful case, and almost the only case in Shaw, of there being no fair fight between the two sides. For instance, the Professor mentions pity. Mr. Undershaft says with melodramatic scorn, "Pity! the scavenger of the Universe!" Now if any gentleman had said this to me, I should have replied, "If I permit you to escape from the point by means of metaphors, will you tell me whether you disapprove of scavengers?" Instead of this obvious retort, the miserable Greek professor only says, "Well then, love," to which Undershaft replies with unnecessary violence that he wont have the Greek professor's love, to which the obvious answer of course would be, "How the deuce can you prevent my loving you if I choose to do so?" Instead of this, as far as I remember, that abject Hellenist says nothing at all. I only mention this unfair dialogue, because it marks, I think, the recent hardening, for good or evil, of Shaw out of a dramatist into a mere philosopher, and whoever hardens into a philosophy may be hardening into a fanatic.

If the reader will now take down the play and refer to the passages in question, he will discover, with a chuckle, first, that

the professor of Greek actually does make the precise retort that
Mr Chesterton says he ought to make, and, second, that "Pity!
the scavenger of the Universe!" is a howling misquotation. I do
not disapprove of scavengers any more than I disapprove of
dentists. But scavenging is only a remedy for dirt, just as dentistry
is only a remedy for decaying teeth. He who aims at a clean
world and sound jaws aims at the extinction of the scavenger and
the dentist. What Undershaft says is, of course, "Pity! the
scavenger of misery!" And my retort to Mr Chesterton is, "If I
refuse to permit you to escape from the point by means of misquotation, will you tell me whether you approve of misery?"
As to the professor making no fight, he stands up to Undershaft all through so subtly and effectually that Undershaft takes
him into partnership at the end of the play. That professor, though
I say it that should not, is one of the most delightful characters in
modern fiction; and that Mr Chesterton, who knows the original
(evidently not so well as I do), has failed to appreciate him, is
nothing less than a public calamity.

Generally speaking, Mr Chesterton's portrait of me has the
limitations of a portrait, which is, perhaps, fortunate in some
respects for the original. As a picture, in the least personal and
most phenomenal sense, it is very fine indeed. As an account of
my doctrine, it is either frankly deficient and uproariously careless
or else recalcitrantly and (I repeat) madly wrong. Madly, because
it misses the one fact that a sane man should postulate about me:
namely, that I am a man, like any other man. And the really
amazing thing about this oversight is that Mr Chesterton is aware
of it, and, in a magnificent Bacchic rhapsody, finally excogitates,
as proof of my superhumanity or sub-humanity, exactly the
reason that would have been given by one of Wellington's
private soldiers. This reason is, that I, having enough money in
my pocket to purchase unlimited beer, do actually pass by public-
house after public-house without going in and drinking my fill. I
know no extravagance in literature comparable to this. Teetotalism is, to Mr Chesterton, a strange and unnatural asceticism
forced on men by an inhuman perversion of religion. Beer drinking is to him, when his imagination runs away with him on paper,
nothing short of the communion. He sees in every public-house

a temple of the true catholic faith; and he tells us that when he comes to one, he enters ostentatiously, throws down all the shields and partitions that make the private bar furtive, and makes libations to the true god and my confusion. And he will see nothing but "cold extravagance" in my sure prevision of the strict regimen of Contrexeville water and saccharine in which his Bacchic priesthood will presently end. I dont drink beer for two reasons: number one, I dont like it, and therefore have no interest to blind me to the plain facts about it; and, number two, my profession is one that obliges me to keep in critical training, and beer is fatal both to training and criticism. It makes men cheaply happy by destroying their consciences. If I did not know how unsafe it is to conclude that men practise what they preach (Mr Chesterton doth protest too much, and may be little better than a hypocritical abstainer), I should challenge him to forswear sack and dispute my laurels as a playwright, instead of lazily writing books about me. Is a man to live on my work, and then tell me I was not drunk enough to do it properly? Have I survived the cry of Art for Art's Sake, and War for War's Sake, for which Mr Chesterton rebukes Whistler and Mr Rudyard Kipling, to fall a victim to this maddest of all cries: the cry of Beer for Beer's Sake?

Another insanity of Mr Chesterton's is his craze for fairy tales. I read every fairy tale I could get hold of when I was a child, and in the normal course took to stodgier literature later on. Mr Chesterton, I suspect, began with Huxley or George Eliot, and was caught in later life by that phase of the Oscar Wilde movement which Du Maurier satirized in his picture of the æsthetes raving about the beauty of Little Bo-Peep. He must have read Jack the Giantkiller for the first time in the budding vigor of his manhood, and read it as a work of art; for no child ever loses its head over a fairy tale as he lost his over this one. He does not seem to have ever read another, or to remember whether that one was really Jack the Giantkiller or Jack and the Beanstalk. Jack was enough for him; and, ever since, he has preached an insane cult of that particular fairy tale. The result is that he falls foul of me for pointing out that the true hero is not an average Englishman miserably mortifying his natural badness, but a superior human being strenuously gratifying his natural virtue. I illustrated this by our myths, which shew the hero triumphing irresistibly because he has a magic sword, an enchanted helmet, a purse of Fortunatas, and a horse beyond all motor-cars. This infuriates Mr Chesterton. He declares that I shall never be nearer to hell than when I wrote this; and I hope he is right, as I was not in the least scorched. Thinking of Jack and forgetting Siegfried, he declares that all the fairy tales shew a little man vanquishing a big one. Now, seriously, nothing can be more horrible than the defeat of the greater by the lesser. Even to see the greater driven to vanquish the lesser by cunning and treachery is not pleasant: it is more endurable to pity Telramund in his helplessness against Lohengrin than to exult in David killing Goliath by what was, by all the rules of the ring, a foul blow. All the stories which represent Jack as killing the giant are mean flatteries of our Jacks and gross and obvious calumnies of our giants. In the great world-significant stories the giants are slain with pitiable certainty by the gods, and not by tailors and hop-o-my-thumbs. There are no consolation prizes for the devil in the book of life. Mr Chesterton has read only one fairy tale, and that a mean one. I have read them all, and I like the ones in which the hero conquers, not because he is a well-plucked little un, but "in this sign."

Mr Chesterton is, at present, a man of vehement reactions; and, like all reactionists, he usually empties the baby out with the bath. And when he sees me nursing the collection of babies I have saved from all the baths, he cannot believe that I have really emptied out their baths thoroughly. He concludes that I am a Calvinist because I perceive the value and truth of Calvin's conviction that once a man is born it is too late to save him or damn him: you may "educate" him and "form his character" until you are black in the face; he is predestinate, and his soul cannot be changed any more than a silk purse can be changed into a sow's ear. Next moment Mr Chesterton is himself Calvinistically scorning me for advocating Herbert Spencer's notion of teaching by experience, and asks, with one of his great Thor-hammer strokes, whether a precipice can be taught by experience, to which I reply, in view of the new railway up the Jungfrau, that I should rather think it can. On another page he is protesting that I exaggerate the force of environment, because I proclaimed the staring fact that Christmas is a gluttonous, spendthrift orgy, foisted upon us by unfortunate tradesmen who can just make both ends meet by the profits of the Christmas trade. He concludes that, in my joyless Puritan home (oh, my father! oh, my mother!) I never melted lead on "Holi-eve," never hid rings in pancakes, never did all those dreary, silly Christmas things, until human nature rebelled against them and they were swept out of our domestic existence, like the exchanging of birthday presents and the rest of the inculcated tribal superstitions of the kitchen; and he would have me believe that every Christmas he turns his happy home into an imitation of the toy department at Gamage's, and burns a Yule log ordered, regardless of expense, from the Vauxhall ship-knackers. Chesterton, Chesterton, these are not the spontaneous delights of childhood: they are the laborious acquirements of bookish maturity. Christmas means: "Thank God Christ was born only once a year; so let us get drunk and have done with it for another twelve months." I would not give twopence for a Christian who does not commemorate Christ's birth every day and keep sober over it.

But I must stop arbitrarily or my review will be longer than the book! For there is endless matter in G. K. C. My last word must be that, gifted as he is, he needs a sane Irishman to look after him. For this portrait essay beginning with the insanity of beer for beer's sake does not stop short of the final far madder lunacy of absurdity for absurdity's sake. I have tried to teach Mr Chesterton that the will that moves us is dogmatic; that our brain is only the very imperfect instrument by which we devise practical means for fulfilling that will; that logic is our attempt to understand it and to reconcile its apparent contradictions with some intelligible theory of its purpose; and that the man who gives to reason and logic the attributes and authority of the will—the Rationalist—is the most hopeless of fools; and all that I have got into his otherwise very wonderful brain, is that whatever is reasonable and logical is false, and whatever is nonsensical is true.

I therefore ask the Editor of The Nation to open a subscription
to send him to Ireland for two years. As I write, with the Kerry
coast under my eyes, I can see, breathe, and feel that climate, that
weather (changing every twenty minutes more than the stiff,
fierce, brain-besotting weather of England can change in a
month), which he calls "material and mechanical," mere "mud
and mist." His English will, his English hope, he says, are
stronger than these mere physical things. Are they? What about
the Scotch will, the Yorkshire hope of the Shaws? have they
prevailed against that most mystical of all mystical things: the
atmosphere of the Island of the Saints? Let Mr Chesterton try
that atmosphere for a while. In ten minutes—no more—he will
feel a curious letting down, ending with an Englishman's first
taste of common sense. In ten months there will not be an atom
of English will or hope anywhere in his ventripotent person. He
will eat salmon and Irish stew and drink whiskey prosaically,
because he will hunger and thirst for food and drink instead of
drinking beer poetically because he thirsts for righteousness. And
the facts will be firm under his feet, whilst the heavens are open
over his head; and his soul will become a torment to him, like
the soul of the Wandering Jew, until he has achieved his appointed work, which is not that of speculating as to what I am
here for, but of discovering and doing what he himself is here
for.

1909

Ferrero and the Decline of Civilisations

by IGNAZIO SILONE [1900–1978]

TOWARDS 1898 Ferrero set himself to study the history of the
Roman Empire with the express intention, as he himself has
frankly admitted, of discovering in it some kind of fundamental

law about the evolution and decline of human societies. And since whenever a convinced believer seeks he invariably finds, Ferrero likewise managed to discover a truth which for the rest of his life was to remain the food of his meditations. In reading Sallust, Livy, Virgil, he was immediately struck by the fact that the things which we today usually appreciate and admire, such as building-up of power, acquisition of wealth, refinement of social customs, were by them, on the contrary, defined and regarded as corruption. The ancient authors were therefore far from being unaware of the causes which were about to determine the ruin of the Roman Empire and Ferrero took on himself the mission of reviving this consciousness, developing it, deepening it, and deriving from it a universal criterion. After the completion of his vast work, *The Greatness and Decline of Rome,* he returned to the scrutiny of his own times. His travels on both sides of the Atlantic showed him a world in the flower of civil and economic development. Enlightened by Sallust, Livy, Virgil, he was prompt to discern in this world the symptoms of its future disintegration. In the general optimism then prevailing, his warnings rang like those of a hysterical Cassandra, and he was mocked and derided, especially by his compatriots; but it was not long before events confirmed his words.

The fact that a forecast has proved accurate is of course inadequate to establish as scientific the theories on which it is based. People endowed with extreme physical sensibility, rheumatic people for instance, can often predict storms; but it is not the rheumatism that produces the storm, and a meteorological observatory cannot base its conclusions on rheumatism. Nevertheless, he is often and justly punished who, on leaving home in the morning, laughs at his rheumatic friend because the latter warns him, despite the clear sky and radiant sunshine, to go back and fetch his raincoat.

Ferrero collected his judgments and prophecies on the modern world in a series of dialogues which he entitled *Between Two Worlds* because the interlocutors were passengers on board a transatlantic luxury liner sailing from Europe to America. They were society people, adventurers, profiteers, people who had "arrived"; optimistic, ingenious and also rather grotesque, as vulgar people almost always are when they think themselves happy; people of unlimited material possibilities. But it was this very absence of limits, seemingly guaranteeing to modern man an absolute sovereignty over nature and society, that began to alarm Ferrero. He defined modern civilisation as *quantitative*, in contrast to ancient civilisations which were *qualitative*. In Ferrero's mind, a qualitative civilisation is one which has clearly defined limits, has models of moral and esthetic perfection, is based on certain virtues, draws its inspiration from certain forms of beauty. Up to the time of the French Revolution and the nineteenth century, humanity, according to Ferrero, had created only qualitative civilisations; but the French Revolution brought chaos in its wake, it gave rise to a civilisation aimed exclusively at riches and power, it swept away the ancient boundaries and was incapable of creating new ones. A quantitative civilisation, in the eyes of Ferrero, is not a real civilisation, but a tumultuous transition, a parenthesis, a fearful interregnum, a tragic adventure; in it there can be no security.

Ferrero was the poet of conservative anguish in an epoch of transition. In giving voice to the longing of every man for a just and ordered society, he struck profoundly human chords, but he could never overcome his horror of everything new, of adventure, as he called it, and his deep attachment to antiquity. Without a minimum of common assurances, it is not possible for men to live together in society. If they are not to massacre each other, men must agree on a certain number of fundamental questions; what is good, what evil; what is true, what false; what is beautiful, what ugly. Ferrero wanted to be the historian of transition periods. He studied and analysed the decline and fall of the Roman Empire in the third century, the end of the French monarchy in the eighteenth, the collapse of the Central and Eastern European monarchies in our own century, and the subsequent defeat of the democracies. He made his personal drama out of the death of civilisations. These events, in themselves far apart and unconnected, were in his vision of them bound together by the same chain of causes. Isolating them from their concrete and historical backgrounds, he gave himself up to the study of their formal and psychological elements. The old principles are breaking down, the old religion leaves the souls of men indifferent, the old morality has grown ridiculous, the old art leaves people cold; but the new class which is gaining the upper hand in society is incapable of founding a new discipline and of fixing boundaries which will be accepted by everyone because recognised by everyone as being true, just and good. Up to the time of the first world war Ferrero's thought had been chiefly busied with the moral and esthetic aspects of the death of civilisations; the reading of Tallyrand suggested to him a complementary theory that fitted its political aspects. He read Tallyrand's memoirs when ill in bed in the early days of November 1918, in the very week, therefore, that saw the military collapse of the Central Powers; and this reading was for him a "tremendous flash of lightning" as he himself has said. Pages 155 to 162 of the second volume were a revelation to him. They are the pages in which Talleyrand expounds his doctrine of legitimate power and shows that a system of balance and a stable peace among European states are possible only if all these states are governed by legitimate powers, that is, powers conforming to a principle of right accepted by the subjects and respected by the rulers.

The definition of legitimacy found in Talleyrand completed those of quality and boundaries already formulated by Ferrero. Quality, boundaries, legitimacy; these became his trinomial. The world is in chaos because we no longer know on what principles the right of command and the duty of obedience are founded. Either men learn to live subordinating power to justice, or they perish. A society can have peace and security only if it is grounded on a legitimate order. We must not let ourselves be deceived by the grandiose constructions of modern political activism: they are edifices built on sand. The old monarchies have been destroyed, but sham democracies have crept into their places, mere show-window democracies; the old generals are still in command, they have replaced the plumed helmet by the Phrygian cap, they no longer believe in the emperor, but neither do they believe in the people. The instruments of democracy, such as universal suffrage, plebiscites, mass organisations, have turned against democracy; there is no longer accordance between end and means, between path and goal. The contradictions of the age of transition which Ferrero brought to light are the internal contradictions of the superstructure; the contradictions are real and his analysis of them is competent, but the roots of the crisis and the solution of the crisis lie beneath them. Ferrero's preachings resemble the custom, formerly prevalent in some Catholic countries, of ringing the church-bells in times of pestilence in order to ward off the disease.

Ferrero's fate has been that of the "disarmed prophet" of whom Machiavelli spoke. The inefficacy of his apostolate came in the end to steep his soul in bitterness and steel his spirit towards the extreme consequences of his innate pessimism. In the end, the substance of history appeared to him as being, under different forms, always one and the same. Man is incapable of reconciling force with righteousness, matter with spirit, quantity with quality, measure with progress. In vain does culture seek to dam the onrush of innate human folly; its dikes are too fragile to stem the impetus of the forces tending to chaos. To what end does man exist? What are we doing here on earth? In his novels: *The Two Truths, The Revolt of the Soul, Blood and Sweat, Liberation,* Ferrero sought to give artistic form to this anguish of his. Here man is shown as a sort of prisoner and human life as a sort of prison. From the narrow windows of his prison man sees a limited horizon, but he knows that beyond there lies a vast, an infinite world, "his" world, the world from which he has been exiled and which he longs to know, but cannot. The torment of man is therefore the typical torment of the prisoner. He sets himself problems which he cannot solve, he aspires to a justice which is not of this world, to a perfection which eludes him, but which leaves him with a lingering nostalgia. The tragedy is that he is condemned for life to this prison and can leave it only as a corpse.

There is, I think, no need to say that in an epoch when thought is dominated by propaganda and optimism is obligatory even in cemeteries, the life of a man like Ferrero is inevitably hard. Ferrero has died in exile, but if the truth must be told, even in Italy he was already an exile. All his life Ferrero was alone. It can almost be said that he was a man born in exile, a man of a bygone age. He was the pathetic and mournful reincarnation, in our epoch, of an eighteenth-century moralist, with a few "scientific" notions borrowed from Saint-Simon and Auguste Comte. He won for himself a certain renown as a historian in France and the South American republics, countries in which historiography is still largely influenced by nineteenth-century ideas; but in Italy, after 1900, after Antonio Labriola, Benedetto Croce, and Giovanni Gentile, he was a solitary wanderer in the world of culture. Stripped of its outdated theories, the real and undying value of Ferrero's work remains in the testimony of his own human destiny. He lived his life within the closed circle of his dreams. In Geneva he found asylum in an eighteenth-century mansion built by Italian artists in the old aristocratic and Calvinist quarter of the ramparts, where in former times there lived the families of refugees hunted from Italy by the Counter-Reformation. His house was always crowded with visitors. He usually sat in a corner, his arms folded, his face sad, remote, overcast; when he began to speak, everyone else was silent, and then he would pronounce grave sentences and peremptory judgment. He never failed to make a deep impression: the impression of a man absorbed by a sombre vision and living in that vision and seeing in it the passage of the centuries. The proud tenor and the integrity of his life inspired everyone with respect, but few even among the Italian emigrants were convinced by his ideas. Even in the opposition he was without a home.

The same criticism may be made of Ferrero as of the conservative humanism of Ortega y Gasset, Borgese, Huizinga; the criticism of all those who seek the Living among the dead. A society is renewed, on the contrary, when its humblest element acquires a value. Today the Living is to be found among the Negroes, in the Polish ghettos, among the Chinese coolies, among the peons, among the cafoni, among the proletarians. But for the aristocratic Ferrero, all this was sordid materialism. He was fond of quoting the invective of the dying Orlando from his son Leo's play "Angelica": "Interest, ignoble filthy crust of the world. Men, why have you no longer any faith in anything? Because you are nothing and you would measure the world by the yardstick of yourselves. You will always be unhappy if you persist in cherishing so mean a conception of happiness." He derived, as befitted his rôle, a certain satisfaction from his exile and his isolation, but it needed no great power of insight to see that, like the dying Orlando, he was tortured by homesickness for the great sun of his country, for its blond vineyards, for its twilights steeped in an immemorial languor, for its sea shimmering in a haze beyond the plains, for its gentle and devoted women, for its marble ruins, for its silences, for the desperate splendor of its cities. He loved his country, but in secret, like a lover that has been rejected.

1942   Translated by
                                            DARINA SILONE

The Old Pacific Capital

by ROBERT LOUIS STEVENSON [1850–1894]

THE WOODS AND THE PACIFIC

THE BAY OF MONTEREY has been compared by no less a person than General Sherman to a bent fishing-hook; and the comparison, if less important than the march through Georgia, still shows the eye of a soldier for topography. Santa Cruz sits exposed at the shank; the mouth of the Salinas river is at the middle of the bend; and Monterey itself is cosily ensconced beside the barb. Thus the ancient capital of California faces across the bay, while the Pacific Ocean, though hidden by low hills and forests, bombards her left flank and rear with never-dying surf. In front of the town, the long line of seabeach trends north and north-west, and then westward to enclose the bay. The waves which lap so quietly about the jetties of Monterey grow louder and larger in the distance; you can see the breakers leaping high and white by day; at night, the outline of the shore is traced in transparent silver by the moonlight and the flying foam; and from all round, even in quiet weather, the low, distant, thrilling roar of the Pacific hangs over the coast and the adjacent country like smoke above a battle.

These long beaches are enticing to the idle man. It would be hard to find a walk more solitary and at the same time more exciting to the mind. Crowds of ducks and sea-gulls hover over the sea. Sandpipers trot in and out by troops after the retiring waves, trilling together in a chorus of infinitesimal song. Strange sea-tangles, new to the European eye, the bones of whales, or sometimes a whole whale's carcase, white with carrion-gulls and poisoning the wind, lie scattered here and there along the sands. The waves come in slowly, vast and green, curve their translucent necks, and burst with a surprising uproar, that runs, waxing and waning, up and down the long key-board of the beach. The foam of these great ruins mounts in an instant to the ridge of the sand glacis, swiftly fleets back again, and is met and buried by the next breaker. The interest is perpetually fresh. On no other coast that I know shall you enjoy, in calm, sunny weather, such a spectacle of Ocean's greatness, such beauty of changing colour, or such degrees of thunder in the sound. The very air is more than usually salt by this Homeric deep.

Inshore, a tract of sand-hills borders on the beach. Here and there a lagoon, more or less brackish, attracts the birds and hunters. A rough, spotty undergrowth partially conceals the sand. The crouching, hardy, live-oaks flourish singly or in thickets— the kind of wood for murderers to crawl among—and here and there the skirts of the forest extend downward from the hills with a floor of turf and aisles of pine-trees hung with Spaniard's Beard. Through this quaint desert the railway cars drew near to Monterey from the junction at Salina City—though that and so many other things are now for ever altered—and it was from here that you had the first view of the old township lying in the sands, its white windmills bickering in the chill, perpetual wind, and the first fogs of the evening drawing drearily around it from the sea.

The one common note of all this country is the haunting

presence of the ocean. A great faint sound of breakers follows you high up into the inland cañons; the roar of water dwells in the clean, empty rooms of Monterey as in a shell upon the chimney; go where you will, you have but to pause and listen to hear the voice of the Pacific. You pass out of the town to the south-west, and mount the hill among pine woods. Glade, thicket, and grove surround you. You follow winding sandy tracks that lead nowhither. You see a deer; a multitude of quail arises. But the sound of the sea still follows you as you advance, like that of wind among the trees, only harsher and stranger to the ear; and when at length you gain the summit, out breaks on every hand and with freshened vigour, that same unending, distant, whispering rumble of the ocean; for now you are on the top of the Monterey peninsula, and the noise no longer only mounts to you from behind along the beach towards Santa Cruz, but from your right also, round by Chinatown and Pinos lighthouse, and from down before you to the mouth of the Carmello river. The whole woodland is begirt with thundering surges. The silence that immediately surrounds you where you stand is not so much broken as it is haunted by this distant, circling rumour. It sets your senses upon edge; you strain your attention; you are clearly and unusually conscious of small sounds near at hand; you walk listening like an Indian hunter; and that voice of the Pacific is a sort of disquieting company to you in your walk.

When once I was in these woods I found it difficult to turn homeward. All woods lure a rambler onward; but in those of Monterey it was the surf that particularly invited me to prolong my walks. I would push straight for the shore where I thought it to be nearest. Indeed, there was scarce a direction that would not, sooner or later, have brought me forth on the Pacific. The emptiness of the woods gave me a sense of freedom and discovery in these excursions. I never in all my visits met but one man. He was a Mexican, very dark of hue, but smiling and fat, and he carried an axe, though his true business at that moment was to seek for straying cattle. I asked him what o'clock it was, but he seemed neither to know nor care; and when he in his turn asked me for news of his cattle, I showed myself equally indifferent. We stood and smiled upon each other for a few seconds, and then turned without a word and took our several ways across the forest.

One day—I shall never forget it—I had taken a trail that was new to me. After a while the woods began to open, the sea to sound nearer hand. I came upon a road, and, to my surprise, a stile. A step or two farther, and, without leaving the woods, I found myself among trim houses. I walked through street after street, parallel and at right angles, paved with sward and dotted with trees, but still undeniable streets, and each with its name posted at the corner, as in a real town. Facing down the main thoroughfare—"Central Avenue," as it was ticketed—I saw an open-air temple, with benches and sounding-board, as though for an orchestra. The houses were all tightly shuttered; there was no smoke, no sound but of the waves, no moving thing. I have never been in any place that seemed so dreamlike. Pompeii is all in a bustle with visitors, and its antiquity and strangeness deceive the imagination; but this town had plainly not been built above a year or two, and perhaps had been deserted overnight. Indeed, it was not so much like a deserted town as like a scene upon the stage by daylight, and with no one on the boards. The barking of a dog led me at last to the only house still occupied, where a Scotch pastor and his wife pass the winter alone in this empty theatre. The place was "The Pacific Camp Grounds, the Christian Seaside Resort." Thither, in the warm season, crowds come to enjoy a life of teetotalism, religion, and flirtation, which I am willing to think blameless and agreeable. The neighbourhood at least is well selected. The Pacific booms in front. Westward is Point Pinos, with the lighthouse in a wilderness of sand, where you will find the lightkeeper playing the piano, making models and bows and arrows, studying dawn and sunrise in amateur oil-painting, and with a dozen other elegant pursuits and interests to surprise his brave, old-country rivals. To the east, and still nearer, you will come upon a space of open down, a hamlet, a haven among rocks, a world of surge and screaming sea-gulls. Such scenes are very similar in different climates; they appear homely to the eyes of all; to me this was like a dozen spots in Scotland. And yet the boats that ride in the haven are of strange outlandish design; and, if you walk into the hamlet, you will behold costumes and faces and hear a tongue that are unfamiliar to the memory. The joss-stick burns, the opium pipe is smoked, the floors are strewn with slips of coloured paper—prayers, you would say, that had somehow missed their destination—and a man guiding his upright pencil from right to left across the sheet, writes home the news of Monterey to the Celestial Empire.

The woods and the Pacific rule between them the climate of this seaboard region. On the streets of Monterey, when the air does not smell salt from the one, it will be blowing perfumed from the resinous treetops of the other. For days together a hot, dry air will overhang the town, close as from an oven, yet healthful and aromatic in the nostrils. The cause is not far to seek, for the woods are afire, and the hot wind is blowing from the hills. These fires are one of the great dangers in California. I have seen from Monterey as many as three at the same time, by day a cloud of smoke, by night a red coal of conflagration in the distance. A little thing will start them, and, if the wind be favourable, they gallop over miles of country faster than a horse. The inhabitants must turn out and work like demons, for it is not only the pleasant groves that are destroyed; the climate and the soil are equally at stake, and these fires prevent the rains of the next winter and dry up perennial fountains. California has been a land of promise in its time, like Palestine; but if the woods continue so swiftly to perish, it may become, like Palestine, a land of desolation.

To visit the woods while they are languidly burning is a strange piece of experience. The fire passes through the underbrush at a run. Every here and there a tree flares up instantaneously from root to summit, scattering tufts of flame, and is quenched, it seems, as quickly. But this last is only in semblance. For after this first squib-like conflagration of the dry moss and twigs, there remains behind a deep-rooted and consuming fire in the very entrails of the tree. The resin of the pitch-pine is principally condensed at the base of the bole and in the spreading roots. Thus, after the light, showy, skirmishing flames, which are only as the match to the explosion, have already scampered down the wind into the distance, the true harm is but beginning for this giant of the woods. You may approach the tree from one side, and see it, scorched indeed from top to bottom, but apparently survivor of the peril. Make the circuit, and there, on the other side of the column, is a clear mass of living coal, spreading like an ulcer; while underground, to their most extended fibre, the roots are being eaten out by fire, and the smoke is rising through the fissures to the surface. A little while, and, without a nod of warning, the huge pine-tree snaps off short across the ground and falls prostrate with a crash. Meanwhile the fire continues its silent business; the roots are reduced to a fine ash; and long afterwards, if you pass by, you will find the earth pierced with radiating galleries, and preserving the design of all these subterranean spurs, as though it were the mould for a new tree instead of the print of an old one. These pitch-pines of Monterey are, with the single exception of the Monterey cypress, the most fantastic of forest trees. No words can give an idea of the contortion of their growth; they might figure without change in a circle of the nether hell as Dante pictured it; and at the rate at which trees grow, and at which forest fires spring up and gallop through the hills of California, we may look forward to a time when there will not be one of them left standing in that land of their nativity. At least they have not so much to fear from the axe, but perish by what may be called a natural although violent death; while it is man in his short-sighted greed that robs the country of the nobler red-wood. Yet a little while and perhaps all the hills of sea-board California may be as bald as Tamalpais.

I have an interest of my own in these forest fires, for I came so near to lynching on one occasion, that a braver man might have retained a thrill from the experience. I wished to be certain whether it was the moss, that quaint funereal ornament of Californian forests, which blazed up so rapidly when the flame first touched the tree. I suppose I must have been under the influence of Satan, for instead of plucking off a piece for my experiment, what should I do but walk up to a great pine-tree in a portion of the wood which had escaped so much as scorching, strike a match, and apply the flame gingerly to one of the tassels. The tree went off

simply like a rocket; in three seconds it was a roaring pillar of
fire. Close by I could hear the shouts of those who were at work
combating the original conflagration. I could see the waggon that
had brought them tied to a live oak in a piece of open; I could even
catch the flash of an axe as it swung up through the underwood
into the sunlight. Had any one observed the result of my experiment
my neck was literally not worth a pinch of snuff; after a few
minutes of passionate expostulation I should have been run up to
a convenient bough.

> To die for faction is a common evil;
> But to be hanged for nonsense is the devil.

I have run repeatedly, but never as I ran that day. At night I
went out of town, and there was my own particular fire, quite
distinct from the other, and burning as I thought with even
greater vigour.

But it is the Pacific that exercises the most direct and obvious
power upon the climate. At sunset, for months together, vast, wet,
melancholy fogs arise and come shoreward from the ocean. From
the hill-top above Monterey the scene is often noble, although it
is always sad. The upper air is still bright with sunlight; a glow
still rests upon the Gabelano Peak; but the fogs are in possession
of the lower levels; they crawl in scarves among the sand-
hills; they float, a little higher, in clouds of a gigantic size and
often of a wild configuration; to the south, where they have
struck the seaward shoulder of the mountains of Santa Lucia,
they double back and spire up skyward like smoke. Where their
shadow touches, colour dies out of the world. The air grows
chill and deadly as they advance. The trade-wind freshens, the
trees begin to sigh, and all the windmills in Monterey are whirling
and creaking and filling their cisterns with the brackish water of
the sands. It takes but a little while till the invasion is complete.
The sea, in its lighter order, has submerged the earth. Monterey
is curtained in for the night in thick, wet, salt, and frigid clouds,
so to remain till day returns; and before the sun's rays they slowly
disperse and retreat in broken squadrons to the bosom of the
sea. And yet often when the fog is thickest and most chill, a few

steps out of the town and up the slope, the night will be dry and warm and full of inland perfume.

MEXICANS, AMERICANS, AND INDIANS

The history of Monterey has yet to be written. Founded by Catholic missionaries, a place of wise beneficence to Indians, a place of arms, a Mexican capital continually wrested by one faction from another, an American capital when the first House of Representatives held its deliberations, and then falling lower and lower from the capital of the State to the capital of a county, and from that again, by the loss of its charter and town lands, to a mere bankrupt village, its rise and decline is typical of that of all Mexican institutions and even Mexican families in California.

Nothing is stranger in that strange State than the rapidity with which the soil has changed hands. The Mexicans, you may say, are all poor and landless, like their former capital; and yet both it and they hold themselves apart and preserve their ancient customs and something of their ancient air.

The town, when I was there, was a place of two or three streets, economically paved with sea-sand, and two or three lanes, which were watercourses in rainy season, and were, at all times, rent up by fissures four or five feet deep. There were no street lights. Short sections of wooden sidewalk only added to the dangers of the night, for they were often high above the level of the roadway, and no one could tell where they would be likely to begin or end. The houses were, for the most part, built of unbaked adobe brick, many of them old for so new a country, some of very elegant proportions, with low, spacious, shapely rooms, and walls so thick that the heat of summer never dried them to the heart. At the approach of the rainy season a deathly chill and a graveyard smell began to hang about the lower floors; and diseases of the chest are common and fatal among housekeeping people of either sex.

There was no activity but in and around the saloons, where people sat almost all day long playing cards. The smallest excursion was made on horseback. You would scarcely ever see the main street without a horse or two tied to posts, and making a fine figure with their Mexican housings. It struck me oddly to come across some of the *Cornhill* illustrations to Mr. Blackmore's *Erema,* and see all the characters astride on English saddles. As a matter of fact, an English saddle is a rarity even in San Francisco, and, you may say, a thing unknown in all the rest of California. In a place so exclusively Mexican as Monterey, you saw not only Mexican saddles but true Vaquero riding—men always at the hand-gallop up hill and down dale, and round the sharpest corner, urging their horses with cries and gesticulations and cruel rotatory spurs, checking them dead with a touch, or wheeling them right-about-face in a square yard. The type of face and character of bearing are surprisingly un-American. The first ranged from something like the pure Spanish, to something, in its sad fixity, not unlike the pure Indian, although I do not suppose there was one pure blood of either race in all the country. As for the second, it was a matter of perpetual surprise to find, in that world of absolutely mannerless Americans, a people full of deportment, solemnly courteous, and doing all things with grace and decorum. In dress they ran to colour and bright sashes. Not even the most Americanised could always resist the temptation to stick a red rose into his hatband. Not even the most Americanised would descend to wear the vile dress hat of civilisation. Spanish was the language of the streets. It was difficult to get along without a word or two of that language for an occasion. The only communications in which the population joined were with a view to amusement. A weekly public ball took place with great etiquette, in addition to the numerous fandangoes in private houses. There was a really fair amateur brass band. Night after night serenaders would be going about the street, sometimes in a company and with several instruments and voices together, sometimes severally, each guitar before a different window. It was a strange thing to lie awake in nineteenth-century America, and hear the guitar accompany, and one of these old, heart-breaking Spanish love songs mount into the night air, perhaps in a deep baritone, perhaps in that high-pitched, pathetic, womanish alto which is so common among Mexican men, and which strikes on the unaccustomed ear as something not entirely human but altogether sad.

The town, then, was essentially and wholly Mexican; and yet almost all the land in the neighbourhood was held by Americans, and it was from the same class, numerically so small, that the principal officials were selected. This Mexican and that Mexican would describe to you his old family estates, not one rood of which remained to him. You would ask him how that came about, and elicit some tangled story back-foremost, from which you gathered that the Americans had been greedy like designing men, and the Mexicans greedy like children, but no other certain fact. Their merits and their faults contributed alike to the ruin of the former landholders. It is true they were improvident, and easily dazzled with the sight of ready money; but they were gentlefolk besides, and that in a way which curiously unfitted them to combat Yankee craft. Suppose they have a paper to sign, they would think it a reflection on the other party to examine the terms with any great minuteness; nay, suppose them to observe some doubtful clause, it is ten to one they would refuse from delicacy to object to it. I know I am speaking within the mark, for I have seen such a case occur, and the Mexican, in spite of the advice of his lawyer, has signed the imperfect paper like a lamb. To have spoken in the matter, he said, above all to have let the other party guess that he had seen a lawyer, would have "been like doubting his word." The scruple sounds oddly to one of ourselves, who have been brought up to understand all business as a competition in fraud, and honesty itself to be a virtue which regards the carrying out but not the creation of agreements. This single unworldly trait will account for much of that revolution of which we are speaking. The Mexicans have the name of being great swindlers, but certainly the accusation cuts both ways. In a contest of this sort, the entire booty would scarcely have passed into the hands of the more scrupulous race.

Physically the Americans have triumphed; but it is not entirely seen how far they have themselves been morally conquered. This is, of course, but a part of a part of an extraordinary problem now in the course of being solved in the various States of the American Union. I am reminded of an anecdote. Some years ago, at a great sale of wine, all the odd lots were purchased by a grocer in a small way in the old town of Edinburgh. The agent had the curiosity to visit him some time after and inquire what possible use he could have for such material. He was shown, by way of answer, a huge vat where all the liquors, from humble Gladstone to imperial Tokay, were fermenting together. "And what," he asked, "do you propose to call this?" "I'm not very sure," replied the grocer, "but I think it's going to turn out port." In the older Eastern States, I think we may say that this hotchpotch of races is going to turn out English, or thereabout. But the problem is indefinitely varied in other zones. The elements are differently mingled in the south, in what we may call the Territorial belt, and in the group of States on the Pacific coast. Above all, in these last, we may look to see some monstrous hybrid—whether good or evil, who shall forecast? but certainly original and all their own. In my little restaurant at Monterey, we have sat down to table day after day, a Frenchman, two Portuguese, an Italian, a Mexican, and a Scotchman: we had for common visitors an American from Illinois, a nearly pure blood Indian woman, and a naturalised Chinese; and from time to time a Switzer and a German came down from country ranches for the night. No wonder that the Pacific coast is a foreign land to visitors from the Eastern States, for each race contributes something of its own. Even the despised Chinese have taught the youth of California, none indeed of their virtues, but the debasing use of opium. And chief among these influences is that of the Mexicans.

The Mexicans although in the State are out of it. They still preserve a sort of international independence, and keep their affairs snug to themselves. Only four or five years ago Vasquez, the bandit, his troops being dispersed and the hunt too hot for him in other parts of California, returned to his native Monterey, and was seen publicly in her streets and saloons, fearing no man. The year that I was there there occurred two reputed murders. As the Montereyans are exceptionally vile speakers of each other and of every one behind his back, it is not possible for me to judge how much truth there may have been in these reports; but in the one case every one believed, and in the other some suspected, that there had been foul play; and nobody dreamed for an instant of taking the authorities into their counsel. Now this is, of course, characteristic enough of the Mexicans; but it is a noteworthy feature that all the Americans in Monterey acquiesced without a word in this inaction. Even when I spoke to them upon the subject, they seemed not to understand my surprise; they had forgotten the traditions of their own race and upbringing, and become, in a word, wholly Mexicanised.

Again, the Mexicans, having no ready money to speak of, rely almost entirely in their business transactions upon each other's worthless paper. Pedro the penniless pays you with an IOU from the equally penniless Miguel. It is a sort of local currency by courtesy. Credit in these parts has passed into a superstition. I have seen a strong, violent man struggling for months to recover a debt, and getting nothing but an exchange of waste paper. The very storekeepers are averse to asking for cash payments, and are more surprised than pleased when they are offered. They fear there must be something under it, and that you mean to withdraw your custom from them. I have seen the enterprising chemist and stationer begging me with fervour to let my account run on, although I had my purse open in my hand; and partly from the commonness of the case, partly from some remains of that generous old Mexican tradition which made all men welcome to their tables, a person may be notoriously both unwilling and unable to pay, and still find credit for the necessaries of life in the stores of Monterey. Now this villainous habit of living upon "tick" has grown into Californian nature. I do not mean that the American and European storekeepers of Monterey are as lax as Mexicans; I mean that American farmers in many parts of the State expect unlimited credit, and profit by it in the meanwhile, without a thought for consequences. Jew storekeepers have already learned the advantage to be gained from this; they lead on the farmer into irretrievable indebtedness, and keep him ever after as their bond-slave hopelessly grinding in the mill. So the whirligig of time brings in its revenges, and except that the Jew knows better than to foreclose, you may see Americans bound in the same chains with which they themselves had formerly bound the Mexican. It seems as if certain sorts of follies, like certain sorts of grain, were natural to the soil rather than to the race that holds and tills it for the moment.

In the meantime, however, the Americans rule in Monterey County. The new county seat, Salinas City, in the bald, corn-bearing plain under the Gabelano Peak, is a town of a purely American character. The land is held, for the most part, in those enormous tracts which are another legacy of Mexican days, and form the present chief danger and disgrace of California; and the holders are mostly of American or British birth. We have here in England no idea of the troubles and inconveniences which flow from the existence of these large landholders—land-thieves, land-sharks, or land-grabbers, they are more commonly and plainly called. Thus the townlands of Monterey are all in the hands of a single man. How they came there is an obscure, vexatious question, and, rightly or wrongly, the man is hated with a great hatred. His life has been repeatedly in danger. Not very long ago, I was told, the stage was stopped and examined three evenings in succession by disguised horsemen thirsting for his blood. A certain house on the Salinas road, they say, he always passes in his buggy at full speed, for the squatter sent him warning long ago. But a year since he was publicly pointed out for death by no less a man than Mr. Dennis Kearney. Kearney is a man too well known in California, but a word of explanation is required for English readers. Originally an Irish drayman, he rose, by his command of bad language, to almost dictatorial authority in the State; throned it there for six months or so, his mouth full of oaths, gallowses, and conflagrations; was first snuffed out last winter by Mr. Coleman, backed by his San Francisco Vigilantes and three gatling guns; completed his own ruin by throwing in his lot with the grotesque Greenbacker party; and had at last to be rescued by his old enemies, the police, out of the hands of his rebellious followers. It was while he was at the top of his fortune that Kearney visited Monterey with his battle-cry against Chinese labour, the railroad monopolists, and the land-thieves; and his one articulate counsel to the Montereyans was to "hang David Jacks." Had the town been American, in my private opinion, this would have been done years ago. Land is a subject on which there is no jesting in the West, and I have seen my friend the lawyer drive out of Monterey to adjust a competition of titles with the face of a captain going into battle and his Smith-and-Wesson convenient to his hand.

On the ranch of another of these landholders you may find our old friend, the truck system, in full operation. Men live there, year in year out, to cut timber for a nominal wage, which is all consumed in supplies. The longer they remain in this desirable service the deeper they will fall in debt—a burlesque injustice in a new country, where labour should be precious, and one of those typical instances which explains the prevailing discontent and the success of the demagogue Kearney.

In a comparison between what was and what is in California, the praisers of times past will fix upon the Indians of Carmel. The valley drained by the river so named is a true California valley, bare, dotted with chaparral, overlooked by quaint, unfinished hills. The Carmel runs by many pleasant farms, a clear and shallow river, loved by wading kine; and at last, as it is falling towards a quicksand and the great Pacific, passes a ruined mission on a hill. From the mission church the eye embraces a great field of ocean, and the ear is filled with a continuous sound of distant breakers on the shore. But the day of the Jesuit has gone by, the day of the Yankee has succeeded, and there is no one left to care for the converted savage. The church is roofless and ruinous, seabreezes and sea-fogs, and the alternation of the rain and sunshine, daily widening the breaches and casting the crockets from the wall. As an antiquity in this new land, a quaint specimen of missionary architecture, and a memorial of good deeds, it had a triple claim to preservation from all thinking people; but neglect and abuse have been its portion. There is no sign of American interference, save where a headboard has been torn from a grave to be a mark for pistol bullets. So it is with the Indians for whom it was erected. Their lands, I was told, are being yearly encroached upon by the neighbouring American proprietor, and with that exception no man troubles his head for the Indians of Carmel. Only one day in the year, the day before our Guy Fawkes, the *padre* drives over from Monterey; the little sacristy, which is the only covered portion of the church, is filled with seats and decorated for the service; the Indians troop together, their bright dresses contrasting with their dark and melancholy faces; and there, among a crowd of somewhat unsympathetic holiday-makers, you may hear God served with perhaps more touching circumstances than in any other temple under heaven. An Indian, stone-blind and about eighty years of age, conducts the singing; other Indians compose the choir; yet they have the Gregorian music at their finger ends, and pronounced the Latin so correctly that I could follow the meaning as they sang. The pronunciation was odd and nasal, the singing hurried and staccato. "In sæcula sæculo-ho-horum," they went, with a vigorous aspirate to every additional syllable. I have never seen faces more vividly lit up with joy than the faces of these Indian singers. It was to them not only the worship of God, nor an act by which they recalled and commemorated better days, but was besides an exercise of culture, where all they knew of art and letters was united and expressed. And it made a man's heart sorry for the good fathers of yore who had taught them to dig and to reap, to read and to sing, who had given them European mass-books which they still preserve and study in their cottages, and who had now passed away from all authority and influence in that land—to be succeeded by greedy land-thieves and sacrilegious pistol-shots. So ugly a thing may our Anglo-Saxon Protestantism appear beside the doings of the Society of Jesus.

But revolution in this world succeeds to revolution. All that I say in this paper is in a paulo-past tense. The Monterey of last year exists no longer. A huge hotel has sprung up in the desert by the railway. Three sets of diners sit down successively to table. Invaluable toilettes figure along the beach and between the live oaks; and Monterey is advertised in the newspapers, and posted in the waiting-rooms at railway stations, as a resort for wealth and fashion. Alas for the little town! it is not strong enough to resist the influence of the flaunting caravanserai, and the poor, quaint, penniless native gentlemen of Monterey must perish, like a lower race, before the millionaire vulgarians of the Big Bonanza.

From *Across the Plains,* 1880.

East and West

by RABINDRANATH TAGORE [1861–1941]

I

IT IS NOT ALWAYS a profound interest in man that carries travellers nowadays to distant lands. More often it is the facility for rapid movement. For lack of time and for the sake of convenience we generalise and crush our human facts into the packages within the steel trunks that hold our traveller's reports.

Our knowledge of our own countrymen and our feelings about them have slowly and unconsciously grown out of innumerable facts which are full of contradictions and subject to incessant change. They have the elusive mystery and fluidity of life. We cannot define to ourselves what we are as a whole, because we know too much; because our knowledge is more than knowledge. It is an immediate consciousness of personality, any evaluation of which carries some emotion, joy or sorrow, shame or exaltation. But in a foreign land we try to find our compensation for the meagreness of our data by the compactness of the generalisation which our imperfect sympathy itself helps us to form. When a stranger from the West travels in the Eastern world he takes the facts that displease him and readily makes use of them for his rigid conclusions, fixed upon the unchallengeable authority of his personal experience. It is like a man who has his own boat for crossing his village stream, but, on being compelled to wade across some strange watercourse, draws angry comparisons as he goes from every patch of mud and every pebble which his feet encounter.

Our mind has faculties which are universal, but its habits are insular. There are men who become impatient and angry at the least discomfort when their habits are incommoded. In their idea of the next world they probably conjure up the ghosts of their slippers and dressing-gowns, and expect the latchkey that opens their lodging-house door on earth to fit their front door in the other world. As travellers they are a failure; for they have grown too accustomed to their mental easy-chairs, and in their intellectual nature love home comforts, which are of local make, more than the realities of life, which, like earth itself, are full of ups and downs, yet are one in their rounded completeness.

The modern age has brought the geography of the earth near to us, but made it difficult for us to come into touch with man. We go to strange lands and observe; we do not live there. We hardly meet men: but only specimens of knowledge. We are in haste to seek for general types and overlook individuals.

When we fall into the habit of neglecting to use the understanding that comes of sympathy in our travels, our knowledge of foreign people grows insensitive, and therefore easily becomes both unjust and cruel in its character, and also selfish and contemptuous in its application. Such has, too often, been the case with regard to the meeting of Western people in our days with others for whom they do not recognise any obligation of kinship.

It has been admitted that the dealings between different races of men are not merely between individuals; that our mutual understanding is either aided, or else obstructed, by the general emanations forming the social atmosphere. These emanations are our collective ideas and collective feelings, generated according to special historical circumstances.

For instance, the caste-idea is a collective idea in India. When we approach an Indian who is under the influence of this collective idea, he is no longer a pure individual with his conscience fully awake to the judging of the value of a human being. He is more or less a passive medium for giving expression to the sentiment of a whole community.

It is evident that the caste-idea is not creative; it is merely institutional. It adjusts human being according to some mechanical arrangement. It emphasises the negative side of the individual—his separateness. It hurts the complete truth in man.

In the West, also, the people have a certain collective idea that obscures their humanity. Let me try to explain what I feel about it.

II

Lately I went to visit some battlefields of France which had been devastated by war. The awful calm of desolation, which still bore wrinkles of pain—death-struggles stiffened into ugly ridges—brought before my mind the vision of a huge demon, which had no shape, no meaning, yet had two arms that could strike and break and tear, a gaping mouth that could devour, and bulging brains that could conspire and plan. It was a purpose, which had a living body, but no complete humanity to temper it. Because it was passion—belonging to life, and yet not having the wholeness of life—it was the most terrible of life's enemies.

Something of the same sense of oppression in a different degree, the same desolation in a different aspect, is produced in my mind when I realise the effect of the West upon Eastern life—the West which, in its relation to us, is all plan and purpose incarnate, without any superfluous humanity.

I feel the contrast very strongly in Japan. In that country the old world presents itself with some ideal of perfection, in which man has his varied opportunities of self-revelation in art, in ceremonial, in religious faith, and in customs expressing the poetry of social relationship. There one feels that deep delight of hospitality which life offers to life. And side by side, in the same soil, stands the modern world, which is stupendously big and powerful, but inhospitable. It has no simple-hearted welcome for man. It is living; yet the incompleteness of life's ideal within it cannot but hurt humanity.

The wriggling tentacles of a cold-blooded utilitarianism, with which the West has grasped all the easily yielding succulent portions of the East, are causing pain and indignation throughout the Eastern countries. The West comes to us, not with the imagination and sympathy that create and unite, but with a shock of passion—passion for power and wealth. This passion is a mere force, which has in it the principle of separation, of conflict.

I have been fortunate in coming into close touch with individual men and women of the Western countries, and have felt with them their sorrows and shared their aspirations. I have known that they seek the same God, who is my God—even those who deny Him. I feel certain that, if the great light of culture be extinct in Europe, our horizon in the East will mourn in darkness. It does not hurt my pride to acknowledge that, in the present age, Western humanity has received its mission to be the teacher of the world; that her science, through the mastery of laws of nature, is to liberate human souls from the dark dungeon of matter. For this very reason I have realised all the more strongly, on the other hand, that the dominant collective idea in the Western countries is not creative. It is ready to enslave or kill individuals, to drug a great people with soul-killing poison, darkening their whole future with the black mist of stupefaction, and emasculating entire races of men to the utmost degree of helplessness. It is wholly wanting in spiritual power to blend and harmonise; it lacks the sense of the great personality of man.

The most significant fact of modern days is this, that the West has met the East. Such a momentous meeting of humanity, in order to be fruitful, must have in its heart some great emotional idea, generous and creative. There can be no doubt that God's choice has fallen upon the knights-errant of the West for the service of the present age; arms and armour have been given to them; but have they yet realised in their hearts the single-minded loyalty to their cause which can resist all temptations of bribery from the devil? The world to-day is offered to the West. She will destroy it, if she does not use it for a great creation of man. The materials for such a creation are in the hands of science; but the creative genius is in Man's spiritual ideal.

III

When I was young, a stranger from Europe came to Bengal. He chose his lodging among the people of the country, shared with them their frugal diet, and freely offered them his service.

He found employment in the houses of the rich, teaching them French and German, and the money thus earned he spent to help poor students in buying books. This meant for him hours of walking in the mid-day heat of a tropical summer; for, intent upon exercising the utmost economy, he refused to hire conveyances. He was pitiless in his exaction from himself of his resources, in money, time, and strength, to the point of privation; and all this for the sake of a people who were obscure, to whom he was not born, yet whom he dearly loved. He did not come to us with a professional mission of teaching sectarian creeds; he had not in his nature the least trace of that self-sufficiency of goodness, which humiliates by gifts the victims of its insolent benevolence. Though he did not know our language, he took every occasion to frequent our meetings and ceremonies; yet he was always afraid of intrusion, and tenderly anxious lest he might offend us by his ignorance of our customs. At last, under the continual strain of work in an alien climate and surroundings, his health broke down. He died, and was cremated at our burning ground, according to his express desire.

The attitude of his mind, the manner of his living, the object of his life, his modesty, his unstinted self-sacrifice for a people who had not even the power to give publicity to any benefaction bestowed upon them, were so utterly unlike anything we were accustomed to associate with the Europeans in India, that it gave rise in our mind to a feeling of love bordering upon awe.

We all have a realm, a private paradise, in our mind, where dwell deathless memories of persons who brought some divine light to our life's experience, who may not be known to others, and whose names have no place in the pages of history. Let me confess to you that this man lives as one of those immortals in the paradise of my individual life.

He came from Sweden, his name was Hammargren. What was most remarkable in the event of his coming to us in Bengal was the fact that in his own country he had chanced to read some works of my great countryman, Ram Mohan Roy, and felt an immense veneration for his genius and his character. Ram Mohan Roy lived in the beginning of the last century, and it is no exaggeration when I describe him as one of the immortal personalities of modern time. This young Swede had the unusual gift of a far-sighted intellect and sympathy, which enabled him even from his distance of space and time, and in spite of racial differences, to realise the greatness of Ram Mohan Roy. It moved him so deeply that he resolved to go to the country which produced this great man, and offer her his service. He was poor, and he had to wait some time in England before he could earn his passage money to India. There he came at last, and in reckless generosity of love utterly spent himself to the last breath of his life, away from home and kindred and all the inheritances of his motherland. His stay among us was too short to produce any outward result. He failed even to achieve during his life what he had in his mind, which was to found by the help of his scanty earnings a library as a memorial to Ram Mohan Roy, and thus to leave behind him a visible symbol of his devotion. But what I prize most in this European youth, who left no record of his life behind him, is not the memory of any service of goodwill, but the precious gift of respect which he offered to a people who are fallen upon evil times, and whom it is so easy to ignore or to humiliate. For the first time in the modern days this obscure individual from Sweden brought to our country the chivalrous courtesy of the West, a greeting of human fellowship.

The coincidence came to me with a great and delightful surprise when the Nobel prize was offered to me from Sweden. As a recognition of individual merit it was of great value to me, no doubt; but it was the acknowledgment of the East as a collaborator with the Western continents, in contributing its riches to the common stock of civilisation, which had the chief significance for the present age. It meant joining hands in comradeship by the two great hemispheres of the human world across the sea.

IV

To-day the real East remains unexplored. The blindness of contempt is more hopeless than the blindness of ignorance; for contempt kills the light which ignorance merely leaves unignited. The East is waiting to be understood by the Western races, in order not only to be able to give what is true in her, but also to be confident of her own mission.

In Indian history, the meeting of the Mussulman and the Hindu produced Akbar, the object of whose dream was the unification of hearts and ideals. It had all the glowing enthusiasm of a religion, and it produced an immediate and a vast result even in his own lifetime.

But the fact still remains that the Western mind, after centuries of contact with the East, has not evolved the enthusiasm of a chivalrous ideal which can bring this age to its fulfilment. It is everywhere raising thorny hedges of exclusion and offering human sacrifices to national self-seeking. It has intensified the mutual feelings of envy among Western races themselves, as they fight over their spoils and display a carnivorous pride in their snarling rows of teeth.

We must again guard our minds from any encroaching distrust of the individuals of a nation. The active love of humanity and the spirit of martyrdom for the cause of justice and truth which I have met with in the Western countries have been a great lesson and inspiration to me. I have no doubt in my mind that the West owes its true greatness, not so much to its marvellous training of intellect, as to its spirit of service devoted to the welfare of man. Therefore I speak with a personal feeling of pain and sadness about the collective power which is guiding the helm of Western civilisation. It is a passion, not an ideal. The more success it has brought to Europe, the more costly it will prove to her at last, when the accounts have to be rendered. And the signs are unmistakable, that the accounts have been called for. The time has come when Europe must know that the forcible parasitism which she has been practising upon the two large Continents of the world—the two most unwieldy whales of humanity —must be causing to her moral nature a gradual atrophy and degeneration.

As an example, let me quote the following extract from the concluding chapter of *From the Cape to Cairo,* by Messrs. Grogan and Sharp, two writers who have the power to inculcate their doctrines by precept and example. In their reference to the African they are candid, as when they say, "We have stolen his land. Now we must steal his limbs." These two sentences, carefully articulated, with a smack of enjoyment, have been more clearly explained in the following statement, where some sense of that decency which is the attenuated ghost of a buried conscience, prompts the writers to use the phrase "compulsory labour" in place of the honest word "slavery"; just as the modern politician adroitly avoids the word "injunction" and uses the word "mandate." "Compulsory labour in some form," they say, "is the corollary of our occupation of the country." And they add: "It is pathetic, but it is history," implying thereby that moral sentiments have no serious effect in the history of human beings.

Elsewhere they write: "Either we must give up the country commercially, or we must make the African work. And mere abuse of those who point out the impasse cannot change the facts. We must decide, and soon. Or rather the white man of South Africa will decide." The authors also confess that they have seen too much of the world "to have any lingering belief that Western civilisation benefits native races."

The logic is simple—the logic of egoism. But the argument is simplified by lopping off the greater part of the premise. For these writers seem to hold that the only important question for the white men of South Africa is, how indefinitely to grow fat on ostrich feathers and diamond mines, and dance jazz dances over the misery and degradation of a whole race of fellow-beings of a different colour from their own. Possibly they believe that moral laws have a special domesticated breed of comfortable concessions for the service of the people in power. Possibly they ignore the fact that commercial and political cannibalism, profitably practised upon foreign races, creeps back nearer home; that the cultivation of unwholesome appetites has its final reckoning with the stomach which has been made to serve it. For, after all, man is a spiritual being, and not a mere living money-bag jumping from profit to profit, and breaking the backbone of human races in its financial leapfrog.

Such, however, has been the condition of things for more than a century; and to-day, trying to read the future by the light of the European conflagration, we are asking ourselves everywhere in the East: "Is this frightfully overgrown power really great? It can bruise us from without, but can it add to our wealth of spirit? It can sign peace treaties, but can it give peace?"

It was about two thousand years ago that all-powerful Rome in one of its eastern provinces executed on a cross a simple teacher of an obscure tribe of fishermen. On that day the Roman governor felt no falling off of his appetite or sleep. On that day there was, on the one hand, the agony, the humiliation, the death; on the other, the pomp of pride and festivity in the Governor's palace.

And to-day? To whom, then, shall we bow the head?

> Kasmai devaya havisha vidhema?
> (To which God shall we offer oblation?)

We know of an instance in our own history of India, when a great personality, both in his life and voice, struck the keynote of the solemn music of the soul—love for all creatures. And that music crossed seas, mountains, and deserts. Races belonging to different climates, habits, and languages were drawn together, not in the clash of arms, not in the conflict of exploitation, but in harmony of life, in amity and peace. That was creation.

When we think of it, we see at once what the confusion of thought was to which the Western poet, dwelling upon the difference between East and West, referred when he said, "Never the twain shall meet." It is true that they are not yet showing any real sign of meeting. But the reason is because the West has not sent out its humanity to meet the man in the East, but only its machine. Therefore the poet's line has to be changed into something like this:

> Man is man, machine is machine,
> And never the twain shall wed.

You must know that red tape can never be a common human bond; that official sealing-wax can never provide means of mutual attachment; that it is a painful ordeal for human beings to have to receive favours from animated pigeonholes, and condescensions from printed circulars that give notice but never speak. The presence of the Western people in the East is a human fact. If we are to gain anything from them, it must not be a mere sum-total of legal codes and systems of civil and military services. Man is a great deal more to man than that. We have our human birth-right to claim direct help from the man of the West, if he has anything great to give us. It must come to us, not through mere facts in a juxtaposition, but through the spontaneous sacrifice made by those who have the gift, and therefore the responsibility.

Earnestly I ask the poet of the Western world to realise and sing to you with all the great power of music which he has, that the East and the West are ever in search of each other, and that they must meet not merely in the fulness of physical strength, but in fulness of truth; that the right hand, which wields the sword, has the need of the left, which holds the shield of safety.

The East has its seat in the vast plains watched over by the snow-peaked mountains and fertilised by rivers carrying mighty volumes of water to the sea. There, under the blaze of a tropical sun, the physical life has bedimmed the light of its vigour and lessened its claims. There man has had the repose of mind which has ever tried to set itself in harmony with the inner notes of existence. In the silence of sunrise and sunset, and on the star-crowded nights, he has sat face to face with the Infinite, waiting for the revelation that opens up the heart of all that there is. He has said, in a rapture of realisation:

"Hearken to me, ye children of the Immortal, who dwell in the Kingdom of Heaven. I have known, from beyond darkness, the Supreme Person, shining with the radiance of the sun."

The man from the East, with his faith in the eternal, who in his soul had met the touch of the Supreme Person—did he never come to you in the West and speak to you of the Kingdom of Heaven? Did he not unite the East and the West in truth, in the unity of one spiritual bond between all children of the Immortal, in the realisation of one great Personality in all human persons?

Yes, the East did once meet the West profoundly in the growth of her life. Such union became possible, because the East came to the West with the ideal that is creative, and not with the passion that destroys moral bonds. The mystic consciousness of the Infinite, which she brought with her, was greatly needed by the man of the West to give him his balance.

On the other hand, the East must find her own balance in Science—the magnificent gift that the West can bring to her. Truth has its nest as well as its sky. That nest is definite in structure, accurate in law of construction; and though it has to be changed and rebuilt over and over again, the need of it is never-ending and its laws are eternal. For some centuries the East has neglected the nest-building of truth. She has not been attentive to learn its secret. Trying to cross the trackless infinite, the East has relied solely upon her wings. She has spurned the earth, till, buffeted by storms, her wings are hurt and she is tired, sorely needing help. But has she then to be told that the messenger of the sky and the builder of the nest shall never meet?

1922

On Being Found Out

by WILLIAM MAKEPEACE THACKERAY
[1811–1863]

AT THE CLOSE (let us say) of Queen Anne's reign, when I was a boy at a private and preparatory school for young gentlemen, I remember the wiseacre of a master ordering us all, one night, to march into a little garden at the back of the house, and thence to proceed one by one into a tool or hen house (I was but a tender little thing just put into short clothes, and can't exactly say whether the house was for tools or hens), and in that house to put our hands into a sack which stood on a bench, a candle burning beside it. I put my hand into the sack. My hand came out quite black. I went and joined the other boys in the schoolroom; and all their hands were black too.

By reason of my tender age (and there are some critics who, I hope, will be satisfied by my acknowledging that I am a hundred and fifty-six next birthday) I could not understand what was the meaning of this night excursion—this candle, this tool-house, this bag of soot. I think we little boys were taken out of our sleep to be brought to the ordeal. We came, then, and showed our little hands to the master; washed them or not—most probably, I should say, not—and so went bewildered back to bed.

Something had been stolen in the school that day; and Mr. Wiseacre having read in a book of an ingenious method of finding out a thief by making him put his hand into a sack (which, if guilty, the rogue would shirk from doing), all we boys were subjected to the trial. Goodness knows what the lost object was, or who stole it. We all had black hands to show the master. And the thief, whoever he was, was not Found Out that time.

I wonder if the rascal is alive—an elderly scoundrel he must be by this time; and a hoary old hypocrite, to whom an old schoolfellow presents his kindest regards—parenthetically remarking what a dreadful place that private school was; cold, chillblains, bad dinners, not enough victuals, and caning awful!— Are you alive still, I say, you nameless villain, who escaped discovery on that day of crime? I hope you have escaped often since, old sinner. Ah, what a lucky thing it is, for you and me, my man, that we are *not* found out in all our peccadilloes; and that our backs can slip away from the master and the cane!

Just consider what life would be, if every rogue was found out, and flogged *coram populo!* What a butchery, what an indecency, what an endless swishing of the rod! Don't cry out about my misanthropy. My good friend Mealymouth, I will trouble you to tell me, do you go to church? When there, do you say, or do you not, that you are a miserable sinner? and saying so do you believe or disbelieve it? If you are a M. S., don't you deserve correction, and aren't you grateful if you are to be let off? I say again, what a blessed thing it is that we are not all found out!

Just picture to yourself everybody who does wrong being found out, and punished accordingly. Fancy all the boys in all the schools being whipped; and then the assistants, and then the headmaster

(Dr. Badford let us call him). Fancy the provost-marshal being tied up, having previously superintended the correction of the whole army. After the young gentlemen have had their turn for the faulty exercises, fancy Dr. Lincolnsinn being taken up for certain faults in *his* Essay and Review. After the clergyman has cried his peccavi, suppose we hoist up a bishop, and give him a couple of dozen! (I see my Lord Bishop of Double-Gloucester sitting in a very uneasy posture on his right reverend bench.) After we have cast off the bishop, what are we to say to the Minister who appointed him? My Lord Cinqwarden, it is painful to have to use personal correction to a boy of your age; but really— *Siste tandem, carnifex!* The butchery is too horrible. The hand drops powerless, appalled at the quantity of birch which it must cut and brandish. I am glad we are not all found out, I say again; and protest, my dear brethren, against our having our deserts.

To fancy all men found out and punished is bad enough; but imagine all women found out in the distinguished social circle in which you and I have the honor to move. Is it not a mercy that a many of these fair criminals remain unpunished and undiscovered! There is Mrs. Longbow, who is forever practising, and who shoots poisoned arrows, too; when you meet her you don't call her a liar, and charge her with the wickedness she has done and is doing. There is Mrs. Painter, who passes for a most respectable woman, and a model in society. There is no use in saying what you really know regarding her and her goings on. There is Diana Hunter—what a little haughty prude it is; and yet *we* know stories about her which are not altogether edifying. I say it is best, for the sake of the good, that the bad should not all be found out. You don't want your children to know the history of that lady in the next box, who is so handsome, and whom they admire so. Ah me, what would life be if we were all found out, and punished for all our faults? Jack Ketch would be in permanence; and then who would hang Jack Ketch?

They talk of murderers being pretty certainly found out. Psha! I have heard an authority awfully competent vow and declare that scores and hundreds of murders are committed, and nobody is the wiser. That terrible man mentioned one or two ways of committing murder, which he maintained were quite common, and were scarcely ever found out. A man, for instance, comes home to his wife, and—but I pause—I know that this Magazine * has a very large circulation. Hundreds and hundreds of thousands— why not say a million of people at once?—well, say a million, read it. And amongst these countless readers, I might be teaching some monster how to make away with his wife without being found out, some fiend of a woman how to destroy her dear husband. I will *not* then tell this easy and simple way of murder, as communicated to me by a most respectable party in the confidence of private intercourse. Suppose some gentle reader were to try this most simple and easy receipt—it seems to me almost infallible—and come to grief in consequence, and be found out and hanged? Should I ever pardon myself for having been the means of doing injury to a single one of our esteemed subscribers? The prescription whereof I speak—that is to say, whereof I *don't* speak—shall be buried in this bosom. No, I am a humane man. I am not one of your Bluebeards to go and say to my wife, "My dear! I am going away for a few days to Brighton. Here are all the keys of the house. You may open every door and closet, except the one at the end of the oak-room opposite the fireplace, with the little bronze Shakspeare on the mantel-piece (or what not)." I don't say this to a woman—unless, to be sure, I want to get rid of her—because, after such a caution, I know she'll peep into the closet. I say nothing about the closet at all. I keep the key in my pocket, and a being whom I love, but who, as I know, has many weaknesses, out of harm's way. You toss up your head, dear angel, drub on the ground with your lovely little feet, on the table with your sweet rosy fingers, and cry, "Oh, sneerer! You don't know the depth of woman's feeling, the lofty scorn of all deceit, the entire absence of mean curiosity in the sex, or never, never would you libel us so!" Ah, Delia! dear, dear Delia! It is because I fancy I *do* know something about you (not all, mind—no, no; no man knows that)— Ah, my bride, my ringdove, my rose, my poppet—choose, in fact, whatever name you like—bulbul of my grove, fountain of my desert, sunshine of

* *The Cornhill Magazine,* in which this essay first appeared.

my darkling life, and joy of my dungeoned existence, it is because I *do* know a little about you that I conclude to say nothing
of that private closet, and keep my key in my pocket. You take
away that closet-key then, and the house-key. You lock Delia in.
You keep her out of harm's way and gadding, and so she never
can be found out.

And yet by little strange accidents and coincidences how we are
being found out every day. You remember that old story of the
Abbé Kakatoes, who told the company at supper one night how
the first confession he ever received was—from a murderer let
us say. Presently enters to supper the Marquis de Croquemitaine.
"Palsambleu, Abbé!" says the brilliant marquis, taking a pinch of
snuff, "are you here? Gentlemen and ladies! I was the abbé's first
penitent, and I made him a confession, which I promise you
astonished him."

To be sure how queerly things are found out! Here is an
instance. Only the other day I was writing in these "Roundabout
Papers" about a certain man, whom I facetiously called Baggs,
and who had abused me to my friends, who of course told me.
Shortly after that paper was published another friend—Sacks
let us call him—scowls fiercely at me as I am sitting in perfect
good-humor at the club, and passes on without speaking. A cut.
A quarrel. Sacks thinks it is about him that I was writing:
whereas, upon my honor and conscience, I never had him once
in my mind, and was pointing my moral from quite another man.
But don't you see, by this wrath of the guilty-conscienced Sacks,
that he had been abusing me too? He has owned himself guilty,
never having been accused. He has winced when nobody thought
of hitting him. I did but put the cap out, and madly butting and
chafing, behold my friend rushes out to put his head into it! Never
mind, Sacks, you are found out; but I bear you no malice, my
man.

And yet to be found out, I know from my own experience,
must be painful and odious, and cruelly mortifying to the inward
vanity. Suppose I am a poltroon, let us say. With fierce mustache,
loud talk, plentiful oaths, and an immense stick, I keep up nevertheless a character for courage. I swear fearfully at cabmen

and women; brandish my bludgeon, and perhaps knock down a little man or two with it: brag of the images which I break at the shooting-gallery, and pass amongst my friends for a whiskery fire-eater, afraid of neither man nor dragon. Ah me! Suppose some brisk little chap steps up and gives me a caning in St. James's Street, with all the heads of my friends looking out all the club windows. My reputation is gone, I frighten no man more. My nose is pulled by whipper-snappers, who jump up on a chair to reach it. I am found out. And in the days of my triumphs, when people were yet afraid of me, and were taken in by my swagger, I always knew that I was a lily-liver, and expected that I should be found out some day.

That certainty of being found out must haunt and depress many a bold braggadocio spirit. Let us say it is a clergyman, who can pump copious floods of tears out of his own eyes and those of his audience. He thinks to himself, "I am but a poor swindling, chattering rogue. My bills are unpaid. I have jilted several women whom I have promised to marry. I don't know whether I believe what I preach, and I know I have stolen the very sermon over which I have been snivelling. Have they found me out?" says he, as his head drops down on the cushion.

Then your writer, poet, historian, novelist, or what not? The "Beacon" says that "Jones's work is one of the first order." The "Lamp" declares that "Jones's tragedy surpasses every work since the days of Him of Avon." The "Comet" asserts that "J's 'Life of Goody Twoshoes' is a κτῆμα ἐς ἀεὶ, a noble and enduring monument to the fame of that admirable Englishwoman," and so forth. But then Jones knows that he has lent the critic of the "Beacon" five pounds; that his publisher has a half-share in the "Lamp;" and that the "Comet" comes repeatedly to dine with him. It is all very well. Jones is immortal until he is found out; and then down comes the extinguisher, and the immortal is dead and buried. The idea (*dies iræ!*) of discovery must haunt many a man, and make him uneasy, as the trumpets are puffing in his triumph. Brown, who has a higher place than he deserves, cowers before Smith, who has found him out. What is a chorus

of critics shouting "Bravo?"—a public clapping hands and fling-
ing garlands? Brown knows that Smith has found him out.
Puff, trumpets! Wave, banners! Huzza, boys, for the immortal
Brown! "This is all very well," B. thinks (bowing the while,
smiling, laying his hand to his heart); "but there stands Smith at
the window: *he* has measured me; and some day the others
will find me out too." It is a very curious sensation to sit by a man
who has found you out, and who, as you know, has found you
out; or *vice versâ*, to sit with a man whom *you* have found out.
His talent? Bah! His virtue? We know a little story or two about
his virtue, and he knows we know it. We are thinking over
friend Robinson's antecedents, as we grin, bow and talk; and we
are both humbugs together. Robinson a good fellow, is he? You
know how he behaved to Hicks? A good-natured man, is he?
Pray do you remember that little story of Mrs. Robinson's black
eye? How men have to work, to talk, to smile, to go to bed, and try
and sleep, with this dread of being found out on their consciences!
Bardolph, who has robbed a church, and Nym, who has taken a
purse, go to their usual haunts, and smoke their pipes with their
companions. Mr. Detective Bullseye appears, and says, "Oh, Bardolph! I want you about that there pyx business!" Mr. Bardolph
knocks the ashes out of his pipe, puts out his hands to the little
steel cuffs, and walks away quite meekly. He is found out. He
must go. "Good-by, Doll Tearsheet! Good-by, Mrs. Quickly,
Ma'am!" The other gentlemen and ladies *de la société* look on and
exchange mute adieux with the departing friends. And an assured
time will come when the other gentlemen and ladies will be
found out too.

What a wonderful and beautiful provision of nature it has been
that, for the most part, our womankind are not endowed with
the faculty of finding us out! *They* don't doubt, and probe, and
weigh, and take your measure. Lay down this paper, my benevo-
lent friend and reader, go into your drawing-room now, and utter
a joke ever so old, and I wager sixpence the ladies there will all
begin to laugh. Go to Brown's house, and tell Mrs. Brown and
the young ladies what you think of him, and see what a welcome

you will get! In like manner, let him come to your house, and tell *your* good lady his candid opinion of you, and fancy how she will receive him! Would you have your wife and children know you exactly for what you are, and esteem you precisely at your worth? If so, my friend, you will live in a dreary house, and you will have but a chilly fireside. Do you suppose the people round it don't see your homely face as under a glamour, and, as it were, with a halo of love round it? You don't fancy you *are,* as you seem to them? No such thing, my man. Put away that monstrous conceit, and be thankful that *they* have not found you out.

From *Roundabout Papers,* 1863.

On Art

by LEO TOLSTOI [1828-1910]

> *What is and what is not Art; And when is*
> *Art Important, and when is it Trivial?*

I

IN OUR LIFE there are many insignificant or even harmful activities which enjoy a respect they do not deserve, or are tolerated merely because they are considered to be of importance. The copying of flowers, horses, and landscapes, such clumsy learning of musical pieces as is carried on in most of our so-called educated families, and the writing of feeble stories and bad verses, hundreds of which appear in the newspapers and magazines, are obviously not artistic activities; and the painting of indecent, pornographic pictures stimulating sensuality, or the composition of songs and stories of that nature, even if they have artistic qualities, is not a worthy activity deserving of respect.

And therefore, taking all the productions which are considered among us to be artistic, I think it would be useful, first, to separate what really is art from what has no right to that name; and secondly, taking what really is art, to distinguish what is important and good from what is insignificant and bad.

The question of how and where to draw the line separating Art from the Non-Art, and the good and important in art from the insignificant and evil, is one of enormous importance in life.

A great many of the wrong-doings and mistakes in our life result from our calling things Art which are not Art. We accord an unmerited respect to things which not only do not deserve it, but deserve condemnation and contempt. Apart from the enormous amount of human labour spent on the preparation of articles needed for the production of art—studios, paints, canvas, marble, musical instruments, and the theatres with their scenery and appliances—even the lives of human beings are actually perverted by the one-sided labours demanded in the preparation of those who train for the arts. Hundreds of thousands if not millions of children are forced to one-sided toil, practising the so-called arts of dancing and music. Not to speak of the children of the educated classes who pay their tribute to art in the form of tormenting lessons—children devoted to the ballet and musical professions are simply distorted in the name of Art to which they are dedicated. If it is possible to compel children of seven or eight to play an instrument, and for ten or fifteen years to continue to do so for seven or eight hours a day; if it is possible to place girls in the schools for the ballet,* and then to make them cut capers during the first months of their pregnancy, and if all this is done in the name of art, then it is certainly necessary to define, first of all, what really is art—lest under the guise of art a counterfeit should be produced—and then also to prove that art is a matter of importance to mankind.

Where then is the line dividing art, an important and necessary matter valuable to humanity, from useless occupations, commercial productions, and even from immorality? In what does the essence and importance of true art lie?

* The schools for training ballet-dancers, as well as the theatres where the chief ballets were performed, were State institutions in Russia.

II

One theory—which its opponents call "tendencious"—says that the essence of true art lies in the importance of the subject treated of: that for art to be art, it is necessary that its content should be something important, necessary to man, good, moral, and instructive.

According to that theory the artist—that is to say the man who possesses a certain skill—by taking the most important theme which interests society at the time, can, by clothing it in what looks like artistic form, produce a work of true art. According to that theory religious, moral, social, and political truths clothed in what seems like artistic form are artistic productions.

Another theory, which calls itself "æsthetic," or "art for art's sake," holds that the essence of true art lies in the beauty of its form; that for art to be true, it is necessary that what it presents should be beautiful.

According to that theory it is necessary for the production of art that an artist should possess technique, and should depict an object which produces in the highest degree a pleasant impression; and therefore a beautiful landscape, flowers, fruit, a nude figure, and ballets, will be works of art.

A third theory—which calls itself "realistic"—says that the essence of art consists in the truthful, exact, presentation of reality: that for art to be true it is necessary that it should depict life as it really is.

According to that theory, it follows that works of art may be anything an artist sees or hears, all that he is able to make use of in his function of reproduction, independently of the importance of the subject or beauty of the form.

Such are the theories; and on the basis of each of them so-called works of art appear which fit the first, the second, or the third. But, apart from the fact that each of these theories contradicts the others, not one of them satisfies the chief demand, namely, to ascertain the boundary which divides art from commercial, insignificant, or even harmful productions.

In accordance with each of these theories, works can be produced unceasingly, as in any handicraft, and they may be insignificant or harmful.

As to the first theory ("tendency"), important subjects—religious, moral, social, or political—can always be found ready to hand, and therefore one can continually produce works of so-called art. Moreover, such subjects may be presented so obscurely and insincerely that works treating of the most important of them will prove insignificant and even harmful, the lofty content being degraded by insincere expression.

Similarly according to the second theory ("æsthetic") any man having learned the technique of any branch of art can incessantly produce something beautiful and pleasant, but again this beautiful and pleasant thing may be insignificant and harmful.

Just in the same way according to the third theory ("realistic"), every one who wishes to be an artist can incessantly produce objects of so-called art, because everybody is always interested in something. If the author is interested in what is insignificant and evil, then his work will be insignificant and evil.

The chief point is that, according to each of these three theories, "works of art" can be produced incessantly, as in every handicraft, and that they actually are being so produced. So that these three dominant and discordant theories not merely fail to fix the line that separates art from non-art, but on the contrary they, more than anything else, serve to stretch the domain of art and bring within it all that is insignificant and harmful.

III

Where then is the boundary dividing art that is needful, important, and deserving of respect, from that which is unnecessary, unimportant, and deserving not of respect but of contempt—such as productions which have a plainly depraving effect? In what does true artistic activity consist?

To answer this question clearly we must first discriminate between artistic activity and another activity (usually confused with it), namely, that of handing on impressions and perceptions received from preceding generations—separating such activity as that, from the reception of new impressions: those, namely, which will thereafter be handed on from generation to generation.

The handing on of what was known to former generations, in the sphere of art as in the sphere of science, is an activity of teaching and learning. But the production of something *new* is creation—the real artistic activity.

The business of handing on knowledge—teaching—has not an independent significance, but depends entirely on the importance people attach to that which has been created—what it is they consider necessary to hand on from generation to generation. And therefore the definition of what a creation is, will also define what it is that should be handed on. Moreover, the teacher's business is not usually considered to be artistic; the importance of artistic activity is properly attributed to creation—that is, to artistic production.*

What then is artistic (and scientific) creation?

Artistic (and also scientific) creation is such mental activity as brings dimly-perceived feelings (or thoughts) to such a degree of clearness that these feelings (or thoughts) are transmitted to other people.

The process of "creation"—one common to all men and there-

* The most usual and widely diffused definition of art is that art is a particular activity not aiming at material utility, but affording pleasure to people; a pleasure, it is usually added, "ennobling and elevating to the soul."

This definition corresponds to the conception of art held by the majority of people; but it is inexact and not quite clear, and admits of very arbitrary interpretation.

It is not clear, for it fuses in one conception art as a human activity producing objects of art, and also the feelings of the recipient; and it admits of arbitrary interpretation, because it does not define wherein lies the pleasure that "ennobles and elevates the soul." So that one person may declare that he receives such pleasure from a certain production from which another does not receive it at all.

And therefore to define art it is necessary to define the peculiarity of that activity, both in its origin in the soul of the producer and in the peculiarity of its action on the souls of the recipients. This activity is distinguished from any other activity of craftsmanship, or trade, or even science (though it has great affinity with this last), in that it is not evoked by any material need, but supplies to both producer and recipient a special kind of so-called "artistic satisfaction." To explain to oneself this characteristic one must understand what impels people to this activity—that is, how artistic production originates.

fore known to each of us by inner experience—occurs as follows: a man surmises or dimly feels something that is perfectly new to him, which he has never heard of from anybody. This something new impresses him, and in ordinary conversation he points out to others what he perceives, and to his surprise finds that what is apparent to him is quite unseen by them. They do not see or do not feel what he tells them of. This isolation, discord, disunion from others, at first disturbs him, and verifying his own perception the man tries in different ways to communicate to others what he has seen, felt, or understood; but these others still do not understand what he communicates to them, or do not understand it as he understands or feels it. And the man begins to be troubled by a doubt as to whether he imagines and dimly feels something that does not really exist, or whether others do not see and do not feel something that does exist. And to solve this doubt he directs his whole strength to the task of making his discovery so clear that there cannot be the smallest doubt, either for himself or for other people, as to the existence of that which he perceives; and as soon as this elucidation is completed and the man himself no longer doubts the existence of what he has seen, understood, or felt, others at once see, understand, and feel as he does, and it is this effort to make clear and indubitable to himself and to others what both to others and to him had been dim and obscure, that is the source from which flows the production of man's spiritual activity in general, or what we call works of art—which widen man's horizon and oblige him to see what had not been perceived before.*

It is in this that the activity of an artist consists; and also to this activity is related the feeling of the recipient. This feeling has its source in imitativeness, or rather in a capacity to be infected, and in a certain hypnotism—that is to say in the fact that the artist's stress of spirit elucidating to himself the subject that had

---

* The division of the results of man's mental activity into scientific, philosophic, theological, hortatory, artistic, and other groups, is made for convenience of observation. But such divisions do not exist in reality; just as the divisions of the River Vólga into the Tver, Nizhnigórod, Simbírsk and Sarátov sections, are not divisions of the river itself, but divisions we make for our own convenience.

been doubtful to him, communicates itself, through the artistic production, to the recipients. A work of art is then finished when it has been brought to such clearness that it communicates itself to others and evokes in them the same feeling that the artist experienced while creating it.

What was formerly unperceived, unfelt, and uncomprehended by them, is by intensity of feeling brought to such a degree of clearness that it becomes acceptable to all, and the production is a work of art.

The satisfaction of the intense feeling of the artist who has achieved his aim gives pleasure to him. Participation in this same stress of feeling and in its satisfaction, a yielding to this feeling, the imitation of it and infection by it (as by a yawn), the experiencing in brief moments what the artist has lived through while creating his work, is the enjoyment those who assimilate a work of art obtain.

Such in my opinion is the peculiarity that distinguishes art from any other activity.

IV

According to this division, all that imparts to mankind something new, achieved by an artist's stress of feeling and thought, is a work of art. But that this mental activity should really have the importance people attach to it, it is necessary that it should contribute what is good to humanity, for it is evident that to a new evil, to a new temptation leading people into evil, we cannot attribute the value given to art as to something that benefits mankind. The importance, the value, of art consists in widening man's outlook, in increasing the spiritual wealth that is humanity's capital.

Therefore, though a work of art must always include something new, yet the revelation of something new will not always be a work of art. That it should be a work of art, it is necessary:

(1) That the new idea, content of the work, should be of importance to mankind.

(2) That this content should be expressed so clearly that people may understand it.

(3) That what incites the author to work at his production should be an inner need and not an external inducement.

And therefore that in which no new thing is disclosed will not be a work of art; and that which has for its content what is insignificant and therefore unimportant to man will not be a work of art however intelligibly it may be expressed, and even if the author has worked at it sincerely from an inner impulse. Nor will that be a work of art which is so expressed as to be unintelligible, however sincere may be the author's relation to it; nor that which has been produced by its author not from an inner impulse but for an external aim, however important may be its content and however intelligible its expression.

That is a work of art which discloses something new and at the same time in some degree satisfies the three conditions: content, form, and sincerity.

And here we come to the problem of how to define that lowest degree of content, beauty, and sincerity, which a production must possess to be a work of art.

To be a work of art it must, in the first place, be a thing which has for its content something hitherto unknown but of which man has need; secondly, it must show this so intelligibly that it becomes generally accessible; and thirdly, it must result from the author's need to solve an inner doubt.

A work in which all three conditions are present even to a slight degree, will be a work of art; but a production from which even one of them is absent will not be a work of art.

But it will be said that every work contains something needed by man, and every work will be to some extent intelligible, and that an author's relation to every work has some degree of sincerity. Where is the limit of needful content, intelligible expression, and sincerity of treatment? A reply to this question will be given us by a clear perception of the highest limit to which art may attain: the opposite of the highest limit will show the lowest limit, dividing all that cannot be accounted art from what is art. The highest limit of content is such as is always necessary to all men. That which is always necessary to all men is what is good or moral.* The lowest limit of content, consequently, will be such as is not needed by men, and is a bad and immoral content. The highest limit of expression will be such as is always intelligible to all men. What is thus intelligible is that which has nothing in it obscure, superfluous, or indefinite, but only what is clear, concise, and definite—what is called beautiful. Conversely, the lowest limit of expression will be such as is obscure, diffuse, and indefinite—that is to say formless. The highest limit of the artist's relation to his subject will be such as evokes in the soul of all men an impression of reality—the reality not so much of what exists, as of what goes on in the soul of the artist. This impression of reality is produced by truth only, and therefore the highest relation of an author to his subject is *sincerity*. The lowest limit, conversely, will be that in which the author's relation to his subject is not genuine but false. All works of art lie between these two limits.

A perfect work of art will be one in which the content is important and significant to all men, and therefore it will be *moral*. The expression will be quite clear, intelligible to all, and therefore *beautiful;* the author's relation to his work will be altogether sincere and heartfelt, and therefore true. Imperfect works, but still works of art, will be such productions as satisfy all three conditions though it be but in unequal degree. That alone will be no work of art, in which either the content is quite insignificant and unnecessary to man, or the expression quite unintelli-

* Half-a-century ago no explanation would have been needed of the words "important," "good," and "moral," but in our time nine out of ten educated people, at these words, will ask with a triumphant air: "What *is* important, good or moral?" assuming that these words express something conditional and not admitting of definition, and therefore I must answer this anticipated objection.

That which unites people not by violence but by love: that which serves to disclose the joy of the union of men with one another, is "important," "good," or "moral." "Evil" and "immoral" is that which divides them, that leads men to the suffering produced by disunion. "Important" is that which causes people to understand and to love what they previously did not understand or love.

gible, or the relation of the author to the work quite insincere. In the degree of perfection attained in each of these respects lies the difference in quality between all true works of art. Sometimes the first predominates, sometimes the second, and sometimes the third.

All the remaining imperfect productions fall naturally, according to the three fundamental conditions of art, into three chief kinds: (1) those which stand out by the importance of their content, (2) those which stand out by their beauty of form, and (3) those which stand out by their heartfelt sincerity. These three kinds all yield approximations to perfect art, and are inevitably produced wherever there is art.

Thus among young artists heartfelt sincerity chiefly prevails, coupled with insignificance of content and more or less beauty of form. Among older artists, on the contrary, the importance of the content often predominates over beauty of form and sincerity. Among laborious artists beauty of form predominates over content and sincerity.

All works of art may be appraised by the prevalence in them of the first, the second, or the third quality, and they may all be subdivided into (1) those that have content and are beautiful, but have little sincerity; (2) those that have content, but little beauty and little sincerity; (3) those that have little content, but are beautiful and sincere, and so on, in all possible combinations and permutations.

All works of art, and in general all the mental activities of man, can be appraised on the basis of these three fundamental qualities; and they have been and are so appraised.

The differences in valuation have resulted, and do result, from the extent of the demand presented to art by certain people at a certain time in regard to these three conditions.

So for instance in classical times the demand for significance of content was much higher, and the demand for clearness and sincerity much lower than they subsequently became, especially in our time. The demand for beauty became greater in the Middle Ages, but on the other hand the demand for significance and sincerity became lower; and in our time the demand for sincerity and truthfulness has become much greater, but on the other hand the demand for beauty, and especially for significance, has been lowered.

v

The evaluation of works of art is necessarily correct when all three conditions are taken into account, and inevitably incorrect when works are valued not on the basis of all three conditions but only of one or two of them.

And yet such evaluation of works of art on the basis of only one of the three conditions is an error particularly prevalent in our time, lowering the general level of what is demanded from art to what can be reached by a mere imitation of it, and confusing the minds of critics, and of the public, and of artists themselves, as to what is really art and as to where its boundary lies—the line that divides it from craftsmanship and from mere amusement.

This confusion arises from the fact that people who lack the capacity to understand true art, judge of works of art from one side only, and according to their own characters and training observe in them the first, the second, or the third side only, imagining and assuming that this one side perceptible to them—and the significance of art based on this one condition—defines the whole of art. Some see only the importance of the content, others only the beauty of form, and others again only the artist's sincerity and therefore truthfulness. And according to what they see they define the nature of art itself, construct their theories, and praise and encourage those who, like themselves, not understanding wherein a work of art consists, turn them out like pancakes and inundate our world with foul floods of all kinds of follies and abominations which they call "works of art."

Such are the majority of people, and, as representatives of that majority, such were the originators of the three æsthetic theories already alluded to, which meet the perceptions and demands of that majority.

All these theories are based on a misunderstanding of the whole importance of art and on severing its three fundamental conditions; and therefore these three false theories of art clash, as a result of the fact that real art has three fundamental conditions of which each of those theories accepts but one.

The first theory, of so-called "tendencious" art, accepts as a work of art one that has for its subject something which, though it be not new, is important to all men by its moral content, independently of its beauty and spiritual depth.

The second ("art for art's sake") recognizes as a work of art only that which has beauty of form, independently of its novelty, the importance of its content, or its sincerity.

The third theory, the "realistic," recognizes as a work of art only that in which the author's relation to his subject is sincere, and which is therefore truthful. The last theory says that however insignificant or even foul may be the content, with a more or less beautiful form the work will be good, if the author's relation to what he depicts is sincere and therefore truthful.

VI

All these theories forget one chief thing—that neither importance, nor beauty, nor sincerity, provides the requisite for works of art, but that the basic condition of the production of such works is that the artist should be conscious of something new and important; and that therefore, just as it always has been, so it always will be, necessary for a true artist to be able to perceive something quite new and important. For the artist to see what is new, it is necessary that he should observe and think, and not occupy his life with trifles which hinder his attentive penetration into, and meditation on, life's phenomena. In order that the new things he sees may be important ones, the artist must be a morally enlightened man, and he must not live a selfish life but must share the common life of humanity.

If only he sees what is new and important he will be sure to find a form which will express it, and the sincerity which is an essential content of artistic production will be present. He must be able to express the new subject so that all may understand it. For this he must have such mastery of his craft that when working he will think as little about the rules of that craft as a man when walking thinks of the laws of motion. And in order to attain this, the artist must not look round on his work and admire it, must not make technique his aim—as one who is walking should not contemplate and admire his gait—but should be concerned only to express his subject clearly, and in such a way as to be intelligible to all.

Finally, to work at his subject not for external ends but to satisfy his inner need, the artist must rise superior to motives of avarice and vanity. He must love with his own heart and not with another's, and not pretend that he loves what others love or consider worthy of love.

And to attain all this the artist must do as Balaam did when the messengers came to him and he went apart awaiting God so as to say only what God commanded; and he must not do as that same Balaam afterwards did when, tempted by gifts, he went to the king against God's command, as was evident even to the ass on which he rode, though not perceived by him while blinded by avarice and vanity.

VII

In our time nothing of that kind is demanded. A man who wishes to follow art need not wait for some important and new perception to arise in his soul, which he can sincerely love and having loved can clothe in suitable form. In our time a man who wishes to follow art either takes a subject current at the time and praised by people who in his opinion are clever, and clothes it as best he can in what is called "artistic form"; or he chooses a subject which gives him most opportunity to display his technical skill, and with toil and patience produces what he considers to be a work of art; or having received some chance impression he takes what caused that impression for his subject, imagining that it will yield a work of art since it happened to produce an impression on him.

And so there appear an innumerable quantity of so-called works of art which, as in every mechanical craft, can be produced without the least intermission. There are always current fashionable notions in society, and with patience a technique can always be learnt, and something or other will always seem interesting to some one. Having separated the conditions that should be united in a true work of art, people have produced so many works of pseudo-art that the public, the critics, and the pseudo-artists themselves, are left quite without any definition of what they themselves hold to be art.

The people of to-day have, as it were, said to themselves: "Works of art are good and useful; so it is necessary to produce more of them." It would indeed be a very good thing if there were more; but the trouble is that you can only produce to order works which are no better than works of mere craftsmanship because of their lack of the essential conditions of art.

A really artistic production cannot be made to order, for a true work of art is the revelation (by laws beyond our grasp) of a new conception of life arising in the artist's soul, which, when expressed, lights up the path along which humanity progresses.

c. 1895–1897   Translated by
                                                  AYLMER MAUDE

Hamlet and Don Quixote

by IVAN TURGENEV [1818–1883]

THE FIRST EDITION of Shakespeare's tragedy, *Hamlet,* and the first part of Cervantes' *Don Quixote* appeared in the same year at the very beginning of the seventeenth century.

This coincidence seems to me significant . . . It seems to me that in these two types are embodied two opposite fundamental peculiarities of man's nature—the two ends of the axis about which it turns. I think that all people belong, more or less, to one of these two types; that nearly every one of us resembles either Don Quixote or Hamlet. In our day, it is true, the Hamlets have become far more numerous than the Don Quixotes, but the Don Quixotes have not become extinct.

Let me explain.

All people live—consciously or unconsciously—on the strength of their principles, their ideals; that is, by virtue of what they regard as truth, beauty, and goodness. Many get their ideal all ready-made, in definite, historically-developed forms. They live trying to square their lives with this ideal, deviating from it at times, under the influence of passions or incidents, but neither reasoning about it nor questioning it. Others, on the contrary, subject it to the analysis of their own reason. Be this as it may, I think I shall not err too much in saying that for all people this ideal—this basis and aim of their existence—is to be found either outside of them or within them; in other words, for every one of us it is either his own *I* that forms the primary consideration or something else which he considers superior. I may be told that reality does not permit of such sharp demarcations; that in the very same living being both considerations may alternate, even becoming fused to a certain extent. But I do not mean to affirm the impossibility of change and contradiction in human nature; I wish merely to point out two different attitudes of man to his ideal. And now I will endeavor to show in what way, to my mind, these two different relations are embodied in the two types I have selected.

Let us begin with Don Quixote.

What does Don Quixote represent? We shall not look at him with the cursory glance that stops at superficialities and trifles. We shall not see in Don Quixote merely "the Knight of the sorrowful figure"—a figure created for the purpose of ridiculing the old-time romances of knighthood. It is known that the meaning of this character had expanded under its immortal creator's own hand, and that the Don Quixote of the second part of the romance is an amiable companion to dukes and duchesses, a wise preceptor to the squire-governor—no longer the Don Quixote he appears in the first part, especially at the beginning of the work; not the odd and comical crank, who is constantly belabored by a rain of blows. I will endeavor, therefore, to go to the very heart of the matter. I repeat: What does Don Quixote represent?

Faith, in the first place; faith in something eternal, immutable; faith in the truth, in short, existing *outside* of the individual, which cannot easily be attained by him, but which is attainable only by constant devotion and the power of self-abnegation. Don Quixote is entirely consumed with devotion to his ideal, for the sake of which he is ready to suffer every possible privation and to sacrifice his life; his life itself he values only in so far as it can become a means for the incarnation of the ideal, for the establishment of truth and justice on earth. I may be told that this ideal is borrowed by his disordered imagination from the fanciful world of knightly romance. Granted—and this makes up the comical side of Don Quixote; but the ideal itself remains in all its immaculate purity. To live for one's self, to care for one's self, Don Quixote would consider shameful. He lives—if I may so express myself—outside of himself, entirely for others, for his brethren, in order to abolish evil, to counteract the forces hostile to mankind—wizards, giants, in a word, the oppressors. There is no trace of egotism in him; he is not concerned with himself, he is wholly a self-sacrifice—appreciate this word; he believes, believes firmly, and without circumspection. Therefore is he fearless, patient, content with the humblest fare, with the poorest clothes—what cares he for such things! Timid of heart, he is in spirit great and brave; his touching piety does not restrict his freedom; a stranger to variety, he doubts not himself, his vocation, or even his physical prowess; his will is indomitable. The constant aiming after the same end imparts a certain monotonousness to his thoughts and onesidedness to his mind. He knows little, but need not know much; he knows what he is about, why he exists on earth—and this is the chief sort of knowledge. Don Quixote may seem to be either a perfect madman, since the most indubitable materialism vanishes before his eyes, melts like tallow before the fire of his enthusiasm (he really does see living Moors in the wooden puppets, and knights in the sheep); or shallow-minded, because he is unable lightly to sympathize or lightly to enjoy; but, like an ancient tree, he sends his roots deep into the soil, and can neither change his convictions nor pass from one subject to another. The stronghold of his moral constitution (note that this demented, wandering knight is everywhere and on all occasions the moral being) lends especial weight and dignity to all his judgments and speeches, to his whole figure, despite the ludicrous and humiliating situations into which he endlessly falls. Don Quixote is an enthusiast, a servant of an idea, and therefore is illuminated by its radiance.

Now what does Hamlet represent?

Analysis, first of all, and egotism, and therefore incredulity. He lives entirely for himself; he is an egotist. But even an egotist cannot believe in himself. We can only believe in that which is outside of and above ourselves. But this *I*, in which he does not believe, is dear to Hamlet. This is the point of departure, to which he constantly returns, because he finds nothing in the whole universe to which he can cling with all his heart. He is a skeptic, and always pothers about himself; he is ever busy, not with his duty, but with his condition. Doubting everything, Hamlet, of course, spares not himself; his mind is too much developed to be satisfied with what he finds within himself. He is conscious of his weakness; but even this self-consciousness is power: from it comes his irony, in contrast with the enthusiasm of Don Quixote. Hamlet delights in excessive self-depreciation. Constantly concerned with himself, always a creature of introspection, he knows minutely all his faults, scorns himself, and at the same time lives, so to speak, nourished by this scorn. He has no faith in himself, yet is vainglorious; he knows not what he wants nor why he lives, yet is attached to life. He exclaims:

> O that the Everlasting had not fix'd
> His canon 'gainst self-slaughter . . .
> Most weary, stale, flat, and unprofitable
> Seem to me all the uses of this world.

But he will not sacrifice this flat and unprofitable life. He contemplates suicide even before he sees his father's ghost, and receives the awful commission which breaks down completely his already weakened will—but he does not take his life. The love of life is expressed in the very thought of terminating it. Every youth of eighteen is familiar with such feelings as this: "When the blood boils, how prodigal the soul!"

I will not be too severe with Hamlet. He suffers, and his sufferings are more painful and galling than those of Don Quixote. The latter is pummeled by rough shepherds and convicts whom he has liberated; Hamlet inflicts his own wounds—teases himself. In his hands, too, is a lance—the two-edged lance of self-analysis.

Don Quixote, I must confess, is positively funny. His figure is perhaps the most comical that ever poet has drawn. His name has become a mocking nickname even on the lips of Russian peasants. Of this our own ears could convince us. The mere memory of him raises in our imagination a figure gaunt, angular, rugged-nosed, and clad in a caricature armor, and mounted on the withered skeleton of the pitiable Rocinante, a poor, starved and beaten nag, to whom we cannot deny a semi-amusing and semi-pathetic co-operation. Don Quixote makes us laugh, but there is a conciliatory and redeeming power in this laughter; and if the adage be true, "You may come to worship what you now deride," then I may add: Whom you have ridiculed, you have already forgiven—are even ready to love.

Hamlet's appearance, on the contrary, is attractive. His melancholia; his pale though not lean aspect (his mother remarks that he is stout, saying, "Our son is fat"); his black velvet clothes, the feather crowning his hat; his elegant manners; the unmistakable poetry of his speeches; his steady feeling of complete superiority over others, alongside of the biting humor of his self-denunciation —everything about him pleases, everything captivates. Everybody flatters himself on passing for a Hamlet. None would like to acquire the appellation of "Don Quixote." "Hamlet Baratynski," * wrote Pushkin to his friend. No one ever thought of laughing at Hamlet, and herein lies his condemnation. To love him is almost impossible; only people like Horatio become attached to

* Baratynski was a Russian lyric poet, a contemporary and successful follower of Pushkin, whom contemplation of "the riddles of the universe" had made very disconsolate.—TRANSLATOR.

Hamlet. Of these I will speak later. Everyone sympathizes with Hamlet, and the reason is obvious: nearly everyone finds in Hamlet his own traits; but to love him is, I repeat, impossible, because he himself does not love anyone.

Let us continue our comparison.

Hamlet is the son of a king, murdered by his own brother, the usurper of the throne; his father comes forth from the grave— from "the jaws of Hades"—to charge Hamlet to avenge him; but the latter hesitates, keeps on quibbling with himself, finds consolation in self-depreciation, and finally kills his stepfather by chance. A deep psychological feature, for which many wise but short-sighted persons have ventured to censure Shakespeare! And Don Quixote, a poor man, almost destitute, without means or connections, old and lonely, undertakes the task of destroying evil and protecting the oppressed (total strangers to him) all over the world. It matters not that his first attempt to free innocence from the oppressor brings redoubled suffering upon the head of innocence. (I have in mind that scene in which Don Quixote saves an apprentice from a drubbing by his master, who, as soon as the deliverer is gone, punishes the poor boy with tenfold severity.) It matters not that, in his crusades against harmful giants, Don Quixote attacks useful windmills. The comical setting of these pictures should not distract our eyes from their hidden meaning. The man who sets out to sacrifice himself with careful forethought and consideration of all the consequences— balancing all the probabilities of his acts proving beneficial—is hardly capable of self-sacrifice. Nothing of the kind can happen to Hamlet; it is not for him, with his penetrative, keen, and skeptical mind, to fall into so gross an error. No, he will not wage war on windmills; he does not believe in giants, and would not attack them if they did exist. We cannot imagine Hamlet exhibiting to each and all a barber's bowl, and maintaining, as Don Quixote does, that it is the real magic helmet of Mambrin. I suppose that, were truth itself to appear incarnate before his eyes, Hamlet would still have misgivings as to whether it really was the truth. For who knows but that truth, too, is perhaps non-existent, like giants? We laugh at Don Quixote, but, my dear sirs, which of us, after having conscientiously interrogated himself, and taken into account his past and present convictions, will make bold to say that he always, under all circumstances, can distinguish a barber's pewter bowl from a magic golden helmet? It seems to me, therefore, that the principal thing in life is the sincerity and strength of our convictions—the result lies in the hands of fate. This alone can show us whether we have been contending with fantoms or real foes, and with what armor we covered our heads. Our business is to arm ourselves and fight.

Remarkable are the attitudes of the mob, the so-called mass of the people, toward Hamlet and Don Quixote. In *Hamlet* Polonius, in *Don Quixote* Sancho Panza, symbolize the populace.

Polonius is an old man—active, practical, sensible, but at the same time narrow-minded and garrulous. He is an excellent chamberlain and an exemplary father. (Recollect his instructions to his son, Laertes, when going abroad—instructions which vie in wisdom with certain orders issued by Governor Sancho Panza on the Island of Barataria.) To Polonius Hamlet is not so much a madman as a child. Were he not a king's son, Polonius would despise him because of his utter uselessness and the impossibility of making a positive and practical application of his ideas. The famous cloud-scene, the scene where Hamlet imagines he is mocking the old man, has an obvious significance, confirming this theory. I take the liberty of recalling it to you:

> POLONIUS: My lord, the queen would speak with you, and presently.
> HAMLET: Do you see yonder cloud, that's almost in shape of a camel?
> POLONIUS: By the mass, and 'tis like a camel, indeed.
> HAMLET: Methinks it is like a weasel.
> POLONIUS: It is backed like a weasel.
> HAMLET: Or, like a whale?
> POLONIUS: Very like a whale.
> HAMLET: Then will I come to my mother by and by.

Is it not evident that in this scene Polonius is at the same time a courtier who humors the prince and an adult who would not cross a sickly, capricious boy? Polonius does not in the least believe Hamlet, and he is right. With all his natural, narrow presumptiveness, he ascribes Hamlet's capriciousness to his love for Ophelia, in which he is, of course, mistaken, but he makes no mistake in understanding Hamlet's character. The Hamlets are really useless to the people; they give it nothing, they cannot lead it anywhere, since they themselves are bound for nowhere. And, besides, how can one lead when he doubts the very ground he treads upon? Moreover, the Hamlets detest the masses. How can a man who does not respect himself respect any one or anything else? Besides, is it really worth while to bother about the masses? They are so rude and filthy! And much more than birth alone goes to make Hamlet an aristocrat.

An entirely different spectacle is presented by Sancho Panza. He laughs at Don Quixote, knows full well that he is demented; yet thrice forsakes the land of his birth, his home, wife and daughter, that he may follow this crazy man; follows him everywhere, undergoes all sorts of hardships, is devoted to him to his very death, believes him and is proud of him, then weeps, kneeling at the humble pallet where his master breathes his last. Hope of gain or ultimate advantage cannot account for this devotion. Sancho Panza has too much good sense. He knows very well that the page of a wandering knight has nothing save beatings to expect. The cause of his devotion must be sought deeper. It finds its root (if I may so put it) in what is perhaps the cardinal virtue of the people—in its capability of a blissful and honest blindness (alas! it is familiar with other forms of blindness), the capability of a disinterested enthusiasm, the disregard of direct personal advantages, which to a poor man is almost equivalent to scorn for his daily bread. A great, universally-historic virtue!

The masses of the people invariably end by following, in blind confidence, the very persons they themselves have mocked, or even cursed and persecuted. They give allegiance to those who fear neither curses nor persecution—nor even ridicule—but who go straight ahead, their spiritual gaze directed toward the goal which they alone see—who seek, fall, and rise, and ultimately find. And rightly so; only he who is led by the heart reaches the ultimate goal. "Les grandes pensées viennent du cœur," said Vo-venarg. And the Hamlets find nothing, invent nothing, and leave no trace behind them, save that of their own personality—no achievements whatsoever. They neither love nor believe, and what can they find? Even in chemistry—not to speak of organic nature—in order that a third substance may be obtained, there must be a combination of two others; but the Hamlets are concerned with themselves alone—they are lonely, and therefore barren.

"But," you will interpose, "how about Ophelia—does not Hamlet love her?"

I shall speak of her, and, incidentally, of Dulcinea.

In their relations to woman, too, our two types present much that is noteworthy.

Don Quixote loves Dulcinea, a woman who exists only in his own imagination, and is ready to die for her. (Recall his words when, vanquished and bruised, he says to the conqueror, who stands over him with a spear: "Stab me, Sir Knight . . . Dulcinea del Tobosco is the most beautiful woman in the world, and I the most unfortunate knight on earth. It is not fit that my weakness should lessen the glory of Dulcinea.") He loves purely, ideally; so ideally that he does not even suspect that the object of his passion does not exist at all; so purely that, when Dulcinea appears before him in the guise of a rough and dirty peasant-woman, he trusts not the testimony of his eyes, and regards her as transformed by some evil wizard.

I myself have seen in my life, on my wanderings, people who laid down their lives for equally non-existent Dulcineas or for a vulgar and oftentimes filthy something or other, in which they saw the realization of their ideal, and whose transformation they likewise attributed to evil—I almost said bewitching—events and persons. I have seen them, and when their like shall cease to exist, then let the book of history be closed forever: there will be nothing in it to read about. Of sensuality there is not even a trace in Don Quixote. All his thoughts are chaste and innocent, and in the secret depths of his heart he hardly hopes for an ultimate union with Dulcinea—indeed, he almost dreads such a union.

And does Hamlet really love? Has his ironic creator, a most profound judge of the human heart, really determined to give this egotist, this skeptic, saturated with every decomposing poison of self-analysis, a loving and devout heart? Shakespeare did not fall into this contradiction; and it does not cost the attentive reader much pains to convince himself that Hamlet is a sensual man, and even secretly voluptuous. (It is not for nothing that the courtier Rosencrantz smiles slily when Hamlet says in his hearing that he is tired of women.) Hamlet does not love, I say, but only pretends—and mawkishly—that he loves. On this we have the testimony of Shakespeare himself. In the first scene of the third act Hamlet says to Ophelia: "I did love you once." Then ensues the colloquy:

> OPHELIA: Indeed, my lord, you made me believe so.
> HAMLET: You should not have believed me . . . I loved you not.

And having uttered this last word, Hamlet is much nearer the truth than he supposed. His feelings for Ophelia—an innocent creature, pure as a saint—are either cynical (recollect his words, his equivocal allusions, when, in the scene representing the theater, he asks her permission to lie . . . in her lap), or else hollow (direct your attention to the scene between him and Laertes, when Hamlet jumps into Ophelia's grave and says, in language worthy of Bramarbas or of Captain Pistol: "Forty thousand brothers could not, with all their quality of love, make up my sum. . . . Let them throw millions of acres on us," etc.). All his relations with Ophelia are for Hamlet only the occasions for preoccupation with his own self, and in his exclamation, "O, Nymph! in thy orisons be all my sins remembered!" we see but the deep consciousness of his own sickly inanition, a lack of strength to love, on the part of the almost superstitious worshiper before "the Saint of Chastity."

But enough has been said of the dark sides of the Hamlet type, of those phases which irritate us most because they are nearer and more familiar to us. I will endeavor to appreciate whatever may be legitimate in him, and therefore enduring. Hamlet embodies the doctrine of negation, that same doctrine which another great poet has divested of everything human and presented in the form of Mephistopheles. Hamlet is the self-same Mephistopheles, but a Mephistopheles embraced by the living circle of human nature: hence his negation is not an evil, but is itself directed against evil. Hamlet casts doubt upon goodness, but does not question the existence of evil; in fact, he wages relentless war upon it. He entertains suspicions concerning the genuineness and sincerity of good; yet his attacks are made not upon goodness, but upon a counterfeit goodness, beneath whose mask are secreted evil and falsehood, its immemorial enemies. He does not laugh the diabolic, impersonal laughter of Mephistopheles; in his bitterest smile there is pathos, which tells of his sufferings and therefore reconciles us to him. Hamlet's skepticism, moreover, is not indifferentism, and in this consists his significance and merit. In his makeup good and evil, truth and falsehood, beauty and ugliness, are not blurred into an accidental, dumb and vague something or other. The skepticism of Hamlet, which leads him to distrust things contemporaneous—the realization of truth, so to speak—is irreconcilably at war with falsehood, and through this very quality he becomes one of the foremost champions of a truth in which he himself cannot fully believe. But in negation, as in fire, there is a destructive force, and how can we keep it within bounds or show exactly where it is to stop, when that which it must destroy and that which it should spare are frequently blended and bound up together inseparably? This is where the oft-observed tragedy of human life comes into evidence: doing presupposes thinking, but thought and the will have separated, and are separating daily more and more. "And thus the native hue of resolution is sicklied o'er with the pale cast of thought," Shakespeare tells us in the words of Hamlet.

And so, on the one side stand the Hamlets—reflective, conscientious, often all-comprehensive, but as often also useless and doomed to immobility; and on the other the half-crazy Don Quixotes, who help and influence mankind only to the extent that they see but a single point—often non-existent in the form they see it. Unwillingly the questions arise: Must one really be a lunatic to believe in the truth? And, must the mind that has obtained control of itself lose, therefore, all its power?

We should be led very far indeed even by a superficial consideration of these questions.

I shall confine myself to the remark that in this separation, in this dualism which I have mentioned, we should recognize a fundamental law of all human life. This life is nothing else than an eternal struggle and everlasting reconcilement of two ceaselessly diverging and continually uniting elements. If I did not fear startling your ears with philosophical terms, I would venture to say that the Hamlets are an expression of the fundamental centripetal force of nature, in accordance with which every living thing considers itself the center of creation and looks down upon everything else as existing for its sake. Thus the mosquito that settled on the forehead of Alexander the Great, in calm confidence of its right, fed on his blood as food which belonged to it; just so Hamlet, though he scorns himself—a thing the mosquito does not do, not having risen to this level—always takes everything on his own account. Without this centripetal force—the force of egotism—nature could no more exist than without the other, the centrifugal force, according to whose law everything exists only for something else. This force, the principle of devotion and self-sacrifice, illuminated, as I have already stated, by a comic light, is represented by the Don Quixotes. These two forces of inertia and motion, of conservatism and progress, are the fundamental forces of all existing things. They explain to us the growth of a little flower; they give us a key to the understanding of the development of the most powerful peoples.

I hasten to pass from these perhaps irrelevant speculations to other considerations more familiar to us.

I know that, of all Shakespeare's works, *Hamlet* is perhaps the most popular. This tragedy belongs to the list of plays that never fail to crowd the theater. In view of the modern attitude of our public and its aspiration toward self-consciousness and reflection, its scruples about itself and its buoyancy of spirit, this phenomenon is clear. But, to say nothing of the beauties in which this most excellent expression of the modern spirit abounds, one cannot help marveling at the master-genius who, though himself in many respects akin to his Hamlet, cleft him from himself by a free sweep of creative force, and set up his model for the lasting study of posterity. The spirit which created this model is that of a northern man, a spirit of meditation and analysis, a spirit heavy and gloomy, devoid of harmony and bright color, not rounded into exquisite, oftentimes shallow, forms; but deep, strong, varied, independent, and guiding. Out of his very bosom he has plucked the type of Hamlet; and in so doing has shown that, in the realm of poetry, as in other spheres of human life, he stands above his child, because he fully understands it.

The spirit of a southerner went into the creation of Don Quixote, a spirit light and merry, naïve and impressionable—one that does not enter into the mysteries of life, that reflects phenomena rather than comprehends them.

At this point I cannot resist the desire, not to draw a parallel between Shakespeare and Cervantes, but simply to indicate a few points of likeness and of difference. Shakespeare and Cervantes—how can there be any comparison? some will ask. Shakespeare, that giant, that demigod! . . . Yes, but Cervantes is not a pigmy beside the giant who created "King Lear." He is a man— a man to the full; and a man has the right to stand on his feet even before a demigod. Undoubtedly Shakespeare presses hard upon Cervantes—and not him alone—by the wealth and power of his imagination, by the brilliancy of his greatest poetry, by the depth and breadth of a colossal mind. But then you will not find in Cervantes' romance any strained witticisms or unnatural comparisons or feigned concepts; nor will you meet in his pages with decapitations, picked eyes, and those streams of blood, that dull and iron cruelty, which are the terrible heirloom of the Middle Ages, and are disappearing less rapidly in obstinate northern natures. And yet Cervantes, like Shakespeare, lived in the epoch that witnessed St. Bartholomew's night; and long after that time heretics were burned and blood continued to flow—shall it ever cease to flow? *Don Quixote* reflects the Middle Ages, if only in the provincial poetry and narrative grace of those romances which Cervantes so good-humoredly derided, and to which he himself paid the last tribute in *Persiles and Sigismunda*. Shakespeare takes his models from everywhere—from heaven and earth —he knows no limitations; nothing can escape his all-pervading glance. He seizes his subjects with irresistible power, like an eagle pouncing upon its prey. Cervantes presents his not over-numerous characters to his readers gently, as a father his children. He takes only what is close to him, but with that how familiar he is! Everything human seems subservient to the mighty English poet; Cervantes draws his wealth from his own heart only—a heart sunny, kind, and rich in life's experience, but not hardened by it. It was not in vain that during seven years of hard bondage * Cervantes was learning, as he himself said, the science of patience. The circle of his experience is narrower than Shakespeare's, but in that, as in every separate living person, is reflected all that is human. Cervantes does not dazzle you with thundering words; he does not shock you with the titanic force of triumphant inspiration; his poetry—sometimes turbid, and by no means Shakespearean—is like a deep river, rolling calmly between variegated banks; and the reader, gradually allured, then hemmed in on every side by its transparent waves, cheerfully resigns himself to the truly epic calm and fluidity of its course.

The imagination gladly evokes the figures of these two contemporary poets, who died on the very same day, the 26th of April, 1616.* Cervantes probably knew nothing of Shakespeare, but the great tragedian in the quietude of his Stratford home, whither he had retired for the three years preceding his death, could have read through the famous novel, which had already been translated into English. A picture worthy of the brush of a contemplative artist—Shakespeare reading *Don Quixote!* Fortunate are the countries where such men arise, teachers of their generation and of posterity. The unfading wreath with which a great man is crowned rests also upon the brow of his people.

A certain English Lord—a good judge in the matter—once

---

* Recent biographies of Cervantes give the period of his captivity as *five* years, and the date of his death *April 23rd.*—TRANSLATOR.

spoke in my hearing of Don Quixote as a model of a real gentle-man. Surely, if simplicity and a quiet demeanor are the distin-guishing marks of what we call a thorough gentleman, Don Quixote has a good claim to his title. He is a veritable hidalgo—a hidalgo even when the jeering servants of the prince are lath-ering his whole face. The simplicity of his manners proceeds from the absence of what I would venture to call his self-love, and not his *self-conceit*. Don Quixote is not busied with himself, and, re-specting himself and others, does not think of showing off. But Hamlet, with all his exquisite setting, is, it seems to me—excuse the French expression—*ayant des airs de parvenu;* he is trouble-some—at times even rude—and he poses and scoffs. To make up for this, he was given the power of original and apt expression, a power inherent in every being in whom is implanted the habit of reflection and self-development—and therefore utterly unat-tainable so far as Don Quixote is concerned. The depth and keen-ness of analysis in Hamlet, his many-sided education (we must not forget that he studied at the Wittenburg University), have developed in him a taste almost unerring. He is an excellent critic; his advice to the actors is strikingly true and judicious. The sense of the beautiful is as strong in him as the sense of duty in Don Quixote.

Don Quixote deeply respects all existing orders—religions, mon-archs, and dukes—and is at the same time free himself and recog-nizes the freedom of others. Hamlet rebukes kings and courtiers, but is in reality oppressive and intolerant.

Don Quixote is hardly literate; Hamlet probably kept a diary. Don Quixote, with all his ignorance, has a definite way of think-ing about matters of government and administration; Hamlet has neither time nor need to think of such matters.

Many have objected to the endless blows with which Cervantes burdens Don Quixote. I have already remarked that in the second part of the romance the poor knight is almost unmolested. But I will add that, without these beatings, he would be less pleasing to children, who read his adventures with such avidity; and to us grownups he would not appear in his true light, but rather in a cold and haughty aspect, which would be incompatible with his character. Another interesting point is involved here. At the very end of the romance, after Don Quixote's complete discomfiture by the Knight of the White Moon, the disguised college bachelor, and following his renunciation of knight-errantry, shortly before his death, a herd of swine trample him under foot. I once happened to hear Cervantes criticized for writing this, on the ground that he was repeating the old tricks already abandoned; but herein Cervantes was guided by the instinct of genius, and this very ugly incident has a deep meaning. The trampling under pigs' feet is always encountered in the lives of Don Quixotes, and just before their close. This is the last tribute they must pay to rough chance, to indifference and cruel misunderstanding; it is the slap in the face from the Pharisees. Then they can die. They have passed through all the fire of the furnace, have won immortality for themselves, and it opens before them.

Hamlet is occasionally double-faced and heartless. Think of how he planned the deaths of the two courtiers sent to England by the king. Recall his speech on Polonius, whom he murdered. In this, however, we see, as already observed, a reflection of the medieval spirit recently outgrown. On the other hand, we must note in the honest, veracious Don Quixote the disposition to a half-conscious, half-innocent deception, to self-delusion—a disposition almost always present in the fancy of an enthusiast. His account of what he saw in the cave of Montesinos was obviously invented by him, and did not deceive the smart commoner, Sancho Panza.

Hamlet, on the slightest ill-success, loses heart and complains; but Don Quixote, pummelled senseless by galley slaves, has not the least doubt as to the success of his undertaking. In the same spirit Fourier is said to have gone to his office every day, for many years, to meet an Englishman he had invited, through the newspapers, to furnish him with a million francs to carry out his plans; but, of course, the benefactor of his dreams never appeared. This was certainly a very ridiculous proceeding, and it calls to mind this thought: The ancients considered their gods jealous, and, in case of need, deemed it useful to appease them by voluntary offerings (recollect the ring cast into the sea by Polycrates); why, then, should we not believe that some share of the ludicrous must inevitably be mingled with the acts, with the very character, of people moved unto great and novel deeds— as a bribe, as a soothing offering, to the jealous gods? Without these comical crank-pioneers, mankind could not progress, and there would not be anything for the Hamlets to reflect upon.

The Don Quixotes discover; the Hamlets develop. But how, I shall be asked, can the Hamlets evolve anything when they doubt all things and believe in nothing? My rejoinder is that, by a wise dispensation of Nature, there are neither thorough Hamlets nor complete Don Quixotes; these are but extreme manifestations of two tendencies—guide-posts set up by the poets on two different roads. Life tends toward them, but never reaches the goal. We must not forget that, just as the principle of analysis is carried in Hamlet to tragedy, so the element of enthusiasm runs in Don Quixote to comedy; but in life, the purely comic and the purely tragic are seldom encountered.

Hamlet gains much in our estimation from Horatio's attachment for him. This character is excellent, and is frequently met with in our day, to the credit of the times. In Horatio I recognize the type of disciple, the pupil, in the best sense of the word. With a stoical and direct nature, a warm heart, and a somewhat limited understanding, he is aware of his shortcomings, and is modest— something rare in people of limited intellect. He thirsts for learning, for instruction, and therefore venerates the wise Hamlet, and is devoted to him with all the might of his honest heart, not demanding even reciprocation. He defers to Hamlet, not as to a prince but as to a chief. One of the most important services of the Hamlets consists in forming and developing persons like Horatio; persons who, having received from them the seeds of thought, fertilize them in their hearts, and then scatter them broadcast through the world. The words in which Hamlet acknowledges Horatio's worth, honor himself. In them is expressed his own conception of the great worth of Man, his noble aspirations, which no skepticism is strong enough to weaken.

> Give me that man
> That is not passion's slave, and I will wear him
> In my heart's core, ay, in my heart of hearts,
> As I do thee.

The honest skeptic always respects a stoic. When the ancient world had crumbled away—and in every epoch like unto that—the best people took refuge in stoicism as the only creed in which it was still possible to preserve man's dignity. The skeptics, if they lacked the strength to die—to betake themselves to the "undiscovered country from whose bourn no traveler returns"—turned epicureans; a plain, sad phenomenon, with which we are but too familiar.

Both Hamlet and Don Quixote die a touching death; and yet how different are their ends! Hamlet's last words are sublime. He resigns himself, grows calm, bids Horatio live, and raises his dying voice in behalf of young Fortinbras, the unstained representative of the right of succession. Hamlet's eyes are not turned forward. "The rest is silence," says the dying skeptic, as he actually becomes silent forever. The death of Don Quixote sends an inexpressible emotion through one's heart. In that instant the full significance of this personality is accessible to all. When his former page, trying to comfort Don Quixote, tells him that they shall soon again start out on an expedition of knight-errantry, the expiring knight replies: "No, all is now over forever, and I ask everyone's forgiveness; I am no longer Don Quixote, I am again Alonzo the good, as I was once called—Alonso el Bueno."

This word is remarkable. The mention of this nickname for the first and last time makes the reader tremble. Yes, only this single word still has a meaning, in the face of death. All things shall pass away, everything shall vanish—the highest station, power, the all-inclusive genius—all to dust shall crumble. "All earthly greatness vanishes like smoke." But noble deeds are more enduring than resplendent beauty. "Everything shall pass," the apostle said, "love alone shall endure."

1860   Translated by
                                                       DAVID MODELL

Traveling with a Reformer

by MARK TWAIN [1835–1910]

LAST SPRING I went out to Chicago to see the Fair, and although I did not see it my trip was not wholly lost—there were compensations. In New York I was introduced to a major in the regular army who said he was going to the Fair, and we agreed to go together. I had to go to Boston first, but that did not interfere; he said he would go along, and put in the time. He was a handsome man, and built like a gladiator. But his ways were gentle, and his speech was soft and persuasive. He was companionable, but exceedingly reposeful. Yes, and wholly destitute of the sense of humor. He was full of interest in everything that went on around him, but his serenity was indestructible; nothing disturbed him, nothing excited him.

But before the day was done I found that deep down in him somewhere he had a passion, quiet as he was—a passion for reforming petty public abuses. He stood for citizenship—it was his hobby. His idea was that every citizen of the republic ought to consider himself an unofficial policeman, and keep unsalaried watch and ward over the laws and their execution. He thought that the only effective way of preserving and protecting public rights was for each citizen to do his share in preventing or punishing such infringements of them as came under his personal notice.

It was a good scheme, but I thought it would keep a body in trouble all the time; it seemed to me that one would be always trying to get offending little officials discharged, and perhaps getting laughed at for all reward. But he said no, I had the wrong idea; that there was no occasion to get anybody discharged; that in fact you *mustn't* get anybody discharged; that that would itself be a failure; no, one must reform the man—reform him and make him useful where he was.

"Must one report the offender and then beg his superior not to discharge him, but reprimand him and keep him?"

"No, that is not the idea; you don't report him at all, for then you risk his bread and butter. You can act as if you are *going* to report him—when nothing else will answer. But that's an extreme case. That is a sort of *force,* and force is bad. Diplomacy is the effective thing. Now if a man has tact—if a man will exercise diplomacy—"

For two minutes we had been standing at a telegraph wicket, and during all this time the Major had been trying to get the attention of one of the young operators, but they were all busy skylarking. The Major spoke now, and asked one of them to take his telegram. He got for reply:

"I reckon you can wait a minute, can't you?" and the skylarking went on.

The Major said yes, he was not in a hurry. Then he wrote another telegram:

> *President Western Union Tel. Co.:*
> Come and dine with me this evening. I can tell you how business is conducted in one of your branches.

Presently the young fellow who had spoken so pertly a little before reached out and took the telegram, and when he read it he lost color and began to apologize and explain. He said he would lose his place if this deadly telegram was sent, and he might never get another. If he could be let off this time he would give no cause of complaint again. The compromise was accepted.

As we walked away, the Major said:

"Now, you see, that was diplomacy—and you see how it worked. It wouldn't do any good to bluster, the way people are always doing—that boy can always give you as good as you send, and you'll come out defeated and ashamed of yourself pretty nearly always. But you see he stands no chance against diplomacy. Gentle words and diplomacy—those are the tools to work with."

"Yes, I see; but everybody wouldn't have had your opportunity. It isn't everybody that is on those familiar terms with the president of the Western Union."

"Oh, you misunderstand. I don't know the president—I only used him diplomatically. It is for his good and for the public good. There's no harm in it."

I said, with hesitation and diffidence:

"But is it ever right or noble to tell a lie?"

He took no note of the delicate self-righteousness of the question, but answered, with undisturbed gravity and simplicity:

"Yes, sometimes. Lies told to injure a person, and lies told to profit yourself are not justifiable, but lies told to help another person, and lies told in the public interest—oh, well, that is quite another matter. Anybody knows that. But never mind about the methods: you see the result. That youth is going to be useful now, and well behaved. He had a good face. He was worth saving. Why, he was worth saving on his mother's account if not his own. Of course, he has a mother—sisters, too. Damn those people who are always forgetting that! Do you know, I've never fought a duel in my life—never once—and yet have been challenged, like other people. I could always see the other man's unoffending women folks or his little children standing between him and me. *They* hadn't done anything—I couldn't break *their* hearts, you know."

He corrected a good many little abuses in the course of the day, and always without friction—always with a fine and dainty "diplomacy" which left no sting behind; and he got such happiness and such contentment out of these performances that I was obliged to envy him his trade—and perhaps would have adopted it if I could have managed the necessary deflections from fact as confidently with my mouth as I believe I could with a pen, behind the shelter of print, after a little practice.

Away late that night we were coming up-town in a horse-car when three boisterous roughs got aboard, and began to fling hilarious obscenities and profanities right and left among the timid passengers, some of whom were women and children. Nobody resisted or retorted; the conductor tried soothing words and moral suasion, but the roughs only called him names and laughed at him. Very soon I saw that the Major realized that this was a matter which was in his line; evidently he was turning over his stock of diplomacy in his mind and getting ready. I felt that the first dip-

lomatic remark he made in this place would bring down a land-
slide of ridicule upon him and maybe something worse; but before
I could whisper to him and check him he had begun, and it was too
late. He said, in a level and dispassionate tone:

"Conductor, you must put these swine out. I will help you."

I was not looking for that. In a flash the three roughs plunged
at him. But none of them arrived. He delivered three such blows
as one could not expect to encounter outside the prize-ring, and
neither of the men had life enough left in him to get up from
where he fell. The Major dragged them out and threw them off
the car, and we got under way again.

I was astonished; astonished to see a lamb act so; astonished at
the strength displayed, and the clean and comprehensive result;
astonished at the brisk and business-like style of the whole thing.
The situation had a humorous side to it, considering how much
I had been hearing about mild persuasion and gentle diplomacy
all day from this pile-driver, and I would have liked to call his attention to that feature and do some sarcasms about it; but when I
looked at him I saw that it would be of no use—his placid and contented face had no ray of humor in it; he would not have understood. When we left the car, I said:

"That was a good stroke of diplomacy—three good strokes of
diplomacy, in fact."

"*That?* That wasn't diplomacy. You are quite in the wrong.
Diplomacy is a wholly different thing. One cannot apply it to that
sort; they would not understand it. No, that was not diplomacy; it
was force."

"Now that you mention it, I—yes, I think perhaps you are
right."

"Right? Of course I am right. It was just force."

"I think, myself, it had the outside aspect of it. Do you often
have to reform people in that way?"

"Far from it. It hardly ever happens. Not oftener than once in
half a year, at the outside."

"Those men will get well?"

"Get well? Why, certainly they will. They are not in any danger. I know how to hit and where to hit. You noticed that I did not
hit them under the jaw. That would have killed them."

I believed that. I remarked—rather wittily, as I thought—that he had been a lamb all day, but now had all of a sudden developed into a ram—battering-ram; but with dulcet frankness and simplicity he said no, a battering-ram was quite a different thing and not in use now. This was maddening, and I came near bursting out and saying he had no more appreciation of wit than a jackass—in fact, I had it right on my tongue, but did not say it, knowing there was no hurry and I could say it just as well some other time over the telephone.

We started to Boston the next afternoon. The smoking-compartment in the parlor-car was full, and we went into the regular smoker. Across the aisle in the front seat sat a meek, farmer-looking old man with a sickly pallor in his face, and he was holding the door open with his foot to get the air. Presently a big brakeman came rushing through, and when he got to the door he stopped, gave the farmer an ugly scowl, then wrenched the door to with such energy as to almost snatch the old man's boot off. Then on he plunged about his business. Several passengers laughed, and the old gentleman looked pathetically shamed and grieved.

After a little the conductor passed along, and the Major stopped him and asked him a question in his habitually courteous way:

"Conductor, where does one report the misconduct of a brakeman? Does one report to you?"

"You can report him at New Haven if you want to. What has he been doing?"

The Major told the story. The conductor seemed amused. He said, with just a touch of sarcasm in his bland tones:

"As I understand you, the brakeman didn't *say* anything."

"No, he didn't say anything."

"But he scowled, you say."

"Yes."

"And snatched the door loose in a rough way."

"Yes."

"That's the whole business, is it?"

"Yes, that is the whole of it."

The conductor smiled pleasantly, and said:

"Well, if you want to report him, all right, but I don't quite make out what it's going to amount to. You'll say—as I understand you—that the brakeman insulted this old gentleman. They'll ask you what he *said*. You'll say he didn't say anything at all. I reckon they'll say, how are you going to make out an insult when you acknowledge yourself that he didn't say a word."

There was a murmur of applause at the conductor's compact reasoning, and it gave him pleasure—you could see it in his face. But the Major was not disturbed. He said:

"There—now you have touched upon a crying defect in the complaint system. The railway officials—as the public think and as you also seem to think—are not aware that there are any kind of insults except *spoken* ones. So nobody goes to headquarters and reports insults of manner, insults of gesture, look, and so forth; and yet these are sometimes harder to bear than any words. They are bitter hard to bear because there is nothing tangible to take hold of; and the insulter can always say, if called before the railway officials, that he never dreamed of intending any offense. It seems to me that the officials ought to specially and urgently request the public to report *unworded* affronts and incivilities."

The conductor laughed, and said:

"Well, that *would* be trimming it pretty fine, sure!"

"But not too fine, I think. I will report this matter at New Haven, and I have an idea that I'll be thanked for it."

The conductor's face lost something of its complacency; in fact, it settled to a quite sober cast as the owner of it moved away. I said:

"You are not really going to bother with that trifle, are you?"

"It isn't a trifle. Such things ought always to be reported. It is a public duty, and no citizen has a right to shirk it. But I sha'n't have to report this case."

"Why?"

"It won't be necessary. Diplomacy will do the business. You'll see."

Presently the conductor came on his rounds again, and when he reached the Major he leaned over and said:

"That's all right. You needn't report him. He's responsible to me, and if he does it again I'll give him a talking to."

The Major's response was cordial:

"Now that is what I like! You mustn't think that I was moved by any vengeful spirit, for that wasn't the case. It was duty—just a sense of duty, that was all. My brother-in-law is one of the directors of the road, and when he learns that you are going to reason with your brakeman the very next time he brutally insults an unoffending old man it will please him, you may be sure of that."

The conductor did not look as joyous as one might have thought he would, but on the contrary looked sickly and uncomfortable. He stood around a little; then said:

"I think something ought to be done to him *now*. I'll discharge him."

"Discharge him? What good would that do? Don't you think it would be better wisdom to teach him better ways and keep him?"

"Well, there's something in that. What would you suggest?"

"He insulted the old gentleman in presence of all these people. How would it do to have him come and apologize in their presence?"

"I'll have him here right off. And I want to say this: If people would do as you've done, and report such things to me instead of keeping mum and going off and blackguarding the road, you'd see a different state of things pretty soon. I'm much obliged to you."

The brakeman came and apologized. After he was gone the Major said:

"Now, you see how simple and easy that was. The ordinary citizen would have accomplished nothing—the brother-in-law of a director can accomplish anything he wants to."

"But are you really the brother-in-law of a director?"

"Always. Always when the public interests require it. I have a brother-in-law on all the boards—everywhere. It saves me a world of trouble."

"It is a good wide relationship."

"Yes. I have over three hundred of them."

"Is the relationship never doubted by a conductor?"

"I have never met with a case. It is the honest truth—I never have."

"Why didn't you let him go ahead and discharge the brakeman, in spite of your favorite policy? You know he deserved it."

The Major answered with something which really had a sort of distant resemblance to impatience:

"If you would stop and think a moment you wouldn't ask such a question as that. Is a brakeman a dog, that nothing but dog's methods will do for him? He is a man, and has a man's fight for life. And he always has a sister, or a mother, or wife and children to support. Always—there are no exceptions. When you take his living away from him you take theirs away too—and what have they done to you? Nothing. And where is the profit in discharging an uncourteous brakeman and hiring another just like him? It's unwisdom. Don't you see that the rational thing to do is to *reform* the brakeman and keep him? Of course it is."

Then he quoted with admiration the conduct of a certain division superintendent of the Consolidated road, in a case where a switchman of two years' experience was negligent once and threw a train off the track and killed several people. Citizens came in a passion to urge the man's dismissal, but the superintendent said:

"No, you are wrong. He has learned his lesson, he will throw no more trains off the track. He is twice as valuable as he was before. I shall keep him."

We had only one more adventure on the trip. Between Hartford and Springfield the train-boy came shouting in with an armful of literature and dropped a sample into a slumbering gentleman's lap, and the man woke up with a start. He was very angry, and he and a couple of friends discussed the outrage with much heat. They sent for the parlor-car conductor and described the matter, and were determined to have the boy expelled from his situation. The three complainants were wealthy Holyoke merchants, and it was evident that the conductor stood in some awe of them. He tried to pacify them, and explained that the boy was not under his authority, but under that of one of the news companies; but he accomplished nothing.

Then the Major volunteered some testimony for the defense. He said:

"I saw it all. You gentlemen have not meant to exaggerate the circumstances, but still that is what you have done. The boy has done nothing more than all train-boys do. If you want to get his ways softened down and his manners reformed, I am with you and ready to help, but it isn't fair to get him discharged without giving him a chance."

But they were angry, and would hear of no compromise. They were well acquainted with the president of the Boston & Albany, they said, and would put everything aside next day and go up to Boston and fix that boy.

The major said he would be on hand too, and would do what he could to save the boy. One of the gentlemen looked him over, and said:

"Apparently it is going to be a matter of who can wield the most influence with the president. Do you know Mr. Bliss personally?"

The Major said, with composure:

"Yes; he is my uncle."

The effect was satisfactory. There was an awkward silence for a minute or more; then the hedging and the half-confessions of over-haste and exaggerated resentment began, and soon everything was smooth and friendly and sociable, and it was resolved to drop the matter and leave the boy's bread-and-butter unmolested.

It turned out as I had expected: the president of the road was not the Major's uncle at all—except by adoption, and for this day and train only.

We got into no episodes on the return journey. Probably it was because we took a night train and slept all the way.

We left New York Saturday night by the Pennsylvania road. After breakfast the next morning we went into the parlor-car, but found it a dull place and dreary. There were but few people in it and nothing going on. Then we went into the little smoking-compartment of the same car and found three gentlemen in there. Two of them were grumbling over one of the rules of the road— a rule which forbade card-playing on the trains on Sunday. They had started an innocent game of high-low-jack and been stopped. The Major was interested. He said to the third gentleman:

"Did you object to the game?"

"Not at all. I am a Yale professor and a religious man, but my prejudices are not extensive."

Then the Major said to the others:

"You are at perfect liberty to resume your game, gentlemen; no one here objects."

One of them declined the risk, but the other one said he would like to begin again if the Major would join him. So they spread an overcoat over their knees and the game proceeded. Pretty soon the parlor-car conductor arrived, and said brusquely:

"There, there, gentlemen, that won't do. Put up the cards—it's not allowed."

The Major was shuffling. He continued to shuffle, and said:

"By whose order is it forbidden?"

"It's my order. I forbid it."

The dealing began. The Major asked:

"Did you invent the idea?"

"What idea?"

"The idea of forbidding card-playing on Sunday."

"No—of course not."

"Who did?"

"The company."

"Then it isn't your order, after all, but the company's. Is that it?"

"Yes. But you don't stop playing; I have to require you to stop playing immediately."

"Nothing is gained by hurry, and often much is lost. Who authorized the company to issue such an order?"

"My dear sir, that is a matter of no consequence to me, and—"

"But you forget that you are not the only person concerned. It may be a matter of consequence to me. It is indeed a matter of very great importance to me. I cannot violate a legal requirement of my country without dishonoring myself; I cannot allow any man or corporation to hamper my liberties with illegal rules—a thing which railway companies are always trying to do—without dishonoring my citizenship. So I come back to that question: By whose authority has the company issued this order?"

"I don't *know*. That's *their* affair."

"Mine, too. I doubt if the company has any right to issue such a rule. This road runs through several states. Do you know what state we are in now, and what its laws are in matters of this kind?"

"Its laws do not concern me, but the company's orders do. It is my duty to stop this game, gentlemen, and it *must* be stopped."

"Possibly; but still there is no hurry. In hotels they post certain rules in the rooms, but they always quote passages from the state laws as authority for these requirements. I see nothing posted here of this sort. Please produce your authority and let us arrive at a decision, for you see yourself that you are marring the game."

"I have nothing of the kind, but I have my orders, and that is sufficient. They must be obeyed."

"Let us not jump to conclusions. It will be better all around to examine into the matter without heat or haste, and see just where we stand before either of us makes a mistake—for the curtailing of the liberties of a citizen of the United States is a much more serious matter than you and the railroads seem to think, and it cannot be done in my person until the curtailer proves his right to do so. Now—"

"My dear sir, *will* you put down those cards?"

"All in good time, perhaps. It depends. You say this order must be obeyed. *Must.* It is a strong word. You see yourself how strong it is. A wise company would not arm you with so drastic an order as this, of *course,* without appointing a penalty for its infringement. Otherwise it runs the risk of being a dead letter and a thing to laugh at. What is the appointed penalty for an infringement of this law?"

"Penalty? I never heard of any."

"Unquestionably you must be mistaken. Your company orders you to come here and rudely break up an innocent amusement, and furnishes you no way to enforce the order? Don't you see that that is nonsense? What do you *do* when people refuse to obey this order? Do you take the cards away from them?"

"No."

"Do you put the offender off at the next station?"

"Well, no—of course we couldn't if he had a ticket."

"Do you have him up before a court?"

The conductor was silent and apparently troubled. The Major started a new deal, and said:

"You see that you are helpless, and that the company has placed you in a foolish position. You are furnished with an arrogant order, and you deliver it in a blustering way, and when you come to look into the matter you find you haven't any way of enforcing obedience."

The conductor said, with chill dignity:

"Gentlemen, you have heard the order, and my duty is ended. As to obeying it or not, you will do as you think fit." And he turned to leave.

"But wait. The matter is not yet finished. I think you are mistaken about your duty being ended; but if it really is, I myself have a duty to perform yet."

"How do you mean?"

"Are you going to report my disobedience at headquarters in Pittsburgh?"

"No. What good would that do?"

"You must report me, or I will report you."

"Report me for what?"

"For disobeying the company's orders in not stopping this game. As a citizen it is my duty to help the railway companies keep their servants to their work."

"Are you in earnest?"

"Yes, I am in earnest. I have nothing against you as a man, but I have this against you as an officer—that you have not carried out that order, and if you do not report me I must report you. And I will."

The conductor looked puzzled, and was thoughtful a moment; then he burst out with:

"I seem to be getting *myself* into a scrape! It's all a muddle; I can't make head or tail of it; it's never happened before; they always knocked under and never said a word, and so *I* never saw how ridiculous that stupid order with no penalty is. *I* don't want to report anybody, and I don't want to *be* reported—why, it might do me no end of harm! Now *do* go on with the game—play the whole day if you want to—and don't let's have any more trouble about it!"

"No, I only sat down here to establish this gentleman's rights—he can have his place now. But before you go won't you tell me what you think the company made this rule for? Can you imagine an excuse for it? I mean a rational one—an excuse that is not on its face silly, and the invention of an idiot?"

"Why, surely I can. The reason it was made is plain enough. It is to save the feelings of the other passengers—the religious ones

among them, I mean. They would not like it, to have the Sabbath
desecrated by card-playing on the train."

"I just thought as much. They are willing to desecrate it themselves by traveling on Sunday, but they are not willing that other
people—"

"By gracious, you've hit it! I never thought of that before. The
fact is, it *is* a silly rule when you come to look into it."

At this point the train-conductor arrived, and was going to shut
down the game in a very high-handed fashion, but the parlor-car
conductor stopped him and took him aside to explain. Nothing
more was heard of the matter.

I was ill in bed eleven days in Chicago and got no glimpse of
the Fair, for I was obliged to return east as soon as I was able to
travel. The Major secured and paid for a stateroom in a sleeper
the day before we left, so that I could have plenty of room and be
comfortable; but when we arrived at the station a mistake had
been made and our car had not been put on. The conductor had
reserved a section for us—it was the best he could do, he said. But
the Major said we were not in a hurry, and would wait for the
car to be put on. The conductor responded, with pleasant irony:

"It may be that *you* are not in a hurry, just as you say, but we
are. Come, get aboard, gentlemen, get aboard—don't keep us waiting."

But the Major would not get aboard himself nor allow me to do
it. He wanted his car, and said he must have it. This made the
hurried and perspiring conductor impatient, and he said:

"It's the best we can *do*—we can't do impossibilities. You will
take the section or go without. A mistake has been made and can't
be rectified at this late hour. It's a thing that happens now and then,
and there is nothing for it but to put up with it and make the best
of it. Other people do."

"Ah, that is just it, you see. If they had stuck to their rights and
enforced them you wouldn't be trying to trample mine under foot
in this bland way now. I haven't any disposition to give you unnecessary trouble, but it is my duty to protect the next man from
this kind of imposition. So I must have my car. Otherwise I will
wait in Chicago and sue the company for violating its contract."

"Sue the company?—for a thing like that!"

"Certainly."

"Do you really mean that?"

"Indeed, I do."

The conductor looked the Major over wonderingly, and then said:

"It beats me—it's bran-new—I've never struck the mate to it before. But I swear I think you'd do it. Look here, I'll send for the station-master."

When the station-master came he was a good deal annoyed—at the Major, not at the person who had made the mistake. He was rather brusque, and took the same position which the conductor had taken in the beginning; but he failed to move the soft-spoken artilleryman, who still insisted that he must have his car. However, it was plain that there was only one strong side in this case, and that that side was the Major's. The station-master banished his annoyed manner, and became pleasant and even half apologetic. This made a good opening for a compromise, and the Major made a concession. He said he would give up the engaged stateroom, but he must have *a* stateroom. After a deal of ransacking, one was found whose owner was persuadable; he exchanged it for our section, and we got away at last. The conductor called on us in the evening, and was kind and courteous and obliging, and we had a long talk and got to be good friends. He said he wished the public would make trouble oftener—it would have a good effect. He said that the railroads could not be expected to do their whole duty by the traveler unless the traveler would take some interest in the matter himself.

I hoped that we were done reforming for the trip now, but it was not so. In the hotel-car, in the the morning, the Major called for broiled chicken. The waiter said:

"It's not in the bill of fare, sir; we do not serve anything but what is in the bill."

"That gentleman yonder is eating a broiled chicken."

"Yes, but that is different. He is one of the superintendents of the road."

"Then all the more must I have broiled chicken. I do not like these discriminations. Please hurry—bring me a broiled chicken."

The waiter brought the steward, who explained in a low and polite voice that the thing was impossible—it was against the rule, and the rule was rigid.

"Very well, then, you must either apply it impartially or break it impartially. You must take that gentleman's chicken away from him or bring me one."

The steward was puzzled, and did not quite know what to do. He began an incoherent argument, but the conductor came along just then, and asked what the difficulty was. The steward explained that here was a gentleman who was insisting on having a chicken when it was dead against the rule and not in the bill. The conductor said:

"Stick by your rules—you haven't any option. Wait a moment —is this the gentleman?" Then he laughed and said: "Never mind your rules—it's my advice, and sound; give him anything he wants—don't get him started on his rights. Give him whatever he asks for; and if you haven't got it, stop the train and get it."

The Major ate the chicken, but said he did it from a sense of duty and to establish a principle, for he did not like chicken.

I missed the Fair, it is true, but I picked up some diplomatic tricks which I and the reader may find handy and useful as we go along.

1893

Large and Small Towns

by MIGUEL DE UNAMUNO [1864-1936]

I REGRET THAT I have not by me a certain essay dealing with this subject by Guglielmo Ferrero. I read it in some review the name of which I have forgotten, but I preserve a clear recollection of it, for it interested me greatly. Ferrero treated the subject from the historical and sociological point of view, and I, who am neither an historian nor a sociologist, intend to treat it, as is my custom, from the point of view of purely personal opinion and individual impression. (This is my custom, and yet in spite of the fact I cannot prevent people from insisting on calling me a savant and talking about my theories. I have no theories. I have only impressions and sensations.)

But, since I am unable to put some quotation from Ferrero at the head of this essay—this habit of basing our assertions upon authority is the conventional way of giving them a deceptive air of objectivity—I will head it by a sentence from George Meredith, that extremely subtle English novelist. In "The Egoist" it is stated that Willoughby "abandoned London as the burial-place of the individual man."

I, to-day, am one with Willoughby in believing that great cities de-individualize, or rather de-personalize, us. This may perhaps be due to the fact that, though not an egoist like the hero of Meredith's novel, I still remain, according to Ramiro de Maeztu, an incorrigible egotist.

Great cities are levelling; they lift up the low and depress the high; they exalt mediocrity and abase superlativeness—the result of the action of the mass, as powerful in social life as in chemistry.

Soon after I came to this ancient city of Salamanca which has now become so dear to me, a city of some thirty thousand souls, I wrote to a friend and told him that if after two year's residence here he should be informed that I spent my time playing cards, taking siestas and strolling round the square for a couple of hours every day, he might give me up for lost; but if at the end of that time I should still be studying, meditating, writing, battling for culture in the public arena, he might take it that I was better off here than in Madrid. And so it has proved to be.

I remember that Guglielmo Ferrero's conclusion, based upon a review of ancient Greece, of the Italy of the Renaissance and of the Germany of a century ago, is that for the life of the spirit, small cities of a population like that of Salamanca are the best—better than very small towns or large ones of over a hundred thousand inhabitants.

This depends, of course, upon the quality of the spirit in question. I am convinced that the monastic cloister, which so often atrophies the soul and reduces the average intelligence to a lamentable slavery to routine, has in certain exceptional cases exalted the spirit by its arduous discipline.

Great cities are essentially democratic, and I must confess that I feel an invincible platonic mistrust of democracies. In great cities culture is diffused but vulgarized. People abandon the quiet reading of books to go to the theatre, that school of vulgarity; they feel the need of being together; the gregarious instinct enslaves them; they must be seeing one another.

I think it was Taine who observed that the majority of French geniuses were either themselves country-born or the sons of country-born parents. And I assure you that I should find it difficult to believe in the genius of a Parisian born of Parisians.

Guerra Junqueiro said to me: "You are fortunate in living in a city in which you can walk along the streets dreaming, without fear of people disturbing your dream!" And certainly in Madrid it is impossible to walk along the streets dreaming, not so much for fear of motors, trams and carriages as because of the continual stream of unknown faces. The distraction of a great city, so agreeable to those who must have something, no matter what, to occupy their imagination, is necessarily vexatious to those whose chief concern is not to have their imagination diverted. Personally I find nothing more monotonous than a Paris boulevard. The people seem to me like shadows. I cannot endure a crowd of unknown faces.

I am afraid of Madrid. That is to say, I am afraid of myself when I go there. It is easy to say that in great cities everyone can live the life that suits him best, but it is easier to say it than to do it. When I am in the capital, I return home every night regretting having gone to the party or to the meeting that I went to and resolving never to go again, but only to break my vow the very next day. I am surrounded, hemmed in and invaded by a lethal atmosphere of compliance, an atmosphere that is generated by this so-called life of society.

I have always felt an aversion from this so-called life of society, which has for its object the cultivation of social relationships. Is there anything more terrible than a "call"? It affords an occasion for the exchange of the most threadbare commonplaces. Calls and the theatre are the two great centres for the propagation of platitudes.

A man of society, a drawing-room man who can make himself agreeable to women when he pays a call, is always a man whose principal concern is to suppress any arresting spontaneity, not to let his own personality show through. For it is a man's own personality that people find irritating. People like to meet the average man, the normal man, the man who has nothing exceptional about him. The exception is always irritating. How many times I have heard the terrible phrase: "This man irritates me." Yes, it is "the man" that irritates, and the hardest fight for the man who feels that he is a man is the fight to win respect for his own individuality.

And in a small town? Its stage is very restricted; the players soon tire of playing the parts allotted to them and the real men begin to appear underneath, with all their weaknesses—that is to say, with precisely that which makes them men. I have a great liking for provincial life, for there it is easiest to discern tragedy lurking beneath an appearance of calm. And just as much as I abhor comedy, I love tragedy. And, above all, tragi-comedy.

I have heard it said that there are no such seething intestine rancours and dissensions as in a merchant vessel or a monastery; that whenever men are obliged to live together, cut off from the rest of the world, their personalities, their most real and intimate selves, immediately clash against one another. And I dare say that this is the only way of attaining that knowledge of ourselves which ought to be our chief aim. It seems to me scarcely possible that a man should get to know himself by shutting himself up in the wilderness, contemplating—what? The best way of knowing one's self is to clash, heart against heart, that is to say, rock against rock, with one's fellow.

I know that I shall be told that I am indulging my love of paradox, but nevertheless I maintain that if it is true that the most ardent admirations are those which are disguised in the form of envy, very often the strongest attractions are those which take the appearance of hate. In one of these tragi-comic, or rather comi-tragic, small towns I know two men who, though obliged to see one another constantly in the way of business, never greet one another in the street and profess a mutual detestation. Nevertheless at bottom they feel themselves reciprocally attracted to one another and each one is continually preoccupied by the other.

These irreconcilable feuds into which small towns are so often divided are much more favourable to the development of strong personalities than the bland comedy of a great metropolis, where those who fight a duel to the death on the public stage embrace one another behind the scenes. Do you suppose that the tragedy of Romeo and Juliet is possible in a city that counts its inhabitants by the million?

And I ask you, do you suppose that anyone who sees a multitude of people in the course of the day, listens to this man to-day, to another man to-morrow and to another man the day after, and attends twenty or thirty conferences—do you think that such a one can preserve his spiritual integrity without any leakage? In such a life a hedgehog would end by becoming a lamb, its quills would turn into softest fleece, and for my part I would rather be a hedgehog than a lamb.

I understand why Willoughby fled from London as from the burial-place of the individual man. Is it not a terrible thing to walk through two or three miles of city streets and pass two or three thousand people without meeting a single known face to set a spark to a train of human thought? A glance of hate from a known enemy is sweeter than a glance of indifference, if not of disdain, from an unknown stranger. For man has acquired the habit of disdaining those whom he does not know, and seems to suppose that every stranger must be presumed to be an imbecile until he proves himself otherwise.

And those who say that they are bored in a small town? The reason is because they have not dug down to its tragic roots, to the august severity of the depths of its monotony.

It is my belief that in great cities proud natures become vain, that is to say, the quills become fleece.

And for the man who is engaged in any kind of work in which

he can exercise his influence from a distance, for the writer or the painter, the small town offers the inestimable advantage of enabling him to live far from his public and of its being possible that the effects which his work produces either do not reach him or reach him only after a searching process of filtration. He can live more or less independently of his public, without allowing himself to be influenced by it, and this is the only way of making a public for oneself instead of adapting oneself to it.

If this be the case, it may be urged that a village would be better than a small town, a hamlet or perhaps even a remote farmhouse. But no, for then there would be lacking that minimum of organic society without which our personality runs as much risk as it runs in the heart of a metropolis.

Essentially, in the sphere of psychologico-sociological relations —this is for the benefit of those who insist on labelling me savant— it is a question of what is perhaps the most fundamental of all problems, the problem of maxima and minima. This is the problem that is the nerve of physical mechanics and the nerve also of social mechanics or economics. The problem always is how to obtain the maximum result or profit with the minimum effort or expense, the largest return with the least expenditure. It is also the fundamental problem of æsthetics; it is at the root of all the problems of life.

And with regard to the subject I am now considering, it is a question of obtaining the maximum of our own personality with the minimum of others' society. Less society, or a society less complex, would diminish our personality, and so also would more society, or a society apparently more complex. And I say apparently, for I am not aware that an elephant is more complex than a fox.

Very well then—he who has no sense of his own personality and is willing to sacrifice it on the altar of sociability, let him go and lose himself among the millions of a metropolis. For the man who has a longing for Nirvana the metropolis is better than the desert. If you want to submerge your own "I," better the streets of a great city than the solitudes of the wilderness.

It is not a bad thing now and again to visit the great city and plunge into the sea of its crowds, but in order to emerge again upon terra firma and feel the solid ground under one's feet. For my part, since I am interested in individuals—in John and Peter and Richard, in you who are reading this book—but not in the masses which they form when banded together, I remain in the small town, seeing every day at the same hour the same men, men whose souls have clashed, and sometimes painfully, with my soul; and I flee from the great metropolis where my soul is whipped with the icy whips of the disdainful glances of those who know me not and who are unknown to me. People whom I cannot name . . . horrible!

1917   Translated by
                                          J. E. CRAWFORD FLITCH

The Bible as Poetry

by WALT WHITMAN [1819-1892]

I SUPPOSE one cannot at this day say anything new, from a literary point of view, about those autochthonic bequests of Asia—the Hebrew Bible, the mighty Hindu epics, and a hundred lesser but typical works (not now definitely including the *Iliad*—though that work was certainly of Asiatic genesis, as Homer himself was—considerations which seem curiously ignored). But will there ever be a time or place—ever a student, however modern, of the grand art, to whom those compositions will not afford profounder lessons than all else of their kind in the garnerage of the past? Could there be any more opportune suggestion, to the current popular writer and reader of verse, what the office of poet was in primeval times—and is yet capable of being, anew, adjusted entirely to the modern?

All the poems of Orientalism, with the Old and New Testaments at the centre, tend to deep and wide (I don't know but the deep

est and widest) psychological development—with little, or nothing at all, of the mere esthetic, the principal verse-requirement of
our day. Very late, but unerringly, comes to every capable student
the perception that it is not in beauty, it is not in art, it is not
even in science, that the profoundest laws of the case have their
eternal sway and outcropping.

In his discourse on "Hebrew poets" De Sola Mendes said:

> The fundamental feature of Judaism, of the Hebrew na-
> tionality, was religion; its poetry was naturally religious. Its
> subjects, God and Providence, the covenants with Israel, God
> in Nature, and as reveal'd, God the Creator and Governor,
> Nature in her majesty and beauty, inspired hymns and odes
> to Nature's God. And then the checker'd history of the nation
> furnish'd allusions, illustrations, and subjects for epic display
> —the glory of the sanctuary, the offerings, the splendid ritual,
> the Holy City, and lov'd Palestine with its pleasant valleys and
> wild tracts.

Dr. Mendes said that

> rhyming was not a characteristic of Hebrew poetry at all.
> Metre was not a necessary mark of poetry. Great poets dis-
> carded it; the early Jewish poets knew it not.

Compared with the famed epics of Greece, and lesser ones since,
the spinal supports of the Bible are simple and meagre. All its
history, biography, narratives, &c., are as beads, strung on and
indicating the eternal thread of the Deific purpose and power.
Yet with only deepest faith for impetus, and such Deific purpose
for palpable or impalpable theme, it often transcends the masterpieces of Hellas, and all masterpieces. The metaphors daring beyond account, the lawless soul, extravagant by our standards, the
glow of love and friendship, the fervent kiss—nothing in argument or logic, but unsurpass'd in proverbs, in religious ecstasy, in
suggestions of common mortality and death, man's great equal-
izers—the spirit everything, the ceremonies and forms of the
churches nothing, faith limitless, its immense sensuousness immensely spiritual—an incredible, all-inclusive non-worldliness and

dew-scented illiteracy (the antipodes of our Nineteenth Century business absorption and morbid refinement)—no hair-splitting doubts, no sickly sulking and sniffing, no *Hamlet,* no *Adonais,* no *Thanatopsis,* no *In Memoriam.*

The culminated proof of the poetry of a country is the equality of its personnel, which, in any race, can never be really superior without superior poems. The finest blending of individuality with universality (in my opinion nothing out of the galaxies of the *Iliad,* or Shakspere's heroes, or from the Tennysonian *Idylls,* so lofty, devoted and starlike), typified in the songs of those old Asiatic lands. Men and women as great columnar trees. Nowhere else the abnegation of self towering in such quaint sublimity; nowhere else the simplest human emotions conquering the gods of heaven, and fate itself. (The episode, for instance, toward the close of the *Mahabharata*—the journey of the wife Savitri with the god of death, Yama,

> One terrible to see—blood-red his garb,
> His body huge and dark, bloodshot his eyes,
> Which flamed like suns beneath his turban cloth,
> Arm'd was he with a noose,

who carries off the soul of the dead husband, the wife tenaciously following, and—by the resistless charm of perfect poetic recitation!—eventually redeeming her captive mate.)

I remember how enthusiastically William H. Seward, in his last days, once expatiated on these themes, from his travels in Turkey, Egypt, and Asia Minor, finding the oldest Biblical narratives exactly illustrated there to-day with apparently no break or change along three thousand years—the veil'd women, the costumes, the gravity and simplicity, all the manners just the same. The veteran Trelawney said he found the only real *nobleman* of the world in a good average specimen of the mid-aged or elderly Oriental. In the East the grand figure, always leading, is the *old man,* majestic, with flowing beard, paternal, &c. In Europe and America, it is, as we know, the young fellow—in novels, a handsome and interesting hero, more or less juvenile—in operas, a tenor with blooming cheeks, black mustache, superficial animation, and perhaps good lungs, but no more depth than skim milk. But reading folks probably get their information of those Bible areas and current peoples, as depicted in print by English and French cads, the most shallow, impudent, supercilious brood on earth.

I have said nothing yet of the cumulus of associations (perfectly legitimate parts of its influence, and finally in many respects the dominant parts) of the Bible as a poetic entity, and of every portion of it. Not the old edifice only—the congeries also of events and struggles and surroundings, of which it has been the scene and motive—even the horrors, dreads, deaths. How many ages and generations have brooded and wept and agonized over this book! What untellable joys and ecstasies—what support to martyrs at the stake—from it. (No really great song can ever attain full purport till long after the death of its singer—till it has accrued and incorporated the many passions, many joys and sorrows, it has itself arous'd.) To what myriads has it been the shore and rock of safety—the refuge from driving tempest and wreck! Translated in all languages, how it has united this diverse world! Of civilized lands to-day, whose of our retrospects has it not interwoven and link'd and permeated? Not only does it bring us what is clasp'd within its covers; nay, that is the least of what it brings. Of its thousands, there is not a verse, not a word, but is thick-studded with human emotions, successions of fathers and sons, mothers and daughters, of our own antecedents, inseparable from that background of us, on which, phantasmal as it is, all that we are to-day inevitably depends—our ancestry, our past.

Strange, but true, that the principal factor in cohering the nations, eras and paradoxes of the globe, by giving them a common platform of two or three great ideas, a commonalty of origin, and projecting kosmic brotherhood, the dream of all hope, all time—that the long trains, gestations, attempts and failures, resulting in the New World, and in modern solidarity and politics—are to be identified and resolv'd back into a collection of old poetic lore, which, more than any one thing else, has been the axis of civilization and history through thousands of years—and except for which this America of ours, with its polity and essentials, could not now be existing.

No true bard will ever contravene the Bible. If the time ever comes when iconoclasm does its extremest in one direction against the Books of the Bible in its present form, the collection must still survive in another, and dominate just as much as hitherto, or more than hitherto, through its divine and primal poetic structure. To me, that is the living and definite element-principle of the work, evolving everything else. Then the continuity; the oldest and newest Asiatic utterance and character, and all between, holding together, like the apparition of the sky, and coming to us the same. Even to our Nineteenth Century here are the fountainheads of song.

From *November Boughs,* 1888.

Impressions of America

by OSCAR WILDE [1856–1900]

I FEAR I CANNOT picture America as altogether an Elysium—perhaps, from the ordinary standpoint, I know but little about the country. I cannot give its latitude or longtitude; I cannot compute the value of its dry goods, and I have no very close acquaintance with its politics. These are matters which may not interest you, and they certainly are not interesting to me.

The first thing that struck me on landing in America was that if the Americans are not the most well-dressed people in the world, they are the most comfortably dressed. Men are seen there with the dreadful chimney-pot hat, but there are very few hatless men; men wear the shocking swallow-tail coat, but few are to be seen with no coat at all. There is an air of comfort in the appearance of the people which is a marked contrast to that seen in this country, where, too often, people are seen in close contact with rags.

The next thing particularly noticeable is that everybody seems in a hurry to catch a train. This is a state of things which is not favourable to poetry or romance. Had Romeo or Juliet been in a constant state of anxiety about trains, or had their minds been agitated by the question of return-tickets, Shakespeare could not have given us those lovely balcony scenes which are so full of poetry and pathos.

America is the noisest country that ever existed. One is waked up in the morning, not by the singing of the nightingale, but by the steam whistle. It is surprising that the sound practical sense of the Americans does not reduce this intolerable noise. All Art depends upon exquisite and delicate sensibility, and such continual turmoil must ultimately be destructive of the musical faculty.

There is not so much beauty to be found in American cities as in Oxford, Cambridge, Salisbury or Winchester, where are lovely relics of a beautiful age; but still there is a good deal of beauty to be seen in them now and then, but only where the American has not attempted to create it. Where the Americans have attempted to produce beauty they have signally failed. A remarkable characteristic of the Americans is the manner in which they have applied science to modern life.

This is apparent in the most cursory stroll through New York. In England an inventor is regarded almost as a crazy man, and in too many instances invention ends in disappointment and poverty. In America an inventor is honoured, help is forthcoming, and the exercise of ingenuity, the application of science to the work of man, is there the shortest road to wealth. There is no country in the world where machinery is so lovely as in America.

I have always wished to believe that the line of strength and the line of beauty are one. That wish was realised when I contemplated American machinery. It was not until I had seen the water-works at Chicago that I realised the wonders of machinery; the rise and fall of the steel rods, the symmetrical motion of great wheels is the most beautifully rhythmic thing I have ever seen. One is impressed in America, but not favourably impressed, by the inordinate size of everything. The country seems to try to bully one into a belief in its power by its impressive bigness.

I was disappointed with Niagara—most people must be disappointed with Niagara. Every American bride is taken there, and the sight of the stupendous waterfall must be one of the earliest, if not the keenest, disappointments in American married life. One sees it under bad conditions, very far away, the point of view not showing the splendour of the water. To appreciate it really one has to see it from underneath the fall, and to do that it is necessary to be dressed in a yellow oil-skin, which is as ugly as a mackintosh —and I hope none of you ever wears one. It is a consolation to know, however, that such an artist as Madame Bernhardt has not only worn that yellow, ugly dress, but has been photographed in it.

Perhaps the most beautiful part of America is the West, to reach which, however, involves a journey by rail of six days, racing along tied to an ugly tin-kettle of a steam engine. I found but poor consolation for this journey in the fact that the boys who infest the cars and sell everything that one can eat—or should not eat— were selling editions of my poems vilely printed on a kind of grey blotting paper, for the low price of ten cents. Calling these boys on one side I told them that though poets like to be popular they desire to be paid, and selling editions of my poems without giving me a profit is dealing a blow at literature which must have a disastrous effect on poetical aspirants. The invariable reply that they made was that they themselves made a profit out of the transaction and that was all they cared about.

It is a popular superstition that in America a visitor is invariably addressed as "Stranger." I was never once addressed as "Stranger." When I went to Texas I was called "Captain"; when I got to the centre of the country I was addressed as "Colonel," and, on arriving at the borders of Mexico, as "General." On the whole, however, "Sir," the old English method of addressing people, is the most common.

It is, perhaps, worth while to note that what many people call Americanisms are really old English expressions which have lingered in our colonies while they have been lost in our own country. Many people imagine that the term "I guess," which is so common in America, is purely an American expression, but it was used by John Locke in his work on "The Understanding," just as we now use "I think." *

It is in the colonies, and not in the mother country, that the old life of the country really exists. If one wants to realise what English Puritanism is—not at its worst (when it is very bad), but at its best, and then it is not very good—I do not think one can find much of it in England, but much can be found about Boston and Massachusetts. We have got rid of it. America still preserves it, to be, I hope, a short-lived curiosity.

San Francisco is a really beautiful city. China Town, peopled by Chinese labourers, is the most artistic town I have ever come across. The people—strange, melancholy Orientals, whom many people would call common, and they are certainly very poor—have determined that they will have nothing about them that is not beautiful. In the Chinese restaurant, where these navvies meet to have supper in the evening, I found them drinking tea out of china cups as delicate as the petals of a rose-leaf, whereas at the gaudy hotels I was supplied with a delft cup an inch and a half thick. When the Chinese bill was presented it was made out on rice paper, the account being done in Indian ink as fantastically as if an artist had been etching little birds on a fan.

Salt Lake City contains only two buildings of note, the chief being the Tabernacle, which is in the shape of a soup-kettle. It is decorated by the only native artist, and he has treated religious subjects in the naïve spirit of the early Florentine painters, representing people of our own day in the dress of the period side by side with people of Biblical history who are clothed in some romantic costume.

The building next in importance is called the Amelia Palace, in honour of one of Brigham Young's wives. When he died the present president of the Mormons stood up in the Tabernacle and said that it had been revealed to him that he was to have the Amelia

* See *An Essay concerning Human Understanding,* IV. xii. 10.
  A still more striking instance of the use of this expression is to be found in the same writer's *Thoughts concerning Education,* s. 28, where he says: "Once in four and twenty hours, I think, is enough; and nobody, *I guess,* will think it too much."

Palace, and that on this subject there were to be no more revelations of any kind!

From Salt Lake City one travels over the great plains of Colorado, and up the Rocky Mountains, on the top of which is Leadville, the richest city in the world. It has also got the reputation of being the roughest, and every man carries a revolver. I was told that if I went there they would be sure to shoot me or my travelling manager. I wrote and told them that nothing that they could do to my travelling manager would intimidate me. They are miners —men working in metals, so I lectured to them on the Ethics of Art. I read them passages from the autobiography of Benvenuto Cellini and they seemed much delighted. I was reproved by my hearers for not having brought him with me. I explained that he had been dead for some little time which elicited the enquiry: "Who shot him?" They afterwards took me to a dancing saloon where I saw the only rational method of art criticism I have ever come across. Over the piano was printed a notice:

> PLEASE DO NOT SHOOT THE
> PIANIST
> HE IS DOING HIS BEST

The mortality among pianists in that place is marvellous. Then they asked me to supper, and having accepted, I had to descend a mine in a rickety bucket in which it was impossible to be graceful. Having got into the heart of the mountain I had supper, the first course being whiskey, the second whiskey, and the third whiskey.

I went to the Theatre to lecture and was informed that just before I went there two men had been seized for committing a murder, and in that theatre they had been brought on to the stage at eight o'clock in the evening, and then and there tried and executed before a crowded audience. But I found these miners very charming and not at all rough.

Among the more elderly inhabitants of the South I found a melancholy tendency to date every event of importance by the late war. "How beautiful the moon is to-night," I once remarked to a gentleman who was standing next to me. "Yes," was his reply, "but you should have seen it before the war."

So infinitesimal did I find the knowledge of Art, west of the Rocky Mountains, that an art patron—one who in his day had been a miner—actually sued the railroad company for damages because the plaster cast of Venus of Milo, which he had imported from Paris, had been delivered minus the arms. And, what is more surprising still, he gained his case and the damages.

Pennsylvania, with its rocky gorges and woodland scenery, reminded me of Switzerland. The prairies reminded me of a piece of blotting paper.

The Spanish and French have left behind them memorials in the beauty of their names. All the cities that have beautiful names derive them from the Spanish or the French. The English people give intensely ugly names to places. One place had such an ugly name that I refused to lecture there. It was called Grigsville. Supposing I had founded a School of Art there—fancy "Early Grigsville." Imagine a School of Art teaching "Grigsville Renaissance."

As for slang I did not hear much of it, though a young lady who had changed her clothes after an afternoon dance did say that "after the heel kick she shifted her day goods."

American youths are pale and precocious, or sallow and supercilious, but American girls are pretty and charming—little oases of pretty unreasonableness in a vast desert of practical common-sense.

Every American girl is entitled to have twelve young men devoted to her. They remain her slaves and she rules them with charming nonchalance.

The men are entirely given to business; they have, as they say, their brains in front of their heads. They are also exceedingly acceptive of new ideas. Their education is practical. We base the education of children entirely on books, but we must give a child a mind before we can instruct the mind. Children have a natural antipathy to books—handicraft should be the basis of education. Boys and girls should be taught to use their hands to make something, and they would be less apt to destroy and be mischievous.

In going to America one learns that poverty is not a necessary accompaniment to civilisation. There at any rate is a country that has no trappings, no pageants and no gorgeous ceremonies. I saw only two processions—one was the Fire Brigade preceded by the Police, the other was the Police preceded by the Fire Brigade.

Every man when he gets to the age of twenty-one is allowed to vote, and thereby immediately acquires his political education. The Americans are the best politically educated people in the world. It is well worth one's while to go to a country which can teach us the beauty of the word FREEDOM and the value of the thing LIBERTY.

1882

How Should One Read a Book? *

by VIRGINIA WOOLF [1882-1941]

IN THE FIRST PLACE, I want to emphasise the note of interrogation at the end of my title. Even if I could answer the question for myself, the answer would apply only to me and not to you. The only advice, indeed, that one person can give another about reading is to take no advice, to follow your own instincts, to use your own reason, to come to your own conclusions. If this is agreed between us, then I feel at liberty to put forward a few ideas and suggestions because you will not allow them to fetter that independence which is the most important quality that a reader can possess. After all, what laws can be laid down about books? The battle of Waterloo was certainly fought on a certain day; but is *Hamlet* a better play than *Lear?* Nobody can say. Each must decide that question for himself. To admit authorities, however heavily furred and gowned, into our libraries and let them tell us how to read, what to read, what value to place upon what we read, is to destroy the spirit of freedom which is the breath of those sanctu-

* A paper read at a School.

aries. Everywhere else we may be bound by laws and conventions
—there we have none.

But to enjoy freedom, if the platitude is pardonable, we have of
course to control ourselves. We must not squander our powers,
helplessly and ignorantly, squirting half the house in order to
water a single rose-bush; we must train them, exactly and powerfully, here on the very spot. This, it may be, is one of the first difficulties that faces us in a library. What is "the very spot"? There
may well seem to be nothing but a conglomeration and huddle of
confusion. Poems and novels, histories and memoirs, dictionaries
and blue-books; books written in all languages by men and women
of all tempers, races, and ages jostle each other on the shelf. And
outside the donkey brays, the women gossip at the pump, the colts
gallop across the fields. Where are we to begin? How are we to
bring order into this multitudinous chaos and so get the deepest
and widest pleasure from what we read?

It is simple enough to say that since books have classes—fiction,
biography, poetry—we should separate them and take from each
what it is right that each should give us. Yet few people ask from
books what books can give us. Most commonly we come to books
with blurred and divided minds, asking of fiction that it shall be
true, of poetry that it shall be false, of biography that it shall be
flattering, of history that it shall enforce our own prejudices. If
we could banish all such preconceptions when we read, that would
be an admirable beginning. Do not dictate to your author; try to
become him. Be his fellow-worker and accomplice. If you hang
back, and reserve and criticise at first, you are preventing yourself
from getting the fullest possible value from what you read. But if
you open your mind as widely as possible, then signs and hints of
almost imperceptible fineness, from the twist and turn of the first
sentences, will bring you into the presence of a human being unlike any other. Steep yourself in this, acquaint yourself with this,
and soon you will find that your author is giving you, or attempting to give you, something far more definite. The thirty-two chapters of a novel—if we consider how to read a novel first—are an attempt to make something as formed and controlled as a building:
but words are more impalpable than bricks; reading is a longer

and more complicated process than seeing. Perhaps the quickest way to understand the elements of what a novelist is doing is not to read, but to write; to make your own experiment with the dangers and difficulties of words. Recall, then, some event that has left a distinct impression on you—how at the corner of the street, perhaps, you passed two people talking. A tree shook; an electric light danced; the tone of the talk was comic, but also tragic; a whole vision, an entire conception, seemed contained in that moment.

But when you attempt to reconstruct it in words, you will find that it breaks into a thousand conflicting impressions. Some must be subdued; others emphasized; in the process you will lose, probably, all grasp upon the emotion itself. Then turn from your blurred and littered pages to the opening pages of some great novelist—Defoe, Jane Austen, Hardy. Now you will be better able to appreciate their mastery. It is not merely that we are in the presence of a different person—Defoe, Jane Austen, or Thomas Hardy—but that we are living in a different world. Here, in *Robinson Crusoe,* we are trudging a plain high road; one thing happens after another; the fact and the order of the fact is enough. But if the open air and adventure mean everything to Defoe they mean nothing to Jane Austen. Hers is the drawing-room, and people talking, and by the many mirrors of their talk revealing their characters. And if, when we have accustomed ourselves to the drawing-room and its reflections, we turn to Hardy, we are once more spun round. The moors are round us and the stars are above our heads. The other side of the mind is now exposed—the dark side that comes uppermost in solitude, not the light side that shows in company. Our relations are not towards people, but toward Nature and destiny. Yet different as these worlds are, each is consistent with itself. The maker of each is careful to observe the laws of his own perspective, and however great a strain they may put upon us they will never confuse us, as lesser writers so frequently do, by introducing two different kinds of reality into the same book. Thus to go from one great novelist to another—from Jane Austen to Hardy, from Peacock to Trollope, from Scott to Meredith—is to be wrenched and uprooted; to be thrown this way and then that. To read a novel is a difficult and complex art. You must be

capable not only of great fineness of perception, but of great bold-
ness of imagination if you are going to make use of all that the
novelist—the great artist—gives you.

But a glance at the heterogeneous company on the shelf will
show you that writers are very seldom "great artists"; far more
often a book makes no claim to be a work of art at all. These biographies and autobiographies, for example, lives of great men, of
men long dead and forgotten, that stand cheek by jowl with the
novels and poems, are we to refuse to read them because they are
not "art"? Or shall we read them, but read them in a different way,
with a different aim? Shall we read them in the first place to satisfy
that curiosity which possesses us sometimes when in the evening
we linger in front of a house where the lights are lit and the blinds
are not yet drawn, and each floor of the house shows us a different
section of human life in being? Then we are consumed with curiosity about the lives of these people—the servants gossiping, the
gentlemen dining, the girl dressing for a party, the old woman at
the window with her knitting. Who are they, what are they, what
are their names, their occupations, their thoughts, and adventures?

Biographies and memoirs answer such questions, light up innumerable such houses; they show us people going about their
daily affairs, toiling, failing, succeeding, eating, hating, loving,
until they die. And sometimes as we watch, the house fades and
the iron railings vanish and we are out at sea; we are hunting, sailing, fighting; we are among savages and soldiers; we are taking
part in great campaigns. Or if we like to stay here in England, in
London, still the scene changes; the street narrows; the house becomes small, cramped, diamond-paned, and malodorous. We see
a poet, Donne, driven from such a house because the walls were so
thin that when the children cried their voices cut through them.
We can follow him, through the paths that lie in the pages of books,
to Twickenham; to Lady Bedford's Park, a famous meeting-
ground for nobles and poets; and then turn our steps to Wilton, the
great house under the downs, and hear Sidney read the *Arcadia* to
his sister; and ramble among the very marshes and see the very
herons that figure in that famous romance; and then again travel
north with that other Lady Pembroke, Anne Clifford, to her wild

moors, or plunge into the city and control our merriment at the
sight of Gabriel Harvey in his black velvet suit arguing about
poetry with Spenser. Nothing is more fascinating than to grope
and stumble in the alternate darkness and splendour of Elizabethan
London. But there is no staying there. The Temples and the
Swifts, the Harleys and the St. Johns beckon us on; hour upon
hour can be spent disentangling their quarrels and deciphering
their characters; and when we tire of them we can stroll on, past
a lady in black wearing diamonds, to Samuel Johnson and Goldsmith and Garrick; or cross the channel, if we like, and meet
Voltaire and Diderot, Madame du Deffand; and so back to England and Twickenham—how certain places repeat themselves and
certain names!—where Lady Bedford had her Park once and Pope
lived later, to Walpole's home at Strawberry Hill. But Walpole
introduces us to such a swarm of new acquaintances, there are so
many houses to visit and bells to ring that we may well hesitate for
a moment, on the Miss Berrys' doorstep, for example, when behold,
up comes Thackeray; he is the friend of the woman whom Walpole
loved; so that merely by going from friend to friend, from garden
to garden, from house to house, we have passed from one end of
English literature to another and wake to find ourselves here again
in the present, if we can so differentiate this moment from all that
have gone before. This, then, is one of the ways in which we can
read these lives and letters; we can make them light up the many
windows of the past; we can watch the famous dead in their familiar habits and fancy sometimes that we are very close and can
surprise their secrets, and sometimes we may pull out a play or a
poem that they have written and see whether it reads differently
in the presence of the author. But this again rouses other questions.
How far, we must ask ourselves, is a book influenced by its writer's
life—how far is it safe to let the man interpret the writer? How far
shall we resist or give way to the sympathies and antipathies that
the man himself rouses in us—so sensitive are words, so receptive
of the character of the author? These are questions that press upon
us when we read lives and letters, and we must answer them for
ourselves, for nothing can be more fatal than to be guided by the
preferences of others in a matter so personal.

But also we can read such books with another aim, not to throw light on literature, not to become familiar with famous people, but to refresh and exercise our own creative powers. Is there not an open window on the right hand of the bookcase? How delightful to stop reading and look out! How stimulating the scene is, in its unconsciousness, its irrelevance, its perpetual movement—the colts galloping round the field, the woman filling her pail at the well, the donkey throwing back his head and emitting his long, acrid moan. The greater part of any library is nothing but the record of such fleeting moments in the lives of men, women, and donkeys. Every literature, as it grows old, has its rubbish-heap, its record of vanished moments and forgotten lives told in faltering and feeble accents that have perished. But if you give yourself up to the delight of rubbish-reading you will be surprised, indeed you will be overcome, by the relics of human life that have been cast out to moulder. It may be one letter—but what a vision it gives! It may be a few sentences—but what vistas they suggest! Sometimes a whole story will come together with such beautiful humour and pathos and completeness that it seems as if a great novelist had been at work, yet it is only an old actor, Tate Wilkinson, remembering the strange story of Captain Jones; it is only a young subaltern serving under Arthur Wellesley and falling in love with a pretty girl at Lisbon; it is only Maria Allen letting fall her sewing in the empty drawing-room and sighing how she wishes she had taken Dr. Burney's good advice and had never eloped with her Rishy. None of this has any value; it is negligible in the extreme; yet how absorbing it is now and again to go through the rubbish-heaps and find rings and scissors and broken noses buried in the huge past and try to piece them together while the colt gallops round the field, the woman fills her pail at the well, and the donkey brays.

But we tire of rubbish-reading in the long run. We tire of searching for what is needed to complete the half-truth which is all that the Wilkinsons, the Bunburys, and the Maria Allens are able to offer us. They had not the artist's power of mastering and eliminating; they could not tell the whole truth even about their own lives; they have disfigured the story that might have been so shapely. Facts are all that they can offer us, and facts are a very inferior form of fiction. Thus the desire grows upon us to have done with half-statements and approximations; to cease from searching out the minute shades of human character, to enjoy the greater abstractness, the purer truth of fiction. Thus we create the mood, intense and generalised, unaware of detail, but stressed by some regular, recurrent beat, whose natural expression is poetry; and that is the time to read poetry when we are almost able to write it.

> Western wind, when wilt thou blow?
> The small rain down can rain.
> Christ, if my love were in my arms,
> And I in my bed again!

The impact of poetry is so hard and direct that for the moment there is no other sensation except that of the poem itself. What profound depths we visit then—how sudden and complete is our immersion! There is nothing here to catch hold of; nothing to stay us in our flight. The illusion of fiction is gradual; its effects are prepared; but who when they read these four lines stops to ask who wrote them, or conjures up the thought of Donne's house or Sidney's secretary; or enmeshes them in the intricacy of the past and the succession of generations? The poet is always our contemporary. Our being for the moment is centred and constricted, as in any violent shock of personal emotion. Afterwards, it is true, the sensation begins to spread in wider rings through our minds; remoter senses are reached; these begin to sound and to comment and we are aware of echoes and reflections. The intensity of poetry covers an immense range of emotion. We have only to compare the force and directness of

> I shall fall like a tree, and find my grave,
> Only remembering that I grieve,

with the wavering modulation of

> Minutes are numbered by the fall of sands,
> As by an hour glass; the span of time
> Doth waste us to our graves, and we look on it;

An age of pleasure, revelled out, comes home
At last, and ends in sorrow; but the life,
Weary of riot, numbers every sand,
Wailing in sighs, until the last drop down,
So to conclude calamity in rest,

or place the meditative calm of

whether we be young or old,
Our destiny, our being's heart and home,
Is with infinitude, and only there;
With hope it is, hope that can never die,
Effort, and expectation, and desire,
And something evermore about to be,

beside the complete and inexhaustible loveliness of

The moving Moon went up the sky,
And nowhere did abide:
Softly she was going up,
And a star or two beside—

or the splendid fantasy of

And the woodland haunter
Shall not cease to saunter
    When, far down some glade,
Of the great world's burning,
One soft flame upturning
Seems, to his discerning,
    Crocus in the shade,

to bethink us of the varied art of the poet; his power to make us at once actors and spectators; his power to run his hand into character as if it were a glove, and be Falstaff or Lear; his power to condense, to widen, to state, once and for ever.

"We have only to compare"—with those words the cat is out of the bag, and the true complexity of reading is admitted. The first process, to receive impressions with the utmost understanding, is only half the process of reading; it must be completed, if we are to get the whole pleasure from a book, by another. We must pass judgment upon these multitudinous impressions; we must make of these fleeting shapes one that is hard and lasting. But not directly. Wait for the dust of reading to settle; for the conflict and the questioning to die down; walk, talk, pull the dead petals from a rose, or fall asleep. Then suddenly without our willing it, for it is thus that Nature undertakes these transitions, the book will return, but differently. It will float to the top of the mind as a whole. And the book as a whole is different from the book received currently in separate phrases. Details now fit themselves into their places. We see the shape from start to finish; it is a barn, a pig-sty, or a cathedral. Now then we can compare book with book as we compare building with building. But this act of comparison means that our attitude has changed; we are no longer the friends of the writer, but his judges; and just as we cannot be too sympathetic as friends, so as judges we cannot be too severe. Are they not criminals, books that have wasted our time and sympathy; are they not the most insidious enemies of society, corrupters, defilers, the writers of false books, faked books, books that fill the air with decay and disease? Let us then be severe in our judgments; let us compare each book with the greatest of its kind. There they hang in the mind the shapes of the books we have read solidified by the judgments we have passed on them—*Robinson Crusoe, Emma, The Return of the Native.* Compare the novels with these—even the latest and least of novels has a right to be judged with the best. And so with poetry—when the intoxication of rhythm has died down and the splendour of words has faded, a visionary shape will return to us and this must be compared with *Lear,* with *Phèdre,* with *The Prelude;* or if not with these, with whatever is the best or seems to us to be the best in its own kind. And we may be sure that the newness of new poetry and fiction is its most superficial quality and that we have only to alter slightly, not to recast, the standards by which we have judged the old.

It would be foolish, then, to pretend that the second part of reading, to judge, to compare, is as simple as the first—to open the mind wide to the fast flocking of innumerable impressions. To continue reading without the book before you, to hold one

shadow-shape against another, to have read widely enough and
with enough understanding to make such comparisons alive and
illuminating—that is difficult; it is still more difficult to press
further and to say, "Not only is the book of this sort, but it is
of this value; here it fails; here it succeeds; this is bad; that is
good." To carry out this part of a reader's duty needs such imagination, insight, and learning that it is hard to conceive any one
mind sufficiently endowed; impossible for the most self-confident
to find more than the seeds of such powers in himself. Would it
not be wiser, then, to remit this part of reading and to allow the
critics, the gowned and furred authorities of the library, to decide the question of the book's absolute value for us? Yet how
impossible! We may stress the value of sympathy; we may try
to sink our own identity as we read. But we know that we cannot sympathise wholly or immerse ourselves wholly; there is
always a demon in us who whispers, "I hate, I love," and we
cannot silence him. Indeed, it is precisely because we hate and
we love that our relation with the poets and novelists is so intimate
that we find the presence of another person intolerable. And even
if the results are abhorrent and our judgments are wrong, still
our taste, the nerve of sensation that sends shocks through us, is
our chief illuminant; we learn through feeling; we cannot suppress our own idiosyncrasy without impoverishing it. But as time
goes on perhaps we can train our taste; perhaps we can make it
submit to some control. When it has fed greedily and lavishly
upon books of all sorts—poetry, fiction, history, biography—and
has stopped reading and looked for long spaces upon the variety,
the incongruity of the living word, we shall find that it is changing a little; it is not so greedy, it is more reflective. It will begin
to bring us not merely judgments on particular books, but it will
tell us that there is a quality common to certain books. Listen, it
will say, what shall we call *this*? And it will read us perhaps *Lear*
and then perhaps the *Agamemnon* in order to bring out that
common quality. Thus, with our taste to guide us, we shall
venture beyond the particular book in search of qualities that
group books together; we shall give them names and thus frame
a rule that brings order into our perceptions. We shall gain a

further and a rarer pleasure from that discrimination. But as a rule only lives when it is perpetually broken by contact with the books themselves—nothing is easier and more stultifying than to make rules which exist out of touch with facts, in a vacuum —now at last, in order to steady ourselves in this difficult attempt, it may be well to turn to the very rare writers who are able to enlighten us upon literature as an art. Coleridge and Dryden and Johnson, in their considered criticism, the poets and novelists themselves in their unconsidered sayings, are often surprisingly relevant; they light up and solidify the vague ideas that have been tumbling in the misty depths of our minds. But they are only able to help us if we come to them laden with questions and suggestions won honestly in the course of our own reading. They can do nothing for us if we herd ourselves under their authority and lie down like sheep in the shade of a hedge. We can only understand their ruling when it comes in conflict with our own and vanquishes it.

If this is so, if to read a book as it should be read calls for the rarest qualities of imagination, insight, and judgment, you may perhaps conclude that literature is a very complex art and that it is unlikely that we shall be able, even after a lifetime of reading, to make any valuable contribution to its criticism. We must remain readers; we shall not put on the further glory that belongs to those rare beings who are also critics. But still we have our responsibilities as readers and even our importance. The standards we raise and the judgment we pass steal into the air and become part of the atmosphere which writers breathe as they work. An influence is created which tells upon them even if it never finds its way into print. And that influence, if it were well instructed, vigorous and individual and sincere, might be of great value now when criticism is necessarily in abeyance; when books pass in review like the procession of animals in a shooting gallery, and the critic has only one second in which to load and aim and shoot and may well be pardoned if he mistakes rabbits for tigers, eagles for barndoor fowls, or misses altogether and wastes his shot upon some peaceful cow grazing in a further field. If behind the erratic gunfire of the press the author felt that there was another kind of criticism, the opinion of people reading for the love of reading, slowly and unprofessionally, and judging with great sympathy and yet with great severity, might this not improve the quality of his work? And if by our means books were to become stronger, richer, and more varied, that would be an end worth reaching.

Yet who reads to bring about an end, however desirable? Are there not some pursuits that we practise because they are good in themselves, and some pleasures that are final? And is not this among them? I have sometimes dreamt, at least, that when the Day of Judgment dawns and the great conquerors and lawyers and statesmen come to receive their rewards—their crowns, their laurels, their names carved indelibly upon im- perishable marble—the Almighty will turn to Peter and will say, not without a certain envy when He sees us coming with our books under our arms, "Look, these need no reward. We have nothing to give them here. They have loved reading."

From *The Common Reader,*
Second Series, 1932.

Magic

by WILLIAM BUTLER YEATS [1865-1939]

I

I BELIEVE in the practice and philosophy of what we have agreed to call magic, in what I must call the evocation of spirits, though I do not know what they are, in the power of creating magical illusions, in the visions of truth in the depths of the mind when the eyes are closed; and I believe in three doctrines, which have, as I think, been handed down from early times, and been the founda- tions of nearly all magical practices. These doctrines are—

(1) That the borders of our mind are ever shifting, and that

many minds can flow into one another, as it were, and create or reveal a single mind, a single energy.

(2) That the borders of our memories are as shifting, and that our memories are a part of one great memory, the memory of Nature herself.

(3) That this great mind and great memory can be evoked by symbols.

I often think I would put this belief in magic from me if I could, for I have come to see or to imagine, in men and women, in houses, in handicrafts, in nearly all sights and sounds, a certain evil, a certain ugliness, that comes from the slow perishing through the centuries of a quality of mind that made this belief and its evidences common over the world.

II

Some ten or twelve years ago, a man with whom I have since quarrelled for sound reasons, a very singular man who had given his life to studies other men despised, asked me and an acquaintance, who is now dead, to witness a magical work. He lived a little way from London, and on the way my acquaintance told me that he did not believe in magic, but that a novel of Bulwer Lytton's had taken such a hold upon his imagination that he was going to give much of his time and all his thought to magic. He longed to believe in it, and had studied, though not learnedly, geomancy, astrology, chiromancy, and much cabalistic symbolism, and yet doubted if the soul outlived the body. He awaited the magical work full of scepticism. He expected nothing more than an air of romance, an illusion as of the stage, that might capture the consenting imagination for an hour. The evoker of spirits and his beautiful wife received us in a little house, on the edge of some kind of garden or park belonging to an eccentric rich man, whose curiosities he arranged and dusted, and he made his evocation in a long room that had a raised place on the floor at one end, a kind of dais, but was furnished meagrely and cheaply. I sat with my acquaintance in the middle of the room, and the evoker of spirits on the dais, and his wife between us and him. He held a wooden mace in his hand, and turning to a tablet of many-coloured squares, with a number on each of the squares, that stood near him on a chair, he repeated a form of words. Almost at once my imagination began to move of itself and to bring before me vivid images that, though never too vivid to be imagination, as I had always understood it, had yet a motion of their own, a life I could not change or shape. I remember seeing a number of white figures, and wondering whether their mitred heads had been suggested by the mitred head of the mace, and then, of a sudden, the image of my acquaintance in the midst of them. I told what I had seen, and the evoker of spirits cried in a deep voice, "Let him be blotted out," and as he said it the image of my acquaintance vanished, and the evoker of spirits or his wife saw a man dressed in black with a curious square cap standing among the white figures. It was my acquaintance, the seeress said, as he had been in a past life, the life that had moulded his present, and that life would now unfold before us. I too seemed to see the man with a strange vividness. The story unfolded itself chiefly before the mind's eye of the seeress, but sometimes I saw what she described before I heard her description. She thought the man in black was perhaps a Fleming of the sixteenth century, and I could see him pass along narrow streets till he came to a narrow door with some rusty iron-work above it. He went in, and wishing to find out how far we had one vision among us, I kept silent when I saw a dead body lying upon the table within the door. The seeress described him going down a long hall and up into what she called a pulpit, and beginning to speak. She said, "He is a clergyman, I can hear his words. They sound like Low Dutch." Then after a little silence, "No, I am wrong. I can see the listeners; he is a doctor lecturing among his pupils." I said, "Do you see anything near the door?" and she said, "Yes, I see a subject for dissection." Then we saw him go out again into the narrow streets, I following the story of the seeress, sometimes merely following her words, but sometimes seeing for myself. My acquaintance saw nothing; I think he was forbidden to see, it being his own life, and I think could not in any case. His imagination had no will of its own. Presently the man in black went into a house with two gables facing the road, and up some stairs into a room where a humpbacked woman gave him a key; and then along a corridor, and down some stairs into a large cellar full of retorts and strange vessels of all kinds. Here he seemed to stay a long while, and one saw him eating bread that he took down from a shelf. The evoker of spirits and the seeress began to speculate about the man's character and habits, and decided, from a visionary impression, that his mind was absorbed in naturalism, but that his imagination had been excited by stories of the marvels wrought by magic in past times, and that he was trying to copy them by naturalistic means. Presently one of them saw him go to a vessel that stood over a slow fire, and take out of the vessel a thing wrapped up in numberless cloths, which he partly unwrapped, showing at length what looked like the image of a man made by somebody who could not model. The evoker of spirits said that the man in black was trying to make flesh by chemical means, and though he had not succeeded, his brooding had drawn so many evil spirits about him, that the image was partly alive. He could see it moving a little where it lay upon a table. At that moment I heard something like little squeals, but kept silent, as when I saw the dead body. In a moment more the seeress said, "I hear little squeals." Then the evoker of spirits heard them, but said, "They are not squeals; he is pouring a red liquid out of a retort through a slit in the cloth; the slit is over the mouth of the image and the liquid is gurgling in rather a curious way." Weeks seemed to pass by hurriedly, and somebody saw the man still busy in his cellar. Then more weeks seemed to pass, and now we saw him lying sick in a room upstairs, and a man in a conical cap standing beside him. We could see the image too. It was in the cellar, but now it could move feebly about the floor. I saw fainter images of the image passing continually from where it crawled to the man in his bed, and I asked the evoker of spirits what they were. He said, "They are the images of his terror." Presently the man in the conical cap began to speak, but who heard him I cannot remember. He made the sick man get out of bed and walk, leaning upon him, and in much terror till they came to the cellar. There the man in the conical cap made some symbol over the image, which fell back as if asleep, and putting a knife into the other's hand he said, "I have taken from it the magical life, but you must take from it the life you gave." Somebody saw the sick man stoop and sever the head of the image from its body, and then fall as if he had given himself a mortal wound, for he had filled it with his own life. And then the vision changed and fluttered, and he was lying sick again in the room upstairs. He seemed to lie there a long time with the man in the conical cap watching beside him, then, I cannot remember how, the evoker of spirits discovered that though he would in part recover, he would never be well, and that the story had got abroad in the town and shattered his good name. His pupils had left him and men avoided him. He was accursed. He was a magician.

The story was finished, and I looked at my acquaintance. He was white and awe-struck. He said, as nearly as I can remember, "All my life I have seen myself in dreams making a man by some means like that. When I was a child I was always thinking out contrivances for galvanising a corpse into life." Presently he said, "Perhaps my bad health in this life comes from that experiment." I asked if he had read *Frankenstein,* and he answered that he had. He was the only one of us who had, and he had taken no part in the vision.

III

Then I asked to have some past life of mine revealed, and a new evocation was made before the tablet full of little squares. I cannot remember so well who saw this or that detail, for now I was interested in little but the vision itself. I had come to a conclusion about the method. I knew that the vision may be in part common to several people.

A man in chain armour passed through a castle door, and the seeress noticed with surprise the bareness and rudeness of castle rooms. There was nothing of the magnificence or the pageantry she had expected. The man came to a large hall and to a little chapel opening out of it, where a ceremony was taking place. There were six girls dressed in white, who took from the altar some yellow object—I thought it was gold, for though, like my acquaintance, I was told not to see, I could not help seeing. Somebody else thought that it was yellow flowers, and I think the girls, though I cannot remember clearly, laid it between the man's hands. He went out for a time, and as he passed through the great hall one of us, I forget whom, noticed that he passed over two gravestones. Then the vision became broken, but presently he stood in a monk's habit among men-at-arms in the middle of a village reading from a parchment. He was calling villagers about him, and presently he and they and the men-at-arms took ship for some long voyage. The vision became broken again, and when we could see clearly they had come to what seemed the Holy Land. They had begun some kind of sacred labour among palm-trees. The common men among them stood idle, but the gentlemen carried large stones, bringing them from certain directions, from the cardinal points I think, with a ceremonious formality. The evoker of spirits said they must be making some masonic house. His mind, like the minds of so many students of these hidden things, was always running on masonry and discovering it in strange places.

We broke the vision that we might have supper, breaking it with some form of words which I forget. When supper had ended the seeress cried out that while we had been eating they had been building, and that they had built not a masonic house but a great stone cross. And now they had all gone away but the man who had been in chain armour and two monks we had not noticed before. He was standing against the cross, his feet upon two stone rests a little above the ground, and his arms spread out. He seemed to stand there all day, but when night came he went to a little cell, that was beside two other cells. I think they were like the cells I have seen in the Aran Islands, but I cannot be certain. Many days seemed to pass, and all day every day he stood upon the cross, and we never saw anybody there but him and the two monks. Many years seemed to pass, making the vision flutter like a drift of leaves before our eyes, and he grew old and white-haired, and we saw the two monks, old and white-haired, holding him upon the cross. I asked the evoker of spirits why the man stood there, and before he had time to answer I saw two people, a man and a woman, rising like a dream within a dream, before the eyes of the man upon the cross. The evoker of spirits saw them too, and said that one of them held up his arms and they were without hands. I thought of the two gravestones the man in chain mail had passed over in the great hall when he came out of the chapel, and asked the evoker of spirits if the knight was undergoing a penance for violence, and while I was asking him, and he was saying that it might be so but he did not know, the vision, having completed its circle, vanished.

It had not, so far as I could see, the personal significance of the other vision, but it was certainly strange and beautiful, though I alone seemed to see its beauty. Who was it that made the story, if it were but a story? I did not, and the seeress did not, and the evoker of spirits did not and could not. It arose in three minds, for I cannot remember my acquaintance taking any part, and it rose without confusion, and without labour, except the labour of keeping the mind's eye awake, and more swiftly than any pen could have written it out. It may be, as Blake said of one of his poems, that the author was in eternity. In coming years I was to see and hear of many such visions, and though I was not to be convinced, though half convinced once or twice, that they were old lives, in an ordinary sense of the word life, I was to learn that they have almost always some quite definite relation to dominant moods and moulding events in this life. They are, perhaps, in most cases, though the vision I have but just described was not, it seems, among the cases, symbolical histories of these moods and events, or rather symbolical shadows of the impulses that have made them, messages as it were out of the ancestral being of the questioner.

At the time these two visions meant little more to me, if I can remember my feeling at the time, than a proof of the supremacy of imagination, of the power of many minds to become one, overpowering one another by spoken words and by unspoken thought till they have become a single intense, unhesitating energy. One mind was doubtless the master, I thought, but all the minds gave a little, creating or revealing for a moment what I must call a supernatural artist.

IV

Some years afterwards I was staying with some friends in Paris. I had got up before breakfast and gone out to buy a newspaper. I had noticed the servant, a girl who had come from the country some years before, laying the table for breakfast. As I had passed her I had been telling myself one of those long foolish tales which one tells only to oneself. If something had happened that had not happened, I would have hurt my arm, I thought. I saw myself with my arm in a sling in the middle of some childish adventures. I returned with the newspaper and met my host and hostess in the door. The moment they saw me they cried out, "Why, the *bonne* has just told us you had your arm in a sling. We thought something must have happened to you last night, that you had been run over maybe"—or some such words. I had been dining out at the other end of Paris, and had come in after everybody had gone to bed. I had cast my imagination so strongly upon the servant that she had seen it, and with what had appeared to be more than the mind's eye.

One afternoon, about the same time, I was thinking very intently of a certain fellow-student for whom I had a message, which I hesitated about writing. In a couple of days I got a letter from a place some hundreds of miles away where that student was. On the afternoon when I had been thinking so intently I had suddenly appeared there amid a crowd of people in a hotel and as seeming solid as if in the flesh. My fellow-student had seen me, but no one else, and had asked me to come again when the people had gone. I had vanished, but had come again in the middle of the night and given the message. I myself had no knowledge of either apparition.

I could tell of stranger images, of stranger enchantments, of stranger imaginations, cast consciously or unconsciously over as great distances by friends or by myself, were it not that the greater energies of the mind seldom break forth but when the deeps are loosened. They break forth amid events too private or too sacred for public speech, or seem themselves, I know not why, to belong to hidden things. I have written of these breakings forth, these loosenings of the deep, with some care and some detail, but I shall keep my record shut. After all, one can but bear witness less to convince him who won't believe than to protect him who does, as Blake puts it, enduring unbelief and misbelief and ridicule as best one may. I shall be content to show that past times have believed as I do, by quoting Joseph Glanvil's description of the Scholar Gipsy. Joseph Glanvil is dead, and will not mind unbelief and misbelief and ridicule.

The Scholar Gipsy, too, is dead, unless indeed perfectly wise magicians can live till it please them to die, and he is wandering somewhere, even if one cannot see him, as Arnold imagined, "at some lone ale-house in the Berkshire moors, on the warm ingle-bench," or "crossing the stripling Thames at Bablock Hithe," or "trailing his fingers in the cool stream," or "giving store of flowers —the frail-leaf'd white anemone, dark harebells drenched with dew of summer eves," to the girls "who from the distant hamlets come to dance around the Fyfield elm in May," or "sitting upon the river bank o'ergrown," living on through time "with a free onward impulse." This is Joseph Glanvil's story—

There was very lately a lad in the University of Oxford who, being of very pregnant and ready parts and yet wanting the encouragement of preferment, was by his poverty forced to leave his studies there, and to cast himself upon the wide world for a livelihood. Now his necessities growing daily on him, and wanting the help of friends to relieve him, he was at last forced to join himself to a company of vagabond gipsies, whom occasionally he met with, and to follow their trade for a maintenance. . . . After he had been a pretty while exercised in the trade, there chanced to ride by a couple of scholars, who had formerly been of his acquaintance. The scholar had quickly spied out these old friends among the gipsies, and their amazement to see him among such society had well-nigh discovered him; but by a sign he prevented them owning him before that crew, and taking one of them aside privately, desired him with his friend to go to an inn, not far distant, promising there to come to them. They accordingly went thither

and he follows: after their first salutation his friends inquire
how he came to lead so odd a life as that was, and so joined
himself into such a beggarly company. The scholar gipsy having given them an account of the necessity which drove him
to that kind of life, told them that the people he went with
were not such impostors as they were taken for, but that they
had a traditional kind of learning among them and could do
wonders by the power of imagination, and that himself had
learned much of their art and improved it further than themselves could. And to evince the truth of what he told them, he
said he'd remove into another room, leaving them to discourse
together; and upon his return tell them the sense of what they
had talked of; which accordingly he performed, giving them
a full account of what had passed between them in his absence. The scholars being amazed at so unexpected a discovery, earnestly desired him to unriddle the mystery. In which
he gave them satisfaction, by telling them that what he did was
by the power of imagination, his phantasy leading theirs; and
that himself had dictated to them the discourse they had held
together while he was from them; that there were warrantable
ways of heightening the imagination to that pitch as to bend
another's, and that when he had compassed the whole secret,
some parts of which he was yet ignorant of, he intended to
leave their company and give the whole world an account of
what he had learned.

If all who have described events like this have not dreamed, we
should rewrite our histories, for all men, certainly all imaginative
men, must be for ever casting forth enchantments, glamours, illusions; and all men, especially tranquil men who have no powerful
egotistic life, must be continually passing under their power. Our
most elaborate thoughts, elaborate purposes, precise emotions, are
often, as I think, not really ours, but have on a sudden come up,
as it were, out of hell or down out of heaven. The historian should
remember, should he not? angels and devils not less than kings
and soldiers, and plotters and thinkers. What matter if the angel
or devil, as indeed certain old writers believed, first wrapped itself

with an organised shape in some man's imagination? what matter "if God himself only acts or is in existing beings or men," as
Blake believed? we must none the less admit that invisible beings,
far wandering influences, shapes that may have floated from a
hermit of the wilderness, brood over council-chambers and studies
and battle-fields. We should never be certain that it was not some
woman treading in the wine-press who began that subtle change in
men's minds, that powerful movement of thought and imagination about which so many Germans have written; or that the passion, because of which so many countries were given to the sword,
did not begin in the mind of some shepherd boy, lighting up his
eyes for a moment before it ran upon its way.

v

We cannot doubt that barbaric people receive such influences
more visibly and obviously, and in all likelihood more easily and
fully than we do, for our life in cities, which deafens or kills the
passive meditative life, and our education that enlarges the separated, self-moving mind, have made our souls less sensitive. Our
souls that were once naked to the winds of heaven are now thickly
clad, and have learned to build a house and light a fire upon its
hearth, and shut-to the doors and windows. The winds can, indeed,
make us draw near to the fire, or can even lift the carpet and
whistle under the door, but they could do worse out on the plains
long ago. A certain learned man, quoted by Mr. Lang in his *Making of Religion,* contends that the memories of primitive man and
his thoughts of distant places must have had the intensity of hal-
lucination, because there was nothing in his mind to draw his attention away from them—an explanation that does not seem to
me complete—and Mr. Lang goes on to quote certain travellers to
prove that savages live always on the edges of vision. One Lap-
lander who wished to become a Christian, and thought visions but
heathenish, confessed to a traveller, to whom he had given a minute account of many distant events, read doubtless in that traveller's mind, "that he knew not how to make use of his eyes, since
things altogether distant were present to them." I myself could
find in one district in Galway but one man who had not seen

what I can but call spirits, and he was in his dotage. "There is no man mowing a meadow but sees them at one time or another," said a man in a different district.

If I can unintentionally cast a glamour, an enchantment, over persons of our own time who have lived for years in great cities, there is no reason to doubt that men could cast intentionally a far stronger enchantment, a far stronger glamour, over the more sensitive people of ancient times, or that men can still do so where the old order of life remains unbroken. Why should not the Scholar Gipsy cast his spell over his friends? Why should not St. Patrick, or he of whom the story was first told, pass his enemies, he and all his clerics, as a herd of deer? Why should not enchanters like him in the *Morte d'Arthur* make troops of horse seem but grey stones? Why should not the Roman soldiers, though they came of a civilisation which was ceasing to be sensitive to these things, have trembled for a moment before the enchantments of the Druids of Mona? Why should not the Jesuit father, or the Count Saint Germain, or whoever the tale was first told of, have really seemed to leave the city in a coach and four and by all the Twelve Gates at once? Why should not Moses and the enchanters of Pharaoh have made their staffs as the medicine men of many primitive peoples make their pieces of old rope seem like devouring serpents? Why should not that mediæval enchanter have made summer and all its blossoms seem to break forth in middle winter?

May we not learn some day to rewrite our histories, when they touch upon these things?

Men who are imaginative writers to-day may well have preferred to influence the imagination of others more directly in past times. Instead of learning their craft with paper and a pen they may have sat for hours imagining themselves to be stocks and stones and beasts of the wood, till the images were so vivid that the passers-by became but a part of the imagination of the dreamer, and wept or laughed or ran away as he would have them. Have not poetry and music arisen, as it seems, out of the sounds the enchanters made to help their imagination to enchant, to charm, to bind with a spell themselves and the passers-by? These very words, a chief part of all praises of music or poetry, still cry to us their origin. And

just as the musician or the poet enchants and charms and binds
with a spell his own mind when he would enchant the mind of
others, so did the enchanter create or reveal for himself as well as
for others the supernatural artist or genius, the seeming transitory
mind made out of many minds, whose work I saw, or thought
I saw, in that suburban house. He kept the doors too, as it seems, of
those less transitory minds, the genius of the family, the genius of
the tribe, or it may be, when he was mighty-souled enough, the
genius of the world. Our history speaks of opinions and discov-
eries, but in ancient times when, as I think, men had their eyes ever
upon those doors, history spoke of commandments and revelations.
They looked as carefully and as patiently towards Sinai and its
thunders as we look towards parliaments and laboratories. We are
always praising men in whom the individual life has come to
perfection, but they were always praising the one mind, their
foundation of all perfection.

VI

I once saw a young Irish woman, fresh from a convent school,
cast into a profound trance, though not by a method known to any
hypnotist. In her waking state she thought the apple of Eve was
the kind of apple you can buy at the greengrocer's, but in her
trance she saw the Tree of Life with ever-sighing souls moving in
its branches instead of sap, and among its leaves all the fowl of the
air, and on its highest bough one white fowl wearing a crown.
When I went home I took from the shelf a translation of *The Book
of Concealed Mystery*,* an old Jewish book, and cutting the pages
came upon this passage, which I cannot think I had ever read:
"The Tree, . . . is the Tree of the Knowledge of Good and of
Evil . . . in its branches the birds lodge and build their nests,
the souls and the angels have their place."

I once saw a young Church of Ireland man, a bank clerk in the
west of Ireland, thrown in a like trance. I have no doubt that he,
too, was quite certain that the apple of Eve was a greengrocer's
apple, and yet he saw the tree and heard the souls sighing through
its branches, and saw apples with human faces, and laying his ear

* Translated by Mathers in *The Kabbalah Unveiled*.

to an apple heard a sound as of fighting hosts within. Presently he strayed from the tree and came to the edge of Eden, and there he found himself not by the wilderness he had learned of at the Sunday-school, but upon the summit of a great mountain, of a mountain "two miles high." The whole summit, in contradiction to all that would have seemed probable to his waking mind, was a great walled garden. Some years afterwards I found a mediæval diagram, which pictured Eden as a walled garden upon a high mountain.

Where did these intricate symbols come from? Neither I nor the one or two people present or the seers had ever seen, I am convinced, the description in *The Book of Concealed Mystery,* or the mediæval diagram. Remember that the images appeared in a moment perfect in all their complexity. If one can imagine that the seers or that I myself or another had indeed read of these images and forgotten it, that the supernatural artist's knowledge of what was in our buried memories accounted for these visions, there are numberless other visions to account for. One cannot go on believing in improbable knowledge for ever. For instance, I find in my diary that on December 27, 1897, a seer, to whom I had given a certain old Irish symbol, saw Brigit, the goddess, holding out "a glittering and wriggling serpent," and yet I feel certain that neither I nor he knew anything of her association with the serpent until *Carmina Gadelica* was published a few months ago. And an old Irish woman who can neither read nor write has described to me a woman dressed like Dian, with helmet, and short skirt and sandals, and what seemed to be buskins. Why, too, among all the countless stories of visions that I have gathered in Ireland, or that a friend has gathered for me, are there none that mix the dress of different periods? The seers when they are but speaking from tradition will mix everything together, and speak of Finn mac Cool going to the Assizes at Cork. Almost every one who has ever busied himself with such matters has come, in trance or dream, upon some new and strange symbol or event, which he has afterwards found in some work he had never read or heard of. Examples like this are as yet too little classified, too little analysed, to convince the stranger, but some of them are proof enough for those they have happened to, proof that there is a memory of nature that reveals events and symbols of distant centuries. Mystics of many countries and many centuries have spoken of this memory; and the honest men and charlatans, who keep the magical traditions which will some day be studied as a part of folk-lore, base most that is of importance in their claims upon this memory. I have read of it in *Paracelsus* and in some Indian book that describes the people of past days as still living within it, "thinking the thought and doing the deed." And I have found it in the prophetic books of William Blake, who calls its images "the bright sculptures of Los's Hall"; and says that all events, "all love stories," renew themselves from those images. It is perhaps well that so few believe in it, for if many did many would go out of parliaments and universities and libraries and run into the wilderness to so waste the body, and to so hush the unquiet mind that, still living, they might pass the doors the dead pass daily; for who among the wise would trouble himself with making laws or in writing history or in weighing the earth if the things of eternity seemed ready to hand?

VII

I find in my diary of magical events for 1899 that I awoke at 3 A.M. out of a nightmare, and imagined one symbol to prevent its recurrence, and imagined another, a simple geometrical form, which calls up dreams of luxuriant vegetable life, that I might have pleasant dreams. I imagined it faintly, being very sleepy, and went to sleep. I had confused dreams which seemed to have no relation with the symbol. I awoke about eight, having for the time forgotten both nightmare and symbol. Presently I dozed off again and began half to dream and half to see, as one does between sleep and waking, enormous flowers and grapes. I awoke and recognised that what I had dreamed or seen was the kind of thing appropriate to the symbol before I remembered having used it. I find another record, though made some time after the event, of having imagined over the head of a person, who was a little of a seer, a combined symbol of elemental air and elemental water. This person, who did not know what symbol I was using, saw a pigeon flying with a lobster in his bill. I find that on December 13, 1898, I used a certain star-shaped symbol with a seeress, getting her to look at it intently before she began seeing. She saw a rough stone house, and in the middle of the house the skull of a horse. I find that I had used the same symbol a few days before with a seer, and that he had seen a rough stone house, and in the middle of the house something under a cloth marked with the Hammer of Thor. He had lifted the cloth and discovered a skeleton of gold with teeth of diamonds, and eyes of some unknown dim precious stones. I had made a note to this last vision, pointing out that we had been using a Solar symbol a little earlier. Solar symbols often call up visions of gold and precious stones. I do not give these examples to prove my arguments, but to illustrate them. I know that my examples will awaken in all who have not met the like, or who are not on other grounds inclined towards my arguments, a most natural incredulity. It was long before I myself would admit an inherent power in symbols, for it long seemed to me that one could account for everything by the power of one imagination over another, or by telepathy, as "The Society for Psychical Research" would say. The symbol seemed powerful, I thought, merely because we thought it powerful, and we would do just as well without it. In those days I used symbols made with some ingenuity instead of merely imagining them. I used to give them to the person I was experimenting with, and tell him to hold them to his forehead without looking at them; and sometimes I made a mistake. I learned from these mistakes that if I did not myself imagine the symbol, in which case he would have a mixed vision, it was the symbol I gave by mistake * that produced the vision. Then I met with a seer who could say to me, "I have a vision of a square pond, but I can see your thought, and you expect me to see an oblong pond," or, "The symbol you are imagining has made me see a woman holding a crystal, but it was a moonlight sea I should have seen." I discovered that the symbol hardly ever failed to call up its typical scene, its typical event, its typical person, but that I could

---

* I forgot that my "subconsciousness" would know clairvoyantly what symbol I had really given and would respond to the associations of that symbol. I am, however, certain that the main symbols (symbolic roots, as it were) draw upon associations which are beyond the reach of the individual "subconsciousness."   1924.

practically never call up, no matter how vividly I imagined it, the particular scene, the particular event, the particular person I had in my own mind, and that when I could, the two visions rose side by side.

I cannot now think symbols less than the greatest of all powers whether they are used consciously by the masters of magic, or half unconsciously by their successors, the poet, the musician and the artist. At first I tried to distinguish between symbols and symbols, between what I call inherent symbols and arbitrary symbols, but the distinction has come to mean little or nothing. Whether their power has arisen out of themselves, or whether it has an arbitrary origin, matters little, for they act, as I believe, because the great memory associates them with certain events and moods and persons. Whatever the passions of man have gathered about, becomes a symbol in the great memory, and in the hands of him who has the secret it is a worker of wonders, a caller-up of angels or of devils. The symbols are of all kinds, for everything in heaven or earth has its association, momentous or trivial, in the great memory, and one never knows what forgotten events may have plunged it, like the toadstool and the ragweed, into the great passions. Knowledgeable men and women in Ireland sometimes distinguish between the simples that work cures by some medical property in the herb, and those that do their work by magic. Such magical simples as the husk of the flax, water out of the fork of an elm-tree, do their work, as I think, by awaking in the depths of the mind where it mingles with the great mind, and is enlarged by the great memory, some curative energy, some hypnotic command. They are not what we call faith cures, for they have been much used and successfully, the traditions of all lands affirm, over children and over animals, and to me they seem the only medicine that could have been committed safely to ancient hands. To pluck the wrong leaf would have been to go uncured, but, if one had eaten it, one might have been poisoned.

VIII

I have now described that belief in magic which has set me all but unwilling among those lean and fierce minds who are at war with their time, who cannot accept the days as they pass, simply and gladly; and I look at what I have written with some alarm, for I have told more of the ancient secret than many among my fellow-students think it right to tell. I have come to believe so many strange things because of experience, that I see little reason to doubt the truth of many things that are beyond my experience; and it may be that there are beings who watch over that ancient secret, as all tradition affirms, and resent, and perhaps avenge, too fluent speech. They say in the Aran Islands that if you speak overmuch of the things of Faery your tongue becomes like a stone, and it seems to me, though doubtless naturalistic reason would call it Auto-suggestion or the like, that I have often felt my tongue become just so heavy and clumsy. More than once, too, as I wrote this very essay I have become uneasy, and have torn up some paragraph, not for any literary reason, but because some incident or some symbol that would perhaps have meant nothing to the reader, seemed, I know not why, to belong to hidden things. Yet I must write or be of no account to any cause, good or evil; I must commit what merchandise of wisdom I have to this ship of written speech, and after all, I have many a time watched it put out to sea with not less alarm when all the speech was rhyme. We who write, we who bear witness, must often hear our hearts cry out against us, complaining because of their hidden things, and I know not but he who speaks of wisdom may not sometimes, in the change that is coming upon the world, have to fear the anger of the people of Faery, whose country is the heart of the world—"The Land of the Living Heart." Who can keep always to the little pathway between speech and silence, where one meets none but discreet revelations? And surely, at whatever risk, we must cry out that imagination is always seeking to remake the world according to the impulses and the patterns in that great Mind, and that great Memory? Can there be anything so important as to cry out that what we call romance, poetry, intellectual beauty, is the only signal that the supreme Enchanter, or some one in His councils, is speaking of what has been, and shall be again, in the consummation of time?

1901

TOLSTOY
Tales of Courage and Conflict
Edited by Charles Neider
576 pp.
0-8154-1010-7
$19.95

THE TRAVELS OF MARK TWAIN
Edited by Charles Neider
448 pp., 6 b/w line drawings
0-8154-1039-5
$19.95

LIFE AS I FIND IT
A Treasury of Mark Twain Rarities
Edited by Charles Neider
with a new foreword
343 pp., 1 b/w photo
0-8154-1027-1
$17.95

THE SELECTED LETTERS OF MARK TWAIN
Edited by Charles Neider
352 pp., 1 b/w photo
0-8154-1011-5
$16.95

MARK TWAIN: PLYMOUTH ROCK & THE PILGRIMS
and Other Essays
Edited by Charles Neider
368 pp., 1 b/w photo
0-8154-1104-9
$17.95

ANTARCTICA
Firsthand Accounts of Exploration and Endurance
Edited by Charles Neider
468 pp.
0-8154-1023-9
$18.95

MAN AGAINST NATURE
Firsthand Accounts of Adventure and Exploration
Edited by Charles Neider
512 pp.
0-8154-1040-9
$18.95

GREAT SHIPWRECKS AND CASTAWAYS
Firsthand Accounts of Disasters at Sea
Edited by Charles Neider
256 pp.
0-8154-1094-8
$17.95

THE FABULOUS INSECTS
Essays by the Foremost Nature Writers
Edited by Charles Neider
288 pp.
0-8154-1100-6
$17.95

EDGAR ALLAN POE
A Biography
Jeffrey Meyers
376 pp., 12 b/w photos
0-8154-1038-7
$18.95

HEMINGWAY
Life into Art
Jeffrey Meyers
192 pp.
0-8154-1079-4
$27.95 cloth

THE FAIRY TALE OF MY LIFE
Hans Christian Andersen
New introduction by Naomi Lewis
610 pp., 20 b/w illustrations
0-8154-1105-7
$22.95

THE LANTERN BEARERS AND OTHER ESSAYS
Robert Louis Stevenson
Edited by Jeremy Treglown
320 pp., 27 b/w maps
0-8154-1012-3
$16.95

T. E. LAWRENCE
A Biography
Michael Yardley
308 pp., 71 b/w photos., 5 b/w maps
0-8154-1054-9
$17.95

SHAKESPEARE
The Man and His Achievement
Robert Speaight
416 pp., 24 b/w illustrations
0-8154-1063-8
$19.95

SCOTT FITZGERALD
A Biography
Jeffrey Meyers
432 pp., 25 b/w photos
0-8154-1036-0
$18.95

GRANITE AND RAINBOW
The Hidden Life of Virginia Woolf
Mitchell Leaska
536 pp., 23 b/w photos
0-8154-1047-6
$18.95

Available at bookstores; or call 1-800-462-6420

 Cooper Square Press

150 Fifth Avenue
Suite 911
New York, NY 10011